No Colours or Crest

Peter Kemp

Copyright © 1958 Peter Kemp
All rights reserved.
ISBN: 9798654735744

v. 1

First paperback edition by Mystery Grove Publishing Co. LLC

TO THE MEMORY OF
MY BROTHER NEIL
14th July 1910—10th January 1941

NOTE FROM THE PUBLISHER

First published in 1958, *No Colours or Crest* is legendary British adventurer Peter Kemp's follow-up to Mine *Were of Trouble,* which detailed his combat during the Spanish Civil War. The book recounts Kemp's service with the British Special Operations Executive (SOE) during the Second World War in Europe. While readers of his first book got to see Kemp as a brave but naïve volunteer in the fight against communism, his second is more complex. Kemp begins the war as a commando, but soon becomes a spy trapped in a labyrinth of alliances and betrayals. The threat posed by the Soviets is often far more immediate than that from the Axis. This is not the Second World War you see in the movies.

The book is a firsthand account of the conflict's underbelly, written by a man whose character, bravery, and patriotism is above reproach. Despite its value, *No Colours or Crest* was out-of-print more than 60 years, with the few surviving copies too expensive for the average person. Mystery Grove Publishing Company is happy and proud to finally make this classic available for the first time ever in paperback and ebook form, allowing Kemp's work to be enjoyed by a new generation of readers.

Please note, although we've attempted to recreate Kemp's work, several photographs appeared in the first edition hardback that would have been too costly to reproduce while keeping prices low. These photos are available free of charge on our Twitter account (@MysteryGrove). Furthermore, the maps of Kemp's travels, originally scattered throughout the first edition, have been consolidated at the front of this book for readers' convenience.

We are very grateful for the enthusiasm with which our earlier releases have been received. We hope to make similar lost or rare titles available to a wide audience in the near future. Please follow us on Twitter for information about our upcoming releases and other news.

Thank you for reading!

Special acknowledgement goes to the men of the HWGC, CL, and Grove Street, along with JAM. Without their support and friendship these releases would not be possible.

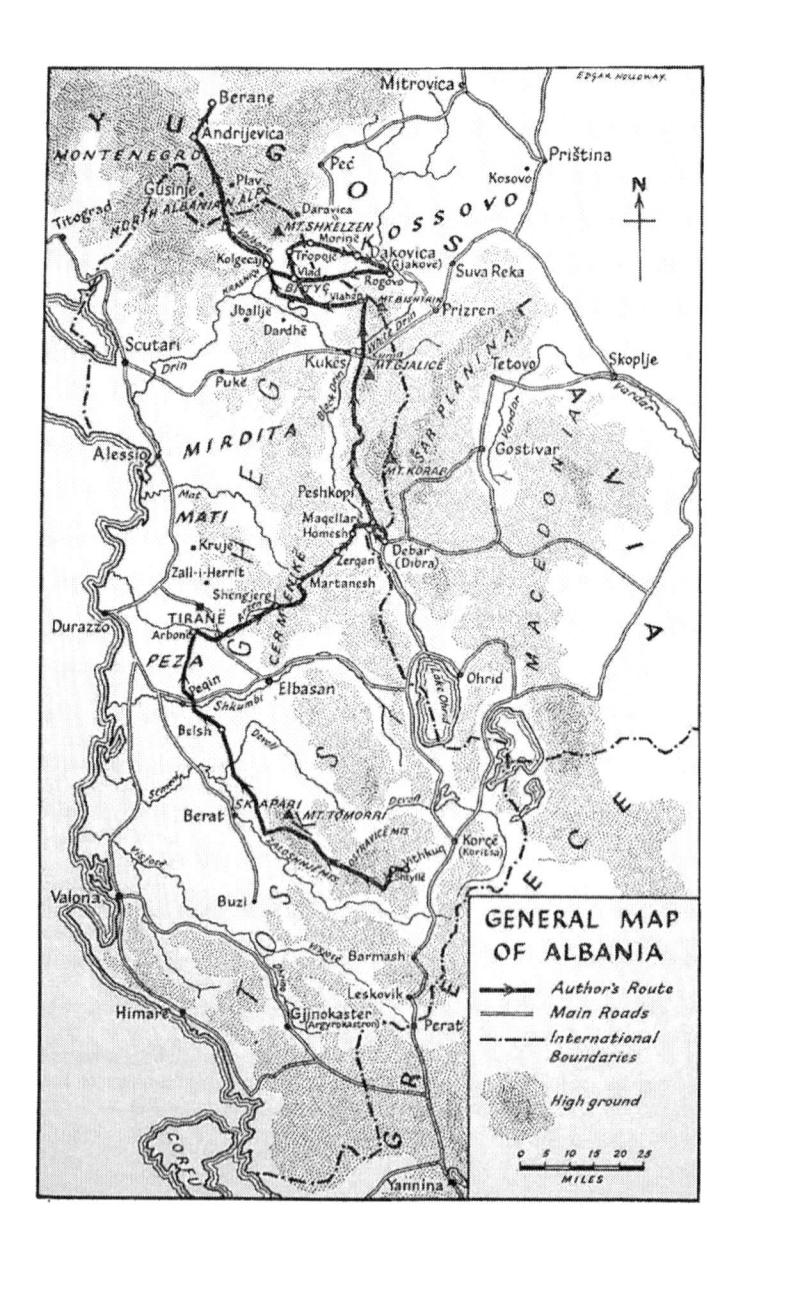

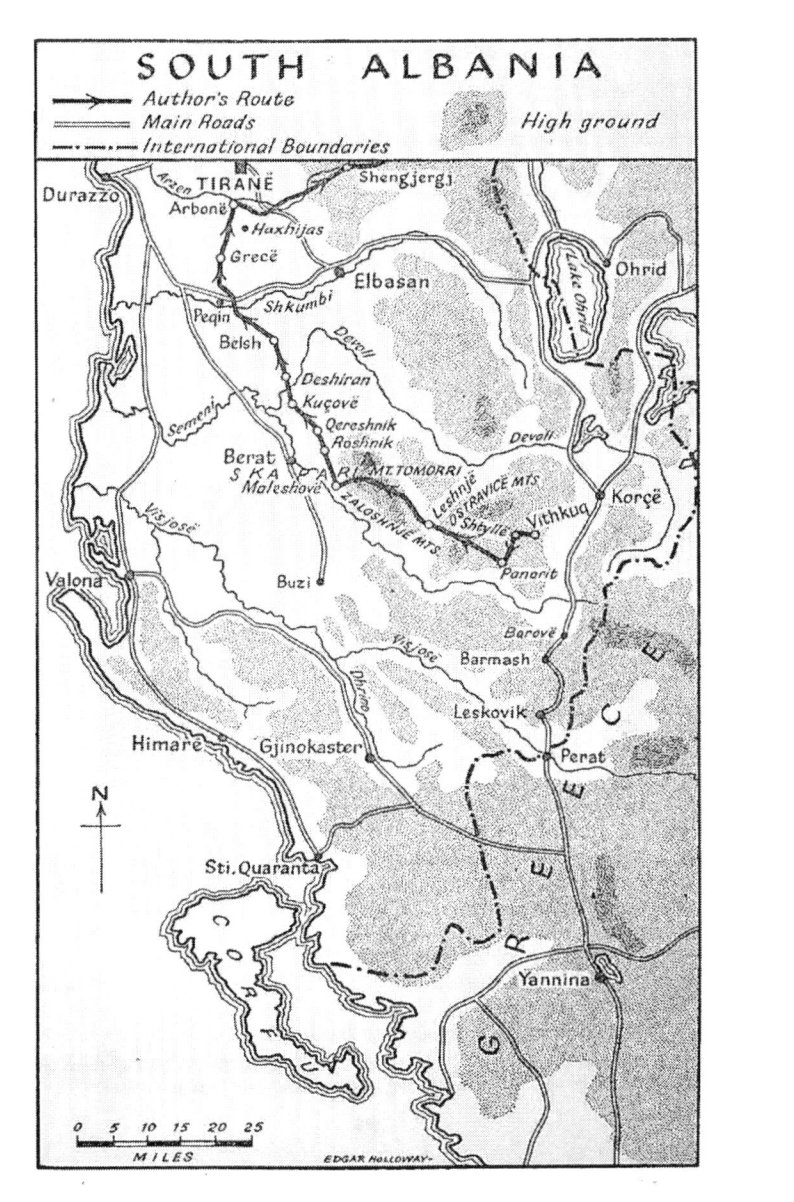

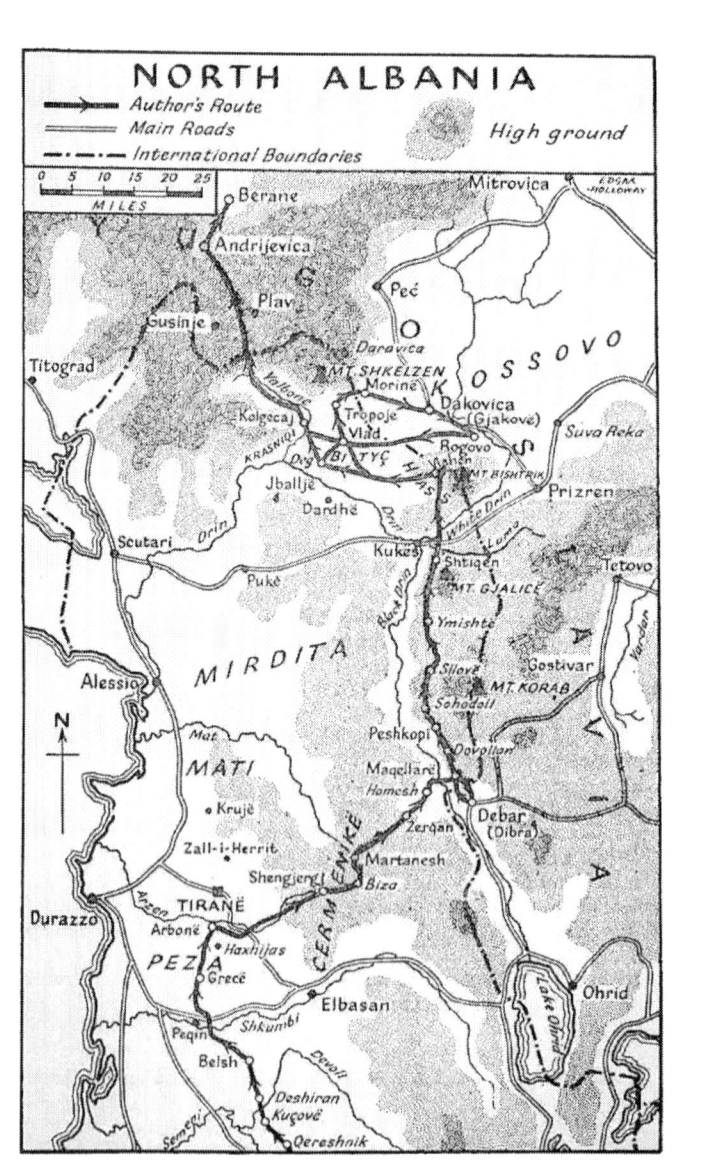

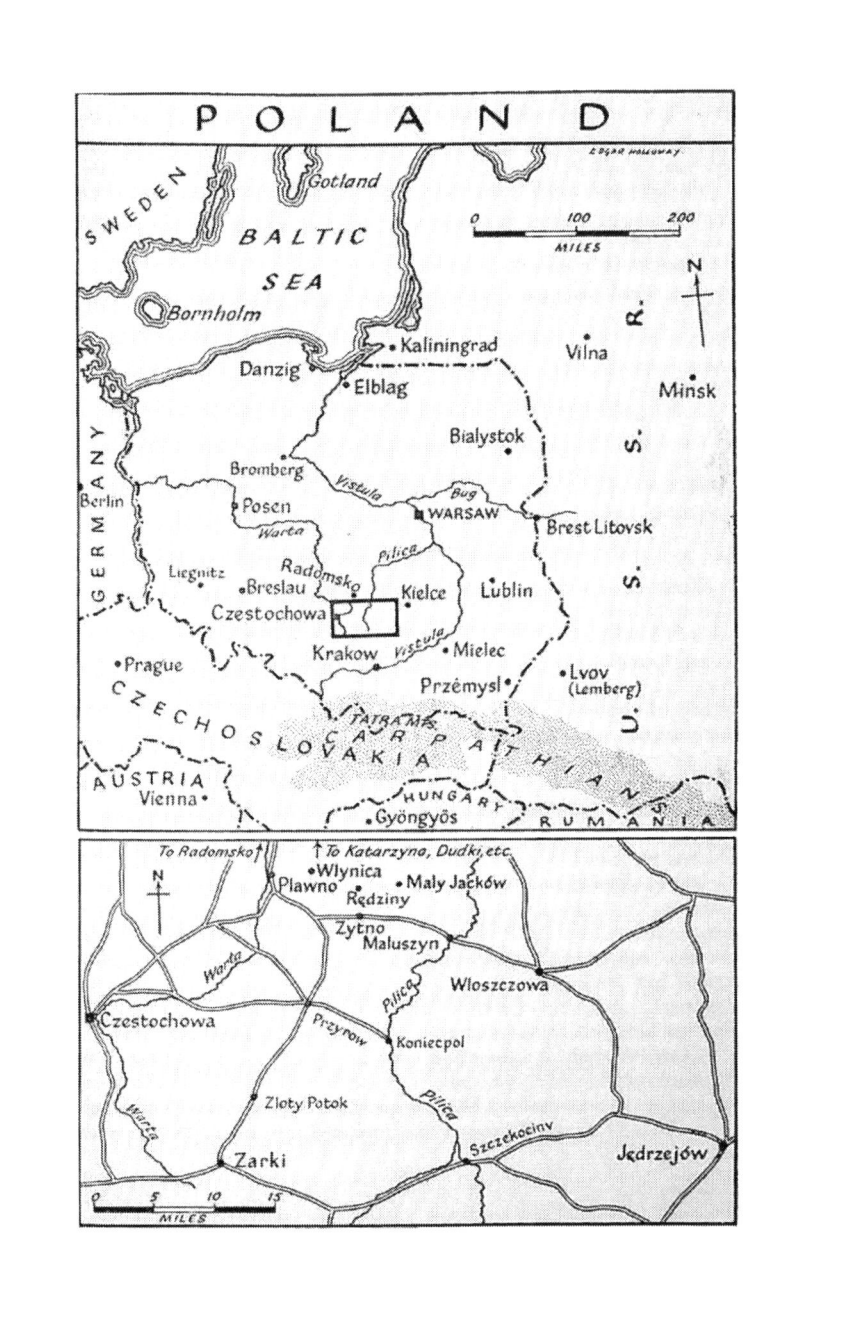

ACKNOWLEDGEMENTS

My particular thanks are to Colonel David Smiley, M.V.O., O.B.E., M.C., some of whose photographs are reproduced in this book; Commander Alastair Mars, D.S.O., D.S.C., R.N., and his First Lieutenant Mr. A. G. Stewart, for their reading and criticism of the passages dealing with my experiences in H.M. submarines; my friend Ihsan Bey Toptani for much valuable help on the chapters concerning Albania; Captain A. R. Glen, D.S.C., R.N.V.R., and to Mr. I. S. Ivonović, aboard whose cargo boats I have done most of my writing; and to the many kind friends, too numerous to mention, who have helped me with their advice, encouragement, and criticism.

PETER KEMP

There's a Legion that never was 'listed,
That carries no colours or crest,
But, split in a thousand detachments,
Is breaking the road for the rest.
Rudyard Kipling

TABLE OF CONTENTS

Chapter 1	English Winter	Pg. 1
Chapter 2	Operation 'Knife'	Pg. 11
Chapter 3	Education of an Agent	Pg. 19
Chapter 4	Small-Scale Raiding Force	Pg. 38
Chapter 5	To the Wilder Shores of War	Pg. 63
Chapter 6	Partisans and Parasites	Pg. 79
Chapter 7	Cloak without Dagger	Pg. 105
Chapter 8	On the Run	Pg. 130
Chapter 9	The Marches of Kossovo	Pg. 156
Chapter 10	Betrayal	Pg. 176
Chapter 11	Montenegro	Pg. 203
Chapter 12	Poland	Pg. 216
Chapter 13	Captivity	Pg. 246

I

ENGLISH WINTER

'Of course they must let you wear your Spanish Civil War medals,' pronounced my uncle in the brisk, cheerful tones that generations of Indian Army subalterns had learnt not to contradict.

'After all, the whole point of campaign ribbons is to indicate that the wearer is a veteran who has seen active service.'

Seated erect in a hard, high-backed chair, with his long, thin legs sprawled wide in front of him, my uncle quizzed me with bright, twinkling eyes; his head was cocked to one side, his deep-lined bony face creased in the half mocking, half affectionate smile that had at once charmed and disconcerted his Sepoys, his relations, and refractory Frontier tribesmen. My gaze wandered round the bleak sitting-room of the suite in the small hotel near the Brompton Road where he had moved when the approach of war drove him from the sunny comfort of the Italian Riviera: plain, deep red carpet; green, flowered wallpaper; drab chintz-covered sofa and armchairs; white net curtains drawn back from the windows to give a dispiriting view of the grimy, uneven Kensington skyline. The street outside was silent and heavy with the gloom of that impending catastrophe which before the end of the next year was to obliterate this unpretentious little family hotel from the face of London.

It was the morning of Sunday, 3rd September, 1939. Germany had invaded Poland; Britain and France had sent an ultimatum to Hitler; King Carol was digging a ditch round Rumania. Within an hour we should hear the sad, tired voice of the Prime Minister announce the beginning of another world war.

A month previously I had returned to London after nearly three years service in Spain, one of the very few Englishmen to fight in the Nationalist armies, defending a cause which enjoyed little popularity among my countrymen. I had joined the Nationalists almost immediately after coming down from Cambridge, partly out of a desire for adventure and partly from the conviction, fostered by the study of early, uncensored reports from newspaper correspondents on the spot, that the vital issue of the civil war was Communism, and that a Republican victory would lead to a Communist government in Spain. A strong Tory myself, I had served in the Carlist militia and the Spanish Foreign Legion, where my friends—Traditionalists, Conservatives and Liberal Monarchists—had no more sympathy than I for totalitarian regimes. But General Franco's friendship with Hitler and

Mussolini and his establishment of the Falange as the only political party in Spain had erased from most British minds all memory of the Communist threat he had defeated; even the Soviet-German Pact had not wholly revived it.

Now the weight of Republican propaganda, backed by the formidable organization of European Communism, had dubbed Franco a Fascist, while many of my British friends regarded me as, at best, a Fascist fellow-traveller. Even those who sympathized with me feared that Spain would enter the war against us, although I had seen enough of the devastation and war-weariness there to believe that she would remain neutral.

When I had left England for the Spanish Civil War, with all the romantic enthusiasm, ingenuousness, and ignorance of my twenty-one years, I had never imagined that six months after it was over I should find myself involved in another and infinitely vaster holocaust. Now, without thinking of myself as a veteran, I knew enough of war to feel no elation at the prospect; I was conscious only of a grave anxiety at the strength of the forces matched against us, a grim realization of what defeat would mean, and the hope that the experience I had acquired in the face of much disapproval and ridicule might not prove entirely useless to my country.

I left my uncle to go to his club in Pall Mall, and sauntered morosely through dismal, deserted streets to the house in Brompton Square which an aged great-aunt had lent me while she and her husband relaxed in the milder atmosphere of Brighton. Greta, the amiable young Austrian cook, panted upstairs from the kitchen, her plump, round peasant face split in a wide, careless grin.

'Please do not look so sad, sir. I think there will not be a war.'

Poor Greta. She was a wonderful cook. But her naïve optimism did not save her from nearly six years in an internment camp.

I walked across the road to listen to the wireless over drinks with a girl-friend and her mother and sister. When the Prime Minister had finished speaking and we knew we were at war there was absolute stillness in the softly lit grey-green drawing-room; under a picture light above the fireplace a charming portrait of a doll-like little Infanta seemed to mock us from the security of a distant age of privilege and faith. I saw my hostess weeping silently and took her hand in a clumsy gesture meant to comfort.

'Oh, I don't mind for myself,' she whispered, looking past me to her daughters. 'But it does seem so hard that these children should have their lives blighted a second time.' I remembered that she had lost her husband from wounds in the first war. Her son was to be killed in this.

When the siren screamed from the Walton Street police station a few yards away, I knew with shame that I was afraid. In Spain I had experienced heavy air attack and I had seen the damage in the dock area of Barcelona; those bombardments would seem like pigeon droppings, I reckoned, compared to what we could now expect. As we trooped downstairs to join the servants in the basement kitchen I must have cut a pretty poor figure, clutching in each hand a bottle snatched in passing from the drinks tray; and in the forced, embarrassed conversation that followed I was all too conscious of my failure to set a proper example of indifference and courage. When the All Clear sounded I reflected sorrowfully that the last three years had left their mark upon my nerves.

I was never granted permission to wear my Spanish decorations; nor even, at first, a uniform on which to wear them. In July 1938 a mortar bomb had shattered my jaw and severely damaged both hands; now, when I joined the general scramble for a commission, the members of the medical board that examined me told me sympathetically but firmly to come back in six months' time. My consequent feeling of frustration was exacerbated by the sight of friends in uniform and the knowledge that my only brother, five years my senior and a lieutenant in the Fleet Air Arm, was already at sea in the carrier *Courageous*. With humiliation I pictured them battling on the fields of Flanders or leading torpedo attacks on pocket battleships or locked in desperate dog-fights in the sky, while I loitered uselessly in England, put out of action by injuries received in an alien war.

As it turned out, I need not have worried; after six months of peace indistinguishable from war it seemed that we were to have six months of war indistinguishable from peace. While the German armies swept eastward and Stalin agreed with Hitler that Poland must never rise again, in England the British Expeditionary Force prepared to cross the Channel, the Women's Services demonstrated that girls could retain their allure and chic in battle-dress and trousers, and the Committee of the Royal Thames Yacht Club announced that in view of the national emergency, smoking would in future be permitted in the Members' Dining-room at eight-fifteen every evening instead of eight-thirty.

In the interval since my return from Spain I had begun work on a book about the Spanish Civil War for the publishing house of Macmillan; now there seemed to be little point in continuing it. My publishers were evidently of the same opinion, for I received a charming letter from Harold Macmillan saying that his firm would be delighted to discuss the matter again at the end of this war 'should both parties survive hostilities'. As a stop-gap I took a job in the Postal Censorship, where I was employed in the Press Section under the urbane direction of Cosmo Hamilton and the stimulating supervision of his assistant, Benn Levy; Levy was deeply suspicious of my Spanish connection, but never allowed his feelings to affect his natural courtesy or his engaging habit of addressing me, like the rest of us, as 'ducky'.

I remained in London for another two months. I was fortunate in the companionship of Archibald Lyall, author, traveller, and epicure, whose robust sense of humour and Rabelaisian wit kept me from brooding on my disappointment. A conspicuous and impressive figure, tall, blond, and corpulent, with a high, bald forehead above a plump and florid face and a carefully trimmed Mephistophelian moustache, Lyall concealed an able and inquisitive mind behind the mischievously complacent expression of a dissipated baby. We had become close friends two years before, when he was visiting Salamanca, at that time the Nationalist G.H.Q., where I was awaiting my posting to the Foreign Legion. During a period when time had hung heavy on my hands he had shown a remarkable flair for discovering interesting and unusual sources of drink and diversion; and in our joint explorations of the night life of that beautiful but usually placid university town he had proved himself an inspired connoisseur of the picaresque.

His works included several travel books on the Balkans, the U.S.S.R., and Portuguese West Africa; *Lyall's Languages of Europe*, a multi-lingual phrase-book; and an unpublished treatise on women, entitled *The Enemies of Englishmen*. On the strength of *Lyall's Languages* his publishers had recently asked him to compile a phrase-book for the Forces, which he was now preparing in the comparative seclusion of a flat in Mount Royal; it was a practical little hand-book, called *Soldier's Speakeasy*, and catered for all the warrior's needs from '*When does the next train leave for Paris?*' to '*How much is that girl with red hair?*'

He nursed a particular resentment against Hitler for what he regarded as an intolerable interruption of his private life. 'Up to the age of thirty-five,' he explained to me, 'a man can work and drink and copulate; but at thirty-five he has to make up his mind which of the three he is going to give up. I had just passed my thirty-fifth birthday and made all my arrangements to give up work when that bloody Hun started the war.'

He sympathized with my impatience at my enforced inactivity. 'How would it be if I took you to see the Dame one of these days?'

Dame Beatrice Lyall was his mother, a formidable woman of strong mind and noble character, who distinguished herself in the Red Cross in both world wars. She was the only person from whom Lyall felt it necessary to conceal the more lurid details of his life.

'She's got quite a bit of influence and might be able to fix you up in something more active than Postal Censorship. But he went on, tapping my arm urgently, 'there's one thing I must emphasize: from the moment we cross the Dame's threshold I, Archie, am a teetotal eunuch of rather low Anglican views.'

For all her kindness there was nothing she could do against the verdict of the medical board. My bitterness was intensified at the end of September, when *Courageous* was sunk by a U-boat; although my brother was a survivor, picked up by a destroyer after swimming for two hours, the event drove home to me the futility of my own war effort.

Returning from work one evening I ran into Douglas Dodds-Parker, whom I had met in Spain during the summer; because he had also been in Prague at the time of the Sudeten crisis I suspected that he was connected with Intelligence. My spirits rose when he asked me:

'Would you like me to give your name to my people at the War Office?'

Early in October I received a letter from a room number in the War Office, which began, as far as I remember:

'Your name has been given to us by Mr. Dodds-Parker as having qualifications which may be of interest to this Department.'

The department seemed to have no name. But the letter requested me to present myself for interview at the above address, and concluded with regrets that the department was not authorized to defray the cost of my travelling expenses.

The interview took place in a large room full of desks, at each of which sat a Staff Captain. The officer who interviewed me, a solicitor in private life, asked me a long succession of questions, writing down my answers on a buff foolscap form; he recorded minutely every detail of my service in Spain. When he had finished he looked up at me:

'I think we might be able to use you. We haven't a job for you at the moment—frankly we haven't a job for anybody at this stage of the war. But if the war spreads, as we believe it will, we are going to need officers with your special experience. Have you any idea of joining a particular regiment at the moment?'

He went on: 'From what I know about you I should say that you would have a more interesting time with us than you would in regimental soldiering. If I can get authority to recruit you, and if you agree, we would commission you and send you in your commissioned rank to an O.C.T.U., where you would get your basic training and fill in the time until we needed you.'

'That would suit me,' I said.

'Good. Now, supposing we accept you, which would you rather go to—the Horsed Cavalry O.C.T.U. at Weedon, where we have a few vacancies, or an infantry O.C.T.U. at Aldershot?'

'Weedon,' I answered emphatically.

I told him about the Postal Censorship, adding that we were supposed to be moving to Liverpool at the end of the month.

'You might as well go with them. It will take us a month or two to commission you and fit you into a course at Weedon. Leave an address where we can get in touch with you.'

As I rose to go I heard my name called from the other end of the room. Standing by a fireplace was a tall captain, whom I recognized as Peter Wilkinson, with whom I had been at Cambridge; he had been commissioned into the Royal Fusiliers from the University. With him was a trim, dark, wiry officer with a neat, clipped moustache and alert, bright eyes, whom he introduced as Lieutenant-Colonel Gubbins; this officer was to have a profound, even decisive influence on the course of thousands if not millions of lives—among them my own. Speaking in staccato, precise sentences he questioned me about the Spanish War, where we had friends in common. He had just returned from Poland, where he had commanded the British Military Liaison Mission with the Polish Army.

Liverpool in November is perhaps not the most attractive city in the British Isles; but my work in the Postal Censorship had become more interesting, or at least more amusing, since my transfer to a new department, known as 'Impounded Baggage'. This ambiguous title signified that our duties were to examine luggage taken at airports and seaports from travellers between neutral countries and the British Isles. My knowledge of Spanish was more useful here than in the Press Section. In addition to letters, books, and newspapers we often had to censor gramophone records and cinema films, for which purpose we were provided with a gramophone and a cinema projector. We had a room to ourselves at the top of a tower in Littlewoods Pools Building; here, comparatively immune from official surveillance, our director was able to run the department to his own and our complete satisfaction. As relief from the routine work we could censor a few gramophone records, or run through a film. Among the latter we had some quaint examples of the *cinema bleu*. These we found particularly useful for the entertainment of visiting mandarins from civilian or Service Ministries. After a quick run through of *His First Affair* or *La Petite Ingenue* the V.I.P.s would depart in a chorus of sniggers, well satisfied with the work of Impounded Baggage.

A week before Christmas I received a bulky O.H.M.S. envelope with the initials M.I.(R.) stamped on the back. M.I.(R.) proved to be the department that had interviewed me in October; to this day I do not know what the (R.) stood for: Recherché? Revolutionary? Reactionary? The envelope contained, among other documents, an official letter informing me that it was proposed to commission me as a second lieutenant (General List) with effect from 19th January, 1940; that I should report on that date at the 110th (Horsed Cavalry) O.C.T.U., Weedon, Northants, informing them of the time of my arrival; that I should first provide myself with the uniform of my rank, including riding-breeches and field boots, for which I might claim the sum of £40 uniform allowance; lastly—and this was the snag—that I was required to attend a medical board in Liverpool in the first week in January and that I was to inform 'this Department' immediately, should I receive any lesser grading than A.I.

I romped through the medical board with an A.I rating, managing this simply by following the old maxim of not speaking unless spoken to: in other words I volunteered no information about Spain or my wounds because I was asked for none, and took care not to expose my hands or jaw to anybody's attention.

On 10th January, having said good-bye to my colleagues in Impounded Baggage, I went south for a few days' leave, most of which I passed at home. My last two days I spent in London with Archie Lyall, who was about to leave for Belgrade, where he had been appointed Press Attaché. For his new assignment he borrowed my treasured Spanish cloak, which I had bought in Madrid the previous summer.

'You can have it, Archie,' I told him, 'on the one condition that you promise to save it, even though you can't save yourself, if the Germans invade Jugoslavia.'

'Agreed. And will you promise to bequeath it to me if you should croak before I do?'

On this exchange of promises we parted and did not meet again for more than three years; but over the next fourteen months reports reached me from Belgrade of the huge, amorphous figure enveloped in a dark blue cloak with green and crimson lining who was a familiar and popular spectacle at public functions and private parties. He fulfilled his part of the bargain the following year, sending the cloak to Athens in the diplomatic bag the day before the German invasion. From Athens it travelled, via Cairo, to England. Lyall remains my heir to this fetish.

The cavalry barracks at Weedon were built, I believe, in the reign of George II, to quarter troops sent to oppose the advance of Prince Charles Edward's highlanders; sometime before the First World War they were considered to have outlived their usefulness and were condemned as unfit for habitation, even by soldiers. A succession of inter-war governments—alternately abused as 'warmongers' and 'appeasers'—so effectively reduced military expenditure that the War Office had no money to spare for new barracks. In January 1940, therefore, the two-hundred-year-old buildings housed the Officer Cadets of the 110th (Horsed Cavalry) O.C.T.U. The winter of 1939-40 was probably the most rigorous of the war. Standing conspicuously on a hill above the town, exposed to every bitter wind and inadequately heated by diminutive coal fires, our new quarters gave us an icy reception. Our block warmed up a little after we had lived in it for a few days; but during our first week-end—we arrived on a Friday—I remember having to abandon the attempt to write a letter because my fingers were too frozen to hold the pen. We were, however, fortunate in that new washrooms had been installed, with an unlimited supply of hot water.

Each troop of twenty-five to thirty cadets occupied a separate block of barrack rooms. Whereas all the other troops consisted of officer cadets between the ages of eighteen and twenty-one, destined for horsed cavalry regiments, ours—known locally as 'the M.I. Troop'—was composed of men varying in age between twenty and forty, recruited by M.I.(R.) in much the same manner as myself; some of us were already commissioned, the remainder would be commissioned at the end of the course. Drawn from every walk of civilian life, with widely different backgrounds and experience, we were something of a puzzle to our instructors, who treated us with more leniency than they showed to the embryo cavalrymen. This was just as well, for most of us had no previous military training apart from our school O.T.C.s, and some had never been on a horse.

The most distinguished among us was Professor Pendlebury of Pembroke College, Cambridge, an archaeologist whose researches in Crete and Egypt were well-known before the war. A quiet man of great charm and sense of humour, he proved his adaptability by becoming a most efficient soldier. He had a house in Crete, where he was sent, after leaving Weedon, to make certain preparations against enemy invasion. His murder at the hands of Gestapo or *Sicherheitsdienst*, as he lay incapacitated by wounds in a peasant's hut a few days after the German occupation, was a tragic blow to learning and a wanton crime.

The most ebullient, by contrast, was Harold Perkins, a former master mariner who had abandoned the sea before the war to graduate in engineering at the University of Prague and become the proprietor of a textile factory in Poland; on the outbreak of hostilities he was attached to Colonel Gubbins's mission, making his escape with Gubbins and Wilkinson through Hungary and Rumania. A solid ball of muscle, gifted with remarkable administrative ability and physical stamina, he was also blessed with a schoolboy sense of fun which, although it endeared him to our instructors as much as to ourselves, nearly landed him, later in the war, in serious trouble. His work when he left Weedon involved the planning of subversive operations in Poland. He was relaxing from his duties one evening in the room of a senior officer of the Polish Air Force, on the first floor of a famous London hotel; after a few drinks they became involved in one of those friendly free-for-alls which have as their object the removal of the adversary's trousers. Both contestants were successful, and two pairs of trousers—one khaki, the other blue—floated gracefully from the window into the busy street below; a moment later guests in the lobby were astonished to see two trouserless but otherwise impeccably uniformed officers dive down the stairs and out into the street, to return in a few seconds clutching their trousers as they darted for the safety of the first floor.

Perkins's friend, Mike Pickles, had been through a bad time during his escape from Poland, travelling from Silesia across the country to the Baltic States dressed as a peasant and riding mostly in haycarts. He and his Polish companions were overtaken by the advancing Germans, but passed through the lines when the Germans halted, only to meet the Russians. Their worst troubles came from the latter, who were looking for Polish officers and shooting all above the rank of lieutenant; the party was frequently stopped and the hands of each one examined to see if they showed a proper proletarian horniness; luckily, by that time they did.

One of my closest friends in the troop was John Bennett, a barrister who had stood for Parliament in the Socialist interest against Neville Chamberlain; a scintillating but polemic character, he had precipitated a riot at one of his election meetings when, carried away by his own indignant eloquence, he had referred to his illustrious opponent as 'that Edgbaston parrot.'

Whatever the limitations of horsed cavalry in modern warfare, the training filled three of the pleasantest months of my career in the British Army. The full O.C.T.U. course lasted five or six months, but ours was a shorter version; the Commandant, Major R. H. Sheppard, 9th Lancers, himself an outstanding horseman, had devised for us a course at once practical and interesting, cutting out such unnecessary items as sword drill and ceremonial order. The two instructors of whom we saw most were Sergeant-Major Sennett and Sergeant Rourke; under the supervision of Captain Hamilton-Russell, the Equitation Officer, they attempted to teach us the elements of riding and horse mastership, to which the greater—and by far the most useful—part of our training was devoted. They taught us a great deal in a short time, using a balanced blend of patient encouragement and ferocious bullying, the latter reinforced by a superb flow of vituperation and an armoury of blasphemous taunts which had probably been handed down from generation to generation of N.C.O.s since the days of Rupert of the Rhine. We often found it hard to believe that the two warm-hearted and genial fellows with whom we had been exchanging pints of beer and dirty stories in the 'Globe' the previous evening could become next morning the pair of furious and sadistic Tartars who insulted us in the riding school.

For dismounted drill we came under a delightful highlander from the Scots Greys, Sergeant Stewart. These parades could never be wholly dull because of his practice of marching our squad across the square, as far away from himself as possible, and then shouting an order in what, from that distance, sounded like pure Gaelic; each of us would place his own interpretation on the command, and the squad would break up in disorder. An angry bellow would come from the stocky, purple figure at the other end of the square.

'Nae! A' didna say "Whah whooh!" A' said "Whah whu-u-h!"'

Our theoretical training might have been of use to cavalrymen in or before 1919. We heard lectures on tactics from an earnest young officer in the Inns of Court Regiment who took his chief illustration from an incident in the First Battle of Mons; lectures on animal management from the Veterinary Officer, who was inaudible; lectures on Military Law, which were incomprehensible, and lectures on the light machine-gun (Hotchkiss 1913 model).

The R.S.M., who controlled our conduct and discipline, was an austere Yorkshireman known as 'Gentleman Joe' Taylor; formerly an equitation instructor at Sandhurst, he was the personification of smartness and efficiency. Not a single detail escaped his eagle eye—a cliché which might have been coined expressly for him—not the smallest speck of dust in a barrack-room or the faintest blemish on a button, boot, or belt. He had that dour North Country humour which gleams brightest when administering a reprimand or dealing out a punishment.

His strongest weapon was his power to stop our week-end leave, and he used it mercilessly to punish slackness. Week-end leave lasted from Saturday midday until, theoretically, Sunday midnight. In fact, the last train that would get us back in time from London left soon after eight o'clock; if we missed that—and we often did—we had to take a tube to the north of London, and thumb a lift from one of the lorries that travelled by night up the Great North Road and passed through Weedon; it was easy to slip into the barracks unobserved in time for a quick brush-up and shave and a mug of tea before the first parade on Monday morning. But the first parade was always Riding School, when Sennett and Rourke would be at their fiercest, knowing that they had a number of sleepless and hung-over gentlemen at their mercy. Trotting round the riding school on my uncomfortable army saddle with its high bridge, I would hear with sinking heart the merciless order, 'Ride! Quit and cross your stirrups!' Often this exercise would last for forty-five minutes—a severe strain at any time. After half an hour Sennett would call out in a conversational tone:

'You married, Mr. Kemp, sir?'

'No, Sergeant-Major.'

His voice would swell triumphantly:

'Nor you never will be neither if you don't sit down in that there bloody saddle!'

II

OPERATION 'KNIFE'

One morning in the middle of April, shortly after the German invasion of Norway, I was ordered to report to the R.S.M. Expecting to lose another week-end's leave I was cheered to hear him say:

'War Office for you, Mr. Kemp, sir! Report to the Orderly Room right away and draw your warrant.'

Next morning I was sitting at another desk in the room where I had been recruited, receiving from Captains Davies and Kennedy a remarkable briefing. Davies's grim, heavy face was unusually grave; he began impressively:

'It's very possible, Kemp, that you may not feel like proceeding with this operation when you hear what we have to say; we shall quite understand if you don't. It involves going somewhere by submarine.'

Assuming an indifference that I did not really feel, I asked him to continue. Later on I came to realize that a submarine is no more dangerous a form of transport than a surface vessel—often, indeed, safer; but at the time I confess the idea scared me. Although it was clear, even from the communiques, that the German invasion was making uncomfortably good progress, it was not yet certain that the Allies would have to evacuate their Expeditionary Force. German land communications were peculiarly vulnerable to 'paramilitary' or 'partisan' warfare—both terms were new in British Army phraseology at this time; Operation 'Knife' was to be one of the first experiments. Briefly, the plan was to land a party of six officers, of which I was to be one, by submarine at a point on the southern shore of the Sogne Fjord, where Norwegian army officers and local guides would meet us. Our first task would be to make our way south across country on skis to the Bergen-Oslo railway, which we were to blow up in such a manner as to render it unserviceable for a long time. In addition to our own requirements we should take with us substantial supplies of explosives, Bren guns, rifles, grenades, and small-arms ammunition to equip local partisan units. After the destruction of the railway we should reconnoitre a lake farther east to see if it would be possible to land seaplanes. Our subsequent plans would depend on circumstances: we might stay in the country to help the partisans, or try to make our way to the Swedish frontier.

'How does this appeal to you?' asked Kennedy.

I said that it suited me well.

'Then we'd better see if Colonel Brian will take you.' Lieutenant-Colonel Brian Mayfield, Scots Guards, who was to command the expedition, was a regular soldier who had left the Army before the war to go into business. An experienced skier, he had recently been Second in Command to Colonel Jimmy Coats in the '5th Scots Guards'—a composite ski battalion raised by the War Office at the end of 1939, consisting almost entirely of officers from various units of the British Army; intended for operations in Finland, it was disbanded early in 1940.

For a few minutes Mayfield studied the written information about me that Kennedy showed him; then he asked: 'Can you ski?'

I hesitated. 'I used to be able to, sir, some years ago. I haven't tried recently but I expect I should be all right on skis.'

He looked at me thoughtfully: 'I think we'll make you our Bren gun instructor. Do you know about Brens?'

I thought it better to admit straight away that I had never even seen one.

'No matter. They're very easy. I suggest you go along to Wellington Barracks this afternoon and get a bit of instruction. I'll give them a ring and let them know you're coming. When you've finished you can come back here and meet the rest of the boys.'

After the complexities of the Hotchkisses and Fiats that we had used in Spain I was astonished at the simplicity, as well as the lightness, of this new weapon. By half past four that afternoon I was able to report to Colonel Mayfield that I felt myself competent to fire, strip, demonstrate and instruct in the Bren. Easily the most junior of our party, I was delighted to find myself promoted overnight to the rank of Captain, which seemed to be the lowest rank on our Establishment. After me the most junior was Bill Stirling, at this time a captain in the Scots Guards; a man of six foot five and proportionately broad, he would, I thought, find a submarine uncomfortably cramped. Our demolitions officer was Jim Gavin, a regular Sapper and skilled mountaineer who had found time off from his duties before the war to take part in one of the Everest expeditions. The remaining two members of the party were Ralph Farrant, a regular officer in a Line regiment, and David Stacey, who in civilian life had been a stockbroker. Not only was I the most junior, but also I had the least skiing experience—apart from Bill Stirling, who have never been on skis in his life. The others had all served in the '5th Scots Guards'.

Two days later we assembled for our final briefing. We were to leave King's Cross that evening for Rosyth, where we were to embark in H.M. Submarine *Truant*. Our stores were already packed and awaiting us there. When Tommy Davies had finished with us he took us along the corridor to see the Director of Military Intelligence. Unfortunately, the passage of time has driven the General's message from my memory, but I am unlikely to forget his opening words:

'I say, you know, it's frightfully nice of you chaps to go on this show.'

No Colours or Crest

H.M.S. *Truant* (Lieutenant-Commander Hutcheson, D.S.O., R.N.) was one of the new 'T' class submarines—the same class as the unlucky *Thetis*. Completed just before the war, she had an extremely strong hull, enabling her to dive to much greater depths than any previous class of submarine. To that extra strength in her hull we were to owe our lives. Lieutenant-Commander Hutcheson was one of the ace submarine commanders of the early months of the war. On his last patrol with *Truant* he had penetrated the Ems estuary, where he had sunk the new German light cruiser *Karlsrühe*, a piece of skill and daring which earned him an immediate award of the D.S.O.; it must have been an exacting experience, for he was obliged to remain submerged for more than forty-eight hours consecutively while making his escape, during which time the enemy dropped over a hundred depth charges around him.

We were introduced to Hutcheson aboard *Truant*'s parent ship, the Submarine Depot Ship *Forth*, where we arrived in time for the pre-lunch gin session in the wardroom; he was a dark, sallow-complexioned, slightly built man who spoke very little and drank nothing. In my experience of submariners I have observed that, whereas they are strictly abstemious on patrol, they delight in making up for lost time aboard their depot ship, where their hospitality is, even among the Navy, outstanding.

In the early part of the afternoon we went aboard *Truant*, where our stores were already stowed. It proved more difficult to find space to stow ourselves. Carrying her full complement of officers and crew—she had to continue on a routine patrol after landing us—*Truant* had little enough space to accommodate even one or two passengers; Hutcheson and his First Lieutenant had to spend a long time finding odd corners where we could lay our heads among the machinery. It was not easy, for we were tall men; Stirling was only able to straighten out during the brief periods when we were allowed on the bridge. I was provided with a mattress of cushions from the wardroom settees, laid at one end of the engine room; at least I could stretch to my full length, but I was deafened by the thunderous hammering of the diesels all the time the submarine was travelling on the surface.

We cast off about an hour before dusk, gliding beneath the Forth Bridge just after a train had passed over. Hutcheson allowed us to stay on deck until we were clear of the estuary, when he dived to trim; thereafter we were only allowed on the bridge for a quarter of an hour, one at a time—any more of us would be an embarrassment in the event of a crash dive. When we dived to fifty feet for trimming I was amazed at the stillness throughout the boat, and the absence of the sea's motion; in a curious way I found it comforting. Although a passenger, I could feel the unity around me—a feeling that captain and crew were working together as a smooth and perfectly controlled machine. The only other time I sailed in a submarine I noticed the same confidence. It was a most inspiring experience.

When Hutcheson was satisfied with the trim he gave the order to surface; in a few minutes we felt the rise and fall of the sea beneath us and heard the diesels begin their deep, regular pounding. We should be on the surface all night, and all the next day unless we sighted an enemy; we ought to reach the entrance of the Sogne Fjord late the following night or in the early hours of the morning after. We were very cramped in the tiny wardroom where we ate our supper; it was a silent meal, for we were all filled with the strangeness of our surroundings and preoccupied with the uncertainties and hazards that lay ahead. We dispersed to our sleeping quarters soon afterwards. I trod carefully along the narrow passage that ran the length of the engine room, edging past the stokers on duty, each of whom stood silently watching his panel of gauges and controls; at the after end of the compartment, by the bulkhead door leading into the stokers' mess, my improvised bed was laid in a small space just wide enough for me to lie down. Taking off my boots and battle-dress blouse, I managed to stow them out of the way of a burly, broad shouldered seaman who was standing over me on duty by one of the electric motors. He gave me a friendly smile:

"Fraid you won't get much sleep there, sir, not with all this 'ere din.'
'Oh yes I will! I can sleep through anything when I'm tired enough.'

I was tired, for I had slept badly in the train the night before; turning my face to the bulkhead I fell asleep within a few minutes. But I was wrong when I said I could sleep through anything. The two explosions, coming hard on top of one another, penetrated my dreamless unconsciousness; through my slumber I was vaguely aware that the first was somewhere quite near me, the second away forward. Suddenly I was fully alert as I heard the order 'Diving Stations!' relayed on loud-speakers through the boat. I realized that the diesels had stopped. In the tense, pervading silence I waited for the diving hooter to sound. I looked at my watch; it was four-thirty, and so I had slept for nearly six hours. Close by, a muffled voice broke the stillness:

'Gawd! We've 'it a bleedin' mine!'

I looked up from my bed to see a stoker standing above me at the nearest diesel; he was stripped to trousers and singlet and the light glistened on the beads of sweat on his muscular arms. His broad, homely face was set in grim lines and he was murmuring out of the corner of his mouth to his companion in short, jerky sentences. From what I could overhear I gathered that the torpedo compartment, right forward, was flooded, but that the watertight bulkhead was holding. After a short interval I saw the tall figure of the First Lieutenant approaching, his friendly features grave and expressionless. Catching sight of me where I lay on my back—there had seemed to be no point in moving—he stopped and grinned.

'Are you comfortable there?'
'Perfectly, thanks. How long am I likely to remain so? Do we know what's happened?'

'I'm trying to find out the full extent of the damage now. It seems there was a U-boat waiting for us. I should say those were magnetic torpedoes she fired. Fortunately, the first one didn't go off as close to us as the second, and our rudder and screws don't appear to have been damaged. We're lucky not to have been blown up.'

'What are we going to do now?'

'Well, the Captain was hoping we might be able to hunt the U-boat; but I'm sorry to say that's impossible in view of the damage. I'm afraid it looks like home, James—with whatever horses we can get out of her. Ah, well! Pretty adjacent, what?' He turned back to his duties.

The big stoker beside me chuckled in admiring imitation:

'Pretty adjacent, what? Don't nothin' ever worry 'im?'

My brother had often told me that during a crisis aboard ship the perfect passenger keeps out of the way and does nothing unless he is told. I decided to stay where I was; asking my stoker friend to let me know if anything happened, I turned over and tried to sleep again. Half an hour later I was much relieved to hear the diesels start; rightly or wrongly it seemed to me an indication that our immediate danger was over. Soon afterwards I fell asleep.

Someone was prodding me in the ribs. As I sat up in sudden alarm I heard a cheerful voice shouting above the pounding of the engines:

'Breakfast ready in the wardroom, sir!'

It was eight o'clock. Breakfast proved to be a picnic which we had to take in relays, for almost all the wardroom crockery had been shattered by the two explosions. This was the least of the damage we had suffered, in addition to the flooded torpedo room, Hutcheson told us, there was some flooding aft, and several rivets were started amidships:

'If this had been any boat but one of these new T-class,' he said, 'we shouldn't have remained afloat.' He added thoughtfully, 'I wonder if that Hun was really laying for us, or just happened to be there?'

There was serious damage to the machinery, details of which I did not understand. But the batteries of the electric motors were cracked, causing them to give off quantities of chlorine gas from the action of the sea water— unpleasant enough while we were on the surface, extremely dangerous if we should have to submerge for any length of time. Hutcheson had no choice but to turn for home. Much later he told us that he had concluded his signal to *Forth*, reporting the incident, with the words, 'will require at least three weeks' refit and new Commanding Officer.'

Apart from an uncomfortable ten minutes while we dived for trim, and one false alarm when an aircraft flew over us as we were approaching the Firth of Forth, we met with no further incident on the way home; but the strained expressions on the faces of Hutcheson and his officers told us that they looked forward to the end of the trip. Just before dark we limped into Rosyth and berthed alongside H.M.S. *Forth*.

We were filled with gin and plied with questions by incredulous submariners, who seemed astonished that *Truant* had managed to get home in such a condition; meanwhile Bill Stirling telephoned to his home at Keir, near Dunblane, and arranged for us all to stay there while new plans were hatched for Operation 'Knife'.

During the next few days we remained in a state of instant readiness; we heard that the Admiralty were providing one of the large 'River' class submarines to take us on a second attempt. It was a very pleasant interlude. Exhilarated by the recollection of our recent escape and stimulated by the hope of another, more successful venture, we were yet able to relax enough to enjoy the superb hospitality which the Stirlings, undismayed by the imminent conversion of Keir into a hospital, lavished upon us.

Once the decision had been taken to withdraw Allied troops from Norway our own small mission clearly had no further purpose; nevertheless, the order to abandon Operation 'Knife' came as a severe blow. Besides the anti-climax of our return to London, we were saddened by the imminent break-up of a party so closely knit by a common purpose and the experience of a common danger. It was thanks to Stirling's imagination and initiative that our partnership was not, in fact, immediately dissolved. Accompanied by Mayfield he preceded us to London for conferences with Colonel Holland, the head of M.I.(R.), and a number of influential friends of his own; when the rest of us arrived he already had a plan for our useful employment as well as the necessary authority to carry it out.

The invasion of Norway showed clearly the possibilities of partisan warfare. Paramilitary formations known as 'Independent Companies'—the forerunners of Commandos—had been employed in the last stages of the Norwegian campaign; Colin Gubbins had commanded a brigade largely composed of them. In spite of a good deal of angry controversy they were considered to have proved their usefulness. There was, however, no organized instruction in this kind of warfare, no school or centre where troops could be trained in its principles; there was a certain amount of theory—Gubbins himself had written a pamphlet—and there must be an untapped reservoir of officers and men with the necessary qualifications and experience to act as instructors: Indian Army officers who had served on the North-West Frontier, 'bush-whackers' from the West African Frontier Force or the King's African Rifles, Polar explorers, ghillies from Lovat's Scouts, and the like. There should be no difficulty in finding a suitable location for the project; the Scottish highlands abounded in what Boswell has described as 'fine and noble prospects', ideal country for training in irregular or amphibious operations; also in half-derelict houses which in size and architecture might have been designed as barracks.

It was Stirling's idea that the six of us, reinforced by a few selected officers and N.C.O.s, should form the nucleus of the new training school; we should begin with cadre courses for junior officers from different units of the Army. Mayfield was to be Commandant, Stirling Chief Instructor. There was no fear, Stirling assured us, of our having to remain instructors for the rest of the war; when the first few cadres were trained there would be a plentiful supply of officers to fill our posts as and when we wished to be released for operational duties; moreover, he added, we should be in a strong position to choose our own operational theatres. By the time the Battle of France opened, Stirling and Mayfield had obtained War Office approval for our Establishment, selected the training area and set the requisitioning machinery in motion; the first cadres would report for training at the end of the month.

Some twenty-five miles west of Fort William as the crow flies—rather more as the road and railway run—stands Inverailort House, a large square building of plain grey stone. It is situated at the head of Lochailort, on the south shore, where the gloom of its natural surroundings matches the chill austerity of its design. The front of the house faces north to the sea loch, whose sombre waters, alternately wrapped in mist and whipped by rainstorms, blend with the leaden tones of walls and roof. The back is overshadowed by a grim black cliff, surmounted by a thick, forbidding growth of trees, which rises from the back door to well above the height of the roof, blotting out the light of the sun at all times except high noon in summer. The rainfall at Glenfinnan, ten miles to the east, is the highest in the British Isles. But on the few fine days at this time of the year the shores of Lochailort and the Sound of Arisaig reveal a wild, bleak beauty of scoured grey rock and cold blue water, of light green bracken and shadowed pine, that is strangely moving in its stark simplicity and grandeur.

In May and June of 1940 the same clear weather that favoured the German offensive in France brought warmth and sunshine to Inverailort, where, at the beginning of the last week in May, we arrived to prepare for the first training course. With the help of the War Office Stirling had been able to recruit some outstanding officers and N.C.O.s to bring our staff of instructors to full strength.

Training in amphibious operations formed an important part of each course, and was supervised by a naval commander. The senior instructor in field-craft was Stirling's cousin, Lord Lovat, to whom I was appointed assistant. In view of his epic career later in the war he needs no introduction here; a brilliant instructor as well as a superb fighting soldier, he taught me in the three weeks I was with him all I know about movement across country and the principles of natural camouflage. Gavin, now a major, was in charge of demolitions; his assistant was another regular Sapper, Mike Calvert, who had just had the satisfaction of seeing himself reported in the official War Office casualty list as killed in Norway; three years later 'Mad Mike', at the age of twenty-five, was one of Wingate's brigadiers. Major Munn, a Gunner officer who had served on the North-West Frontier, instructed in map reading and allied subjects. He brought with him two lean, bronzed, hard-bitten officers of the Guides. They were supposed to instruct in the practice of irregular warfare, but it turned out that their experience had all been the other way—in suppressing guerrillas; they exasperated their pupils by making them climb to the tops of the hills and march along the crests, where they were visible for miles against the skyline. They left us after a few weeks.

Our first students arrived at the beginning of June—twenty-five keen but puzzled subalterns, some of them volunteers, others arbitrarily dispatched by their commanding officers. Among them was Stirling's brother David, later to become famous as the founder of the Special Air Service Regiment in North Africa. Each course was to last a month, with a few days break before the arrival of the next. From this small beginning developed the series of Special Training Schools which was later established throughout Great Britain, in the Middle and Far East, in Australia and the North American Continent.

III

EDUCATION OF AN AGENT

In the year 1941 began with the greatest personal tragedy of my life. On 10th January, the aircraft carrier *Illustrious* was heavily bombed by Stukas in the Sicilian Channel: among the dead was my brother. The previous November he had flown a Swordfish in the Fleet Air Arm attack on Taranto, and torpedoed one of the new *Littorio* class battleships, for which he was posthumously awarded a D.S.C. My mother's telegram reached me in Edinburgh, where I was convalescing after a prolonged illness following my return from Portugal. As I read it again and again, numb and sick with shock, it seemed absurd that so much human misery could be carried on a crumpled piece of buff-coloured paper. My mother, four years a widow, never recovered from the blow. It was a long time before I could bring myself to realize that Neil was dead. Throughout his life he had exercised a profound, even decisive influence on me; it was easier to imagine that the sky should fall than that he should be killed. Not yet thirty-one he had already earned recognition as an historian and writer on naval affairs, and a column and a half of tributes to him in The Times showed that his death was a severe loss to the Service as well as to ourselves. I tried to console myself with the words of Clarendon's epitaph on Lord Falkland:

'And whosoever leads such a life need not care upon how short warning it be taken from him.'

Early in February I was ordered to report in London to Captain Kennedy, one of the officers who had briefed us for Operation 'Knife'. M.I.(R.) was now dissolved and its place taken by a much larger organization, combining elements of M.I.(R.) with other departments that had previously been working along the same lines, but so often at cross purposes that their efforts had seemed directed against each other rather than against the Germans. This new organization, known as S.O.E., became responsible for all subversive activities in enemy-occupied territory. It received its directives through the Minister of Economic Warfare, and was staffed, surprisingly, by senior executives from several large banking and business houses, with a small but useful leavening of Regular Army officers, a few of whom had received Staff College training.

'We're preparing a party,' said Kennedy, 'to go on an operation that I think might interest you. Are you quite fit again?'

I was, except for a sharp attack of gout, an inherited complaint which caused me much annoyance later.

'I can't give you any details about the operation now,' he went on. 'You will join the rest of the party at Lochailort and do the paramilitary course with them as a student. While you're up there you'll be told more about the scheme.'

I arrived at Lochailort on a clear frosty morning three days later. The instructing staff had changed a great deal since I was last there. Mayfield was commanding a brigade in North Africa, Stirling was in Cairo, Gavin on his way to Singapore; Lovat was about to start his spectacular career in Commandos; Calvert was in India.

I had at first supposed that the operation for which we were being prepared would take place in Spain; but my eighteen companions did not seem to have been chosen for their knowledge of that country or language. In fact, we seemed to have no common background. Not all of us could speak Spanish, and the majority of those who could had learnt it in South America; one or two had been to Spain for a short holiday. The majority had been plucked without explanation from regimental soldiering and given a brief interview in London; they had been asked a few obscure questions, such as 'Would you rather be General Wavell or Lawrence of Arabia?' Then they had been ordered to report to Lochailort. They felt they had been better employed in their old units; some, who had been company commanders, were indignant at the change. One officer, known to the rest of us as 'Slogger', was frankly apprehensive; he was a quiet, meticulous man with a nervous manner, a literal mind and no sense of humour.

It was, therefore, a bewildered and resentful audience that assembled in one of the lecture rooms towards the end of February to hear what was in store for us. For the past three weeks we had undergone extremely rigorous training, making forced marches across country carrying fifty-pound rucksacks, sweating up steep hillsides, plunging into deep ravines and across rock-strewn torrents, pretending to blow up bridges with dummy explosives, and once nearly destroying a bridge and ourselves with real explosive that had been substituted in error. We had spent hours listening to lectures on map-reading, demolitions, and German Army Order of Battle; and we had been taught pistol-shooting and 'unarmed combat' by two ex-detectives from the Shanghai International Police. The senior detective had the manner and appearance of an elderly, amiable clergyman, combined with the speed and ferocity of a footpad; lulled by his soft tones and charmed by his benevolent smile, we would be startled to hear him conclude some demonstration with a snarled, 'Then you bring up your right knee smartly into his testicles.'

Now at last we were to know the object of our training: a senior officer of S.O.E. had come all the way from London to tell us. There was some ribald speculation as to whether he would be a banker or a business tycoon;

he proved to be neither, but a rising young lawyer, now wearing the badges of a lieutenant-colonel. His manner jarred on us, probably because he had little military experience. He seemed anxious for us to realize that he was a jolly good fellow, just like one of us, a simple, friendly chap with no nonsense about him. To emphasize this he began his talk with one of the oldest dirty jokes in the legal profession. He continued, in a tone half ingratiating, half patronizing, to explain that it was very probable that the Germans would invade Spain. If they did there would be a surprise for them; we were going to be the surprise. He himself would control our activities from not too far away, and he would be with us all the time in spirit.

We should soon be leaving for Gibraltar, there to await the German invasion. We should be divided into parties of two, each party to be provided with a wireless set, a wireless operator, and quantities of arms, ammunition and explosives. When the German invasion seemed imminent each party would move as fast as possible to a previously determined operational area; it was not quite clear what we should do when we arrived there, but it seemed that there would be anti-German resistance groups with whom we could work and whom we would supply with arms. We might be interested to know that we were already spoken of in the Office as 'Ali Baba and the Forty Thieves'; 'Ali Baba' was the officer detailed to command us inside the country, with whom we should keep in contact by wireless. We should meet him in Gibraltar. Another piece of good news, he told us, was that we were all to be made captains with effect from 16th March. Those of his audience who were already captains received this *bonne bouche* without enthusiasm.

'As for what the future holds for you,' he summed up, as though he had not already made it clear, 'I can only tell you'—his voice took on a deeper, sterner tone—'Hardship shall be your mistress, Danger your constant companion.'

If we had any qualms about the venture he urged us to withdraw from it now, before the irrevocable step was taken.

'Slogger' rose to his feet. This was not at all the sort of thing, he explained in low, precise tones, for which he would consider volunteering. In the first place, he had not been consulted before being sent on this course; he felt himself to be quite unsuited for this kind of operation, and he would be grateful if he could be returned as soon as possible to his work with the Intelligence Corps.

As we suspected, and as it turned out, 'Slogger' had the laugh on us.

After a few days' leave we reassembled at Fawley Court, near Henley-on-Thames, an S.O.E. holding school for operational parties such as ours; the commandant was Major Tommy Lindsay, an Irish Guards officer gifted with the very necessary qualities of tact, patience and charm. Here we discovered that, in addition to being 'Ali Baba and the Forty Thieves,' we were Operation 'Relator'.

We were told to choose our partners for the operational parties. I found myself paired with John Burton, a tall, burly, ginger-haired officer from the Lincolnshire Regiment; it was a partnership that was to last a long time, through operations much more serious than 'Relator'. Burton's quiet, almost gentle manner concealed surprising determination, courage and powers of endurance; despite an austere appearance he combined a sense of humour with a genuine personal humility, while his natural common sense and efficiency provided a valuable counter to the volatility of my own temperament.

At the end of the second week in March we received our embarkation orders. The prospect of a fortnight at sea during the Battle of the Atlantic and at such a time of year filled some of us with dismay; others, like myself, who were good sailors and enjoyed the sea, fortified ourselves with thoughts of comfortable bunks, congenial company and unlimited quantities of duty-free liquor. The reality, when we boarded the tramp steamer *Fidelity* at Liverpool, proved a shock to the most pessimistic of us.

Although she flew the White Ensign *Fidelity* had recently belonged to the French mercantile marine. Her captain, officers and crew were all French; but they appeared on the ships manifest under incongruous Scottish or Irish names and were supposed to pass as Canadians in the event of their being taken by the Germans. Although they spoke no English they gallantly tried to call each other by their assumed names, so that the ship would ring with such cries as '*Merde! Où est ce sale Maconzee?*' At the time of the fall of France her captain had smuggled *Fidelity* out of Marseilles with this volunteer crew; now she was in the service of a similar organization to S.O.E.. Naturally, there was no love lost between the two organizations, which may have accounted for some of our discomfort.

We arrived in Liverpool on a raw, rainy evening and went straight to the Adelphi for dinner. About ten o'clock we were driven to the ship.

We were received on board by Lieutenant-Commander Milner-Gibson, R.N., who was sailing as liaison officer. He was both apologetic and indignant.

'I don't know how to break it to you chaps,' he began. 'Until an hour ago, when I got here myself, nobody in this ship had the least idea that there would be passengers. There's nowhere for you to sleep, but the crew are clearing space in two of the holds, and you'll just have to park your camp-beds there. At least it's a lucky thing that you've brought camp equipment. I'm afraid you're going to be hellish uncomfortable. Of course the Captain's furious, but that's not your fault. Another thing—I don't know how we're going to fit you in for meals, as there's no room in the saloon; I don't even know if there's enough food, because we're sailing tomorrow and there's no time to order extra stores.'

'Oh well!' somebody said, 'I expect we'll survive till Gibraltar on gin.'

'You won't!' he retorted. 'Not unless you've brought it with you. There's no time to get Customs clearance for extra liquor and the ship's officers have barely enough for themselves. The whole thing's a damn disgrace,' he concluded sympathetically, 'and I can assure you I'm going to send in a strong report about it!'

We set up our camp-beds and sleeping bags in the holds, where there was just enough space to accommodate all of us, with two feet between each bed. We turned in immediately, by the light of kerosene lanterns; next day the electricians rigged up a few lights, enabling us to see enough for dressing and moving about, but barely enough for reading. Neither daylight nor fresh air could penetrate to lighten the frosty atmosphere of our dormitories.

After dropping us at Gibraltar *Fidelity* was bound for secret operations in the Mediterranean. She had been converted into something between a 'Q' ship and a flak-ship; her decks and superstructure fairly bristled with guns of varying calibres, from the clumsy four-inch fore and aft to light Oerlikon anti-aircraft cannon, pom-poms, and machine-guns; most of them were concealed behind dummy bulwarks.

The ensuing fortnight was among the most unpleasant in my experience at sea. *Fidelity* was not a happy ship. Officers and crew alike were terrified of their Captain, a stocky, black-bearded pirate with a reputation for ferocity and courage which he seemed resolved to impress upon us all. Slung from a belt round his uniform jacket he carried an automatic pistol, with which he claimed to be a deadly shot and with which he would blaze away at anything that caught his eye—a seagull on the mast, a piece of flotsam on the sea or an offending member of the crew; he would stride about the bridge, his hands in the pockets of his jacket, his beard thrust out aggressively and a malignant expression on his brick-red face, screaming invective at the Officer of the Watch, the guns' crews at practice, the quartermaster at the wheel or anybody unlucky enough to cross his line of vision. During these black moods, and they were more frequent than his bright ones, he would aim savage kicks and blows at the nearest officer or man within reach. He never actually assaulted any of us, contenting himself with abuse. Only to Milner-Gibson was he always polite. I do not ever remember seeing him smile.

For defaulting officers he had a special treatment: when all were assembled for a meal in the saloon the Captain would bellow the offender's name. A trembling 'O'Flaherty' or 'Mackenzie' would present himself at attention in front of the angry little man, who would launch into voluble details of his offence, his character and the less creditable habits of his parents, concluding with three or four heavy slaps across the face in dismissal;

often, as the victim turned to go, a well-directed kick in the seat of the pants would send him sprawling among his colleagues.

The only person who could control the Captain was his mistress, a sharp-faced little blonde with a metallic voice and vicious tongue; he had smuggled her out of Marseilles with the ship and had persuaded our sister organization to invest her with the uniform and two rings of an officer of the W.R.N.S. She was the real ruler of the ship, and she let us know it. Towards us soldiers she showed a particular animosity, reviling us on every possible pretext and resorting, when she felt that words were inadequate, to typewritten announcements on the saloon notice-board; these began usually with the phrase: '*Messieurs les officiers anglais sont avisés que...*' followed by a list of our misdemeanours—chiefly being late for meals, and spilling cigarette ash on the saloon deck. Space in the saloon was so restricted that the eighteen of us were divided into three watches for our meals, the first watch going to lunch at eleven-fifteen, the second at twelve o'clock and the third at twelve forty-five; we changed our mealtimes in rotation. The slightest unpunctuality on the part of any of us would invoke a tirade from this harpy, followed by some such announcement on the notice-board as: '*Messieurs les officiers anglais sont avisés que nous ne sommes pas sur un paquebot et que l'Empire est en guerre!*'

In the early afternoon following our arrival on board we sailed, one of a slow convoy that made its way round the north coast of Ireland and well out into the Atlantic. While we were in port the crew had worked hard to make our sleeping quarters habitable; but despite all their efforts the holds, with their bare iron decks and bulkheads, remained a grim reminder to us that we were not '*sur un paquebot*'. In good weather we should not have been too uncomfortable, but as soon as we entered the Western Ocean we ran into the first of a series of gales which lasted until we had rounded Cape St. Vincent. Through the ill-caulked decks above, rain and sea-water poured in unceasing streams, drenching our beds and clothes and swirling about the floor with each roll of the ship. Because of her heavy armament aloft *Fidelity* rolled with a savage, plunging violence, sending our camp-beds and their occupants skidding across the floor and often upsetting us into the water which had collected at one or other side of the hold. Seasickness did not affect me, but it prostrated poor Burton, whose bed was next to mine and for whom the whole voyage was unbroken hell. We found buckets for him and other sufferers to be sick into, but no ingenuity could prevent the buckets themselves from overturning and adding their contents to the mess swilling about the floor.

I think we were all haunted by a nagging fear of being trapped in those holds if the ship were torpedoed. However, although the convoy was attacked on more than one occasion, we in *Fidelity* were disturbed by nothing more menacing than the distant explosions of depth-charges.

No Colours or Crest

The Rock of Gibraltar has never seemed so beautiful to my eyes as when it appeared, wrapped in a faint haze, in the shining forenoon of 5th April. *Fidelity* dropped anchor in the bay with the rest of the convoy, a launch drew alongside and a middle-aged lieutenant-colonel, wearing Gunner badges, climbed on deck. In a Canadian accent he introduced himself as our new commanding officer—the 'Ali Baba' of whom we had heard at Lochailort.

The news with which he greeted us killed whatever hopes we might have had for the success of our operation. He had just returned from a visit to Madrid, where he had tried to persuade our Ambassador to let us make a few preparations in Spain for our reception after the German invasion. The Ambassador's answer had been an emphatic refusal to countenance any S.O.E. activity whatsoever.

'Ali Baba' sugared this bitter pill with the news that our Director—the officer who had addressed us so disarmingly at Inverailort—was now in Gibraltar, having followed us from England, V.I.P. fashion, in a battle-cruiser. He was giving a cocktail party that evening for us at the Rock Hotel.

Our quarters had been prepared under canvas on the North Front, on a strip of ground beside the military cemetery, bordering the new and rapidly growing airfield. This was the site of the old race-course, which had disappeared at the beginning of the war, together with such peacetime luxuries as the Calpe Hunt. By the time we had installed ourselves, two to a tent in our operational pairs, it was time to leave for the Rock Hotel and our party with the Director.

Smooth and well-groomed in a Palm Beach suit, he greeted us effusively, hoping that we had had a pleasant voyage. It was a good party, but no one had foreseen the impact of unlimited martinis or whisky upon young men recently accustomed to one glass of Suze a week. Officers gathered in groups of two or three to celebrate their release from the discomforts of *Fidelity* and the tyranny of her Captain and his mistress; soon, flushed faces and raised voices began to indicate the general dissatisfaction with Operation 'Relator', its planners and commanders. In retrospect this appears rather ungrateful, seeing that those we were reviling were paying for our drink; but at the time it seemed to us that we had been brought a long way to execute a plan that was already stillborn.

Our host came to the entrance hall of the hotel to say good-bye; he stood at the head of the steps which led down to the drive, to shake hands with each of us. When my turn came I marched up to him very erect, extended my hand and, trying to look him in the eyes, uttered a thick 'Goodnight, sir! Thank you very much!' Then I did a smart about turn and fell headlong down the flight of marble steps, to land in a heap on the gravel, where I was collected by John Burton and David Muirhead, and bundled into their waiting taxi.

Next morning the whole party assembled in the large mess tent for briefing; we were joined by our wireless operators, who had travelled out separately with their equipment. 'Ali Baba' presided. It was regrettable, he explained that the Ambassador's attitude made it impossible for us to prepare for our task inside Spain; but we must be ready to do our duty whenever the situation should arise. He would now proceed to allot our operational areas. The one to which Burton and I were going was in the western province of Extremadura. It was a part of the country that I did not know. Nothing, it seemed, was known about our proposed collaborators beyond the fact that there was a group of people living there in the mountains who, it was hoped, could be persuaded to work for us against the Germans; for all we knew, they might be remnants of the Republican Army against which I had fought for nearly three years.

It was difficult for us to feel great enthusiasm for such a vague and ill-planned scheme, or to take much interest in its preparation. The method by which it was proposed that we should reach our areas had the one merit of simplicity: as soon as the German invasion began, each party would climb into its lorry—already loaded with arms, explosives and wireless—and drive by the shortest route to its destination; how many of us would get there, or even succeed in crossing the International Zone to La Línea, was anybody's guess. The assembly broke up in a mood approaching alarm and despondency.

Our chief problem during the succeeding weeks was how to fill in time; we had no troops to train, and after our course at Lochailort we required little more instruction ourselves. But 'Ali Baba' wished our establishment to be run on Regular Army lines; he devised a training programme which, sensibly, included wireless instruction—a subject I could never understand—demolition practice, shooting with tommy-gun and pistol, and lorry-driving. At times we were sent to scale the north-western face of the Rock, each carrying a Tommy-gun and a fifty-pound rucksack—a terrifying performance for anyone, like myself, with a poor head for heights. In addition to this collective training we each had separate, specialist duties. Mine was the preparation of an English-Spanish dictionary of military terms, on which I worked every free morning in a room at the Joint Intelligence Centre. It was an uninspiring task, the more so because I was sternly forbidden to include the most interesting phrases from Archie Lyall's *Soldier's Speakeasy*.

The problem of our spare time was more difficult. A large part of the civilian population had been evacuated, but the strength of the garrison had swollen to many times its normal size. We were no longer allowed to visit Spain or Tangier. Apart from the Yacht Club, the Rock Hotel, the Bristol, and a few bars, Gibraltar offered little in the way of evening entertainment. I spent most of my afternoons swimming off one of the beaches on the east side of the Rock, or sailing in the bay of Algeciras with a Cambridge friend of mine from the Meteorological Office, who owned a Star; we had to keep our distance from the Spanish shore, because we were liable to be fired on if we approached too close. In the evening, as the sun was sinking behind the dark hills above Algeciras, reminding me with bitter nostalgia of the Western Highlands where I used to spend my holidays before the Spanish War, Burton and I would stroll out of camp, past the sentries at the concrete roadblocks, towards the harbour and the Yacht Club. We always knew whom we should meet there, just as we knew whom we should see in the Bristol or any of the other bars. The tension of waiting for a hazardous operation and the exasperation of feeling that it could never come off increased our urge to look for relief in gin and whisky, which were plentiful and cheap, in frivolous conversation and forced geniality. Worst of all, I was in love. The pain of separation had been bearable as long as my mind was occupied with thoughts of hazard and adventure in Spain; but now idleness gave me too much time to brood, and the bottle was a simple anodyne.

We often had friends to dine in Mess in our camp, where the food was poor but the drink lavish. The Mess tent, a large marquee, stood on the very edge of the airfield; behind it were the rows of sleeping tents, their guy-ropes almost overlapping; some distance beyond them were the latrines. Every guest night at the end of dinner the darkness would ring with cries of pain or indignation as we and our guests tripped over guy-ropes or the iron staples supporting them, on our tipsy journey to relieve ourselves. My most frequent guest was Hugh Sidebottom, a Newmarket trainer in civilian life, now a Captain in command of the Pack Transport Company on the Upper Rock; a broad, powerfully built man with an inexhaustible fund of good humour and a boisterous but endearing manner, he had the distinction, in which he took great pride, of being the only mounted officer on the Rock. He exulted in his surname and would shake his head sadly over a relation who had changed it to Edgedale.

'Not a true Bottom,' was his comment.

The Navy—chiefly submariners attached to the depot ship *Maidstone* and officers from Admiral Somerville's famous Force H—provided us with some diversion. Theirs were faces we did not see every evening in the bars, for the submariners were often away on patrols and the ships of Force H only put in to Gibraltar for a few days between their visits to the 'Men's End' of the Mediterranean. They meant to make the best of their time ashore. Most of our friends were from the carrier Ark Royal—Fleet Air Arm pilots whose enjoyment of life was not impaired by their slender expectation of survival. It was they who initiated an incident subsequently known as 'The Battle of the Bristol'.

One evening I was dining in the Bristol Hotel with Sidebottom and a captain in the Devonshire Regiment. There were a few Army Officers at tables near us; the rest of the room seemed to be full of pilots from Ark

Royal. Drink was flowing freely; there was a good deal of banter passing across the room, and an atmosphere of vigorous good humour. Just for the fun of it someone slung a glass at the chandelier, shattering the lights. In a moment everybody joined in the party; the air was full of flying glass and crockery, accompanied by war whoops and hunting calls. Crouched behind our table in the darkness, lobbing our plates and glasses and listening to the splintering of others close around us, we wondered whatever could have made us think Gibraltar dull. Soon the stocks of ammunition were exhausted, and we were wiping lumps of goulash and *sole bonne femme* from our hair and mopping wine from our eyes. Within a quarter of an hour peace reigned, light had been restored and the management was graciously accepting our apologies and promises of compensation. There were no serious casualties, but Force H veterans subsequently swore that not even in their battles up the 'Men's End' had they been more terrified.

One way and another, I did not envy the Assistant Provost Marshal his job of keeping discipline on the Rock. He was a dug-out major of a famous cavalry regiment, whose ideas had crystallized in or about the year 1916 into an almost religious and totally humourless veneration of the outward forms and appearance of soldiering; in his trim, perfectly tailored uniform, gleaming buttons and Sam Browne, and strikingly coloured forage cap he was a figure of half affectionate, half ribald fun to the garrison. On one occasion all officers of Fortress Headquarters had to go through a gas chamber wearing their masks as part of an exercise; afterwards Sidebottom jokingly asked him if his gas mask had fitted.

'I should hope so, indeed!' replied the A.P.M. in genuine surprise. 'I had it made for me at Lock's before I came out here.'

Early in May Lord Gort replaced Sir Clive Liddell as Governor of Gibraltar. The appointment of this tough fighting soldier and disciplinarian gave rise to rumours that a German attack on the Rock was imminent. Soon afterwards the news of the German invasion of Crete with airborne troops shook Gibraltar. It was taken for granted that similar tactics would be used at any moment against us. The whole fortress was put into a state of siege. In the galleries inside the Rock work went on with redoubled speed by day and night; extra roadblocks and anti-tank defences appeared on every road; a curfew was imposed at eleven o'clock and severe penalties threatened against all unauthorized persons found abroad after that hour; at any time after dark there was danger of being shot by some trigger-happy sentry.

All units were obliged to take special security precautions; 'Ali Baba's' took the form of issuing an order that one officer and one sergeant should sit up all night in the Mess tent, armed with tommy-guns. The burden of this duty was light enough until about two in the morning, because there were usually several officers carousing in the ante-room; but the small hours dragged intolerably on this farcical guard. Nevertheless, there was an air of tension and grim purpose for at least ten days after the initial shock. It was dispelled, for us, by the arrival of a brief order, signed by the Garrison Commander, announcing that 'in the event of an enemy airborne invasion of the Rock, all tentage will be returned forthwith to Ordnance.'

One afternoon at the end of May we were all ordered to assemble in the big marquee; the Director had something important to say to us. We had not seen much of him lately; on the few occasions when he had dined with us in Mess he had seemed preoccupied and had spoken little. Now, when he walked into the stuffy Mess tent, dressed as always in a Palm Beach suit, we all felt that we were about to hear something dramatic. Standing at the head of the long trestle table and laying his brief-case carefully in front of him, he began to speak in sombre, heroic periods.

In view of the refusal of His Majesty's representative in Spain to countenance any of our preparations for action in that country, he had decided that it was impossible to pursue our original plan. Once the German invasion was under way we could not hope to penetrate the country in uniform; our only chance would be to infiltrate in civilian clothes. He was already working on new plans to this end. He could not, of course, order us to undertake such an operation, but perhaps some of us would care to volunteer.

'It is my duty to warn you,' he continued, 'that if you are caught in civilian clothes in an enemy-occupied country, you will most certainly be—' At that precise moment the crash of a volley from the adjoining cemetery broke in upon his words.

Even those of us who volunteered were not destined to learn details of the Director's new plans. Well on into June we persisted in our hopes that 'Relator' might yet prove feasible, and we remained in a state of readiness to put it into practice, if necessary, at a few hours' notice. But when on 22nd June we heard the news of the German invasion of Russia, all prospect of the operation vanished. We seemed likely to spend the rest of the war kicking our heels within the narrow frontiers of the Rock, for Lord Gort would not allow any officer or other rank to leave, except on a specific military assignment, whether or not his presence on the Rock was necessary. During the ensuing weeks a few members of our party were sent by the Director on clandestine expeditions to North Africa; they ended in Vichy prison camps, where they remained until the North African landings.

Soon after five o'clock on a bright, brassy evening at the end of June H.M. Submarine *Clyde* (Commander David Ingram, D.S.C., R.N.) slid out of Gibraltar harbour between the South and the Detached Moles into the Bay of Algeciras. Standing on the bridge beside Ingram I felt once again the throb of diesels beneath my feet as we pounded westward towards Tangier and the

Straits; I turned my eyes from the glare of the sun on the water to gaze at the white and yellow houses of the town clustered beneath the great blue bulk of the Rock, and wondered grimly whether this second submarine trip of mine was going to end in such an anti-climax as my first.

Clyde was the submarine which the Admiralty had detailed to take us to Norway in place of *Truant* in April 1940. I had not expected to see her again. But when, after the collapse of our hopes for Operation 'Relator', I had approached 'Ali Baba' with the suggestion that I should go on a submarine patrol in order to study the problems of inter-service liaison and Combined Operations, he had raised no objection. My friends from H.M.S. *Maidstone* made the arrangements for me, introducing me to David Ingram over a few pink gins in the wardroom. Ingram, a serious-minded officer of high seniority and long submarine experience, agreed to take me on his next patrol. He told me, confidentially, that *Clyde* was to sail in twenty-four hours' time to hunt a U-boat which was reported on its way to refuel in the Canary Islands.

'If we can catch her at dusk or in darkness,' he said, 'it would be fun to try to board her and take her alive. In that case, you will come in useful with your cloak and dagger stuff.'

I reported on board next morning, armed with tommy-gun, grenades, and .32 automatic. *Clyde* was a considerably larger boat than Truant; as the only passenger I was given a bunk in the comfortable little wardroom. Over lunch, which we ate aboard H.M.S. *Maidstone*, I met the rest of *Clyde's* officers, a quiet, friendly group who seemed genuinely glad to be taking a 'pongo' with them; they seemed to think it would be a good opportunity of studying the breed at close quarters.

For the first few minutes after casting off, while the crew were at 'Harbour Stations', I was asked to stay below; but as soon as we were in the Bay I was invited up to the bridge. As we swung westward into the Straits I watched the houses and streets of Ceuta glimmering on our port beam under the imposing mass of Gebel Musa; to starboard, on the Spanish coast, rose tiers of dark hills clothed in groves of cork trees; high up, a ruined Moorish watch-tower concealed, some supposed, a German observation post.

We were abeam of Tarifa when we sighted the destroyer approaching from the west. She proved to be H.M.S. *Avon Vale*, one of the new 'Hunt' class. Once she had been identified as a friend I turned my attention from her to watch the changing colours on the African shore glow and fade in the evening light. I was vaguely aware that we were exchanging identification signals with her at a distance of a little over a mile on our starboard beam. Then in a flash of alarm I sensed that something was wrong: there was a mistake in the colour of the recognition flares. I heard the Officer of the Watch shout, 'My God, she's opening fire!' Simultaneously with Ingram's snapped order, 'Crash dive!' I heard the whine of a shell close overhead. I was seized from behind and pushed roughly to the opening of the conning tower hatch. Fearfully alive to the danger I almost threw myself down the vertical iron ladder, with the boots of the next man stamping on my fingers. As my feet touched the floor of the control room and the last man off the bridge slammed the hatch of the conning-tower, there was a violent explosion overhead, followed a second later by the faint report of a gun. I heard someone exclaim, 'Bloody good for a second shot!'

The confined space of the control room, the ship's nerve centre, was crowded with men, each concentrating grimly on his job: the First Lieutenant by the hydroplane controls, anxiously watching the angle of our dive; the helmsman tense at the wheel, listening for Ingram's curt directions; petty officers and ratings with their hands on control levers, their eyes on the dials and gauges. Clearly this was no place for me; I made my way to the wardroom and sank onto a settee at the little dining-table. *Avon Vale* was still firing. Sitting in the silence of the wardroom I could plainly hear the bark of her guns and the rising hum of the shells as they flew towards us, to burst with a curious metallic ringing on the water around us. Over the intercom came the warning, toneless and terrifying:

'Stand by for depth-charge attack. Stand by for depth-charge attack.'

Alone, bewildered, and sweating in anticipation, I wondered what action I was supposed to take. Looking up I caught sight of the ward-room steward in the narrow passageway, bracing himself against a bulkhead; following his example, I braced myself between the wall and one of the supports of the table. I was glad to notice, even from that distance, that he also was sweating. I managed a feeble smile and received a cheerful grin in reply.

The shelling ceased; there was absolute silence. I would never have believed that a crowded ship could be so quiet. It was impossible to tell if we were still diving, or even if we were moving. No sound came from *Avon Vale*. Surely, I tried to comfort myself, if she were closing to attack we should hear the sound of her propellers. I have no idea how long we continued thus before the tension was broken by the Captain's voice:

'Flap seems to be over. Up periscope!'

A minute or two later the welcome orders came through the loudspeaker:

'Stand by to surface!'

'Blow number one!'

'Blow all tanks!'

I heard the rush of water sweeping past our sides as we broke surface, and felt a draught of air blow through the boat when the conning-tower hatch was opened. A few minutes later I was on the bridge, watching *Avon Vale* wallow in the swell while signals of explanation and apology flew between us. *Avon Vale* could certainly be proud of her gunnery: with her second shot she had landed a four-inch shell on our bridge as we were submerging; luckily the damage was only to the superstructure, and we were able to continue our voyage.

'Could it be, Peter,' asked Ingram, who had heard of my journey in *Truant*, 'that you are a Jonah in submarines?'

Passing Cape Spartel we altered course towards the Canaries. At first we travelled on the surface by day as well as at night, but we kept a sharp lookout for enemy aircraft and dived whenever we sighted a ship in the distance; we met no enemy, or any ship suspected of trading with the enemy, but it was important for us to escape detection on our outward journey, lest our destination and the nature of our mission were suspected. Because space on the bridge was limited and everyone needed a spell up there for fresh air, I spent most of my time in the wardroom, where the reading matter varied in subject and quality from the stiff, blue-bound *Mediterranean Pilot* to James Hadley Chase's *Twelve Chinks and a Woman*.

Between meals—the food was excellent and included luxuries unknown in our mess at Gibraltar—we spent most of our time sleeping. No liquor was drunk at sea, apart from one whisky every night before supper; known as the 'evening snodgrass' it gave me more pleasure than a whole day's drinking in Gibraltar. At six o'clock each evening we had prayers, attended by all the ship's company who were not on watch; they would crowd into the control room and the compartments next to it while Ingram read the brief service.

'Save and deliver us, we humbly beseech Thee, from the hands of our enemies; abate their pride, assuage their malice, and confound their devices.' The noble language of the Book of Common Prayer filled me with quiet confidence and pride as I stood bunched with the others in the dim and cramped interior of our pulsating steel shell.

As we neared the Canaries the feeling of tension increased. We travelled submerged during the hours of daylight, surfacing only at night to charge the batteries, when we would be thankful for a short spell on the bridge. It was quiet and restful under water—so restful that I passed nearly all the time asleep on my bunk. Although we sometimes submerged for sixteen hours on end I never felt stifled; the everything was damp with the condensation, and we sweated all the time in the heat. We nosed around the Islands, sometimes less than a mile off shore, searching for indications of our quarry. Through the after periscope, which was fitted with a telescopic lens, we could see people bathing, their dark brown bodies glistening in the bright sun, and watch the fishermen in their gaily coloured boats pulling in their nets; but in the three days of our search we found no sign of a submarine. Ingram's orders did not allow him to remain longer. With a feeling of anticlimax we turned for home, reaching Gibraltar ten days after we had set out.

During the next few weeks Burton and I became more and more impatient with our inactivity on the Rock. I heard from the Director that there was talk of dropping operational parties into northern Spain, should the collapse of Russian resistance enable the Germans to launch an attack through the Peninsula. When I pointed out to him that most of my experience of Spain had been in the north, he agreed to have Burton and myself recalled to England on military grounds.

August the 3rd, 1941, was my happiest day on the Rock; that morning Burton and I received orders to embark for England aboard the French liner *Pasteur*, now converted into a troopship. We went aboard in the afternoon, but when we had stowed our kit in our cabin we were curtly ordered ashore and told not to return before midnight. We learnt the reason next day: *Pasteur* was one of the largest and fastest liners in the world; moored at the South Mole, she would be clearly visible to anyone with a telescope in the neighbourhood of Algeciras. All that afternoon long lines of troops could be seen filing aboard her, obviously bound for the besieged island of Malta. When darkness had fallen the fast mine-laying cruiser *Manxman* glided alongside *Pasteur*. By the time Burton and I boarded her at midnight, all those troops had been transferred to *Manxman*, who carried them safely to Malta, in the early hours of 4th August *Pasteur* sailed for England, full of service men and civilians from Malta, with a few soldiers like ourselves from the Rock. She had as escort the battle-cruiser *Renown*, the aircraft carrier *Furious*, and five Tribal class destroyers. Our homeward course took us well out into the Atlantic, but travelling at nearly thirty knots in good weather, we were only a week on the voyage.

The offices of the Spanish section of S.O.E. were in a large block of requisitioned flats off the Marylebone Road. The two staff officers who interviewed us on our return were solicitors in private life, members of the same firm as our Director in Gibraltar. One was an R.N.V.R. lieutenant with a solemn manner and an enthusiasm for the piano, the other an Army captain whose tastes were simpler; he could usually be found around midnight at a night-club called the Nut House, a bottle of whisky in front of him and a blonde on either side.

'We're going to send you on a series of courses,' said one of them. 'We've got some pretty interesting ones now, which I'm sure you'll like. Let me see. There's a nice little three-day course on industrial sabotage at a place of ours down in Buckinghamshire, which starts at the end of September. We'll send you there first. Then at the end of October there's our parachute course up at Ringway, near Manchester. You'll love that. Then early in November you can go to Beaulieu, where we have a very interesting course for agents, lasting a fortnight. By that time we hope there'll be an operation for you. Meanwhile, you'd better go on leave, but keep us informed of your address.'

I took advantage of my leave to get married. Looking back from time's distance I wonder how I could have been so foolish, complacent, and blind to my own character as to ask any girl, at my age and at such a time, to marry me; it is scarcely less remarkable, I suppose, that any girl who knew me well—

and this one did—should have considered me a suitable husband. Our marriage lasted almost, but not quite, to the end of the European war.

Burton and I reported for our course on industrial sabotage at a comfortable house standing, as estate agents would say, in its own park-like grounds. Three days did not seem a very long time in which to learn so extensive a subject; but we were told that with our previous knowledge of demolitions it should be long enough to teach us the bare essentials; so that if we found ourselves in enemy-occupied country we might at least be able to blow up something. Theory was well combined with practice. For instance a lecture on the sabotage of power stations, illustrated by diagrams, explained the most vulnerable points for the placing of charges; afterwards a tour of a neighbouring power station showed us where these points were, what they looked like, and where we might expect to find sentries. On a visit to the railway yards at Bletchley we were each allowed to drive an engine. When my turn came I started the engine without difficulty, and was approaching a tunnel at fair speed when I found that I could not stop; luckily the engine driver could, but he insisted on driving back himself.

The most interesting character among our instructors was an officer known locally as the Mad Major. He had a particular fondness—and a genius—for elaborate mechanisms of destruction, of which he invented or developed a large number. He had a disquieting habit during lectures of exhibiting to us one of his pets with a live charge attached, placing it on the desk in front of him, cocking it, and announcing, 'this will go off in five minutes'. He would then continue his lecture, apparently unconcerned, while we nervously counted the minutes ticking away. During the last half of the last minute the sound of his voice was almost drowned by shuffling and scraping of chairs, especially from the front rows. When only five seconds remained, and every head in the class was down, he would suddenly remember, pick up the infernal machine, look at it for a moment thoughtfully, and toss it nonchalantly through the window to explode on the lawn with barely a second to spare.

For our parachute course we reported, towards the end of October, at Dunham Massey House, between Altrincham and Knutsford in Cheshire. It was by far the best-run course I ever attended. The Commandant was a Major Edwards of the Northumberland Fusiliers, had served with distinction in the First World War; an industrious and efficient officer whose passion was punctuality and whose relaxation billiards, he instilled into me more of the latter than the former. His Chief Instructor, Captain Wooller, was an enthusiastic young athlete with more than a hundred and fifty parachute drops to his credit.

They were supported by an able and energetic staff of N.C.O.s, under whose direction we did P.T. every morning before breakfast to limber us up, and learnt our parachute drill. The ground training, I seem to remember, was divided into two main exercises: jumping from a height of about fifteen feet to learn how to fall when landing by parachute—the theory was that the impact of a parachute landing was equal to that of jumping from the roof of a train moving at the same speed as the wind—and dropping through a hole in a dummy fuselage in order to learn the correct position for leaving the aircraft. The important points, they told us, were to keep the body rigid, the hands pressed close to the sides and the knees and feet together, in order to brace the body against the force of the slip-stream; also to look up on leaving the exit, because if we looked down we should bang our heads on the opposite side. The exit aperture in the Whitley, which we were using in those days for training, was indeed too narrow; I saw a number of such injuries during the course. On landing we must take care to keep our feet and knees together, to let each leg bear an equal part of the shock; otherwise we should risk breaking a leg or an ankle. Above all, once the parachute had opened we must keep our eyes on the ground all the way down, and resist the temptation to relax and admire the scenery.

The day before we were to make our first drop we drove to Ringway Aerodrome and flew in a Whitley to get 'air experience'. This was supposed to give us confidence, but on me it had the opposite effect. When the covers were taken off the exit aperture as we approached Tatton Park, our dropping ground, and we looked through the hole at the fields and trees eight hundred feet below us, while the aircraft lurched and shuddered as the pilot throttled back, my stomach turned over and I wondered how I should ever be able to face my first drop. I spent a sleepless and apprehensive night.

Next morning, while waiting on the aerodrome for our turn, I looked at my five companions and noted with a little satisfaction that none of them seemed happier than I. Our sergeant-instructor fitted our parachutes; they felt surprisingly heavy on the back. He gave us a few words of encouragement. He was coming with us in the aircraft, he said, to dispatch us. We should be dropped singly from a height of eight hundred feet, which should give us about twenty seconds on the way down. Subsequent drops would be from five hundred feet.

'Nah, don't forget,' he concluded with a sudden leer, 'if yer 'chute don't open there's never any blood! There yer lies spread on the grahnd like a jelly. All yer bones broke. But there's never—any—*blood.*'

For a time it seemed doubtful whether we should take off; there was a fresh wind blowing and at that time it was considered unsafe to drop in a wind of more than twenty-five miles per hour. After half an hour we were ordered aboard the aircraft, and arranged ourselves opposite each other across the fuselage, three of us forward of the exit, three aft. I was dismayed to find that I should be the last to drop. The sergeant clipped the static lines of our parachutes to the 'strong-point', a stout wire running along the fuselage just beneath the roof. In this way the weight of the parachutist's body, as he left the aircraft, would pull on the static line attached to the 'strong point', causing the parachute to open.

The flight to Tatton Park took about ten minutes. As the pilot throttled back, the sergeant stood up beside the exit. A red light came on by his head; raising his hand he shouted, 'Action Stations, Number One!' The first man swung his legs over the hole and sat on the edge, his hands gripping the sides, his head up—looking, I thought, like a man on his way to the gallows. The red light was followed by a green one. As the sergeant dropped his arm and shouted 'Go!' Number One, with a last imploring look upwards, disappeared through the hole. The sergeant peered after him, then nodded to us. "E's okay!'

Between each drop the aircraft made a circuit of the park. When the fifth man had gone, leaving me alone with the dispatcher, I eased over closer to the hole, ready to swing into the 'action stations' position, and gripped the edge with one hand against the bucking of the aircraft. I dared not look down, fearing that if I did I should not have the nerve to jump. I was cold and sweating at the same time. Reason told me that only one parachute in five thousand failed to open, that five people had just dropped before me without mishap, and that I was being a fool and a cissy; but reason failed to comfort me in the face of an unknown experience, against the background of the aircraft's hammering vibration and the startling backfires of the engines. I may add here that, among all the parachutists I know, I have never met one who did not find his first drop a frightening experience.

The sergeant gave me an encouraging smile, then turned to watch the lights above me. The red flashed. Swinging my legs over the edge, I sat tense and rigid, fixing my attention on the sergeant's arm, as I had been told, and not on the lights. During the next ten seconds I felt no sensation, not even fear, so fierce was my concentration. As his arm swept down and his shout rang in my ears, I thrust myself upwards and outwards with my hands and heels, jerking my head back in my anxiety not to look down. For a ghastly two seconds I felt myself falling, then the slip-stream hit me like a battering-ram and I turned a complete somersault. Next moment I felt a strong pull above me, the sensation of falling ceased, and my parachute was floating like a brilliant white mushroom against the sky.

In the first surge of relief I forgot all my instructions about keeping my feet and knees together and my eyes on the ground; I just relaxed and watched the panorama, enjoying the delicious sensation of gliding slowly earthwards. Even when a loud-hailer on the ground sharply recalled my attention to the drill I remained happy in the thought that my troubles were over. I was gravely mistaken. What I did not know was that the pilot had failed to see a red Verey light, fired from the ground while he was on his last circuit, warning him not to drop me; the wind had risen rapidly and was now gusting up to thirty-five miles an hour. The ground, which a moment before had seemed comfortably far away, suddenly rose up to strike me. I took a frantic pull on my liftwebs to ease the impact, then I landed in a sprawl, partially stunned and totally winded, face down on a cinder-track. Before I could get to my feet and run round behind the parachute to let it collapse, it had billowed out in a great gust of wind and was dragging me over the cinders at the speed of a racehorse. Jerking myself onto my back I struck the quick-release plate on my chest and began to tear with frenzied, shaking fingers at my leg-harness, striving to keep my head off the ground. When my legs were free I twisted back onto my stomach in accordance with the drill, my arms extended straight in front of me, and prayed for the shoulder-harness to slip off before all the skin was torn from my face. In a few seconds my parachute and harness were flying across the park and, after ploughing through some fifty yards of cinders I came to rest.

I lay still until two members of the ground staff, who had been chasing me since my landing, arrived to help me up and escort me to Major Edwards and Captain Wooller; they greeted me with deep concern and warm sympathy. During my descent the wind had carried me beyond the edge of the dropping-zone onto the foundations of a new road. My face, hands and knees were lacerated and black with dirt; I was slightly concussed, but not seriously damaged. When my injuries had been dressed, Edwards drove me back to Dunham and ordered me straight to bed.

'According to medical opinion', he told me, 'the first parachute drop is normally equivalent to the loss of eight hours' sleep. I don't know how much you've lost. You are excused P.T. tomorrow.'

In London, when we arrived after completing the course, my greeting from the staff officers of the Spanish section was not such as a hero might expect. Coldly the R.N.V.R. lieutenant said to me, 'Perhaps you would care to read the concluding words of Major Edwards's report on you?'

They ran simply: 'Not once, nor twice, but three times have I seen this officer punctual.'

IV

SMALL-SCALE RAIDING FORCE

Our intensive courses did not lead, as we had expected, to immediate operations; the Spanish Section, lacking opportunities rather than ideas, had no employment for us. The end of 1941 found Burton and me living in London, reporting daily by telephone to receive each time the same answer. Perhaps, we thought, one of the other Country Sections of S.O.E. might have use for us. We approached in turn the French, Norwegian, Polish, Czech, Russian, and—after Pearl Harbour—Far Eastern Sections, all without success; some had no vacancies, others no work.

Towards the end of February 1942 our spell of unemployment came at last to an end. While job-hunting in one of the several buildings in Baker Street that comprised S.O.E. headquarters we met Colonel Munn, who had been an instructor with me at Lochailort in 1940.

'You had better join my old friend, Gus March-Phillipps', he said after hearing our story. 'He is recruiting officers for a scheme of his which should be just up your street. I'll give your names to him.'

A few days later we were interviewed by Major March-Phillipps and his second-in-command, Captain Geoffrey Appleyard. However overworked and misapplied the words 'personality' and 'genius' may be, it is difficult to avoid their use in a description of those two remarkable characters. A regular officer in the Royal Artillery, March-Phillipps had served in India before the war, where he had experienced both the glamour of action with his battery on the North-West Frontier, and the glitter of social life in various hill stations. Wearying of the latter he had sent in his papers and retired to the English countryside to write novels, only to be recalled on the outbreak of war. After winning the M.B.E. in France in 1940 he had been posted as a Troop Commander to Number 7 Commando on its formation that autumn. In the spring of 1941, with the help of Brigadier Gubbins, he had persuaded S.O.E. to allow him to fit out a Brixham trawler, the *Maid Honor*, and sail her with a crew of seven from Poole Harbour to Freetown in West Africa. Such a voyage would have been extraordinary in peacetime; March-Phillipps and his party completed it without incident at the height of the Battle of the Atlantic. They carried out some brilliant *coup-de-main* operations along the African coast, for which March-Phillipps was awarded the D.S.O. He had returned to England at the beginning of the year.

By religion a deeply sincere Roman Catholic, by tradition an English country gentleman, he combined the idealism of a Crusader with the severity of a professional soldier. He was slightly built and of medium height; his eyes, puckered from straining against tropical glare, gave him an enquiring, piercing and even formidable expression, only slightly mitigated by his tendency to stammer. Despite an unusually hasty temper he had a great sense of fairness towards his subordinates. In battle he was invariably calm. He was intelligent, without any great academic ability. Above all, he had the inspiration to conceive great enterprises, combined with the skill and daring to execute them; he was also most fortunate in his second-in-command.

Of calmer temperament but similarly romantic nature, less impetuous but more obstinate, Appleyard combined a flair for organization and planning with superb skill in action and a unique ability to instill confidence in time of danger. Beneath a broad forehead his deep-set blue eyes gazed on the world with a quiet steadiness matched by the low timbre of his voice. He had the agility and stamina of a champion skier, which his extraordinary will-power subjected to inhuman strains.

The son of a leading Yorkshire industrialist, he had entered his father's engineering business on leaving Cambridge, but had been commissioned in the R.A.S.C. in 1939. Having met March-Phillipps for the first time with the B.E.F. in France, he became one of his troop officers in Number 7 Commando. Landed from a submarine near the Loire estuary early in 1941, he collected two of our agents and brought them back to safety in peculiarly difficult conditions; for this he was awarded the M.C. For the *Maid Honor* operation, when he was March-Phillipps's second-in-command, he received a Bar to his M.C.

The scheme which March-Phillipps and Appleyard had conceived, and for which they had already received official approval, was to raise and train a force to carry out small-scale raids on selected points along the enemy-occupied coasts of Europe. The size of each raiding-party would be about a dozen men, the objectives small strong-points or signal stations thinly held and comparatively easy of access by parties of trained and determined men approaching silently under cover of darkness.

The short-term object of these raids was to take prisoners for information, to shake the morale of the enemy and to raise that of our European allies; the long-term object was, by launching a series of small raids almost nightly along the whole length of coast from the Texel to Brest, to force the enemy to redeploy his forces in Europe, and so relieve some of the pressure on the Russian front. March-Phillipps's eventual ambition was to command a chain of small-scale raiding groups operating from bases scattered along the English coast; his immediate intention was to raise a nucleus of officers and N.C.O.s, to train them in the principles of this kind of warfare, and to give them practical experience by leading them himself in raids across the Channel. As we ourselves acquired experience, he explained, we should be able to train and lead others in similar operations. In this way would the force expand.

As I listened to the details of this plan and realized its enormous possibilities the clouds of frustration that had hung over me during the last few months vanished. Glancing at Burton I saw by his expression how much the idea appealed to him. Before we left the office we were enrolled on the establishment of the Small-Scale Raiding Force.

'We've seen a house in Dorset,' Appleyard told us, 'that would do admirably for our headquarters; I think we shall be allowed to requisition it. Our early raids will be mounted from Portland, Poole and Gosport, so that Anderson Manor, which is between Blandford and Poole, is ideally situated. We shan't be able to get down to our training for at least another six weeks, so what would you like to do with yourselves in the meantime?'

The most sensible thing, we decided, would be to get ourselves fit again, and refresh our memories on demolitions and other useful paramilitary activities; and so, two days later, Burton and I left for the Western Highlands.

The S.O.E. paramilitary training centre was now at Arisaig, a few miles north of Lochailort. After reporting there we were sent to one of the outlying establishments, hard by the shores of Loch Morar. Here, under the direction of Major Young and the expert instruction of Captains Gavin Maxwell and Matthew Hodgart, we started a course of hard and intensive training. Carrying tommy-guns and fifty-pound rucksacks we tramped across the hills in dense mist and darkness, trying to find our way by compass, stumbling over invisible obstacles, sinking into bogs and falling into gullies and ravines. On one of these schemes the Adjutant from Arisaig, an enormous Highlander, broke a leg and lay for six hours in the mist on a mountain top before he could be carried down. Our companions on these exercises were a party of Czech officers, whose enthusiasm, skill and stamina inspired us to yet greater efforts; within three weeks we were thoroughly fit, competent at demolitions and accurate with pistol and tommy-gun.

We did some amphibious training in small boats on Loch Morar. Here we encountered a party of Spanish Republicans, a villainous crowd of assassins; we made no attempt to mix with them. Their conducting officer, a Captain Martin, spoke of them with distaste.

'They seemed to take no interest in anything', he told us, 'until, the other day, I brought them down to one of the beaches for a spot of landing practice. They slouched about apathetically until suddenly one of them found a whelk or mussel or something. He let out a shout and all the others started running around like mad. Believe it or not, inside half an hour they'd eaten every living thing on that damn beach that didn't speak to them!'

We were back in London in time to attend March-Phillipps's wedding in the middle of April. His wife, who had the same adventurous nature as himself, had interrupted a stage career to become the first qualified woman parachutist at Ringway.

At the wedding we met some of the other officers who were to form the nucleus of the Small-Scale Raiding Force. Senior among them was Major John Gwynne of the Sussex Yeomanry, in charge of planning. A teetotaler and vegetarian, obstinate, unwavering, and fearless, he fretted constantly under the restraints of his sedentary occupation; eager to lead an operation in the field, he was always planning for himself some desperate venture into enemy territory. With his lean, dark, ascetic face, gleaming eyes, and thinning, almost tonsured hair, he had the look of some medieval inquisitor; he always shaved in cold water.

Captain Graham Hayes of the Border Regiment, a school friend of Appleyard's, had also won an M.C. in Maid Honor. He was a quiet, serious-minded young man of great personal charm, courage, and strength, who had sailed before the mast in a Finnish grain ship, and was a superb seaman.

Another member of our party was Anders Lassen, a cheerful, lithe young Dane with a thirst for killing Germans and a wild bravery that was to win him the M.C. and two Bars, and at last a posthumous Victoria Cross.

In spite of a competing claim by the Ministry of Health we moved into Anderson Manor towards the end of April. This beautiful Elizabethan house had been cleared of its furniture before we took over, and the walls covered with beaver-boarding; nevertheless March-Phillipps, who was a friend of the owner, and who knew only too well the Army's reputation for vandalism, enjoined the strictest care upon officers and other ranks, so that not only was the house preserved from damage, but the handsome gardens were maintained by us in our spare time. In other parts of the grounds we built a pistol range and an assault course with walls, ditches full of barbed wire, Dannert wire entanglements, and a rope slung across the drive between two tall oaks; wearing full equipment we had to climb one tree, crawl along the rope and clamber down the other.

Our basic training was on the same lines as our course at Arisaig, with emphasis on tests of strength and endurance; but we specialized in map-reading exercises, movement across country by night, and boat training both by day and night. Because our raiding parties would be small their only hope would be in surprise; for this reason our raids must take place during non-moon periods. We must train ourselves to see like cats in the dark, and to move as silently. On our first night exercises we were all very uncertain and noisy, but in a surprisingly short time we became accustomed to the work; within two months we were able to find our way in silence over unknown country at a surprising speed, to crawl noiselessly under barbed wire and to stalk sentries on our stomachs, using elbows and feet to propel us. Rock climbing by day and night was an important and for me a terrifying part of our training.

The Admiralty put at our disposal a small, fast M.T.B. under the command of Lieutenant Freddy Bourne, D.S.C., R.N.V.R. Affectionately known as 'The Little Pisser' she was smaller than most M.T.B.s, was armed only with two Vickers machine-guns and had been stripped of her torpedo tubes. There was space to carry a light landing craft, lashed to the after deck. She would take us across the Channel to within a mile or so of our objective, where we could disembark and row or paddle ourselves ashore. We practiced with various types of landing craft, chiefly the eighteen-foot dory and the Goatley pattern assault craft—a flat-bottomed boat with canvas sides, which proved itself surprisingly seaworthy. We practiced in every kind of weather, under all sorts of conditions, until we had perfected our training in disembarkation, landing, and re-embarkation.

Although we were administered by S.O.E. we came under Combined Operations Headquarters for planning, and under Special Service Brigade—the Commando organization—for discipline; this last control was only a formality, because March-Phillipps arranged our training according to his own ideas, almost free from outside interference. Thus, although we were also known as No. 62 Commando and were issued with green berets, March-Phillipps encouraged us to wear civilian clothes when off duty; this was in keeping with his conception of us as successors to the Elizabethan tradition of the gentleman-adventurer. During training our discipline was extremely strict, March-Phillipps and Appleyard demanding the highest standard of efficiency from everyone. There were no punishments, nor were they necessary: we knew that the lives of all of us would depend on the skill and competence of each. Off parade relations between officers and other ranks were easy and informal, almost casual. We were a very happy unit.

Because we had been recruited as the nucleus of a larger force our establishment comprised more officers than other ranks. Besides those whom I had already met there was Captain Lord Howard of Penrith, quiet, intellectual, and conscientious; Captain Colin Ogden Smith, who had been one of March-Phillipps's troop officers in No. 7 Commando; Captain Hamish Torrance, M.B.E., of the Highland Light Infantry, a veteran S.O.E. officer who had seen service in Norway; a young and earnest Sapper, Paul Dudgeon, who had been through Woolwich; Tony Hall, a subaltern from the London Irish; a Yorkshire neighbour of Appleyard's, Lieutenant Warren; Lieutenant Brinkgreve of the Royal Netherlands Army; André Desgranges, a deep-sea diver and ex-petty officer of the French Navy, who had sailed with *Maid Honor* and had received a commission in the British Army on his return; and Brian Reynolds, newly commissioned as an ensign in the Welsh Guards.

Reynolds was an Irishman, well known before the war as a sportsman, bon viveur, and playboy. On the outbreak of the Russo-Finnish war in 1939 he went to Finland as a volunteer in Major Kermit Roosevelt's International Brigade; having exchanged the comfort and cuisine of Buck's for the icy forests of Lapland and Karelia, he endured bitter hardship with that ill-fated band of idealists before making his way to Sweden after the collapse of Finnish resistance. There he turned his unusual abilities to the service of the Allies, smuggling cargoes of ball-bearings on merchant ships through the Skagerrak from Gothenburg to Britain, under constant attack from the German Navy and Air Force; on his last run he lost four ships out of five, but his arrival with the fifth prevented a serious gap in British tank production. He was awarded the O.B.E. As well as courage he had great personal charm and a delicious sense of humour. His death, the day after the European war ended, was one of those futile tragedies in which fate seems to delight: when the Small-Scale Raiding Force broke up he returned to his old activities in the Skagerrak, this time in fast motor boats. Entering Antwerp harbour to celebrate the victory with some friends, he was killed instantly when his M.T.B. struck a mine.

Outstanding among the other ranks were Sergeant-Major Winter, an amiable but extremely efficient soldier who had also served with March-Phillipps and Appleyard in West Africa; Sergeant Nicholson, by far the oldest man in the force, a grey-haired regular soldier with the D.C.M.; Bruce Ogden Smith, Colin's brother, who had joined us as a private; Adam Orr, a Polish Jew who had taken this English *nom-de-guerre* as a precaution in case of capture, and Rifleman Rowe, an irrepressible little Cockney with a salacious wit who had spent some years in a priest's seminary in Belgium before deciding that the Church was not his vocation.

By the end of July we were fully trained, at the peak of our morale and craving action; plans were already completed for our first raids. But there followed a disheartening period of frustration and delay: our M.T.B. was considered unseaworthy in any wind stronger than Force 3; and two or three nights in the week were 'convoy nights', when we were not allowed to be in the English Channel. Because we were restricted to non-moon periods—a fortnight in each month—it was difficult to find a night when the limitations of weather and convoys did not affect us. Keyed up as we were, standing by night after night, sometimes setting out on a raid only to turn back within an hour or so, we all found this period of waiting a heavy strain on our nerves; for March-Phillipps and Appleyard it must have been nearly intolerable.

Early in August the first raid was launched, with about half of our force, against a small strong-point on the Normandy coast. The approach involved some difficult rock climbing, which caused March-Phillipps, who had noticed my clumsiness, to exclude me from the party; Burton, who had injured a calf muscle, was also left behind. With envy and anxiety we watched the party set out in the dusk for Gosport, each of them festooned with tommy-gun, Colt .45 automatic, and hand-grenades. Next morning before breakfast they returned, strained and exhausted but content with their night's work. They had found the target without difficulty and had crawled undetected to the wire perimeter. Trying to force an entry they alarmed the guard, most of whom they slaughtered with hand-grenades and small-arms fire. After inflicting further casualties on the frightened and bewildered garrison they withdrew without loss and were embarked safely aboard the M.T.B. Although they had taken no prisoners we all felt it was an encouraging start.

Our next target was in the Channel Islands—the German-occupied lighthouse and signal-station on the Casquets, a rocky islet about seven miles west of Alderney. About a week after the first raid our party, this time including Burton and myself, assembled in the Conference Room at Anderson; for several hours we studied charts, aerial photographs and, most important of all, a large and perfectly executed scale model in plasticine of the Casquets Rock with the lighthouse and adjoining buildings clearly shown in detail. March-Phillipps issued his operation orders.

Leaving Portland at 9 p.m. we should arrive off the Casquets just before midnight; Appleyard would be navigating. During the last part of the approach the M.T.B. would travel on her silent auxiliary engine. At half a mile's distance she would anchor, and we should man the Goatley and paddle ourselves ashore. It was likely to be a difficult approach and landing, because we could expect a heavy swell and a fierce tiderace round the rocks. Hayes, as coxswain, would be responsible for letting go the kedge anchor to keep the boat off the rocks; Appleyard as bow-man would take the painter ashore and make her fast while the rest of us landed. Hayes and Warren would stay with the landing-craft. Once ashore we should climb in single file up to the wall surrounding the station buildings. Inside, we were to divide into four parties, each with its separate objective: 'A' party, consisting of March-Phillipps, Dudgeon, Howard and Orr, was to tackle the main building, containing the living and sleeping quarters; 'B' party—Burton and myself—was to make straight for the wireless tower, kill or capture any Germans we found before they could use the wireless, and put the transmitter out of action; 'C' party—Appleyard and Winter—were to take possession of the lighthouse tower, and 'D' party—Brinkgreve and Reynolds—were to occupy the engine room. When we had cleared the enemy from our respective buildings we were to report with our prisoners to March-Phillipps. The prisoners would then be shepherded to the landing-craft by a small escort, while the rest of the party searched the buildings for code-books and other documents. Nobody knew the exact strength of the German garrison, but it was believed to number about eight; there would be ten of us excluding Hayes and Warren, so that if we could achieve surprise we should be able to overpower them.

Although we had now a detailed description of our target and were familiar with its every aspect, none but March-Phillipps and Appleyard knew its exact position; not until the raid was over were the rest of us told where we had been. Without this precaution there might have been a security leak;

in fact, owing to engine trouble in the M.T.B. as well as unfavourable weather, it was nearly a fortnight before we could make the raid. During this time we had several false starts, arriving on one occasion within a mile of the rock before thick fog compelled us to turn home.

Wednesday, 2nd September, was a fine day with a fresh breeze. We had spent a large part of the previous night crawling on our stomachs in the rain, practicing silent movement. I did not sleep well afterwards, and awoke feeling tired and jittery; but a brisk run before breakfast with Burton and Appleyard, followed by the news that we should try to do the raid again that night, revived my spirits. We spent the morning in the conference room, the afternoon resting. Although we had the greatest confidence in our commanders and in each other, it was difficult not to contemplate the numerous possibilities of disaster. Once we were in the M.T.B. I should feel all right, but I found this period of waiting very hard to bear. We spent the time between tea and supper in drawing and preparing our equipment. There was plenty of it. I was carrying a tommy-gun and seven magazines, each with twenty rounds, a pair of wire-cutters, two Mills grenades, a fighting knife, a clasp knife, a torch, emergency rations, and two half-pound explosive charges for the destruction of the wireless transmitter; on top I had to wear a naval lifebelt, an awkward and constricting garment which might save my life in the water but seemed very likely to lose it for me in action. We wore battle-dress, balaclava helmets and felt-soled boots.

After a hurried supper we climbed into our lorry. The whole unit turned out in the stable-yard to see us off; Tony Hall, in an old suit and peaked cap, was ringing the mess dinner bell and shouting in the accents of an American railroad conductor:

'All aboard! All aboard! Minneapolis, Saint Paul, Chicago, and all points east!'

We sang lustily, all tension now relaxed, as we drove through the green and golden countryside towards Portland. The lorry swung into the dockyard, drove onto the quay and halted close alongside our boat; we hurried aboard and dived out of sight below. I found myself in the forecastle with Dudgeon, Reynolds, Warren and Orr; March-Phillipps and Appleyard were on the bridge with Lieutenant Bourne; Burton and the rest were disposed somewhere aft. At nine o'clock we sailed.

With the forecastle hatch battened down to show no light, it was oppressively hot in our cramped quarters. The small craft bounced jarringly across the waves, for the wind, which had been Force 3 when we started, was rising to Force 4, with occasional stronger gusts. My companions lay down to sleep on the two wooden seats and the floor; I sat up and tried to read a thriller.

We had hoped to drop anchor off our target about ten-fifteen to catch the slack of the tide; the moon would be rising at eleven-thirty. But one of the motors again gave trouble, forcing us to reduce speed for part of the way. It was after ten-thirty when Appleyard knocked on the forecastle hatch and warned us to be ready to come on deck when summoned. When we had adjusted our equipment and inspected our weapons we switched out the forecastle lights, to accustom our eyes to the darkness outside; half an hour later the hatch was opened and we were ordered on deck.

It was a beautiful, clear night, bright with stars. The wind had dropped and the sea was moderating. Clustered in a body aft of the bridge, standing by to launch the Goatley as soon as we should anchor, we could make out the dim shapes of some rocks on the starboard beam; Appleyard and March-Phillipps were on the bridge, trying to identify them. The M.T.B. had switched from her main engines to the silent auxiliary. Looking round the horizon and shivering in the chill night breeze, I noticed a flickering light at some distance on our port bow, and another—a bright red one—almost directly ahead of us; the latter, I afterwards heard, was Sark. The moon appeared, low in the sky, on our port quarter. Suddenly I caught sight of our target, straight ahead of us; the tall, thin column of the lighthouse, the whitewashed wall and the buildings of the signal-station gleamed palely above the blackness of the rock.

Slowly the M.T.B. moved in, maneuvering to approach from the northwest; at half a mile's distance she anchored. Silently we pushed our Goatley over the stern and dropped quickly into our places, kneeling with our paddles ready. It was five minutes after midnight when March-Phillipps jumped down beside me and called softly:

'Right! Push off! Paddle up!'

Now the moon was higher, casting a sharp, clear light over the choppy water between us and the island; we could see it distinctly and must ourselves be visible, I thought uncomfortably, to any watchers there. I dismissed such thoughts and concentrated on keeping time with the others, holding my paddle well away from the side of the boat; I took comfort from the silence of our movement through the water and from the knowledge that we were a small object and therefore difficult to pick out among the waves. It was hard work paddling, for the north-east flood was running fast.

Some twenty minutes after leaving the landing-craft I saw that we were entering a small bay. There were splashes of white close ahead, where the surf was breaking on the rocks.

'All right, Apple?' whispered March-Phillipps. Appleyard's voice called back from the bows, low, yet to our tensed minds alarmingly clear:

'Okay. Graham, bring her in just to the right of that white splash of surf.'

Hayes, in the stern, could not hear him above the hiss of the sea, and asked him to repeat his orders more loudly. I could see the landing place, a smooth and gently sloping slab of rock, lighter in colour than the rest, in the right hand corner of the bay. As Hayes let go the kedge anchor Appleyard stood up in the bow, the line in his hand. The swell caught us, sweeping us towards the rock; Appleyard leaned forward to jump for the shore. At this moment, the kedge began to drag, holding us back. We paddled up with all our strength to shorten the distance, but we could make no headway against the weight of the kedge. I saw March-Phillipps glance apprehensively at the buildings above us. We were close under the rock; its black mass towered overhead, the signal station standing out clearly against the sky. It would be awkward to be caught in such a place, as it seemed we must be if the enemy up there were alert. As the swell lifted us again and carried us shore wards Appleyard jumped with the bow-line. He landed on the rock, slipped on the wet surface and almost fell into the sea; recovering just in time, he scrambled up the cliff to make fast the painter. One by one we followed him ashore, timing our jumps to the rise of the swell, while Hayes held the boat off the rock with the stern-line and kedge. Encumbered by our weapons we slithered about, trying to get a purchase on the rock, until March-Phillipps hissed angrily:

'Use the rope, you b-bloody f-fools, to haul yourselves up!'

Leaving Hayes and Warren to look after the Goatley and keep a watch on the M.T.B. through an infra-red receiving set, we started to climb the cliff in single file. I followed Burton, who, prostrated with sea-sickness during the crossing, had made a remarkable recovery as soon as his feet touched land. We had avoided the recognized landing points, fearing that they might be set with mines or booby-traps; we were lucky, therefore, to find an easy way up from the shore. Our only obstacle was some coiled Dannert wire, through which we cut our way without trouble. Any noise we made was probably drowned by the rumble of surf and the booming of the sea in the chasms and gullies round the cave. Nevertheless, my heart was pounding with more than exertion as we came into full view of the buildings. Under different circumstances the white-washed walls and dark roofs must have seemed lovely under the pale moonlight: in those critical moments they loomed cold and menacing, silent and lifeless, yet seemingly ready to spring into life to destroy us.

The entrance to the courtyard was blocked by a heavy 'knife-rest' barbed wire entanglement. Motioning us to follow him, March-Phillipps leaped for the wall, heaved himself over it and dropped on the other side. Within a few seconds we were all in the courtyard. This was the moment for independent action. Burton and I tore across the fifty yards of open ground to the door of the wireless tower, where a light was burning. Inside, on the left, a stone staircase led up to the transmitting room. Without a pause we raced up the stairs to a landing on the first floor, where an open doorway led into a lighted room. Burton was through the door in a second, his pistol in his hand; I was hard on his heels, my finger on the trigger of my tommy-gun.

No Colours or Crest

We found ourselves in a deserted room, crammed with wireless sets, generators and equipment; by the operator's stool, which was thrust back from the table, were some signal pads and an open notebook; code-books were on a shelf on the wall above. I stood on guard at the doorway overlooking the staircase, listening for sounds of firing from the other parties; but everything was quiet. Meanwhile Burton went through the room collecting code-books, signal-books and other documents likely to be of interest. I heard a sound from the entrance below; raising my tommy-gun I peered over the low balustrade, and was relieved to see Appleyard looking up at me.

'All clear here,' I said, 'we haven't seen a soul. How's it gone with you?'

'Splendid! We caught the whole damn bunch with their pants down—or rather, with their pajamas on. Two of them had just come off watch and were turning in, two others were filling up log-books, and the rest were in bed. Just as well, after all, that we didn't get here earlier. I've never seen men look so astonished and terrified—not a show of fight among the lot of them. We're taking them down to the boat now.' He came upstairs to join us.

'What about smashing up all this equipment?' I asked. 'Can I use the tommy-gun to blast it?'

'No. There's been no shooting, so Gus wants us to keep as quiet as possible. John had better use his axe while you and I go back to help with the prisoners. When you've made a nice mess, John, pick up that bumf you've collected and join us in the main building.'

We had indeed achieved complete surprise. Like the wireless tower, the lighthouse and engine-room were both deserted; all seven members of the garrison were in the main building. It seemed extraordinary that they had not posted a sentry, but they explained to us that they had not expected visitors. Nothing could better describe their state of un-preparedness than a sentence from March-Phillipps's official report to the Chief of Combined Operations: 'A characteristic of those in bed was the wearing of hairnets, which caused the Commander of the party to mistake one of them for a woman.'

All the following day and night, we were informed later, Cherbourg was calling up the Casquets, and asking all other stations if they had had any signals from the island. It was a month before the Germans discovered what had happened to the garrison. All the prisoners were naval ratings, under the command of a Chief Petty Officer Muenthe. Among them were two leading telegraphists, one of whom had previously been employed on guided missiles and whose information proved particularly valuable.

While some of us made a thorough search of the buildings, collecting documents and destroying arms and equipment—which included an Oerlikon cannon—others rounded up the prisoners and marched them down to the boat. As time was running short the Germans were not allowed to dress; dejected and tearful they were hurried away with over-coats over their pajamas, one of them keeping on his hairnet until we arrived at Portland, where he proved a willing subject for interrogation.

It was one o'clock when I reached the Goatley, to find the prisoners already embarked. The moon was well up, bathing the Casquets and the sea around in brilliant light; our position now would be desperate if enemy patrol craft were to approach. Although the Goatley was going to be seriously overloaded, with the seven prisoners and ourselves, March-Phillipps decided to take the risk rather than waste time sending for the emergency dory. He ordered me to jump in and stand at the bow to help the rest of the party aboard. With the heavy-swell, the jump from the rock to the landing craft varied from five to twenty feet, so that re-embarkation was not easy. The smallest mistake might cause the swamping of the boat and bring disaster on us all. The last man to jump before March-Phillipps and Appleyard was the Pole, Orr; he had his fighting knife in his hand and, as he dropped, the boat lurched and threw him against me. I felt a sharp, biting pain in my right thigh as the blade went in. However, I had no time to think about it; March-Phillipps dropped into the boat and ordered us to cast off. I crawled to my place and began paddling with the others, under a ceaseless rain of invective from our agitated commander.

With nineteen men aboard, the Goatley was dangerously low in the water; but she rode the swell admirably and we reached the M.T.B. safely after thirty-five minutes. The prisoners were hauled aboard first and sent down to the forecastle with Howard and Dudgeon to guard them; I joined them there, helped along by Orr, who was very contrite about the injury he had accidentally caused. The return journey to Portland was uneventful. The prisoners were docile, huddled together in their misery at one end of the forecastle; indeed, there was no comfort for any of us in the cramped and stifling compartment. Orr's knife had penetrated deep and my wound was stiff and painful; when we reached Portland, just before dawn, I could barely stand. After a while an ambulance took me to the Naval Hospital, where I was immediately put to sleep with a shot of morphia. An operation the next morning removed the blood-clots and greatly relieved the pain. I thought I was the only casualty of the raid, but I was wrong: Appleyard, following March-Phillipps into the boat, had seriously damaged his ankle. These accidents, which temporarily put us out of action, in the event prolonged our lives.

During my convalescence disaster struck the Small-Scale Raiding Force. On the night of 12th September one of our parties sailed in M.T.B. 344 to attack a target on the Cherbourg peninsula. March-Phillipps was in command, with Appleyard, whose damaged ankle would not allow him to land, as navigator. This was the second consecutive night that they had attempted the raid, having run into fog the first time when they were within a mile or two of their objective; this part of the coast was heavily defended, and so it might have been wiser to allow a longer interval.

At that time my wife and I had a cottage at Spettisbury, about five miles from Anderson. Although I had left hospital two days before, I was not yet fit for operations. On the morning of the 12th Reynolds and Torrance, who were not included in the raiding party, drove over to us for dinner. It was an uncomfortable meal; conversation was artificial and constrained, for all our thoughts were with our friends crossing the channel on their desperate mission. As we stood in the garden afterwards silently looking down over the vale of the Stour and watching the shadows creep across the meadows beside the river, Torrance put my fears into words.

'Don't telephone, Peter. As soon as we have any news I'll come over myself and let you know.'

I slept little that night: Burton, my close companion for the last eighteen months, was with March-Phillipps and I hated not to be there beside him in the battle; I half hoped that fog would again defeat them and the operation be postponed until I was fit again. All next day I loafed about, irritable and unhappy, with no word from Anderson. Long after dark I heard a truck draw up at the gate, and rushed out to meet Torrance; his thin, dark face was puckered with anxiety and grief.

'We've lost the lot! Apple came back tonight with Freddy Bourne—I've just left them in the Mess. They aren't sure exactly what happened, but the Germans must have been waiting for them. Gus and his party could hardly have landed when the boys on the M.T.B. heard all hell break loose on shore; they were quite badly shot up themselves. God knows if any of the landing force got away, but it looks as if they're all dead or prisoners.'

It was not for many months that we learned the full story of the tragedy. In the small hours of 13th September March-Phillipps landed with eight others, including Burton, Hayes, Howard, Hall, Winter, and Desgranges. They had barely stepped ashore when heavy fire was directed on them from the cliffs above; machine-guns, hand grenades, mortars and cannon blasted their narrow and exposed strip of beach. In the pitch darkness Bourne and Appleyard, aboard the M.T.B., could see nothing but the enemy flashes and the explosions of shells; but they edged their craft as close inshore as they dared in the shallow water, and stood by to pick up the party. As the firing died down they heard a voice, which they believed to be Hayes's, calling to Appleyard to leave them and save the ship while he could. Nevertheless, the M.T.B. continued to cruise around just off-shore, showing signal lights and blowing whistles in a desperate attempt to rescue survivors. She was under continuous fire from the shore and one of her engines was put out of action. With the approach of daylight there was no alternative but to make for home.

March-Phillipps's death was reported two days later in a communique issued by the German High Command. Afterwards, we heard that the

No Colours or Crest

Goatley had been swamped while carrying the party back to the M.T.B. All but March-Phillipps had swum ashore; he was drowned trying to reach the M.T.B., and his body was recovered by the Germans next morning. Letters from the survivors told of the calmness, skill and courage with which he had faced that desperate situation on the beach and organized the withdrawal of his force. All but one of the others were taken prisoner almost immediately, Hall and Howard with serious wounds. Hayes alone managed to escape, swimming away from the beach and landing farther down the coast; he eluded capture for a while, but was eventually handed over to the Germans, placed in Fresnes prison in solitary confinement for nine months, and shot on 13th July, 1943. Burton made his way inland, but was picked up a day or two later and spent the rest of the European war in a prison camp near Kassel; he emerged, however, in time to fly to the Far East and take part in what were officially and euphemistically called 'post-hostilities operations' against the Indonesians in Sumatra.

We had been prepared for casualties, but not for such a catastrophe as this. The death of the gallant idealist and strange, quixotic genius who had been our commander and our inspiration, together with the loss of so many good friends, all in the space of a few hours, was a crippling calamity which nearly put an end to our activities. Indeed, it probably would have done so but for the energetic reaction of Appleyard, who refused to let our grief for our comrades arrest his determination to avenge them. Our masters in London responded with a heartening display of confidence, appointing Appleyard as temporary commander of the Force, with the rank of Major.

Their confidence was quickly justified. Within a month of the disaster Appleyard took a party, consisting of Ogden Smith, Lassen, Dudgeon and half a dozen others to the island of Sark, leading the raid himself in spite of his injured ankle. They spent more than four hours reconnoitring the island; they also captured two Germans. Realizing that the route back to the landing-craft passed close by some German defences, Appleyard ordered the prisoners' hands to be tied behind their backs, to lessen their chances of escape. At the most critical point on the journey one of the two ran away; Lassen gave chase in the dark, caught him and before he could raise the alarm dispatched him quickly and silently with a fighting knife. The remaining prisoner gave no trouble; he subsequently proved a most valuable source of information. For their work on this and previous raids Appleyard received the D.S.O., Dudgeon the M.C.

There was one unfortunate sequel: when the dead prisoner was found, his hands still tied behind his back, the German High Command raised an outcry, maintaining that it was contrary to International Law to tie the hands of prisoners. In retaliation they put chains on some of the prisoners they had taken in the Dieppe raid.

No Colours or Crest

In October the Chiefs of Staff gave orders for the expansion of the Small-Scale Raiding Force. It seemed that March-Phillipps's dream was coming true. Four more large houses were requisitioned to provide bases for us along the south coast—one in the New Forest, another near Dorchester, a third near Paignton and the fourth between Falmouth and Truro. Bill Stirling, recently returned from Cairo, arrived to take command of the whole force, with the rank of Lieutenant-Colonel; Appleyard became second-in-command and field force commander; John Gwynne was at last allowed to train a party of his own to operate deep into Northern France. Two motor gunboats were put at our disposal, but on operations we preferred to use M.T.B. 344 because she was smaller, more difficult to see, and easier to manœuvre. Two navigating officers were added to our establishment. One of them was an R.A.F. squadron-leader, the other a tubby, red-faced Breton fisherman who spoke no English and whose dialect few of us could understand; a cheerful, friendly little man, he took a touching pride in his new uniform of lieutenant R.N.R., especially in his uniform cap, which he seldom, if ever, removed; sharing a room with him I was fascinated to watch him sitting up in bed reading a book, wearing a suit of thick flannel pajamas, his cap set jauntily on the back of his bald head.

With our expansion came an important change of policy, affecting the composition of our raiding force; in future, selected officers and N.C.O.s from the Commandos would be sent to us for a short period of training in the specialized technique of small-scale raiding, after which we should take them on a raid. This was the logical development of March-Phillipps's original idea. Towards the end of October the first cadres arrived at Anderson Manor—all from No. 12 Commando. The officers, Captains Pinckney and Rooney and Lieutenant Gilchrist, each brought six N.C.O.s from his own troop. Reynolds, Sergeant Nicholson and I were ordered to train Rooney's squad in preparation for a raid in the immediate future.

Rooney, a powerfully built, self-confident officer, who knew his men intimately and commanded their implicit obedience, had little to learn from me. In fact, apart from pistol shooting and movement at night, he and his men knew more about the business than I. However, I was to command them on the forthcoming raid, and so we spent the next two weeks together in unremitting training by day and night. In particular we exercised ourselves in night schemes on land and water, in soundless movement and the use of our eyes in the dark. For such intensive practice we were soon to be thankful.

On 5th November, appropriately enough, we were called to the Conference Room for our operational briefing. Our target was to be a German semaphore station on the Point de Plouezec, about fifteen miles north-west of Saint Brieuc on the Brittany coast. This time we had no scale model of the target, but plenty of maps and aerial photographs, as well as some local intelligence about the station and its defences; the latter was to prove inaccurate in some important details.

Our information from all sources indicated that the semaphore station stood on the top of steep cliffs at the end of the point, which jutted north-eastwards from the Baie de Saint Brieuc. The northern and eastern faces were defended by concrete emplacements, at least one of which mounted a gun; the only practicable landing place seemed to be a small shingle beach below the southern face, where a narrow track appeared to lead up the cliff to join a path running inland from the signal station. On this side of the station, we were told, the defences consisted only of a single belt of barbed wire and, beside the track, just inside the entrance, a small concrete guard-house, where we should probably find a sentry. The entrance itself was not protected by barbed wire. According to local information there were neither mines nor booby-traps. The garrison contained about a dozen soldiers; there would be ten of us, so that surprise would be essential.

Appleyard would accompany us in the M.T.B., but he was forbidden to land, for his ankle was now encased in plaster; I was to command the landing-party, with Rooney as second-in-command and Reynolds as coxswain of the dory in which we should paddle ashore. Stirling particularly impressed on us that he wanted no casualties in our party; afterwards he took Reynolds and me aside to emphasize the point.

'Rooney and his chaps,' he began, 'are very keen and will obviously seize any opportunity for a fight. Naturally we want to inflict casualties and take prisoners; but not, I repeat, at the cost of losing men ourselves; it isn't worth it at this stage. If, when you get there, you don't think you can fight without losing men I promise you I shall be quite satisfied with a recce. Remember, Peter, I don't want any Foreign Legion stuff on this party!'

He did not need to worry: with the lives of nine valuable officers and N.C.O.s in my hands I had no mind to stick my neck out on my first independent command.

With the help of Rooney and Reynolds I drafted my operation orders.

In addition to the usual weapons, my landing-party was issued with a Bren gun, a Sten gun fitted with a silencer, and two hand grenades of a new pattern known officially as "Grenades P.E., No. 6'; these grenades had a thin metal casing and contained a heavy charge of Plastic Explosive; they burst on impact with a very heavy blast, and so should be useful if we had to blow our way through the barbed wire. Once we had gained the cliff top, our most difficult problem would obviously be to approach the sentry close enough to kill him noiselessly before he could raise the alarm; that was the purpose of the silent Sten, which we had already tried out and found satisfactory. The Bren gun was to guard our rear while we were making the attack, and cover our withdrawal afterwards.

No Colours or Crest

I worked out a simple plan: immediately after landing, the party was to form a defensive beach-head at the foot of the cliffs, protecting the landing-craft, while I located the track leading to the top. When we reached the top of the cliff Sergeant Nicholson would take up position with the Bren gun, to cover the path inland and to indicate the point where the track led down. This should be about a hundred and fifty yards from the entrance to the semaphore station. The rest of us would approach the target in three groups, one on either side of the path and one in rear; Rooney would lead the left hand party, I the right. The last part of the approach would have to be made crawling on our stomachs. If we could get near enough, Rooney and I would kill the sentry with our knives; if not, Sergeant Broderson would shoot him with the silenced Sten. We should then invade the station, the party on the right pausing to clear the guard-house, while the remainder attacked the main building.

M.T.B. 344 was lying at Dartmouth, ready to take us across on the first night of favourable weather. At midday on Wednesday, 11th November, heartened by the news of far more important landings in North Africa, we set off from Anderson to carry out our raid.

After a brief halt at Lupton House, our new base near Paignton, where we had a hurried meal and put on our operational clothing and equipment, we drove into Kingswear in the late afternoon. Stirling and Sam Darby, our new Intelligence Officer, were on the quay talking to Freddie Bourne, whose boat lay alongside, her engines already running. As soon as the last of us was on board we cast off and started down the estuary. Waving a silent good-bye to Stirling and Darby I settled myself with Rooney and Reynolds in the lee of the dory on the afterdeck. Appleyard took up his usual station on the bridge with Bourne; Rooney's men were below. Savouring my first moments of relaxation since early morning I gazed at the wooded hills above the Dart, watching their colours soften as we drew away in the last clear light of evening; the old castle above Dartmouth stood black against the fading western sky. Soon distance and darkness hid them; only the bright torrent of our wake showed in the blackness of night and water.

I strove to keep myself from worrying about the work that lay ahead of us, reflecting that we had rehearsed every detail of my plan; but now doubts began to crowd upon me. Rooney and his men were superb, but we had worked together only for a fortnight; on this difficult approach the slightest misunderstanding or mischance, impatience or carelessness, would destroy us before we could launch our attack. Moreover, despite all that Stirling had said, I knew that we should look extremely foolish if we were to return without taking prisoners or inflicting casualties; yet I could not overlook his instructions, which I knew came from headquarters, to bring my party home intact.

No Colours or Crest

Fortunately I was not allowed to immerse myself for long in these unhappy droughts. As we cleared Start Point and increased speed to twenty-eight knots against a Force 3 wind and swell from the southeast, the sea began to break green over the whole length of the boat, drenching us through our protective clothing, and freezing us as we lay under the inadequate cover of the dory. Before long I was too numbed to think about my troubles, and looked forward to our arrival off the Point de Plouezec, which would at least put an end to this discomfort.

The journey took us nearly six hours. For some of the time I stood on the bridge with Appleyard, staring in silence through the spray and darkness, unable to make out the horizon in any direction, so dark was the sky. Two or three times I went below with Rooney to see how his men were faring; finding nearly all of them asleep, I envied their composure.

It was not surprising that we had some difficulty in finding our first landfall, the light tower on the Roches Douvres, and wasted an hour making a 'square search' for it; just before ten o'clock we picked it up at a distance of about a mile. From here Appleyard laid a course to bring us directly to the Baie de Saint Brieuc. At half past eleven we switched onto silent engines, altering course again to approach the Point de Plouezec from the east-south-east. The night was now bright with stars, and as we drew near we could clearly distinguish the headland with its off-lying rocks and islands; on top of the point the squat outline of the semaphore station made a dark silhouette against the sky.

At ten minutes past midnight we dropped anchor about half a mile from the shore; Rooney's men filed noiselessly on deck. Now I realized that the hours we had spent rehearsing the launching of the dory had not been wasted; within twelve minutes, without a word having been spoken, we were all in our places and paddling silently towards the shore.

Fifteen minutes later we ran into the cove we had selected for our landing; we were dismayed to find that the beach was not shingle, as our intelligence had led us to believe, but boulders. The tide was ebbing fast, and if we left the dory on this beach we should be unable to refloat her on our return from the raid. While Reynolds stayed in the boat, to keep her off the rocks, I took the party ashore and established my beach-head at the foot of the cliffs; Rooney went off on a reconnaissance of the cove, in the hope of finding a more suitable beach. He returned ten minutes later to tell me that there was nowhere else possible. The only solution was to leave Reynolds to keep the dory afloat while we made our attack. He accepted the disappointment with his usual good nature. In the end we owed to him our survival.

We formed up in staggered file and began to climb the cliff, myself in the lead, Rooney close behind me; but we soon realized that we could not hope to keep any formation. The track, which had looked so plain in the aerial photographs, did not exist, or, if it did, was invisible in the darkness. We set ourselves to scramble up the face, which I judged was nearly a hundred feet high at this point. It was an arduous climb, for the ascent was almost perpendicular and the cliffs were overgrown with thick gorse bushes whose spikes pierced our clothes and tore our hands and faces; it was alarming too, for the surface was slippery grass and loose shale, which we could not help dislodging with the sound, to our strained ears, of an avalanche.

After twenty minutes we reached the top, where we lay down to look around us and regain our breath. About a hundred yards ahead I could make out a hue of telegraph poles running parallel with the cliff face, indicating the track which led inland from the semaphore station. We made for the track, moving swiftly across the open ground that separated it from the cliff top; we joined it about a hundred and fifty yards away from the barbed wire and the guard-house. I was reflecting with relief that at least we had encountered no mines or booby-traps when I saw Rooney staring fixedly at two small notice-boards, one on each side of the track, facing inland. I went to examine them, and read with horror the warning: '*Achtung! Minen.*' Included in the minefields was the route by which we had approached and by which we must return.

I sent Rooney with one of his men to make a close reconnaissance of the defences of the semaphore station. They returned with the gloomy news that the entrance and guard-house were protected by a double line of barbed wire, which also blocked the path, and by two sentries, who seemed very much on the alert. Our best plan seemed to be to work our way across country on the left of the path and try to get through the wire at some distance from the sentries. This, of course, involved the risk of mines; but we had already crossed one advertised minefield without mishap, and so could reasonably hope that the notices were either a bluff or merely warning of an intention to lay mines. Accordingly, after leaving Nicholson with the Bren gun by the path to guard our rear and to serve as a marker for our return, I started to lead the others across the open ground on our left.

We did not get very far. I had covered only a few yards, crouching low and straining my eyes to watch the ground at every step, when I all but trod on a mine. It was laid, with very little attempt at concealment, under a small mound of turf. Abandoning our hopes that the notices might be a bluff, we returned to the path. A frontal attack was the only solution; whatever the risks, they were at least calculable; we must trust to our luck and skill to bring us close enough to the wire to blast our way through it and kill the sentries before the garrison could turn out. Although I knew that Stirling would not blame me if I abandoned the raid at this point, I agreed with Rooney that it would be pusillanimous of us now to return without putting up a fight.

I split the party into three groups, according to my original plan. I took the right side of the path myself, followed by Sergeant Broderson with his silent Sten; Rooney, Sergeant Barry, and another N.C.O. were to move along the left side, abreast of me, while the rest followed a dozen yards behind. I was to set the pace; as soon as I dropped to the ground the rest of the party would do the same, after which we would complete the approach on our stomachs. We had rehearsed all this beforehand, and so detailed instructions were unnecessary at this point; Rooney was carrying the No. 6 grenade which was to blow our way through the wire, and he would have to decide when to throw it.

As we padded slowly up the path I was appalled at the stillness of the night. At a hundred yards distance the voices of the sentries sounded unnaturally clear; Sergeant Broderson's breathing pounded like a steam-engine at the back of my neck, and I feared my own must be as loud; but our felt-soled boots and long hours of practice enabled us to tread silently, and as long as the sentries went on talking we could move forward in reasonable safety, although slowly. Whenever they stopped speaking we halted and stood motionless, holding our breath. Thirty paces from them I dropped onto my stomach and, waiting until all the others were down, began to edge forward inch by inch on my elbows and the points of my toes. I halted frequently to listen and peer through the gloom at the line of wire and the silhouette of the guard-house ahead. Those last yards seemed like miles, and it needed all my self-control to move without haste; in that still air the least sound would carry to the sentries' ears and give us away. I was glad to note that Rooney and the others were watching me carefully, coordinating their movements with mine; I could see Rooney's dark bulk on the other side of the track exactly level with me.

When we were ten paces from the sentries we came upon a pair of low posts, one on each side of the track, with a trip-wire hanging loosely between them. I judged that we were unlikely to get any nearer without being heard, but I decided to wait awhile in the hope that the guards might move away on a round of the defences. For a full fifteen minutes we lay there, listening to the lazy drawl of their conversation, punctuated all too frequently by periods of silence when they would peer towards us and listen. The nervous strain inside me grew almost intolerable, sometimes bordering on panic when I thought of the peril of our situation; we must carry on now, for I could never turn my party back under the noses of this watchful pair. Clearly we had no hope of killing them quietly. I remember thinking how good the earth and grass smelt as I pressed my face close to the ground; overhead a lone aircraft beat a leisurely way up the coast; from the direction of Paimpol came the distant sound of a dog barking.

Out of the corner of my eye I saw Rooney make a slight movement; then I heard a distinct metallic click as he unscrewed the top of his No. 6 grenade. The sentries heard it too; they stopped their conversation, and one gave a sharp exclamation. I sensed rather than saw Rooney's arm go up, and braced myself for what I knew was coming. There was a clatter as one of the sentries drew back the bolt of his rifle; then everything was obliterated in a vivid flash as a tremendous explosion shattered the silence of the night. The blast hit me like a blow on the head. From the sentries came the most terrible sounds I can ever remember: from one of them a low, pitiful moaning, from the other bewildered screams of agony and terror, an incoherent jumble of sobs and prayers, in which I could distinguish only the words '*Nicht gut! Nicht gut!*' endlessly repeated. Even in those seconds as I leaped to action I felt a shock of horror that those soft, lazy, drawling voices which had floated to us across the quiet night air could have been turned, literally in a flash, to such inhuman screams of pain and fear.

Though they were to haunt me for a long time, I had no leisure for such thoughts now. In a moment I was floundering through the wire by the guardhouse on the heels of Rooney and Sergeant Barry. The wire, mangled by the explosion, was no longer a serious obstacle. A little dog sped out of the open door of the guard-house and ran off into the darkness, giving tongue in shrill, terrified yelps. The guardhouse was empty. The two sentries were sprawled on the ground, one silent with his hands over his face, the other calling on his mother and his Maker until a burst of tommy-gun fire from one of my N.C.O.s quietened him; the grenade must have landed close beside them, for their clothes were terribly burnt.

I wasted no time here, but followed Rooney's party past the guard-house and on to the open courtyard in front of the main building. As I arrived beside Rooney a German loomed up out of the darkness, firing rapidly at us with a small automatic. Rooney and I replied with our .45s, bringing him to his knees; but he courageously continued firing until a burst from Sergeant Barry's tommy-gun finished him off. A door was thrown open in the station building ahead, revealing a light inside and, silhouetted clearly against it, the figure of a man with a sub-machine gun, poised at the top of a flight of steps. He paid for his folly in presenting such a target, because Sergeant Broderson gave him two bursts from the silenced Sten, toppling him forward on his face; as he tried to rise Corporal Howells riddled him with his tommy-gun.

When my rear party arrived I prepared to send half of them round to the back of the station building, while the rest of us stormed the front. But although only a few seconds had passed since we had started the attack, we no longer had the advantage of surprise; the Germans were organizing their defence and, having turned out the lights, began to pour a heavy fire on us from the windows and the open doorway. The garrison was clearly stronger than we had expected. If we stormed the building we should have to cross the open courtyard under heavy fire, with a grave risk of casualties; in any case it was doubtful if we were strong enough to overwhelm the garrison now that they were alert. We had killed four Germans for certain, without loss to ourselves; I decided to disengage now, before I had the added difficulty of carrying wounded through the minefield and down the cliffs.

I shouted the order to withdraw. We raced back across the wire and along the path to the spot where Sergeant Nicholson was waiting impassively with his Bren gun. As we hurried through the minefield I was in a sweat of terror lest we should have a casualty here at the last moment; I do not know how we could have carried a wounded man down those cliffs to the boat. In fact we were lucky, but the descent was dangerous enough as we slid and fell blindly in the gorse-covered gullies leading down to the beach. I was greatly relieved that there were no signs of pursuit from above, although the semaphore station was in an uproar and we could still hear the sound of small-arms fire when we arrived on the beach. The Germans had sent up alarm rockets, and I wondered whether they would have searchlights to intercept us on our way back to the M.T.B.

When we reached the dory I saw how much we owed to Brian Reynolds. While we were away the tide had been going out fast; but for Reynolds the dory would have been left high and dry on the boulders, where she would have been almost impossible to refloat. For two hours he had stood waist-deep in the icy water, holding the boat off the rocks; I wondered that he had any movement left in his legs, but he seemed active enough.

We stumbled to our places in the boat; but when Rooney called the roll there were two men missing. Both had been with us when we started down the cliff, and so presumably they would join us at any moment—unless they had had an accident on the way down, which was not unlikely. As we sat waiting anxiously, a Verey light shot upwards from the cliff top and fell slowly towards the sea, illuminating the bay, the cliffs and ourselves in a vivid magnesium glare. I began to feel desperate. In such a light the Germans could not fail to see us; my stomach contracted as I awaited the spatter of machine-gun bullets that would announce our discovery. There could be no escape for us once we were seen; was I to lose the whole party for the sake of two men, or must we incur the shame of abandoning two of our companions to certain capture and possible death? Fortunately I was not called upon to make the decision: as the last glow from the Verey light faded we heard a clatter on the pebbles; the two missing men heaved themselves painfully over the gunwhale.

There was no need to urge everyone to paddle his hardest. We were three hundred yards off-shore when another Verey light went up from the signal station, lighting up the tense, sweating faces of my companions as though in the glare of footlights. This time, I thought, they're bound to see us, and I waited, almost resigned now, for the hiss and splash of bullets. But once again darkness enveloped us, allowing us to go our way. Reynolds had a pair of very powerful night glasses, with which he had been able to pick out the M.T.B. from the shore; when the second Verey light expired he sent our homing signal—three green flashes from his torch. We were onboard at half past three in the morning, ten minutes after leaving the shore, and received a

No Colours or Crest

warm welcome from Appleyard, who had passed an anxious three hours while we were away. As we turned for home two more alarm rockets went up from the semaphore station, followed by another illuminating flare, but we could see no response anywhere along the coast.

During the homeward journey Rooney and I sat huddled miserably in a pool of water on the bottom of the dory, under the flimsy protection of a tarpaulin. I was feeling the reaction from the excitement of the last few hours; although relieved that I had brought our party back intact I could feel no elation at our small success: instead, I could not rid my ears of the terrible screams that had come from the mangled, wounded sentries, or my mind of the grim memory of our return through the minefield and our wait in the dory under the blazing Verey lights. At the same time I could not shake off a nagging, persistent worry that perhaps I had not acted with sufficient resolution; that if I had pressed home my attack instead of giving the order to withdraw we might have made prisoners of the entire garrison.

At seven-twenty, through the half light of dawn, we made our first landfall on Downend Point; an hour later, on a raw, grey morning, we came alongside the quay at Dartmouth, where Stirling was awaiting us with Darby and a formidable escort of Field Security Police. My spirits sank as I saw the latter and wondered how Darby would take the news that we had no prisoners for him. What he said was:

'Go straight back and get some!'

Stirling listened without interruption to my account of the raid. At the end he said:

'You were fully justified in breaking off the action when you did, in view of the score at the time; I will say so in my covering report. It's bad luck that you couldn't take any prisoners, but you must have given the enemy quite a shock, which is one of our objects.'

Revived by an excellent breakfast in the Y.M.C.A. at Paignton, of scrambled eggs and mugs of tea laced with our rum ration, we drove back to Anderson, arriving in time for lunch. I worked all the after-noon and until late in the evening, composing two reports on the raid—a summary which Stirling wanted to show to the Prime Minister, and a detailed account for Combined Operations Headquarters. Appleyard told me later that the Prime Minister made the simple comment, 'Good!'; and so I suppose that honour, at least, was satisfied.

That was the last raid to be carried out by the Small-Scale Raiding Force from a base in England. During the succeeding months a number of operations were planned for us by Stirling; but on each occasion we were thwarted by weather, by lack of ships or by the overriding priority of other operations, such as the landing of agents by sea along the coasts of Normandy and Brittany—in preparation, as we learnt later, for the Allied invasion. After this change in policy our raids, which kept the Germans on the alert, would be more of a hindrance than a help to the grand design.

A few days after our return from the Point de Plouezec, when Rooney and his men had gone on leave, I was ordered by Brigadier Gubbins to take a party of our officers on the parachute course at Ringway. I had been sleeping badly, with terrible nightmares of those screaming sentries, and I was glad of an opportunity to take my mind off the recent raid. The party included Lassen, Warren, and two Anglo-French officers who were booked to go with John Gwynne on an intelligence mission into France. I was particularly glad, because it was hinted that there might be a parachute operation for me afterwards. Lassen had mixed feelings; on the one hand he was keen to learn about parachuting, on the other he loathed all courses of instruction.

'Tell me, Peter,' he asked nervously when I explained about Dunham Massey, 'is it a much-bullshit place?'

Remembering the report I had received at the end of my last course, I was determined this time to make a favourable impression on Major Edwards. I therefore took particular care to be in time for meals, for parades, and even for early morning P.T.; moreover, with shameless hypocrisy I gave my party short talks on the importance of punctuality. I was rewarded for my sycophancy with a report which concluded: 'He is not entirely the irresponsible officer that he appears at first sight.' I was disappointed in my hopes of a parachute operation. In fact, the only person with the prospect of any action for the moment was John Gwynne. He refused, quite rightly, to give us any details of his proposed mission beyond the fact that it was not planned by Stirling and had nothing to do with Combined Operations Headquarters. He spent much of his time away from Anderson visiting various S.O.E. experimental stations, in particular one concerned with camouflage. He reappeared at the end of his tour with two unusual pieces of equipment. One of them was a lifelike cow's head mask in *papier mâché* with holes pierced through the eyes; the other was a curious arrangement of fine-meshed camouflage netting. He was good enough to reveal to us their purpose. The mask was for road-watching: in other words, he would lie up in a field beside a main road and push his head, enveloped in the mask, through the hedge; thus disguised, he would be able to keep a watch on the road and observe the number and nature of enemy troops using it. The purpose of the netting was even simpler.

'It enables a man to disguise himself at will,' explained Gwynne, 'as a rubbish heap or pile of sticks.'

Not all the products of the extensive research organization maintained by S.O.E. were camouflaged exclusively for protection; almost the whole range of children's joke toys was exploited for some destructive purpose. For instance, imitation turds of horse or camel dung contained small explosive charges which would destroy the tyres of any vehicle that drove over them; and sickeningly realistic dead rats, apparently in the later stages of decomposition, were dropped by the gross over occupied Europe to be smuggled into German barrack rooms and offices. Anyone picking them up by the tail—the natural method when throwing them away—would automatically release a pin, exploding a small but lethal charge.

We were concerned with Gwynne's operation only in that the Small-Scale Raiding Force was to transport Gwynne and his party over to the Brittany coast and provide an escort in case they ran into trouble on landing; once they were safely ashore we should return to England. In early December I spent a week at Paignton with a party including Appleyard, Ogden Smith, Lassen, and Warren, waiting for a chance to land them in France. Once again, however, the weather defeated us, and we all returned in disappointment to Anderson. And so went out the year 1942.

Early in 1943 Stirling conceived the plan of transferring the bulk of the Small-Scale Raiding Force to North Africa, where there were plenty of opportunities for the amphibious operations we were no longer allowed to carry out across the Channel. Among those he took with him were Appleyard, Lassen, Dudgeon, and Philip Pinckney of No. 12 Commando. Together they formed the Second Special Air Service Regiment, following in the footsteps of Stirling's brother, David, who had founded the First S.A.S. in 1941. Operating first from Tunisia, later in Italy, and finally in France, they expanded their activities to include parachute as well as sea-borne raids. They achieved a number of brilliant successes, but at the cost of some of their most valuable lives. Appleyard was killed in Sicily, Pinckney and Lassen in Italy, Dudgeon in France.

Among those who stayed behind with me were Reynolds, Ogden Smith, and the Dutchman, Brinkgreve. After an uneventful and frustrating four months of inactivity we split up towards the end of April. The death of Reynolds I have already recorded. Ogden Smith was parachuted into Brittany with a sabotage party in June 1944; surrounded in a farm-house by a large force of S.S., he and his few companions put up a stout fight for four hours, until they were all killed or incapacitated by wounds. The survivors were shot out of hand by the S.S. In Holland a similar fate overtook poor Brinkgreve.

V

TO THE WILDER SHORES OF WAR

One morning in the middle of May 1943 I was sitting in an office in Baker Street, talking to Lieutenant-Colonel James Pearson, who had been in my troop at Weedon. He had recently returned from a staff appointment in Cairo to take up a post in London concerned with S.O.E. operations in the Balkans.

'We're looking for officers,' he told me, 'who would be prepared to parachute into Greece and Jugoslavia to work with the guerrilla forces there. Would that interest you? If so, which country would you prefer?'

Apart from a brief visit to Greece during my first long vacation from Cambridge, I knew very little about the Balkans; Pearson explained that the present need for British Liaison Officers was greater in Jugoslavia, and so I asked to be sent there. Parachute operations into the Balkans were controlled from Cairo; I should be flown to Egypt about the end of the month. I spent the next three weeks in a basement office in Baker Street, learning about the political and military situation inside the country, reading reports and telegrams from British Liaison Officers already in the field and listening to the views of two of Pearson's staff officers, Major Boughey and Captain Uren.

Hitherto I had believed that Jugoslav resistance centered around General Draža Mihailović and the guerrilla bands, known in the British Press as Chetniks, who had taken to the mountains under his leadership after the German invasion in the spring of 1941. Now I knew that there was another guerrilla leader in the country, a shadowy figure called Tito, who, after the entry of Russia into the war, had rallied the Communists and their sympathizers and taken to the hills in arms against the Germans. For a few months the supporters of Tito and Mihailović had worked together, although with mutual suspicion, for they were fundamentally opposed in outlook and objectives. By the end of 1941 their hostility to each other had flared into open warfare, so that their efforts were wasted in internecine strife. Now British Liaison Officers were being dropped to both sides in the hope of persuading them to concentrate on fighting the Germans rather than each other. Although Mihailović still enjoyed the official support of the British Government, Tito was not without friends in S.O.E.: one staff officer, in fact, so far allowed his enthusiasm to exceed his discretion that he was subsequently tried and convicted under the Official Secrets Act for passing confidential information to the Soviet Embassy in London.

In Boughey's office I met my friend John Bennett, whom I had last seen on the barrack square at Weedon. In June 1940 Bennett had been sent to Belgrade, where he had remained to do valuable work for the Allies until the German invasion in April 1941. For the next two years he had been in charge of the Jugoslav Country Section of S.O.E. in Cairo, a post which he had just left when I met him. When I told him where I was going he shook his head gloomily.

'I don't think you'll enjoy it there; or be able to do anything useful. Nobody can stop this ghastly civil war now. I think you'd prefer Greece. Better still, why don't you try to get into Albania? It's a wonderful country, wonderful people, ideal for guerrilla operations and no civil war. So far as I know we haven't anybody there now, but we ought to have. You'll see Archie Lyall in Cairo, he added. 'Archie should be able to give you a good idea of what goes on in those countries.'

'How did he do in Belgrade?'

'He certainly livened the place up. I remember once the Embassy told him to entertain a delegation of Bishops from England. Archie took them to about the lowest night-club in the place, where the high-spot of the evening is a girl dancing the belly dance. I don't suppose you've ever seen the belly dance, but you can take my word for it that it's all its name implies. Nothing is left to the imagination. The audience applauds the dancer's contortions by shouting "*Mešaj!*" which means, literally, "Mix it!" '

Tired and dirty, in a sticky, crumpled uniform, and sweating in the unaccustomed heat of Cairo, I climbed out of the lorry which had brought me from the airport and walked stiffly up the steps of Shepheards Hotel; I had asked to be taken to Shepheards because it was the only place in Cairo I knew by name. Cringing beneath the supercilious glances of the cool, immaculate officers and their girl friends who were having tea on the terrace, I went straight to the telephone and called a number I had been given in Baker Street; then, as I had been told, I asked to speak to 'Mr. Rose' and gave my name. Having thus established my identity I was told to take a taxi to G.H.Q., where I would be collected.

In Rustum Buildings, the headquarters of M.O.4, as our organization was named in Egypt, I reported to Captain Ionides of the Jugoslav Country Section. He gave me the disappointing news that there was no hope of my being dropped into Jugoslavia in the next moon period, which was in a fortnights time, because all vacancies were already filled; I should therefore have to wait until August. These parachute operations, unlike those of the Small-Scale Raiding Force, could take place only in moonlight, because it was difficult to locate the target in that mountainous region. In the interval, Ionides said, I could stay in his houseboat on the Nile, and occupy my time in learning Serbo-Croat and studying the situation inside the country. He introduced me to Captain James Klugmann, the Country Section Intelligence Officer.

I was surprised to find Klugmann occupying such a confidential position, because when I had last seen him, in 1936, he had been the secretary and inspiration of the Cambridge University Communists. I had innocently supposed that Communists were strictly excluded from S.O.E., for I myself had been required to sign a declaration that I belonged to no Communist or Fascist party before I was enrolled in the organization. However, among my acquaintances at Cambridge there were a number of young men who had joined the Party in a spirit of idealism, only to leave it after the Soviet-German pact of 1939; I assumed that Klugmann was one of them. But I was wrong: like his contemporary, Guy Burgess, he was one of the hard core and today he is a member of the Politburo of the Communist Party of Great Britain.

Although it was impressed upon me from the moment of my arrival in Cairo that when I went into the field I must regard myself simply as a soldier, whose task would be the prosecution of military operations to the exclusion of politics, I could not fail to be aware of the strong political differences which divided the staff officers both in London and Cairo. Nowhere were they more evident than in the Jugoslav Section. Boughey in London had maintained that because Mihailović was the representative of the recognized Jugoslav Government he should be given every support; Major Basil Davidson, on the other hand, the head of the Country Section in Cairo, who later distinguished himself in action with partisan forces in Jugoslavia and in Northern Italy, could not conceal his antipathy to the Chetniks. He wanted me to sign a declaration that I had been subjected in London to indoctrination on behalf of Mihailović; I refused, but the incident warned me of the sort of feeling that was to embitter relations between British officers in the field as well as at headquarters.

With the end of the fighting in North Africa, Cairo had relaxed in an atmosphere of untroubled gaiety; I had plenty of leisure to enjoy it, in the company of Archie Lyall and an old friend from the Spanish Foreign Legion, Bill Nangle. Nangle, who had been a regular officer in the Indian Army before joining the Legion, had at this time just relinquished command of the Indian Squadron of the Long Range Desert Group. He had volunteered for service in the field with S.O.E., but his stubborn refusal to be civil to senior ranks led him to quarrel with the brigadier who controlled the Cairo office, and so he returned to the L.R.D.G. He was killed in action in Italy early the following year.

Lyall had escaped from Jugoslavia, carrying a diplomatic bag to Athens, before the German invasion began. Afterwards he had worked for nearly a year with the S.O.E. organization in Cairo and Jerusalem before returning to Cairo as a major in the Balkan Section of Political Warfare Executive.

He shared John Bennett's pessimism about the future of operations in Jugoslavia, and feared the prospects were no better in Greece.

'I should try for Albania, Peter,' he advised. 'At least the situation there is uncomplicated by civil war. We have two first-class men in there at the moment, Bill McLean and David Smiley, both personal friends of mine. I can't think of a better party for you to join.'

We discussed the failure of S.O.E. preparations against the Germans in Rumania, Bulgaria, Jugoslavia, and Greece before those countries became involved in the war. They had cost us some valuable lives and a great deal of money without inflicting appreciable damage on the enemy.

'I once thought of designing a coat of arms for S.O.E.,' he mused. 'It was to be something like this: Surmounted by an unexploded bomb a cloak and dagger casually left in a bar sinister. The arms supported by two double agents. The motto: "*Nihil quod tetigit non made a balls of it*".'

A day or two later Ionides called me to his office.

'Look, you've a chance of going in during this moon period after all, if you don't mind going to Albania. They're looking for officers at the moment. Come with me now and I'll introduce you to the head of the Section.'

The Albanian Section at that time consisted of two officers, Major Philip Leake and Mrs. Hasluck. The former, a schoolmaster in civilian life, had held an important post with S.O.E. in West Africa in 1941, when March-Phillipps and Appleyard were there with *Maid Honor*, and had worked with them on several operations. A gentle, kindly person with a nice sense of humour, a dry, cynical wit and that 'transcendent capacity of taking trouble' which Carlyle equated with genius, he was a most capable staff officer, well fitted for his post as head of the Cinderella of the Balkan Country Sections.

Mrs. Hasluck, a grey, bird-like woman who made up in energy and determination what she lacked in patience, was an anthropologist who had entered Albania in 1919 and settled near Elbasan in the centre of the country. Until her expulsion by the Italians twenty years later she had lived there very happily, winning the trust of the people and the friendship of many of their leaders. Thereafter she had organized an Albanian office for S.O.E. in Athens and Istanbul, before coming to Cairo to work with Philip Leake. Because of her love for Albania she regarded us B.L.O.s with special affection; we were 'her boys', and when we were in the field we would often receive signals from her, directing our attention to some nearby beauty spot where we could enjoy a picnic.

Among her publications was an English-Albanian grammar, which we were required to study; alas, it was of little use to most of us, who found it scarcely more intelligible than the language it was meant to interpret. Indeed Albanian, which is supposed to be derived from ancient Illyrian, must be one of the most difficult of European languages to learn. Few of us managed to learn it, which was a great hindrance to our work in the field; unable to converse directly with the inhabitants we were nearly always dependent upon interpreters, whom we could trust neither to render faithfully our own words nor to give us a true picture of local reactions.

Most of our knowledge of the current situation in Albania came from signals which McLean and Smiley had sent since their arrival in the country. Dropped to a British headquarters in Epirus during the previous April, their party—known in code as 'Consensus Mission'—had walked across the Albanian frontier about the end of the month, with no knowledge of what they would find on the other side. In the first week of May they were able to establish contact with Albanian guerrillas and set up their wireless. Before describing the situation as they found it I must briefly trace the course of Albanian politics in recent years.[1]

Albania within its present frontiers is about the size of Wales; by far the greater part of it is mountainous. It is a poor country, where under-nourishment is general among the peasantry, who suffer much from tuberculosis in the mountains and from malaria in the marshy coastal plains. The Albanians, or Shqypëtars, as they are properly called, are, in the words of *Chambers's Encyclopedia*, 'the remains of a race which inhabited the Balkan peninsula at the dawn of history, and are of pure Aryan stock.' In spite of nearly five hundred years of Ottoman rule, followed by the frequent attempts of neighbouring powers to absorb their country, they still retain a strong sense of nationality. The race is subdivided into two branches—the Ghegs in the North, the Tosks in the South—speaking slightly different variants of the same language. The river Shkumbi, impassable in winter, divides the two. At this time the social structure in the north was tribal, resembling that of the Scottish highlands before the Forty-five; in the south a rich landowning aristocracy exploited a landless peasantry which since the beginning of Turkish rule had been allowed neither the security of wealth nor the dignity of freedom.

There are three religions in the country, generally confined within geographical limits: in the south the majority of the peasantry is Greek Orthodox, though the land-owning *Beys* are Moslem; the centre and plains are predominantly Moslem, while the north is divided between the Catholic mountaineers of Mirdita and Djukagjin, and the Moslems of Kossovo and the wild north-eastern frontier. But religious differences seemed to be of little importance in comparison with the rivalry of Gheg and Tosk and the age-long hatred of both for their Slav and Greek neighbours.

---

[1] For a fuller account than I am able to give here I would refer readers to Julian Amery's classic study in guerrilla warfare, *Sons of the Eagle* (Macmillan, 1948). pp. 1-71, where they will find a clear, detailed and objective account of Albanian politics and tribal structure, to which I gladly acknowledge my own debt.)

At the end of the Balkan Wars the Ambassadors' Conference of 1913 recognized Albania as an independent State, delineating for it frontiers which were acceptable neither to the Albanians nor to their neighbours. Those boundaries, which were confirmed by the Great Powers in 1926, condemned nearly a million Albanians to live under Greek and Serb rule, without abating the claims of the Serbs and Greeks to most of the rest of Albania; the majority of these irredentist Albanians lived in Kossovo, the borderland between Serbia and north-eastern Albania, a rich and fertile country considered by Albanians to be their natural granary. Nevertheless, Serbia's claim to Kossovo, based on grounds of history and tradition, prevailed over racial and economic considerations.

During the First World War the Albanians, impelled by their hatred of Serbia and Montenegro, contributed troops to the Austrian Army, while various parts of the country were occupied by Serb, French, and Italian forces. The Peace was followed by a period of internal unrest, which was settled, at least nominally, in December 1924, when Ahmed Bey Zogu, subsequently known as King Zog, seized supreme power with the help of the Jugoslav Government and the support of Gheg tribesmen from Kossovo and his own territory of Mati, north of Tirana. Zog, who was not yet thirty when he assumed power, had learnt the art of government in his youth in Constantinople under the tutelage of the Sultan Abdul Hamid. Playing off his rivals against each other, resorting to methods not always applauded by western democracies and relying on a competent gendarmerie trained by British officers, he ruled without interruption for more than fourteen years.

Although he had won his throne with Jugoslav aid, it was upon Italian financial and technical support that he depended during the years of his rule. Albania's foreign policy, the development of her communications and mineral resources, her currency, commerce and education were directly or indirectly under Italian control. So strong was this influence that during my travels throughout the country, from south to north, there were few villages, even in the mountains, where I was unable to exchange a few words of Italian. But Zog was too independent a character to suit Mussolini's imperial ambitions; he retained in his own hands the internal administration of the country, refused to dismiss the British Mission under General Sir Jocelyn Percy and Colonel Frank Stirling which trained and led his gendarmerie, and generally obtained more concessions from the Italians than he gave away. This situation came to an end with the Italian invasion of Albania on Good Friday, 1939. King Zog and Queen Geraldine escaped to Greece with their infant son. Only in the port of Durazzo did the Italians meet organized resistance; there a battalion of gendarmerie and a few tribal levies resisted for thirty-six hours the assault of two divisions supported by heavy naval bombardment. The Albanian Army officer who directed this gallant action was Major Abas Kupi, a stocky, granite-faced, illiterate Gheg from Krujë in the Mati country—the fortress where the national hero, Skanderbeg, raised his revolt against the Turks in the fifteenth century. After the battle Abas Kupi was smuggled by his followers out of the country to Istanbul. Two years later he was back in the mountains of Mati, where he carried on a guerrilla war against the Italians and their German successors until the end of 1944, when he was overrun and driven into exile by the Communists who now dominate his country.

In the summer of 1940, after Italy had entered the war, S.O.E. began to organize from Belgrade an Albanian resistance movement. Foremost amongst its promoters were Colonel Frank Stirling, Lieutenant-Colonel Oakley-Hill—an ex-instructor to the Albanian gendarmerie and a fluent Albanian speaker—and Julian Amery. Recruited from Albanian exiles living in Jugoslavia and from Kossovar irredentists its leaders were Gani, Saïd, and Hasan Kryeziu—three brothers from an influential Kossovar family—Abas Kupi, who had been brought from Istanbul by Stirling, and Mustafa Gjinishi, a leading Communist with a flair for propaganda. Previously the Kryezius had been bitter enemies of Zog and his lieutenant, Abas Kupi, for they believed that Zog had ordered the murder of their eldest brother, Cena Beg, in 1927. But now both parties were prepared to forget their differences and even to ally themselves with the Communists, whom both detested, in the interests of their country.

On 7th April, 1941, immediately after the German invasion of Jugoslavia, Kupi, the Kryezius, and Gjinishi, accompanied by Oakley-Hill led a force of some three hundred Kossovars over the border into Albania. At first the Moslem tribesmen rallied to them, and they advanced westwards towards Scutari, defeating several Italian patrols on the way; but the Catholic clans, who enjoyed a privileged position under the Italians, gave them no support. After the collapse of Jugoslavia even their Moslem allies deserted them. Italian armies occupied the province of Kossovo, which the Axis powers formally incorporated into Albania, thus winning the sympathy of Albanians and Kossovars alike. Within a week Oakley-Hill and his friends were fugitives. He tried to escape to Istanbul with the help of the Kryezius, but the plan miscarried and he was forced into hiding in Belgrade. At length, fearful of the risk he was bringing on his friends, he gave himself up to the Germans.

The leading Albanian conspirators—they were later to become my friends and associates—now scattered in flight. Gani and Saïd Kryeziu were betrayed to the Italians, who imprisoned them in a concentration camp for political offenders on the island of Ventotene; Hasan, who had taken no part in politics before the war, returned to his large estates in Kossovo, where he remained unmolested, but by no means idle, until the end of 1943; Abas Kupi escaped to the Mati country, and Mustafa Gjinishi made his way southward to his native town of Korçë, near the Greek frontier, where he made contact with the principal Albanian Communist leaders.

It was two years before S.O.E. again turned its attention to military operations in Albania. In the meantime such scraps of information as came out of the country were collated by Mrs. Hasluck in her Istanbul office and passed on to Cairo. There was not very much information, but what there was, combined with rumours coming from Jugoslavia, indicated that there were armed bands, or *çetas*, in the Albanian mountains; of the nature of these bands, their politics, location and activities there was little known.

In consequence of the Allied victory in North Africa and the approaching invasion of Italy, S.O.E. began to take a more serious interest in Albania, if only because of the importance to the Axis of her lines of communication. 'Consensus' Mission was therefore dispatched with the primary task of reporting on the situation and strength of the Albanian guerrillas and their potential value to the Allies. From the information they sent out a much clearer picture emerged.

After the outbreak of war between Russia and Germany, the Communists in Albania, as in other Balkan countries, took to the hills for safety. Having established a comparatively secure base in the mountains between Korçë and Gjinokaster they began to form partisan *çetas*, recruited partly from the landless peasantry of the countryside, partly from the young intelligentsia of the towns. Probably their original instructions came from Tito, who maintained two representatives with the Albanian Communist committee; I was to meet these sinister gentlemen, Dušan Mugoša (alias Ali Gostivari) and Miladin Popović, and to note the respect, bordering on veneration, in which they were held by their Albanian colleagues.

Following the general practice, the Partisan leaders declined to call themselves Communists. Their movement, they pretended, was a 'democratic' movement which all who held 'democratic' views were welcome to join. Its true nature, which we came to learn in time, is best described in Julian Amery's own words:[1]

'In practice, exclusive control of the movement was retained in the hands of a small committee, all of whom were Communists. This committee, besides directing policy, appointed the guerrilla commanders, the political commissars, and the regional organizers. The former were most often, and the two latter invariably, Communists; while, in accordance with the best conspiratorial traditions, all three were kept under observation by Party members who held no official position at all. By these methods, seconded by the salutary liquidation of those who disobeyed or disagreed, the Partisan

---

[1] *Sons of the Eagle*, p. 54.

movement presently achieved a degree of discipline and cohesion of which few observers believed Albanians to be capable.[1]

As Amery goes on to point out, the Partisan movement drew its strength entirely from the Tosks. North of the Shkumbi there was little support for Communism; there were, however, various guerrilla groups with which the Communists, for reasons of prestige, wished to ally themselves. Most powerful of these was Abas Kupi with his Mati tribesmen; next in importance was the veteran outlaw, Myslim Peza, who controlled the scrub-covered, malarial hills southwest of Tirana, and who for the past ten years had been defying the central authority; lastly, in the mountains of Martanesh, north-east of Tirana, the hard-drinking old Bektashi abbot, Baba Faja, a bitter enemy of the Italians, commanded a powerful Çeta.

The skilful diplomacy, personal charm and evident sincerity of Mustafa Gjinishi were largely responsible for persuading these three chieftains to join the Partisan movement; a conference between all the guerrilla leaders was held at Peza in September 1942, as a result of which their various groups were amalgamated in a single 'National Liberation Movement', subsequently known as the L.N.C. from the initial letters of its Albanian name. The movement was controlled by a Central Council of ten members, predominantly Communist but including the three Gheg chieftains.

This was a triumph for the Communists: it disarmed the suspicions of those who feared the political affiliations of their movement, for it was now clear that the L.N.C. included known anti-Communists; secondly, it enabled them to extend their influence among the Ghegs and to infiltrate their own supporters into the forces of Myslim Peza and Baba Faja, who soon became mere Communist puppets. Abas Kupi alone refused to allow any Communist penetration or to accept Communist nominees in positions of responsibility; although he served on the L.N.C. Council and collaborated in battle with Partisan units, he kept the control of his forces firmly in his own hands.

There was another resistance movement in southern Albania, known as the Balli Kombëtar, or National Front. Recruited largely from local landowners and their retainers, from merchants, teachers and professional men, and from the non-Communist intelligentsia of the towns, the Ballists viewed the L.N.C. with fear and suspicion. The founder of the party was the venerable statesman, Midhat Bey Frasheri, an outstanding figure in the struggle for Albanian independence during the early years of the century; its leaders included some of the ablest politicians in the country. As convinced Republicans the Ballists were opponents of King Zog, but as staunch nationalists they were enemies of the Italians, although they did not take the field against them until the end of 1942. They were lukewarm in their support

---

[1] Communist tactics are, of course, more widely understood today than they were in 1943.

of the British, for they feared, rightly as it proved, that an allied victory would result at best in the loss of Kossovo, at worst in Communist domination of their country. Moreover, they were especially handicapped in undertaking guerrilla operations by the fact that many of their supporters lived in villages near the main roads, where they and their families were peculiarly vulnerable to reprisals. Nevertheless, in order to justify their demands for arms and money they would on occasion go into action against the Italians.

Thus, at the time when McLean's mission entered Albania there were two separate resistance movements in the south of the country, each viewing the other with suspicion, often inflamed to hostility. For a few months after the fall of Mussolini there seemed to be a chance that the two movements would sink their differences for the duration of the war, in a common effort against the Italians. On the initiative of Abas Kupi and Mustafa Gjinishi delegates from the L.N.C. and Balli Kombëtar met in conference at the village of Mukaj, near Tiranë, and agreed to a truce. This triumph of patriotic moderation was shortlived. The extreme Communists, who really directed the policy of the L.N.C., disapproved of compromise, and had only acquiesced in the meeting for fear of offending Abas Kupi; nor did the leaders of the Balli Kombëtar, in their deep distrust of the Communists, put any faith in the agreement.

It gradually became apparent that the arms and money which S.O.E. was dropping so lavishly into Albania were being conserved by L.N.C. and Balli Kombëtar alike for use against each other. In our briefing it was repeatedly impressed on us that, unlike B.L.O.s in Greece and Jugoslavia, we were going to be dropped to an area, not to a faction; we were to ignore politics and consider ourselves only as soldiers, lending our support impartially to any groups or parties in our area that were prepared to fight the enemy. These instructions, which seemed clear and logical to us in Cairo, were to prove quite unrealistic in the field.

My hopes of dropping into Albania during July were disappointed. I was about to leave when, with my peculiar genius for anticlimax, I fell ill with a sudden and crippling attack of gout, which put me into hospital for a fortnight; by the time I was able to walk again the July moon period was over.

At this time S.O.E. parachute operations were launched from Derna; I arrived there in the first week of August after a hot and crowded train journey of twenty-four hours across the desert to Tobruk, followed by an eight-hour lorry ride. We lived comfortably enough in a camp on top of the escarpment overlooking the shell-battered white buildings of Derna and the brassy sea beyond; half a mile up the road was the aerodrome, where a squadron of Halifaxes, commanded by an old school-friend of mine, Wing-Commander Jimmy Blackburn, waited to carry us to our different destinations in the Balkans.

There were four parties, including my own, going to Albania this month; each of the other three consisted of an officer, a wireless operator, and an N.C.O. who was supposed to be an expert in demolitions and sabotage operations. By far the eldest—and the toughest—of us was Major Tilman, commanding 'Sculptor' Mission. Short and stocky, with a prominent nose and chin and a small fierce moustache, he was an experienced and enthusiastic mountaineer who had taken part in the last pre-war Everest expedition; he had volunteered for Albania, he informed us, in order to keep himself in practice for his next Himalayan attempt. He took not the slightest interest in politics, and so, while he was always glad to blow up a bridge or ambush a convoy, his passion for climbing and the frequent opportunities to indulge it left him happily impervious to the bitter quarrels between the different Albanian factions.

Less fortunate in this respect was Major Gerry Field, in command of 'Sapling' Mission; a serious-minded and enthusiastic officer, he had a positive aversion to political controversy and all who engaged in it. He was particularly unlucky, therefore, to be sent to the Valona area where L.N.C. and Balli Kombëtar were expending all their energies in civil strife, in which they were aggressively determined to involve him.

Major George Seymour, Royal Scots Fusiliers, who commanded 'Sconce' Mission, was, like Tilman and Field, a regular soldier. After five gay years of regimental service in India before the war, he had been through some grim experiences in the Western Desert, culminating in the Battle of Alamein, where he had commanded a company of the Argylls under Colonel Lorne Campbell, V.C., and had been severely wounded by a land mine. Although imbued with a professional distaste for politics and politicians he was prepared to tackle both when necessary, confident that they held no problems which could not be solved by an officer with a gentleman's education, a Sandhurst training, and a sound knowledge of King's Regulations.

Tall and thin in appearance, he had the manner of a military dandy of Crimean days, enriched by a vast handlebar moustache which always reminded me of those anglers' stories of 'the one that got away'.

In my own party, which bore the code name of 'Stepmother', I had as paramilitary expert Sergeant Gregson Allcott, R.A.F., a gentle, soft-spoken young man from Eastbourne; my wireless operator, Corporal Roberts, had dropped in the previous month. Although destined for different parts of the country, our four missions were to be dropped together to McLean and Smiley at the village of Shtyllë in the mountains about ten miles south-west of Korçë. We were to take off in two aircraft, Tilman and Field with their parties in one, Seymour and I in the other.

We passed our days in supervising the packing of our kit, choosing our maps, and studying our operational briefs, and our evenings in drinking, dart-playing, and writing letters. We were allowed to take with us one container of personal clothing and equipment, including any special weapons for our own use; I was taking a Colt .45 automatic and a new type of sub-machine gun, named the Welgun after the S.O.E. experimental station where it was designed. The main load of each aircraft would consist of supplies for McLean and Smiley—chiefly explosives, arms, clothing, and money; the money was in gold sovereigns and Napoleons, for gold was at this time the only readily negotiable currency in the Balkans.

Our operational instructions were drafted in the broadest terms. They bade us, quoting from my own, 'kill Germans and Italians, to lower by every possible means their morale, to contain their forces; to ascertain the requirements in arms and supplies of the Albanian *çetas* resisting the enemy and to give every possible encouragement to all parties, irrespective of politics, who were prepared to co-operate against the enemy; to collect as much intelligence as possible, both political and military'. Reading this last sentence I was reminded that the *Encyclopedia Britannica* listed the word 'intelligence' under three headings: 1. Human; 2. Animal; 3. Military.

An unsatisfactory though necessary feature of our letter-writing was that we were forbidden to give any indication where we were going or what we were about to do. An anxious wife or mother could have gained little satisfaction from such stereotyped phrases as 'I am about to go on active operations in the field and I shall be unable to communicate with you for some time. My headquarters will keep you informed of my health and safety,' which was about all we were allowed to say. While we were in Albania we could hope to receive mail whenever supplies were dropped to us, but of course we could send nothing out. We were, however, told to leave the names and addresses of our next-of-kin and of any other friends or relatives we chose; the Welfare Section of our Cairo office would keep in touch with them by a regular series of formal telegrams, assuring them of our safety and health and, in varying degrees, of our affection. Unfortunately, in the course of time and with the transfer of the Cairo office to Italy the telegrams were sometimes misdirected, occasionally with catastrophic results. A certain officer, arriving back in Italy after six months in Albania, complained to a colleague:

'I don't so much mind that they've divorced me from my wife, but damn it, they've engaged me to another girl!'

The outlines of the Halifaxes ranged by the runway looked like monstrous black locusts against the angry light of the dying sun; the ground shook from the thunder of their warming engines, the grass around them was flattened by the slip-streams. As Seymour and I walked towards them from the station buildings an aircraft carrying a party bound for Bosnia began to taxi, gathered speed and floated into the air above the escarpment; a moment later it turned northward over the sea. Beside our own Halifax stood our dispatcher, a cheerful, fresh-faced young corporal. Telling us to follow him he climbed a short ladder under the belly near the tail, leading through a narrow aperture into the reeking metal interior of the fuselage. When the ladder was removed and the hatch closed I experienced a terrifying moment of claustrophobia at the thought of being trapped within that narrow, windowless shell, a feeling of suffocation which lasted until we were airborne.

It was the night of 10th August. Having fitted our parachutes earlier in the day we need not put them on for at least another three hours, and so we could enjoy a certain freedom of movement in the aircraft. We crowded into the fore part of the fuselage for take-off, but afterwards settled ourselves comfortably among the soft bales of blankets and clothing. These bales were known as 'free drops', as distinct from the containers which required parachutes and were carried in the bomb bays. When we had climbed to our cruising height the roar of the engines softened to an even purr, the vibration eased and, stretched among the blankets in the heated, dimly lit belly of the Halifax I fell asleep....

The dispatcher shook me awake.

'You'll be putting on parachutes in about half an hour, sir. The Skipper wondered if you'd like to go forward to the flight deck for a look around.'

Ten thousand feet below us the coast line of Epirus rose white in the moonlight from an indigo sea. It was a clear and lovely night 'clad in the beauty of a thousand stars'. In a few minutes we should be crossing the coast, turning inland towards Korçë and our dropping zone.

'We can be thankful for this,' said the pilot, following my gaze downwards. 'That dropping zone is in a narrow valley with some nasty hills around. I shouldn't fancy going down through cloud to look for the fires. You'd better get back now. Good luck to you!'

The dispatcher helped us on with our parachutes, clipped each static line to the steel wire running along the roof of the fuselage and pushed the metal safety-pin through the clip, thus ensuring that the clip was not torn from the wire by the weight of the parachutist's body as he left the aircraft. Before the introduction of the safety-pin there had been some nasty accidents. We had already arranged the order of our dropping. On the first run-in the aircraft would loose the containers and the 'free-drops'; she would then make a complete circuit and drop us in two sticks: as senior officer Seymour would go out first, followed by his N.C.O.s, Corporals Smith and Hill; on the next run-in Gregson Allcott would drop, followed immediately by myself; Seymour and I had agreed that, as officers, we ought to be first and last out of the aircraft.

We seated ourselves around the exit hatch in our dropping order; the dispatcher lifted back the covers, letting in the night air to blow chill on our bodies; the roar of the engines struck suddenly at our ears. We had about half an hour to wait before we might expect to sight the signal fires marking our dropping zone. With nothing to distract my mind from contemplation of the immediate future, my spirits began to sink; I wondered how I should withstand mentally and physically whatever stresses and dangers might be awaiting me. For all our study of 'Consensus' signals, Mrs. Hasluck's lectures, and such few books on Albania as had come our way I felt that it was into an utterly unknown country that we were about to launch ourselves; nor could I imagine when or how we should return. It was not so much fear that coloured my thoughts as gloom.

A shout from the dispatcher, who had been talking on the intercom, brought me back to the present.

'We've sighted the fires! We're going to circle now to make the first run-in. Remember, when your turn comes to drop don't watch the signal lights, watch my hand. I'll raise it when the red conies on for Action Stations. As soon as I drop it, you go. I repeat—don't bother about the lights. And remember this is a four-engined kite—so brace yourselves for quite a punch from the slip-stream. We'll be dropping you from a thousand feet, so you'll have plenty of time to look around on your way down.'

The floor tilted steeply as the aircraft banked and began to lose height rapidly, pitching sickeningly in the turbulent air; the engines spluttered and flashed as the pilot throttled back for the approach. One of the crew had come aft to help the dispatcher throw out the 'free drops'. The pair of them stood over the hole, their eyes fixed on the two signal lights in the roof above us; neither man was wearing a parachute. The red light flashed on, gleamed steadily for some ten seconds, then changed to green; as the two men hurriedly bundled out the packages I caught a glimpse through the hole of a line of fires flashing past on the ground. When the last package had disappeared the rhythm of the engines swelled as the aircraft rose steeply and began to bank in a wide turn. Sweating, the dispatcher turned to us with a broad smile.

'That's the containers and bundles gone. Now it's your turn!'

Beneath the handlebar moustache Seymour's lips twisted into a sickly grin.

Once again the beat of the engines slowed as we came out of our turn. When the dispatcher's hand went up I gave Seymour what I hoped was a smile of encouragement; but his eyes were fixed on the upraised hand. There was a shout of 'Go!', the hand dropped, and within five seconds Seymour, Smith, and Hill had disappeared through the hole.

'Lovely!' sighed the dispatcher, looking after them.

It seemed to me that the last circuit would never end. Opposite me across the hole sat Gregson Allcott, his hands gripping the side, his feet dangling into space; as soon as his head was clear of the aperture I must swing my legs over the side and follow him, dropping with my back to the direction of the aircraft's flight. Hastily I tried to fix in my mind all the details I had been taught at Ringway—hands pressed to my sides, body stiff, feet and knees together.... Above my head the dispatcher's hand was raised, in those few remaining moments I noticed thankfully that I felt no longer gloomy or afraid; only quite cold and drained of all emotion. I caught the flash of the green light a fraction of a second before I felt the dispatcher's hand come down on my shoulder. Gregson Allcott toppled rather than dropped through the hole. I gave him one second to fall clear, swung my legs over, stiffened, and pushed myself away from the side; I remembered to look up as I dropped.

There were two seconds of nausea when my stomach seemed to leap into my mouth; then something like the fist of a heavy-weight boxer hit me in the small of the back, I felt a violent pull under the armpits and groins and at last I was floating slowly earthwards with a great white canopy billowing above my head. Instead of the rush of air through my ears the only sound was the hum of the Halifax's engines growing fainter in the distance.

The moonlight shone on rocky, scrub-covered hills rising from a long, narrow valley where, immediately below me, flickered a line of small fires. As I drifted lower there came on my ears the sounds of men shouting in the valley, mingled with the faint tinkle of goat-bells from the surrounding hills. I felt as content, even elated, as before I had been sad and frightened. I beamed upon the happy pastoral scene. My complacency was shattered a few moments later when I realized that I was drifting away from the fires, across what seemed to be a dry water-course, towards the side of a mountain...

The next thing I remember, I was standing unsteadily on a piece of sloping, rocky ground, supported on my feet with difficulty by a grinning, dark, shaggy little man; he seemed to my confused mind like a satyr, and I should not have been surprised to see goat-feet, horns and a tail. I tried to collect my wits and remember where I was and to decide whether I was awake or dreaming; my head swam, my eyes seemed unable to focus. The word 'Albania' flickered through my consciousness and I found myself repeating it aloud, to the delight of the satyr, who broke into excited pidgin French:

'*Albanie, oui! Vous êtes en Albanie! Vous venez parachutiste*'—he pointed upwards—'*Vous frappez tête—poum!*' He indicated the rock where I was standing and my parachute and harness strewn upon it. '*Moi*,' he added, tapping his chest, '*Moi Albanais. Moi Stefan.*'

At this moment I heard Seymour's cheerful tones behind me:

'How do you feel, Peter, old boy?'

'What happened?'

'You missed the D.Z. and landed half-way up the hillside. You came an awful smack and hit your head on a rock. It looks as though you've got a bit of concussion. Come along and we'll see if we can get you onto a mule.'

'Would you mind telling me the date?' Somehow it seemed terribly important.

'Certainly! It's nearly midnight, Tuesday, 10th of August, 1943.'

With one of them on either side of me I limped down the hill, over the bed of the watercourse and onto the smooth grass of the valley, where the fires were being doused and all their traces obliterated by the Albanians. On the farther side a bunch of mules were standing, waiting for the containers to be loaded as they were collected from the dropping ground. Hoisting me onto one of the rough wooden pack saddles, Seymour and Stefan led my mule along a narrow track winding towards the eastern end of the valley. After ten minutes we reached the crest of a low col, where we looked down on another, broader valley in which nestled the low white houses of the village of Shtyllë. Approaching up the hill with long, easy strides came a tall, well-built figure in jodhpurs and a wide crimson cummerbund, a fresh-faced young man with long, fair hair brushed back from a broad forehead and wearing a major's crown on the shoulder-straps of his open-necked army shirt. With a charming smile he introduced himself as Bill McLean and bade us welcome to Albania.

'Stefan will take you to our headquarters,' he went on, 'where you'll find the others, as well as some food and drink, which I expect you need. I'll join you as soon as we've finished clearing up the D.Z. Your kit will be collected and brought to you there. Afterwards I'll send somebody to show you where you're sleeping.'

'Consensus' headquarters was in the disused village mosque and school, a single-storey mud and brick building consisting of three large rooms and standing on a low out-crop of rock which overlooked the valley to the southeast. In the largest room, lit by oil lamps and candles, was a long trestle table laden with plates of hot food, bottles of Italian champagne and brandy and flasks of red chianti—brought from Korçë, it was explained to me, by McLean's Albanian couriers on their biweekly visits to the town. Seated at the table on old ammunition boxes and empty parachute containers were members of McLean's headquarters staff, busily entertaining Field, Tilman and their parties. I was glad to hear that I was the only casualty of the evening's drop, although Gerry Field had achieved the remarkable if not unique distinction of being sick in the air on his way down; it must have been a distressing experience, for it seemed that he descended quicker than his vomit.

By this time I was feeling very sick myself; and so after swallowing two or three mugs of hot sweet tea I asked to be shown my bed. Led by Stefan and accompanied by Seymour, who was sharing my lodgings, I climbed the hill to a small wooden house, where an old woman led us into a narrow, low-ceilinged room; there were two mattresses covered with blankets on the floor. Within five minutes I was asleep.

VI

PARTISANS AND PARASITES

For the next thirty-six hours I slept almost continuously. On the morning of Thursday, 12th August, I awoke feeling refreshed and fit again. After a breakfast of hot sweetened milk and maize bread I walked down to the mosque to report to McLean.

If ever an officer could be described as having, in the colloquialism of the time, a 'good war' that officer was Bill McLean. Entering the Army through Eton and Sandhurst he was commissioned in the Scots Greys in 1939 and was serving with them in Palestine when the war broke out. During the Abyssinian campaign he commanded a battalion of Amhara irregulars, with which he inflicted heavy casualties on the Italians. Now, in his twenty-fifth year, he was commander of the British Mission in Albania, one of the most responsible military appointments in the Balkans. Gifted with outstanding qualities of imagination, leadership, courage and endurance he hid beneath a nonchalant and charming personality a shrewd and ruthless mind.

Captain David Smiley, his second-in-command, had left the morning we arrived to lay an ambush on the main road from Korçë to Yannina with a Balli Kombëtar *Ceta*; but in the mosque I found the Sapper, Lieutenant Garry Duffy. A spare dark young man with a serious cast of expression, Duffy was a very brave and competent officer with an uncanny skill at demolitions and the laying of mines—his two chief interests in life. The other British members of headquarters staff were Sergeant Williamson, McLean's wireless operator, Sergeant Jenkins, a big, bloodthirsty paramilitary expert who had dropped in a month previously, and Sergeant Jones, his inseparable companion who lived in the same street in Liverpool. With them I also met my own wireless operator, Corporal Roberts, a quiet young man, brave and intelligent, in whom I soon grew to have great confidence. Squadron-Leader Neel and Flight-Lieutenant Hands, who had dropped to McLean in July, had already left for the north.

McLean had collected a number of camp followers, some of them Albanians, others Italian deserters; there was a carpenter, an armourer, and several Italian cooks, batmen, and house-servants. More important—for security in guerrilla warfare is vitally dependent on mobility—he had hired a band of Vlach muleteers to look after his pack transport. These Rumanian nomads were exceptionally skilled in the management of mules; they were not particularly honest but were expert in the performance of their contractual duties, which they insisted did not include fighting or the exposure of themselves to danger. There were also three Albanian interpreters: Stefan, who had rescued me when I landed—in the daylight he looked splendidly farouche with a pair of fierce black moustaches; Stiljan Biçi, a gentle, timid youth who spoke excellent French; and, dominating them both—indeed dominating all the Albanians in our camp—the sinister figure of Frederick Nosi. Nephew of the respected elder statesman, Lef Nosi, this young man, still in his early twenties, enjoyed a position of great confidence with the L.N.C.; a thoroughly indoctrinated Marxist with unusual qualities of intelligence and judgment and a fluent knowledge of English, he was selected by Enver Hoxha as liaison officer to McLean's mission—as official interpreter and unofficial spy. Few were the messages we sent to Cairo or to each other that Frederick Nosi did not do his best to read.

Marxist theory teaches that the 'historical process' must lead to the emergence of a Communist society and that the wise man, faced with the alternatives of opposing or assisting the process, will choose the latter. Uninhibited by personal scruple or family tradition Frederick Nosi made his choice. Imperturbably brave, infinitely ambitious, he trampled ruthlessly on all who impeded his progress, allowing no considerations of friendship to stand in his way. He terrorized his subordinates, fawned on his superiors and spied on his comrades; towards the majority of his fellow-countrymen he assumed an attitude of supercilious contempt, emphasizing his superiority to them with the frequent use of the phrase, 'we intellectuals'.

One of the first tasks that McLean and Smiley had commissioned after their occupation of Shtyllë was the erection of a large wooden structure, known as 'the barracks', on the southern side of the valley under the lee of a steep mountain. It was a single storey building skillfully camouflaged with parachutes and containing a kitchen and sleeping quarters for the N.C.O.s, a wireless room, and separate store-rooms for arms and explosives, money and clothing. It had cost sixty gold sovereigns to build. The supplies received in drops were stored there under lock and key, to be doled out to the partisans by Smiley, who as quartermaster kept an exact tally of each item down to the last pair of socks.

We lived very well in McLean's headquarters. In addition to what we received by air we could buy as much fresh food as we needed from the friendly inhabitants of Shtyllë and the neighbouring village of Vithkuq; luxuries such as wine, brandy, and the excellent local cigarettes came from Korçë, brought by McLean's well organized courier service. In short the mission had established a well-found and comfortable base; how long we should be able to enjoy it depended on the sufferance of the Italians.

Vithkuq, some three miles east of Shtyllë, was at this time the headquarters of the L.N.C. Central Council. Although a much larger village it was not so secure a base, for it was accessible by road from Korçë, about twenty miles away, where the Italians maintained a strong garrison. A cart track, winding along a steep mountain-side, connected Vithkuq and Shtyllë; Smiley and Duffy had prepared it for demolition in case of enemy attack.

By the time I arrived various local L.N.C. *Çetas* had been grouped into the nucleus of a striking force, based on Vithkuq and grandiloquently styled 'The First Partisan Brigade'.[1] Totaling no more than eight hundred men, organized in four 'battalions', it was nevertheless formidably equipped with small-arms, heavy machine-guns and mortars captured from the Axis armies in North Africa and dropped to 'Consensus' mission; after a month's intensive training by McLean and his staff it was now ready for action.

The men were of every age from fifteen to sixty. Against a background of peasant misery or artisan squalor the contrast of this free life under arms in the mountains made a strong emotional appeal to each of them. They seemed fit, cheerful and enthusiastic; sitting round their camp fires under the stars they would sing of their courage and endurance, the skill of their officers and the wisdom of their leaders. There were some girls among them, who carried rifles and dressed like the men and whose functions, we were repeatedly assured, were strictly confined to cooking, nursing, and fighting. Dress varied from town or peasant clothes to uniforms captured from the Italians and British battle-dresses issued by Smiley. But all ranks wore the five-pointed red star in their caps. Officers, who wore no other insignia, were saluted with clenched fist and the Partisan slogan, '*Vdekje Fashizmit! Liri Popullit!*' ('Death to Fascism! Freedom to the people!').

The Brigade Commander was Mehmet Shehu, a grim, energetic and efficient soldier who has since become Prime Minister of the Albanian People's Republic. Unlike most of the Partisan leaders he already had some practical experience of serious warfare, for he had commanded a company of the International Brigades in Spain; unlike most of them, also, he spoke good English. A sour, taciturn man of ruthless ambition, outstanding courage, and sickening ferocity—he had personally cut the throats of seventy Italian prisoners after a recent engagement—he tried hard to conceal his dislike and distrust of the British, because he admired the soldierly qualities of McLean and Smiley and valued the help they gave him.

The direction of Partisan military operations was vested in the *Shtabit*, the General Staff of the L.N.C. Central Council. Although, as Commander-in-Chief, Mehmet Shehu was a member, supreme political and military control of the *Shtabit*—and indeed of the whole L.N.C. movement—was in the hands of the Chief Political Commissar, Professor Enver Hoxha, an ex-schoolmaster from the Lycée at Korçë. He was a tall, flabby creature in his early thirties, with a sulky, podgy face and a soft woman's voice. Like Mehmet

---

[1] The term Partisan refers in future to L.N.C. guerrillas, as distinct from the Balli Kombëtar and other resistance groups in Albania and Jugoslavia.

Shehu he was a fanatical Communist, cruel, humourless, and deeply suspicious of the British. He spoke excellent French but no English. Although physically a coward he had absurd military pretentions, which led him two years later, when his forces had made him master of Albania, to arrogate to himself the rank of 'Colonel-General'.

It was only gradually that I came to appreciate the influence exercised by Political Commissars in this guerrilla army; for neither Enver Hoxha nor any of his colleagues would admit to us that the policy of their movement was Communist, even when, later on, they must have realized that it was obvious to us. As the army expanded, every L.N.C. brigade, every battalion and every *çeta* had its own Political Commissar. In theory the responsibilities of the Commissar were limited to political discipline, administration and welfare: in practice, on all matters outside the actual conduct of military operations his authority overrode that of the Commander to whom he was nominally adviser.

When I reported to McLean on the morning of 12th August he took me for a walk, ostensibly to show me the dropping ground, in reality to explain to me in private the political situation in the area and throughout the country and to discuss plans for my own future.

'Relations between the L.N.C. and the Balli Kombëtar,' he told me, 'are daily getting worse. The L.N.C. call the Balli reactionaries, which they may be, and collaborationists, which they certainly are not; they also accuse them of attacking L.N.C. *çetas* when the latter go into their territory to attack the Germans or Italians, and of giving warning to the enemy of ambushes planned by the L.N.C. The Balli accuse the L.N.C., of being Communists and of making unprovoked attacks upon their villages and their *çetas*, they say they're willing to fight the Huns and Ities, but are hindered by the fact that they haven't enough arms unless we give them some; also by the fact that their villages lie alongside or very near the Leskovik—Korçë road, and whenever a convoy is attacked, either by themselves or the L.N.C., one of those villages is burnt in reprisal and its inhabitants slaughtered. The L.N.C., of course, who have no villages, couldn't care less.'

'How much truth is there in the Balli excuses?'

'A good deal in what they say about reprisals. At the beginning of last month, after a series of Partisan attacks on the road, the Germans sent an armoured column down from Korçë to Borovë and Barmash. They went through both those villages with flame-throwers, setting every house on fire with the inhabitants inside; they then surrounded each village and drove the people back into the flames as they tried to escape. There's one little boy of seven in Shtyllë now; both his parents were burnt alive in Borovë and he was twice driven back into the fire before he found a way to crawl out, badly burnt. No wonder the villagers are fed up! They must either take to the hills and lose their property, or stay and be massacred. Sometimes, to escape reprisals, they do warn the enemy of L.N.C. ambushes, and it's hard to blame them.

'It's becoming more and more difficult for us to carry out Cairo's instructions about helping L.N.C. and Balli impartially. In spite of their difficulties the Balli have attempted a few half-hearted and unsuccessful operations, and we've given them some rifles and ammunition, the odd machine-gun and mortar, and a few grenades; but every time we do so Enver raises a howl that we're supporting traitors, collaborationists, and enemies of the Albanian people, and he sulks for a week. Meanwhile the Balli complain that we're arming the L.N.C. for civil war.'

'What are you going to do about it?' I asked gloomily, remembering John Bennett's description of the Civil War in Jugoslavia.

'Well, we're putting pressure on both parties to prove their good faith by undertaking an action against the Germans. If they don't fight they don't get any more arms—or any more sovereigns either, which will shake them! David Smiley left on Wednesday to attack the main road down south, near Barmash, with a Balli Çeta. They're two hundred strong, and David has taken our 20-mm. cannon to support them, so they should be all right. Enver and Mehmet of course are furious and will probably try to sabotage the operation. David should be back tomorrow, so we'll hear then.

'Secondly, David and I have worked out a plan with Mehmet for a large-scale ambush by the whole Brigade on the road, near the same place; there's an ideal stretch where the road runs along the side of the mountain with a sheer precipice below, and if a large convoy comes along we ought to bag the lot. It will be a wonderful blooding for the Brigade and a splendid climax to all our training.'

'When is it to be, and am I in on it?'

'Of course you are, if you like. We've planned it for the end of next week—about the 20th. That brings us to the question of your own future. While you were laid up I discussed with Seymour, Field, and Tilman the areas where they should work. Bill Tilman is going to Gjinokaster, Gerry Field to Valona, and Seymour to Peza to work with Myslim; they'll be moving early next week, as soon as we can get them mules and drivers; Tony Neel went north last month to Abas Kupi in the Mati, and Hands is on his way to Dibra. Have you any ideas for yourself?'

'Well, while I was in Cairo I saw a signal from you suggesting that someone should be sent to the Kossovo area. That's where I should like to go—it's bound to be interesting, that frontier.'

'Right. They haven't come back on that signal yet, but we'll book you for Kossovo if and when they approve. Meanwhile, I suggest you stay with us and help us out in dealing with Enver and the Central Council; there's a lot of political work and it's quite interesting if a bit discouraging at times.'

'What are they like to deal with, those boys?'

'Not very cooperative—suspicious and bloody-minded. It's very hard to get them to agree to anything, and impossible to rely on their carrying out what they do agree to. Apart from our relations with the Balli they're always complaining about something, always demanding more money and more arms. They give us absurd figures of casualties they claim to have inflicted on the enemy in various alleged operations, and get furious when we cast the smallest doubt upon their accuracy; yet they hardly ever bring us an identification disc, as we've asked them to do, nor will they ever warn us in advance of any of their operations, so that one of us can go and observe. The only actions of theirs that David and I have watched have been flops, so of course we don't believe their figures.

'They're incredibly inefficient and sometimes very funny. About a fortnight ago the *Shtabit* came to see us with lists of figures of the oil production from the Kuçovë oil-wells, north of Berat, for which I had asked them. But they wouldn't let us keep them or copy them—sheer bloody-mindedness, of course! However, while I kept them talking, David left the room with some excuse about listening to the wireless, swiped the papers off the tables as he went, made a copy of the lot and returned the original without anyone noticing. The sad thing was that when the *Shtabit* went away they forgot to take the lists with them, so all David's work was unnecessary.'

In brilliant sunlight we stood on the col that separated the two valleys, looking down on the board stretch of grassland and the river bed where I had dropped two nights before. The hills rose steep on either side, the lower slopes covered with scrub and stunted conifer, the summits bare and rocky; at the western end of the valley the blue bulk of a great mountain glittered in the clear air.

'I take off my hat to those Halifax pilots,' said McLean. 'Sometimes they come down to five hundred feet to drop our stuff accurately. God knows how they manage to miss that mountain at the other end, or clear the hills on either side when they make their turns. We had a nasty shock during a drop three weeks ago. There were two Halifaxes, and while the second was making its run-in an Italian aircraft followed it and bombed the dropping ground. Luckily David heard it above the noise of the Halifax and recognized it from the engines as a Caproni. He shouted in French to the Partisans who were on the D.Z. to clear off and take cover, which they did pretty quick; but he forgot that poor Garry Duffy, who was right in the middle flashing the recognition signal, didn't speak French! The Caproni dropped twelve 50-kilo bombs with great accuracy, blowing out more than half the signal fires and making a frightful mess of the dropping ground, but luckily without hurting Garry or anybody else. It was a fantastic sight to see the Halifax and the Caproni making alternate runs, one dropping supplies and the other bombs, and neither of them seeming to notice the other! Needless to say, all the Partisans panicked and ran off, although most of them came back next day to loot our kit and steal our food. You ought to have heard David's language next morning, especially when some Albanian came up to him saying he was the owner of the field and claiming compensation for the damage caused by the bombs!'

'The Ities haven't tried it again?'

'No. The Caproni crashed the same night on landing at Korçë, and all the crew were killed, so I suppose they never had a chance to tell anyone about their exploit.'

We turned and walked back to Shtyllë in silence, listening to the tinkle of goat bells and the distant calls of shepherds. The sun beat strong upon our heads but the air, at three thousand feet above the sea, was sweet and cool, filled with the resinous scent of trees and grass and the tang of wood smoke. As we came to the outskirts of the village McLean took me by the elbow:

'Remember, Peter, be very careful what you say in front of Frederick Nosi. Every word gets back to Enver. Above all, no mention, please, of your part in the Spanish Civil War!'

I spent the following day on 'training walks' with Tilman; in the morning we climbed the hills on the north side of the valley, in the afternoon we scaled those on the south. The exercise left me, as it left others who climbed with that indefatigable alpinist, completely exhausted; for it seemed to be his habit, which I am told he followed throughout his stay in Albania, to climb straight to the top of any peak in his path and straight down the other side, disdaining the tracks used by lesser men and mules.

I was nodding over the dining table after our evening meal when there was a commotion outside and Smiley strode into the room. He gave us all a brief good evening and called for beer.

A regular officer in the Household Cavalry, Smiley had served with his regiment in Syria and the Western Desert and with the Commandos in Abyssinia and Eritrea before coming to Albania. Reserved in manner, economical in speech, he had a shrewd insight and quiet self-confidence which enabled him to make up his mind quickly and speak it with a directness that compelled attention without giving offence. Politics bored him, although he could deal well enough with political problems when they came his way; he was happiest when in action or planning action, when testing a new gun or preparing a demolition. In the most dangerous situations he appeared phlegmatic to the point of indifference, not because he lacked the intelligence to feel fear but because he possessed the priceless self-discipline that can conceal and suppress it.

He had a surprising variety of interests outside his profession, and a remarkably detailed knowledge on such widely differing subjects as the rise and fall of the Mongol Empire and the care and cultivation of cacti and succulents. Square and stocky, with fair hair and very bright blue eyes in a round, tanned, well-polished face, he radiated briskness and efficiency.

Standing in front of us, his feet apart, his head slightly cocked to one side, with the bright, alert look of a bird listening for a worm, he told his story in quick, clipped sentences.

'It was quite successful,' he began, 'but not half as good is it might have been. We got into position on Friday morning—the day before yesterday. The *çeta* commandant and I watched the road all day and made plans for the ambush. In the evening I had a lot of trouble with that bloody man Petrit Duma. He arrived with thirty Partisans, saying he intended to lay an ambush in exactly the same place as ours. Of course this was just to bitch the Balli. I told him so and made him push off, but I had to use a lot of threats. That night I laid sixteen mines on the road, in two places about 250 yards apart and out of sight of one another. The road is cut out of the mountain side and there's no way off it—sheer cliffs above and a ravine below. Perfect for an ambush. While I was laying the mines a Halifax flew over and all the men with me ran away, thinking it was a car, so I had to do all the work myself.

'At six-thirty yesterday morning a Hun troop-carrier full of troops and towing an 88-mm. gun approached from the north. Some of the guerrillas shouted, "A Tank! A Tank!" and ran away. The troop-carrier blew up on my mines, and I've got a photograph of it going up. All the Huns were killed—twelve by the mines and my 20-mm. and six shot while running away. Then the braver guerrillas went onto the road and got identifications from the dead Huns and murdered any wounded ones. They had a wonderful time looting the troop carrier. I tried to get them to push the gun over the ravine, but the mines had damaged the wheels and they couldn't move it. We threw all we could down the ravine. Then we heard a convoy coming from the south and got into position again. There were twenty-three lorries all told, five Germans in the first and two in each of the others. The first was blown to bits on the mines, and all five Germans killed inside it. But by this time all the guerrillas had run away except the two who were with me by the 20-mm. It was heartbreaking, as the remaining Germans ran back down the road, leaving the three of us to destroy the lorries they left behind. I sent two of them up in flames with the 20-mm. and hit a third; but if the *çeta* had stayed there we could have got onto the road and destroyed every one. A bit later a lot more Germans returned and started shooting at us, so we went home; they came too close to be healthy. We got good identifications—all from the 1st Alpine Division.'

The next day we were all invited to attend the ceremony of the 'official inauguration' of the First Partisan Brigade at Vithkuq. The cart-track from Shtyllë followed the contour of the mountain, which rose sharply on the right, and on the left dropped sheer into a deep wooded ravine with a stream at the bottom. Near Vithkuq the ravine broadened into a valley, commanded by a steep hill covered with a monastery, which the Partisans had garrisoned and fortified. It gave me a satisfying feeling of security to see how ideal was this country for defence.

The 'inauguration' turned out to be a parade and march-past at which Enver Hoxha took the salute and Mehmet and other members of the Central Council each in turn made a speech. The speeches, of course, were in Albanian and so we had no idea of what was being said, but all were warmly applauded with clenched fist salutes and shouts of 'Death to Fascism!' After two or three hours of this we sat down on the ground to a *vin d'honneur* and lunch on a lavish scale: There was raki,[1] followed by chianti or beer; pilaff and sheep roasted whole; even coffee and execrable Italian brandy. There were speeches throughout the meal and Partisan songs in chorus at the end of it. The most popular song, which had a stirring, haunting rhythm, commemorated, if I remember rightly, the heroism of a certain Comrade John, who came from Valona; when the rest of his *çeta* ran away he alone stood firm.

The following morning, 16th August, Seymour, Tilman, and Field left for their different areas, each with a string of mules carrying his wireless set and generator and canisters full of stores. At McLean's suggestion I moved my kit and sleeping bag into the mosque, where a mattress was laid for me on the floor of the dining-room.

Once a week the peasants from the surrounding districts came to Shtyllë to sell us mules and horses; any thing from seventy to a hundred animals would arrive, of which not more than ten would be fit for use. When McLean and Smiley had selected those they wanted to buy they would leave the bargaining to one of the camp followers, a Palestinian Arab known as Black George[2]—to distinguish him from the armourer, who was known as Greek George. The price of a mule usually worked out at about five gold napoleons; a horse would cost more. However, I was strongly advised to buy myself a mule to ride rather than a horse, because a mule was surer on the steep and stony tracks across this mountainous country and could see better in the dark. Smiley had a mule named Fanny, to whom he was devoted; whenever he felt depressed or particularly disgusted he would stalk out of the mess and over to the mule-lines, where he would be found with his arm round Fanny's neck, whispering into her ear.

In the course of the next few days we received two supply drops. For their reception we had the help of a detachment of Partisans from the First Brigade, under the command of a certain Xhelal Staravecka, a fierce looking, loud-mouthed braggart in a dirty grey fur hat. He had been a gendarmerie officer under the Italians but had deserted to the Partisans in the middle of a

---

[1] A strong, clear spirit distilled from grapes and drunk as an aperitif.

[2] Black George was a private in the Pioneer Corps who had taken to the mountains in Greece after the British withdrawal.

battle, for which he had been rewarded with the command of one of Mehmet's new battalions. After the German occupation of Albania in September 1943 he deserted again and joined the Germans, perpetrating in his new employment such atrocities against both Albanians and Italians that when I last heard of him, in 1949, he was in the Regina Cocli Prison in Rome awaiting trial as a war criminal.

Hearing that my birthday would fall on 19th August McLean sent a courier into Korçë the day before to buy food and drink for a party. On such occasions he would give the courier a few gold sovereigns or napoleons to change into Albanian paper money at the existing black market rate; it was obviously unsafe to buy from the shops with gold—indeed the couriers ran a considerable risk even in carrying our gold, because they might easily be searched by *carabinieri* on entering or leaving the city.

During these days we had several official meetings with the *Shtabit*, sometimes at Vithkuq, sometimes at Shtyllë. They were the first of many conferences I was to endure with this organization, all of which followed a similar pattern. The first item would be a demand for money. The members of the *Shtabit* rendered no accounts, and gave only evasive answers when we asked for precise statements of their needs; if we did not agree to their demand in full—and some of their figures were outrageous—there was sure to be a period of sulky silence or an outburst of blustering rage from Enver Hoxha. When this had subsided Mehmet Shehu would present his indent for military stores; this matter seldom gave difficulty because we always agreed to pass on his requirements to Cairo. Then the *Shtabit* would give us a report on actions undertaken by its units against Germans or Italians, accompanied by imposing figures of enemy killed, captured, and wounded. The figures were seldom supported by the evidence we had asked for—identification discs and shoulder straps—but the hysteria generated by any signs of skepticism on our part was so exhausting that we developed a technique of smiling politely, congratulating the *Shtabit* and promising to tell Cairo what it had achieved.

The fourth item, which the *Shtabit* clearly enjoyed the most, was complaints. These were divided into complaints against the Balli Kombëtar, and complaints against the British Mission. The one usually led on to the other, with little variation in the form of either: The Balli had refused to allow an L.N.C. *çeta* to pass through their territory on its way to attack an Italian garrison; the Balli had fired on some Partisans who were trying to buy food in a Balli village. (Privately we thought the word 'buy' was good.) The Ballist leader, Abas Ermenje, had betrayed the Partisan plan of attack on Berat to the Italians, causing the Partisans to suffer heavy casualties. There was irrefutable evidence of all these incidents, which we could examine one day. Nevertheless, the *Shtabit* was deeply pained, in fact horrified, to learn that the British Mission had been supplying arms to those Fascist traitors, those enemies of the Albanian people, in particular to that tool of the Italian invaders, the so-called Professor Safet Butkë (the local area commander of the Balli Kombëtar). No wonder there was not enough money or arms for Albanian patriots, when *Monsieur le Majeur* gave so much away to collaborators.

We would reply mildly that we were only carrying out the instructions of the Allied High Command, which were to give arms to all those who were prepared to fight the Axis; if Professor Safet Butkë or any other Ballist would fight, then it was the duty of the British Mission to help them with supplies. It had always seemed to us a great pity, we would add, that the two Albanian patriotic movements could not compose their differences and combine against the real enemies of their country.

Thereupon the whole *Shtabit* would break out in a gabble of angry protest, the gist of which was obvious to us even before Frederick Nosi could translate such parts of it as were not covered by 'Traitors!', 'Fascists!' and 'Collaborationists!' Of course the Balli had no intention of fighting the Germans and Italians; all the tales they told about their battles were lies. Couldn't we understand that they only told us these stories in order to get arms from us with which to fight the L.N.C., who alone represented all true Albanian patriots? This theme, developed with rancorous enthusiasm, would result in a general political discussion, usually lasting into the small hours of the morning.

At our second meeting, however, the *Shtabit* had tangible proof of military success, in the shape of eight Italian prisoners captured in an ambush near Korçë; Smiley had already interrogated them at Vithkuq. They were a captain, three subalterns, two N.C.O.s, and two privates. Smiley obtained from them their names and units and the addresses of their families in Italy; but they refused to divulge any more information.

'I admired their behaviour very much,' he told us afterwards. 'Because they must have had a pretty good idea that they were going to be shot. When we get out of here I'll write to their next-of-kin.' 'Do the Partisans always shoot their prisoners?' I asked him. 'Either that, or cut their throats—which is probably kinder to them as these people are such bad shots. They ambushed a cartload of Huns the other day and took four of them prisoner. One of the Partisans who was there told me they led the Germans into a wood and made them take off their boots, and then lined them up and shot at them with Sten guns. The shooting was so bad that the Germans were able to pick up stones and throw them at the Partisans before being killed. One German ran away, but was caught again.'

'I suppose,' said McLean maliciously, 'the Partisan told you that to show you how brave he was to go on shooting at the Germans while they were throwing stones.'

My twenty-eighth birthday was marked by the first signs I had seen of enemy action. In the morning an Italian two-seater biplane circled over our valley; shortly afterwards we heard the sound of gun-fire from the east. Through our glasses we could see the monastery on the hill near Vithkuq; shells were falling on the slopes around the building and bursting on the walls, while the aircraft circled overhead, presumably spotting for the guns. The shelling, punctuated by the sound of machine-gun fire, continued for most of the morning. At lunch time we heard that the monastery was in Italian hands. Partisan losses had been light.

On the morning of 21st August Smiley and I walked into Vithkuq to see Mehmet Shehu. The Brigade was to leave that evening to carry out the attack McLean had planned on the road near Barmash; we, who could move faster, would leave the following morning. Mehmet Shehu confirmed that his troops were ready, and added the interesting news that the *Shtabit* had departed on the previous day for the region of Elbasan in central Albania. Whatever the defects of the *Shtabit*, its members possessed, as events were to prove, a useful capacity for scenting danger. Back at Shtyllë we spent a busy afternoon in final preparations for the battle.

The target was the same stretch of road that Smiley had attacked eight days before. In retrospect it seems a foolish choice; but Partisan patrols had reported that the sector was still clear of enemy pickets, and. it would be difficult to find a better spot for an ambush. A convoy caught there would be at our mercy because there was no room to turn on the road.

The plan as I remember it was simple. During the night of the 22nd-23rd Mehmet Shehu would dispose his brigade on the heights commanding the road—one battalion on a spur immediately above the road, the remainder across the valley where they would have a clear field of fire. Everyone was to be in position by sunrise. Northbound convoys were to be left alone, but when a large enough convoy appeared travelling southwards it would be shot up from both sides and the road closed behind it by mines. Meanwhile Duffy, with a demolition party of our N.C.O.s, would blow the important bridge at Perat, farther south, closing the road to reinforcements from that direction. With the force and armament at our disposal it should not take long to destroy the largest convoy.

Duffy, whose party had a long way to go, left as soon as our conference was ended. I was to leave at daylight for a meeting on the way with Professor Safet Butkë, the local Balli Kombëtar commander, who had been complaining of increased hostility from the L.N.C. After the meeting I was to meet the others for lunch at a nearby village.

The first sunlight striking on my back as my mule-cleared the ridge above Shtyllë dispelled the bad temper caused by early rising and a hurried breakfast. My companions were Stiljan, the young interpreter, and a Balli guide. I soon learnt that it was impossible to move in Albania without a local guide. For although our maps were good enough they did not show the countless tiny tracks which branched in every direction over the mountains; nor, if we left the tracks, could we have moved very far across that savage terrain, even with the best of compasses; on a long journey it might be necessary to change the guide once or twice a day. It was a waste of time to ask about distances; men would reply vaguely, 'two hours on foot, three hours with mules'. But it was wiser to add several hours to their estimates because their natural politeness would lead them to try and spare a stranger's feelings.

After a couple of hours' ride across desolate, scrub-covered hills our way led down through a forest carpeted with pine needles into a green valley, where we halted to rest our animals and drink from a clear, cool stream. We climbed again through pine forest onto rolling green uplands reminiscent of high pastures in the Alps in summer. About eleven o'clock we came into another valley, where a party of armed men awaited us at the entrance to a small village. As I dismounted, their leader, a tubby old man with a stubbly chin, weak, watery eyes and a worried, nervous manner, came forward and greeted me in French, introducing himself as Professor Safet Butkë.

Obviously distrustful of Stiljan he insisted on talking with me alone. His story ran along the lines I had been led to expect and which I later took for granted from either faction when discussing the other: L.N.C. aggression in his territory was becoming intolerable; they came in bands to steal food and plunder property, taking by violence what they could not secure by stealth; they even tried to conscript young men into their çetas. He had tried to avoid bloodshed, but in truth he could not promise to restrain his men much longer if these bandits continued their depredations. Would I please ask Major McLean to use his influence with the L.N.C. to stop their aggression? Another point: the villages near the Korçë-Leskovik road were Ballist. Every time an attack was made on that road one or more of these defenceless villages would be burnt and its inhabitants massacred. It was all very well for the L.N.C. and ourselves to attack the road, because we could escape into the mountains where the enemy could not reach us; but it was Ballist villages that had to suffer. Could we not in future find some place to attack the road far from any villages?

Sadly I rode on my way with Stiljan to the village where I was to meet McLean and Smiley. Safet Butkë sent a strong escort to accompany us as far as the outskirts. I never saw him again. A month later he shot himself in a lavatory.

We joined the Brigade in the late afternoon. The winding column of guerrillas faded slowly along the broad, sandy bed of a water-course; oleander bushes grew thick on the banks and a thin stream trickled sluggishly between. We were in flat, open country with little cover from the air; but we travelled undisturbed. Riding a little ahead of McLean and Smiley I was beginning to feel acutely uncomfortable on my wooden pack-saddle, my feet thrust into improvised stirrups of thick cord. Snippets of Smiley's talk drifted to my ears; he and Mclean were back in London rehearsing the drill for mounting guard.

'You do that, Billy,' I heard Smiley bark, 'and you go straight back to riding-school for the next six months!'

I admired their detachment before an operation that meant so much to them both.

As the sun was setting we began to climb again into the hills. With darkness came a chill wind that whistled mournfully over the bare ridges. It was hard not to lose touch with one another or stray from the track in the impenetrable blackness. Poised on the edge of some escarpment, unable to discern any way down, I was often in despair; but each time my mule carried me with sure feet to the bottom, while I lurched in the saddle, sweating with fright. About midnight we came to a broad plateau surrounded by hills, where we halted.

We were now within half a mile of the road. After a brief conference Mehmet Shehu dispatched one of his battalions, under Tahir Kadaradja, to cross the road and take up position on the spur beyond. A few minutes later the rest of us moved forward towards the hills overlooking the valley and the road. Leaving our mules in the care of our Vlachs we followed Smiley to the position he had already selected for us on the forward slope of one of the hills. We had just settled ourselves to get what rest we could before dawn when we were disagreeably startled by the sound of machine-gun fire from across the valley.

'Oh God!' sighed Smiley, 'Tahir's run into trouble. Unless of course they're shooting at each other.'

Half an hour later Mehmet Shehu and his staff approached over the hill, shining torches with a lavish disregard for concealment which infuriated Smiley.

'Our plan has failed,' began Mehmet angrily. 'Tahir's battalion has been surprised by a German post on that hill. We must withdraw. There is nothing we can do here.'

'Oh yes, there is!' said Smiley and McLean together. 'You can start by wiping out that German post. There can't be many of them.'

Mehmet Shehu shook his head: 'No. It is impossible. My first operation must be one hundred per cent successful.'

'Just what we mean,' said Smiley. 'Look how easy it's going to be to kill those few Germans with all the men you've got—especially in the dark. Then we can have a crack at a convoy tomorrow.'

Mehmet looked at the ground between his feet. 'I have already given the order to withdraw,' he muttered.

We returned to the plateau, where we lay on the ground wrapped in our blankets and sleeping bags. But none of us slept. Mehmet found himself confronted next morning by three furious and disgusted officers. He brought his entire staff with him, feeling, I suppose, the need of moral support. Our reconnaissance had already shown us that the German post consisted of a platoon party of from eighteen to twenty men with a light machine-gun. With such odds in his favour we could hardly believe that Mehmet would refuse to fight. We urged him to overrun the post that night and carry on with the operation as planned on the following morning.

Mehmet remained unmoved by all our arguments. It was useless, he sullenly maintained, to blind ourselves to the fact that the operation had failed. He argued that although a withdrawal would be a blow to the morale of his men, the heavy losses which would result from carrying out our plan would be a bigger blow. At the end of a morning's argument McLean gave up.

'So eight hundred of your "patriotic Albanians", with all the armament and all the training we have given them, are to be frightened away by twenty Germans!' he exclaimed.

Without a word Mehmet turned and walked away, followed by his staff and some plainly audible comments from Smiley.

In the early afternoon I spent two hours watching the road through my binoculars. No convoy passed; a few solitary staff cars and one or two army lorries were the only traffic during my vigil. When I rejoined McLean the Brigade had moved off, leaving us alone with Stiljan, Stefan, our mules, and their drivers.

'You'll be pleased to hear that the Brigade has been in action,' was Smiley's greeting to me.

I looked at him in astonishment, for I had heard no shooting.

'Yes, they killed a solitary German who had wandered into a village near here in search of food. He was unarmed, of course.'

We spent another chilly and despondent night in the same place; but sunrise warmed us and raised our spirits.

'I'm damned if I'm leaving here without having a crack at something,' McLean said to me over breakfast. 'David's got to get back to Shtyllë to receive the drops we're expecting, but if you agree I thought we might try to shoot up a lone staff car. Of course, it's a purely Boy Scout operation, but at least it should work off some of our bad temper.'

Stiljan volunteered to come with us, and one of the Vlachs agreed to guard our mules out of sight of the road. We decided to lay our ambush just before dusk, in order to have the protection of darkness for our escape should the action go against us.

In the early evening we made our way slowly towards the road, while the dying sunlight dappled the hills in a splendid contrast of ochre and indigo. We chose a spot a mile north and out of sight of the German position; here the hills reached almost to the road, and fern and bushes gave plenty of cover without obstructing our view in either direction. Leaving the Vlach with our mules behind a ridge some five hundred yards back, we hid ourselves behind a bank above the road; Stiljan crouched beside me, McLean stood ten yards to our right watching and listening.

The sun had set. In the still, clear light before dusk the land seemed deserted; the only sound I could hear was Stiljan's heavy breathing, showing that he was feeling the same nervous tension as I. We had agreed to attack only a vehicle travelling by itself; but now I remembered that it was the practice for a staff car to precede a convoy at a few hundred yards distance, and I prayed that we should not find ourselves in a trap. Besides our pistols and submachine-guns each of us carried two phosphorus smoke grenades to cover our retreat in an emergency, but I had little faith in their protection if we should run into serious trouble.

Faintly from the south came the sound of a car. We heard it a long way off, the noise of its engine rising and falling on the twisting mountain road. I saw McLean staring through his field-glasses; then he stiffened:

'It's a German staff car, all alone; don't fire till I give the word.'

The car turned the last bend and came into full view, a grey saloon approaching at about twenty-five miles an hour—a perfect target. As I heard Stiljan cock his Schmeizer I pressed forward the safety-catch of my Welgun. Then McLean stood up, his Schmeizer at his shoulder.

'All right, let 'em have it,' he ordered quietly.

We opened fire simultaneously. Within a few seconds the windscreen and side windows were shattered, the body scoured with the marks of our bullets. The car continued on its way for about twenty yards, then slewed in a cloud of dust and came to a halt at the side of the road. The driver sat slumped over the wheel, two men lay huddled motionless in the back, but from the front seat a figure leapt out and, crouching behind the car, returned our fire with his pistol. Changing their magazines McLean and Stiljan continued firing, but at this moment my Welgun jammed; savagely I cursed George, the armorer, to whom I had given it for adjustment three days before and who, it now appeared, had damaged the mechanism. Throwing it aside I drew my .45 and began to fire carefully aimed shots at the place where I imagined the German to be. Suddenly I heard McLean shout.

'Give me covering fire, boys! I'm going down.'

'For Christ's sake stay where you are!' I shouted back; but I was too late. Throwing one of the smoke grenades, which landed well short of the car, McLean scrambled down the slope; Stiljan, urged by me, redoubled his rate of fire. Unfortunately the thick cloud of phosphorus smoke effectively hid the car from our view, although it did not seem to hide McLean from the German; we could hear the crack of his pistol and see spurts of earth fly from the bullets round McLean's feet. I knew McLean was going down not only to finish off the German, but to collect any documents in the car, and I shuddered to think how we should get him away if he were hit. I threw a smoke grenade, hoping to give him extra cover; but by now McLean himself had thought better of it and was climbing back towards us. In a moment he was safe.

'I think we'd better beat it,' he gasped, 'while the score is still in our favour.'

We raced down into a gully and started to climb the ridge beyond which our mules awaited us. It was an arduous journey until we found a gap with a rough track running through it. The mules were grazing peacefully in the shelter of an outcrop of rock, but the Vlach looked thoroughly frightened; he and Stiljan urged us to be on our way at once. I too was anxious to be gone, remembering that one of the first rules of an ambush is not to linger on the scene of the crime. I wasted no time in climbing onto my mule and begged McLean to hurry. We had a wide patch of open ground to cross, and although darkness was falling there was still enough light for us to present a very good target. McLean, however, was in no mood for haste. The danger, he maintained, was over and now was the time to relax and rest before the long journey home. Pulling a tortoiseshell comb from his breast pocket he began to pass it in long, leisurely strokes through the thick blond hair that swept back from his forehead.

'Don't be so damned windy, Peter,' he protested with a careless laugh.

At that moment, with the crackle of exploding fireworks, a burst of machine-gun fire struck the rocks beside us. For a moment McLean stood rigid, the comb still in his hair, the smile frozen on his face; then he gave me a sheepish grin and seized the head-rope of his mule.

'On our way, boys!' He pointed to a low bank beyond the open ground. 'Meet you on the other side of that.'

The Vlach was already making off at the double, followed by Stiljan and our spare mule, which had broken loose. My own mule took fright and started to follow at a trot across the hideously exposed piece of ground. Feeling uncomfortably naked and conspicuous I tried to dismount; but my right foot was caught in the cord stirrup and I could not free it. The air was full of the hiss of the bullets and the angry red gleam of tracer flying all round me as I bent helplessly over the beast's neck, my useless Welgun, which was slung across my back, beating painfully against my hips and elbows with every movement. The machine-gun was firing from the direction of the road; I could not be sure exactly where it was, nor at that moment was I much interested in finding out. The distance was only two or three hundred yards, but it seemed as many miles with the stream of tracer whistling about my head. The Germans must have found it hard to see us in the gathering gloom; they were shooting high, although one or two bursts struck the ground behind me, ricocheting past with an angry whine. At last I was behind the cover of the bank; I fell rather than climbed from my mule, luckily remembering to keep hold of the head-rope. A few seconds later McLean joined me, panting heavily. The rest of our party had disappeared.

Cautiously we peered over the edge. The shooting had ceased and there was no sign of pursuit. We decided to put a safe distance between ourselves and the road, and then to look for a village where we could sleep. Leading our mules we struck northwards away from the road and into the hills. After half a mile we found a track, which we followed for another mile until we felt it safe to halt for a rest. We were about to move on when McLean seized my arm and pointed back down the path:

'There's someone coming!' he whispered, unslinging his Schmeizer.

Listening, with my pistol ready, I heard the sound of hooves striking against rock; a moment later Stiljan's slight figure loomed out of the darkness, leading our spare mule. He had not seen the Vlach since the firing started.

'Never mind,' said McLean. 'He'll have the sense to find his own way back to Shtyllë. Let's get a move on.'

With Stiljan as guide we rode on for an hour without meeting any-one. There was no moon, but the stars gave enough light to follow the track. At last we came to a village. The houses were shuttered and silent, the street deserted; glimmers of light showed behind a few of the doors.

'We should be safe enough here for the night,' said McLean. 'Let's see if we can get anyone to put us up.'

Leaving Stiljan to try one of the houses on our right, McLean and I rode up the street and dismounted in front of a large wooden door. McLean knocked and called several times in a clear voice, 'O Zot i shtepis!'[1] At first there was no reply, but when he persisted a surly voice from within shouted back, brusquely ordering us away; other voices joined in, angry and frightened.

'I'd better try another house,' sighed McLean. 'You go back and see how Stiljan's getting on.'

I found Stiljan engaged in what was obviously a losing argument with an indignant figure in a half-open doorway. As I came up, the door was slammed in the interpreter's face.

'He will not have us, Captain,' explained Stiljan—superfluously in the circumstances. 'They have heard of the shooting on the road and they are very much afraid, and very enraged with us for causing the trouble.'

We found McLean arguing with a group of gesticulating and hostile villagers. As he caught sight of us he shouted:

'For God's sake hurry up and let's get out of here! These people are going to shoot us if we stay any longer.'

Hastily we mounted and rode on our way, the abuse of the peasants following us as far as the outskirts. We tried two more villages in the next

---

[1] Lit.: 'Master of the House!'

hour, but the inhabitants refused to open their doors to us or even to answer our requests for shelter. Finally, about two in the morning, we came to a hamlet with a Greek Orthodox church, where at last we found a friendly reception in the house of the priest. After a few hours' sleep on the floor and a breakfast of warm sweetened milk, maize bread and yoghourt we went on our journey in the dawn.

The sun was sinking below the hills as we rode into Shtyllë. Smiley greeted us with the news that the aircraft which had dropped our stores the previous night had made their runs across the valley instead of down it, with the result that our stores had been scattered all over the hills. He had spent the whole day searching for them, but a great deal had been lost or looted.

'Really Cairo do make some prize bogs,' he snorted. 'All the boots they sent—which I listed as top priority—are size six! They may be some use for the local school children but none for the Partisans. And, believe it or not, all the hand grenades were dropped ready primed, which is bloody dangerous.'

Duffy had returned from Perat, where he had found the bridge too heavily guarded to attempt a demolition. We worked late, drafting signals to Cairo and checking stores; then, utterly exhausted, we crawled to bed, promising ourselves a long lie-in.

At half past seven next morning I was awakened by two most un-welcome sounds: an aeroplane circling low above the house and the explosion of a shell outside. Smiley, already fully dressed, put his head into the dining-room where I was lying on my mattress. He gave me a friendly grin.

'We're being attacked, but never mind.'

I am not normally quick at getting up, but I made an exception that morning, spurred by two more shells which landed considerably closer than the first, blowing in the windows and part of the roof. As I threw on my clothes I reflected savagely that it was exactly a week since my birthday and my first sight of that aeroplane. With the help of their observation post in the monastery and the spotting aircraft overhead the Italians would not take long to reduce the mosque to rubble; the only course for us was to pack up our essential stores and move as quickly as possible to the barracks across the valley; there, under the lee of a steep mountain, we should be fairly safe from shelling. While we were getting ready Smiley mounted the 20-mm. on a rock outside and started firing at the aeroplane; but his gun had no anti-aircraft mounting and he could not bring it to bear on the aircraft as it banked and turned, so that his shells were always bursting below and behind his target.

'Pack it in, David, and let's get weaving!' cried McLean after another salvo had straddled the mosque. 'There's no future in staying on here.'

We moved off in pairs, making use of what cover the ground afforded. We had a few seconds' warning of each salvo, for we could hear the faint thuds as the guns opened fire; we reckoned them to be a battery of 15.5-cm. howitzers placed about five miles away on the road beyond Vithkuq. Reaching the barracks without loss we sent a messenger to Vithkuq to find out from Mehmet whether he expected an attack in force. During the previous month Smiley had prepared a hide-out for our stores among the pine woods in the hills a mile or two north of Shtyllë. The mule lines were alongside the barracks, and so we should be able to move our stores fairly quickly. For the moment there was no hurry.

From the security of the barracks we watched the shells bursting among the houses of Shtyllë and felt ashamed that the unhappy villagers should have to suffer for the hospitality which they had had no choice but to give us; I began to understand the feelings of the peasants who had chased us away from their doors two nights before. Little groups of men, women, and children were streaming out of the village, some struggling up the steep hillsides, others plodding down the track that led past the barracks to the west, all carrying pathetic little bundles of food and clothing. If I had been entranced before I came to Albania by the romance and glamour of guerrilla warfare, this was a sobering reminder of its squalor and injustice.

A small group left the track and came towards us, bearing the frail figure of an old man which they laid under the tree beside us. One of his legs was shattered at the knee. We gave him a morphia tablet and bandaged the ragged, bone-splintered pulp of his leg, which in our ignorance was all we could do; but he seemed to feel no pain and smiled and chattered away happily until he gradually lost consciousness. We made him as comfortable as we could in the shade of the tree, but he died in the afternoon. The next casualty was a boy of fifteen with shell splinters in his stomach. We put him beside the old man, where he lay groaning and crying for water; Smiley told us not to give him any, but when we saw that there was no hope of saving him we gave him a drink. He died in a few minutes.

At the height of the shelling an old man in military uniform came riding slowly down the track from the west accompanied by a girl on foot; when he saw us he hesitated, then turned his horse towards us. At that moment a shell landed about five yards from him, covering him and the girl in a cloud of smoke and dust. Quite unperturbed they came on, the old man smiling happily, the girl and the horse seemingly indifferent to their narrow escape. When he was a few paces from us the old man dismounted, threw his reins to the girl and came rigidly to attention in a smart salute. McLean explained to me that he was Colonel Osman Gazepi, a rich Bey from Leskovik and a strong supporter of the L.N.C.

'He's quite dotty,' added McLean, 'and has no influence in the area, but he's a nice old thing. The girl's his daughter; she's barmy too.'

The girl, who was about twenty-five, was fair-haired, short and broad. She wore a green forage cap embroidered with the red star, a short jacket, a brown kilted skirt, and woollen stockings below the knee. She carried a rifle and bandolier.

The object of their visit was to tell us that the Colonel had decided to place the produce of his Leskovik farm and estate at our disposal. It seemed unlikely to benefit us much, because the farm was burnt and the estate deserted; but we thanked him warmly, and watched him ride away still smiling happily.

Soon after midday the bombardment ceased, the aeroplane flew off towards Korçë and we supposed that the Italians had knocked off for lunch. There were still some things we wished to salvage from the mosque, and so McLean and I set off along the path to the village, forgetting that we could be seen from the monastery. We found the mosque damaged but not destroyed, the rooms full of broken glass and fallen plaster; the stores we wanted were intact. We had hardly started to collect them when we heard the ominous thuds from beyond Vithkuq. We had just time to throw ourselves to the floor before the salvo arrived. Two of the shells went wide; the other two landed on either side of the house, a yard or two away. Dazed by the explosions and covered in debris and plaster we scrambled to our feet and ran from the mosque into the fields below. Deciding to leave further salvage operations until after dark we made our way cautiously back to the barracks for lunch.

The bombardment continued intermittently throughout the afternoon. In the evening the biplane returned in company with a light bomber. For about an hour they bombed and strafed the villages on the other side of the mountains to the north-west; although they circled our valley between their bombing runs, often flying directly over the barracks, they left us alone; this was just as well, because in one of our rooms we had nearly a hundred canisters of explosives, besides ammunition, mortar bombs and hand grenades. Undeterred by this frightening prospect Sergeants Jones and Jenkins mounted a Bren gun outside and loosed off a stream of tracer at them every time they approached.

At nightfall a message arrived from Mehmet telling us that an Italian force of about two battalions, supported by artillery and heavy-mortars, was attacking Vithkuq; the Partisans were engaging them and expected to hold the town. McLean told me to attach myself to Mehmet next morning and bring back a report on the battle at the end of the day.

The morning was bright, with promise of great heat. As guide and interpreter I took Stefan, the fierce-looking Albanian who had rescued me after my drop. There was no splendour about him now; his moustaches seemed to droop lower with every step we took towards the sound of battle. When I struck the cart-track leading to Vithkuq I realized that the fighting was much nearer than we had supposed. From a hill beyond the gorge on my left came the sound of heavy machine-gun fire; I decided to see what was happening there, and started to scramble down the steep slope towards the stream. Stray shells were bursting on both sides of the ravine as we crossed. Stefan's melancholy deepened; from time to time he stopped to glance longingly back the way we had come.

'*Faut nous éloigner d'ici, monsieur le Capitaine!*' he whispered. '*C'est tres dangereux.*'

Spurred by my own anxiety I bullied him with threats and taunts into following me. Near the top of the slope we came upon a group of Partisans, who told us they were part of Tahir Kadaradja's battalion; we should find Tahir and the rest of the battalion somewhere on the top.

McLean had nicknamed Tahir 'T for Pig', which was a fair comment on his looks. I found him nervous and unhappy, but he greeted me civilly enough. His battalion, he explained, was holding the left flank of the Partisan defence; the centre and right rested on the hills beyond the ravine I had just crossed. The Brigade had engaged the Italians outside Vithkuq last night, but had withdrawn to this line of hills before daylight. He added that his battalion had just beaten off an attack against their position—that must have been the firing I had heard from the road—but he was not sanguine about his chances of holding on for long—'For you see, *monsieur le Capitaine*, there are many of the enemy, and they are powerful in artillery and mortars.'

I pointed out to Tahir that he held a very strong position with plenty of natural cover and a superb field of fire; but he was doubtful whether his troops would stand up to very much shelling. My immediate object now was to find Mehmet; Tahir had no idea where he was to be found, but supposed he must be with one of the battalions on the other side of the valley. He seemed anxious to be rid of me and sent a runner with us to help us find our way.

There was a lull in the fighting as we crossed the ravine and climbed the hills above the road. By steep and devious paths we came, after two hours, to the battalion headquarters of Xhelal Staravecka, who was holding the left centre of the Brigade. Xhelal was manifestly and unashamedly frightened; as a deserter he could expect no mercy from the Italians. He did not know where Mehmet was, nor could he spare a man to help me find him. Fortunately Mehmet chose that moment to pay us a visit. He seemed worried and preoccupied, but readily answered my questions about the progress of the battle. He claimed to have inflicted heavy casualties on the Italians the previous evening, in what he called 'a highly successful mortar action'. He had abandoned Vithkuq under cover of darkness for fear of being surrounded and trapped in the town. He had launched a counter-attack early in the morning with two battalions, to cut off the enemy in a pincer movement.

'But,' he concluded sorrowfully, 'I was obliged to call off the attack when one of the battalions ran into very heavy enemy fire and was forced to withdraw with the loss of'—he hesitated—'of two killed and three wounded.'

Suddenly the fighting flared up again, spreading all along the line of hills. Shells crashed into the mountain side all round us or burst overhead in the branches in a whirr of flying splinters; two biplanes swooped to rake us from tree-top height, their bullets spattering the pine trunks and ricocheting viciously among the rocks. Throughout the afternoon the Italians shelled the ridge, while the aircraft circled overhead machine-gunning the hill tops and upper slopes. Under cover of this barrage their infantry began slowly but steadily to advance. Although the bombardment was uncomfortable enough it would not have sufficed to break a determined opposition. In addition to the guns which had shelled us at Shtyllë the Italians were using one battery of light mountain artillery for the whole operation—not a very heavy concentration against such formidable natural obstacles defended by so strong a force. Moreover, the hills were thickly wooded and even our forward positions were well concealed by scrub and undergrowth. While, therefore, the artillery and even the aircraft were to a large extent firing blind, the Italian infantry had to advance across open country which was swept, or should have been swept, by Partisan fire.

But although Mehmet himself showed an example of coolness and courage his troops and their officers failed to respond; they were utterly demoralized by the shelling and by the continuous strafing from the air. Xhelal in particular cut a ludicrous figure of impotence and fear; he stamped, gesticulated and shouted, but I could not persuade him to accompany me to his own forward positions, so that I began to wonder if he even knew where they were. Stefan kept up his miserable refrain of *'faut nous éloigner d'ici,'* until I swore to ask McLean to dismiss him unless he shut up.

By evening it was clear that the Partisans were going to fall back. The Italians were pressing close and had brought their 81-mm. mortars into action—weapons far more terrifying and deadly than the artillery. I returned with the bad news to McLean.

Back at the barracks I found that McLean had had a far more alarming experience than any of mine: together with Frederick Nosi he had gone to reconnoitre Vithkuq, and had arrived there just at the time when the Italians were setting fire to the town. The two of them had blundered into a party of the enemy in one of the streets; they had almost been cut off but had managed to get away under fire. McLean told me that Nosi had shown great resource and courage on this occasion.

There was little doubt that the Italians would reach Shtyllë some time the following morning. McLean therefore ordered the mules to be loaded with all the stores they could carry and told Smiley and me to take them up into the woods after dark, where we were to spend the night guarding them; Duffy and Jenkins would leave the barracks before dawn to blow the road between Vithkuq and Shtyllë, where it had been prepared for demolition; McLean himself would go tonight to see Mehmet. We would meet again at the barracks at eight o'clock next morning unless the Italians were already there, in which case our rendezvous would be the village of Panarit, five miles south-west of Shtyllë, on the other side of the mountains.

We had to leave behind nearly sixty canisters of explosives; under Smiley's direction these were cunningly concealed among some bushes two hundred yards from the barracks, and skilfully covered with green camouflage parachutes. Smiley was able to recover them four days later.

After a hurried meal Smiley and I moved off with Sergeant Gregson Allcott, Corporal Roberts, Stiljan, Stefan, a few camp-followers, about thirty mules and half that number of Vlach drivers. It took us two hours to find our way in the darkness, stumbling up a narrow track into the hills and feeling our way through the thick gloom of the woods. At last we had the mules unsaddled and the canisters stowed ready for immediate reloading. Spreading my sleeping bag on the most level patch of ground I could find on the hillside, I tried to snatch a little sleep.

Soon after seven Smiley and I started back for Shtyllë, leaving Gregson Allcott and Roberts to guard our stores. The woods smelt delicious in the early morning air, but we had little heart to enjoy scent or scenery. Shells were already falling among the trees below—probably 'overs', for there was no target in the neighbourhood to interest the Italian gunners; but the aeroplane was circling overhead, and so we must move with care. From the direction of Shtyllë came the crash of shells and the crump of heavy mortars.

We passed safely through the woods where the shells were falling, and took a path that led us out onto the dropping ground. Here we were under the fire of the mountain guns, which must by now be shooting from the hills where I had been the day before; I felt uncomfortably exposed, walking across the open grassland towards the col where I had met McLean on my first night in Albania. As we crossed the col and came down into the valley of Shtyllë we saw that the barracks were still intact; there was no sign of life in them. The Partisans seemed to have faded away, but evidently the Italians were taking no chances; shells and mortar bombs were falling thick in the valley and around the barracks, some of them bursting uncomfortably close to us as we hurried forward. I was frankly scared and several times threw myself on my face when I heard a shell coming our way; Smiley, on the other hand, showed an irritating indifference and walked on, his head held high, as though he were being pelted by urchins with snowballs while mounting guard.

After a quick look round the store-rooms we went outside to watch for McLean. I crouched in a ditch, peering over the top, but Smiley sauntered nonchalantly up and down, his hands in his pockets, among the puffs of smoke and dust and erupting earth. After half an hour of waiting, expecting at any time to find the Italians on top of us, we saw his tall figure striding blithely down the hill. As we had guessed, the Partisans were in full retreat. We must move to Panarit.

'We ought to have an officer with the mules,' concluded McLean. 'Peter, will you go back there now and wait for us until we join you, which I hope will be in a couple of hours. If we don't turn up, or if things get too hot for you, take the stuff on to Panarit. David and I will hang around here for a bit to see what happens.'

I spent an anxious morning waiting for them. A few shells dropped around us, none of them within two hundred yards but near enough to alarm the muleteers and to terrify Stefan and Stiljan, who sat one on each side of me begging me to move away from such a dangerous place. At the end of three hours I gave orders to load the mules and be ready to move at a moment's notice; I was worried that the Italians might cut us off or surprise us, for their patrols were reported to be very near. I had posted Albanian guards but had little confidence that they would give us warning. Another half-hour passed without a sign of McLean or Smiley; I was wondering how much longer I could risk waiting and endangering our stores, when my mind was made up for me: Stiljan came to me with a message from the leader of the Vlachs saying that unless I agreed to leave now they would desert us. I wondered if Stiljan had anything to do with the ultimatum, for he knew that I could not afford to let the Vlachs go; then I reflected that if we were caught by the Italians the English might be made prisoners, but the Vlachs and Albanians would almost certainly be shot. I gave the order to leave.

We climbed through the woods for an hour; then the track led onto a bare and rocky ridge with a superb view to north and east over wild, craggy mountain tops and thick, dark forest. We should now be safe from pursuit and so I ordered a halt, for the ascent had been arduous. We were preparing to go on when we were joined by Duffy and Jenkins, both of them wearing the exhausted but happy look of men who have survived great peril. They had indeed: they had reached their objective that morning, quite unaware that the Italians were in occupation of the heights overlooking the road on both sides. The Italians let them get well under way with their preparations before opening up on them from two directions with machine-guns, light machine-guns, rifles, and even mortars. It is a mystery how they managed to reach cover unwounded; but Jenkins had a bullet through the paybook which he kept in his breast pocket.

We reached Panarit the following afternoon, where we found McLean and Smiley, very despondent over the failure of the Brigade to put up a fight after all the training and armament it had received. I tried to comfort them by pointing out that a month's training was hardly enough to turn a rabble of peasants and artisans into disciplined soldiers who could be expected to stand up to shelling; that by trying to fight 'brigade actions' the Partisans were only sacrificing their natural advantages of mobility and knowledge of the country, in order to meet the enemy on his own ground where his superior training and armament were bound to tell; finally that they would do better for the moment to confine themselves to small, carefully planned 'bullying' actions, dispersing whenever the enemy concentrated against them.

There was, of course, one point that was not yet apparent to me: Enver Hoxha and Mehmet Shehu were not building up their military formations in order to fight Germans or Italians, but in order to gain control of Albania for themselves by force; they were not going to risk serious losses in operations which to them were only of secondary importance.

I suppose it was Stefan who had the last word on those three days of battle. As we jolted down the valley that led to Panarit his spirits rose to their normal exuberance.

'*Monsieur le Capitaine*,' he affirmed, nodding his head in wise appreciation, 'now we know that the Italians are no use. But for their artillery they would never have taken Shtyllë. Their soldiers have no stomach for fighting.'

VII

CLOAK WITHOUT DAGGER

In spite of the set-back of the last week we could at least be thankful that we had escaped with our lives and most of our stores. Much of our personal property had been looted, but if the looters were the inhabitants of Shtyllë we were in no position to blame them; they had suffered far worse than we. Those of them who had taken to the hills returned to find their houses in ashes; those who stayed behind were shot by the Italians.

This dilemma was our constant companion in our efforts to promote resistance: if we were to do our job properly we were bound to put innocent people in jeopardy; they had to stay and face reprisals while we found safety in flight. In the service of our country we simply had to harden our hearts. Whether the leaders of the L.N.C. were as squeamish I do not know; in any case our qualms were no protection to the victims.

Our usefulness in this area was over. Both the L.N.C. Central Council and the First Partisan Brigade had moved north; the Balli Kombëtar were becoming increasingly hostile. It was time for us to split up. On 31st August Smiley, with Sergeants Bell and Jenkins, set out north-east for the Mokra area, near Lake Ohrid, to establish a new headquarters for 'Consensus'; Duffy and my paramilitary expert, Gregson Allcott, left for a reconnaissance in the south; McLean decided to reconnoitre the Greek frontier east of Korçë before rejoining Smiley. Cairo had not yet replied to my request to go to Kossovo; in the meantime McLean suggested that I should move north-west into the Berat area to take on the duties of political liaison officer with the L.N.C. Central Council, at the same time keeping in touch with Abas Ermenje, the Balli Kombëtar leader in that region.

On 6th September I set out with Corporal Roberts, Stiljan, an Albanian servant, three Vlachs, and ten mules; I was riding a small but sturdy horse which I had bought in Panarit. The Vlachs proved excellent servants, efficient, tireless, and cheerful; Dimitri, their leader, a tall gaunt figure with a sardonic cast of expression who wore a splendid shepherd's cloak of grey wool, was a genius at loading his animals so that each could carry the maximum load with the least discomfort. This was important because the mules were heavily laden with stores, including a wireless set, clothing, blankets for the approaching winter, food and two canisters of gold. The wireless set presented the greatest problem in loading; it was about the size of an ordinary suitcase and ran off batteries which had to be charged regularly from a heavy and awkward petrol generator. The set, batteries and engine required two mules to transport them. Roberts and I each wore a canvas money-belt under our battledress, filled with gold. McLean gave me a word of warning.

'Take care you don't let any of the locals see you carrying that money; they're quite likely to bump you off to get it.'

'I can imagine they'd try and steal it, but surely they wouldn't go so far as murder?'

'Wouldn't they? Two months ago David gave two hundred sovereigns to a Partisan commissar, Ramiz Aranitas, to organize a *çeta* in this area. David's bodyguard—a man called Ali—saw him do it; he followed Ramiz for a mile, then shot him in the back, pinched the sovereigns and disappeared. My God! One of our Italian camp-followers at Shtyllë was shot in the back by a Partisan just for a pair of boots David had given him. You must never walk around this country on your own. That's why, after you've stayed in a house, your host always sends you on your way with an escort.'

I was to spend the night at the village of Leshnjë, some fifteen miles north-east of Panarit, in the house of Kahraman Ylli, a Partisan commissar; he had been warned of our coming, and sent a small party of his followers to guide us all the way. We climbed steadily for the first half of our journey, passing beneath the bare crags of the Ostravicë range whose tallest peaks, rising above seven thousand feet, glittered majestic and bright in the strong, hard sunlight.

At Leshnjë we were greeted by Kahraman Ylli's father. He was a man of fine physique, over six foot tall, with a fierce white moustache; but his features were predatory, his eyes narrow and shifty. He and his two brothers were rich landowners, whose attachment to the Partisan cause sprang partly from Kahraman's influence, partly from the hope of saving their property from confiscation by the L.N.C. While dinner was being prepared we were led into the guest-room and offered raki and *mezë*—small pieces of goat cheese, slices of hard-boiled egg, onions, and meat balls. Our personal kit was brought in and placed beside us, for this was the room where we should spend the night.

In the morning, when the mules were being loaded for an early start, I noticed that my sleeping bag was missing. I had seen it in the guest-room when I went to bed, but I had not slept in it; no one but our host and our three selves had been in the room since supper. Our host affected deep distress that the property of any guest should have disappeared in his house. I could not conceal my dismay at losing, on the threshold of a winter in the mountains, a sleeping bag at once warm and so light and compact that it could easily be carried in a small haversack. Much later, when I told McLean, he laughed.

'Not one of us has stayed in that house without losing something of value!'

No Colours or Crest

We rode northwards until midday over rough and broken tracks under the enormous grim bulk of the Zaloshnje mountains; then we climbed slowly over a spur of the Tomorri range by a steep path that brought us down to a village nestling in the shadow of Mount Tomorri itself, the highest mountain of southern Albania. Tomorri was an ancient seat of pagan worship before the days when the gods of the Greeks ruled the land; in classical times pilgrims came there to consult an oracle as powerful as the oracle of Dodonian Zeus. Now a Bektashi monastery stood on the slopes. The Bektashi sect, which was influential in Albania, seems to have originated during Turkish times among the Janissaries and contains elements of different religions absorbed into the Islamic faith. In particular, its adherents are not forbidden the use of strong drink.

The area between Tomorri and Berat is called Skapari, a name whose harsh syllables suit well the savage stony country with its bleak mountains and narrow, precipitous valleys. Thick cloud laid the upper slopes of Mount Tomorri and a chill rain blew in our faces as we picked our way down the mountain towards the house of Muharrem Kaplanë, a powerful Bey who under Abas Ermenje commanded the Ballist *çetas* in this area. I had already sent word to him, asking for a meeting. On the borders of his domain an escort of retainers waited to take me to his house.

A solid stone building with, thick walls loopholed for defence, the home of the Kaplanë family stood on a mountainside overlooking a deep valley rich in grain fields and olive groves. We were shown into a cheerful guest-room with white walls and high windows looking onto a courtyard. The floor was spread with thick, richly coloured rugs; round the walls ran a broad divan strewn with silk cushions. In accordance with custom our arms were taken from us when we entered the house. This gesture signified that as long as we were under his roof our host was responsible with his life for our safety; if anyone were to kill us our host must start *Hakmarjë*—a blood feud—with him and would be dishonoured in the eyes of all his neighbours until he avenged our death with that of the murderer.

The *Hakmarjë* existed throughout Albania, among both Tosks and Ghegs. Whenever a man was murdered his family were obliged to start a blood feud, not only with the murderer but with all the murderer's family, one of whom must be killed to wipe out the stain; a man who left a blood feud unavenged was subject to perpetual dishonour and insult. It was not unusual for as many as twenty members of one family to be killed in the same vendetta in the course of two or three generations.[1] More than once an Albanian has said to me:

'I cannot go with you to that house; I have enemies.'

---

[1] Women and children were generally excluded from the *Hakmarjë*.

While a messenger ran down to the valley to tell our host of our arrival Roberts, Stiljan and I sat in the guest-room with the men of the house, sipping Turkish coffee. This was the time, Stiljan explained, when I must decide whether or not I meant to stay the night; if so, I should start to remove my boots. I had intended to press on after my talk with Kaplanë, for I was in a hurry to catch up with Enver Hoxha; but night was closing in and I had no wish to lose my way in that wild country, which would be only too easy in the dark, even with a guide. I began to undo my field boots, whereupon one of our companions took them off for me while another went to give orders to prepare a meal. We were in for a long wait, Stiljan told me, for they would probably kill and roast a sheep in our honour; meanwhile we must sit and make conversation, however tired we felt, until the food was served.

Muharrem Kaplanë was a well-built man in early middle age, with a grave and courteous manner and a quiet air of confidence and authority. He welcomed us cordially, serving us with raki from his own estate and a rich assortment of *mezë*.

I had asked to see him for two reasons: to hear his views on the situation in Skapari, where it was rumoured that the L.N.C. and the Balli Kombëtar were on the verge of civil war; and to ask him to arrange a meeting with Abas Ermenje, who was reputed to be the ablest and most vigorous of the Ballist leaders. However, it turned out that Abas Ermenje had left the district to attend a conference that would keep him away for a week.

I learned from Kaplanë that rumour had not exaggerated the tension in Skapari; he expected to be fighting against the L.N.C. within two or three days. The trouble had become acute after the failure of Abas Ermenje's attack on the Italian garrison at Berat a few weeks previously; according to Kaplanë the L.N.C. had promised their support but had treacherously withdrawn it in the middle of the battle, leaving the Balli out on a limb. At my insistence he promised to use his authority to restrain his men; but he added ominously that a great deal would depend on the Partisans.[1]

My next meeting was with Mestan Ujaniku, the L.N.C. area commander, who entertained me for lunch the following day in the mountain village of Nishovë. He was a picturesque old man with a huge white moustache and a breast covered with decorations of various countries, which he had apparently awarded to himself, for he had been a brigand until he joined the L.N.C. He welcomed me with a kiss on both cheeks, a painful experience because he had not shaved for some days. His account of the present situation confirmed Kaplanë's, although he placed the blame for it on the Balli, who, he said, had attacked prematurely and without giving warning to

---

[1] Kaplanë was captured by the Partisans at the end of the war and, after months of cruel imprisonment, executed.

the L.N.C. He too promised to urge moderation on his forces, but he seemed to have little confidence in the result.

Civil war would surely have broken out already but for the presence in the area of one Isa Toska, a notorious Albanian quisling, whom Balli and L.N.C. were combining to destroy. This man was a brigand who with Italian help had equipped a strong band of mercenaries and turned his own house into a fortress. Having for a long time terrorized the countryside with murder, robbery, and rape he had incurred the extreme hatred of all the people of Skapari. The Italians, having used him to subdue their enemies, as they used others of his type, now abandoned him to the fury of his countrymen; he was surrounded in his house and, after a few days' fighting, taken prisoner. According to one of Mestan's men who was present, he was blinded and his ears and nose cut off before being shot. This was one of the few occasions when I heard of Albanians using torture, until later on the Communists employed it to punish or extract information from 'traitors'.

Mestan now told me that Enver Hoxha and the Central Council had moved to the Peza area, five or six days' journey to the north-west. Because my first task was to make contact with them I abandoned my plans to see Abas Ermenje and contented myself with sending him a letter. I waved a friendly good-bye to Mestan as we rode out of Nishovë escorted by his Partisans; with his cheerful, easy-going manner, flamboyant uniform and obvious attachment to the old Albanian way of life he seemed an incongruous figure to be holding such a responsible position in an organization controlled by ruthless fanatics who proclaimed their contempt for all tradition. Evidently he thought so too, for when the policy of the L.N.C. hardened in favour of the extreme Left he joined Abas Kupi.

On the evening of 10th September we were approaching the village of Roshnik, six miles east of Berat, when we met a merry group of Partisans. They gave us the news of the surrender of Italy. We embraced each other while raki circulated freely; then it occurred to me that I ought to take some immediate and positive action. Roberts had a wireless 'sked' with Cairo at nine-thirty the following morning; I decided to spend the night in Roshnik, hoping to receive instructions from Cairo. Meanwhile I sent a courier into Berat to find out the situation and if possible make contact with the Italian commander; I also summoned the chief of the local Partisan get çeta to meet me.

No instructions came for me over the wireless; moreover my batteries ran out and the charging engine developed a technical fault which Roberts assured me rendered it useless. I was therefore cut off from Cairo until I could find Seymour, who I believed was still in the Peza area at a place called Grecë. When eventually I joined Seymour a week later, I received a message from Cairo ordering me to 'contact the Italian commanders in Berat and persuade them to implement the terms of the Armistice'. By then, of course, it was much too late.

My courier returned early in the morning. It appeared that the Partisans had entered Berat unopposed on 9th September and had invited the Italians to give them arms and to join their ranks. While they were discussing the details a German column swept into the town, causing the Partisans to leave in haste. Now Berat was an important town with a large Italian garrison, and the Germans were not yet established there in strength. During the next two days, therefore, I tried to persuade the Partisans to guide me into the town and put me in touch with their supporters; I hoped to see the Italian commander myself. For two days they vacillated, by which time the Germans were firmly in control. On 13th September we continued our journey north.

During the next three days our route lay through Ballist villages with strange and comic names—Qereshnik, Deshiran, and Belsh. Our Partisan escort proved an embarrassment, for the villagers, though friendly enough to ourselves and willing to provide us with food and guides, would not let us remain in the neighbourhood while we were with Partisans; in consequence we had to keep on the move, and went almost without sleep for three nights. After leaving Qereshnik we came down from the mountains into flat, open country where the going was much easier. Just before dusk we passed through the Kuçovë oilfields, the centre of Albanian oil production on which the Italians had based such hopes before the war; they had been disappointed, and now we rode through a forest of abandoned derricks in a deserted, smelly plain.

We changed guides at every village, but each relay seemed more useless than the last. Even when we lent them mules they held us up by loitering and demanding frequent halts to smoke and rest; at every fork in the path they stopped to argue with each other, chattering like parakeets, and they often lost the way. When we came to the bank of the Devoll river near Deshiran they delayed us for half an hour while they argued who should venture in to test the depth and swiftness of the stream. At last I lost patience and put my own horse into it, leading the string of mules across; but when we reached the other side three of the guides still remained behind, waving their arms and twittering shrilly until one of the Vlachs went back for them with a spare mule.

After the bare mountains the country beyond Deshiran seemed soft and fertile, with newly harvested fields of maize on every side; but the few farms and dwellings we passed were miserable hovels of mud and thatch, where wretched undernourished families lived sunk in apathy, poverty and filth.

At Belsh we took on fresh guides who would see us across the Shkumbi and the main road from Elbasan to Durazzo. This was the only hazardous part of our journey, for the river was broad and deep, the road in constant use and probably guarded; with our long train of mules it would be difficult to escape attention. We planned to make our crossing about midnight, when we could hope that the traffic would have ceased and the guards would be asleep; and we chose a point some two miles east of the town of Peqin, where there were no villages whose dogs might betray our presence.

A bright moon hung in the sky as we approached the bank, shining cold and white and beautiful on the broad stretches of sand beside the river and illuminating faintly the pencil of road beyond. The calm, scented night, the moon and the quiet river carried memories of Andalusia and the *Romancero Gitano*; but the scene that would have stirred Garcia Lorca brought only anxiety to me. If anyone were watching on the road he could hardly fail to see us against the gleaming sand.

I sent across a guide with two Partisan scouts to keep a look-out for us on the other side; then, dividing the mules into three groups, each with a Vlach, I ordered them to follow me at five minute intervals. When all were across I went forward on foot with the guide to reconnoitre the road. On either hand it ran straight and deserted for as far as I could see. I decided to take the whole party across at once, and sent back the guide to bring them on. After a few anxious moments while the mules clattered across the tarmac road we found ourselves on a track climbing gently through low, scrub-covered hills. We continued for an hour, to put a safe distance between ourselves and the road; then I ordered the mules to be unloaded in a small wood and settled down to sleep for the three remaining hours of darkness.

At ten o'clock next morning, 16th September, we rode into Seymour's camp. This consisted of two or three tents pitched in a pine wood among the hills. We were greeted by Bombardier Hill and Sergeant Smith, Seymour's wireless operator and paramilitary specialist. Seymour, they told us, was at the village of Arbonë, some five or six miles south-west of Tirana and six hours' journey from where we were at Grecë, he was engaged in negotiations with General Dalmazzo, G.O.C. Ninth Army and Italian Commander-in-chief in Albania. There were signals awaiting me from Cairo, and others which I must give Roberts to send now that he could re-charge his batteries; I decided to spend the night at Grecë and join Seymour next day.

It was just as well that I made this decision, for a crisis was immediately thrust upon me. Dimitri, the leader of the Vlachs, announced that he and his men could stay with us no longer; with the approach of winter they must get back to their families, who would starve without them. Worse still, the mules belonged to the Vlachs, for the Italian attack on Shtyllë had prevented my buying any for myself and none had been obtainable in Panarit. Not all my entreaties, reinforced by lavish offers of gold, would persuade the Vlachs to stay; courteously, even regretfully, Dimitri pointed out that his original contract with McLean had expired at the beginning of the month, and although they had carried on in order to see us through our journey they could not remain longer; nor dared they sell us their mules, which were their livelihood and which they could not replace at this time of year. I had no choice but to let them go. Their departure left me with one horse and one mule—insufficient to transport even my wireless set; Seymour was very short of mules and there were none to be bought in the district. I could only hope that we should not have to move in a hurry.

Early in the morning a courier arrived from Seymour with messages for Cairo; he was returning immediately and so I asked him to conduct me to Arbonë. I decided to take Stiljan, leaving Roberts to help Smith and Hill, who had more work than they could manage, with the cipher and wireless duties. We travelled for five hours over drab, low hills formed of a kind of black sandstone and covered with stunted mountain oak; we passed no villages or houses, but only an occasional charred ruin. The poor vegetation is attributed to centuries of grazing by goats; the depopulation was caused by an Italian punitive expedition the previous year against Myslim Peza, when nearly every house and village in these hills was burnt.

At noon I reached Arbonë, where I was warmly greeted by Seymour in the house which he shared with Myslim Peza and Colonel Barbi Cinti, who until the surrender had been commandant of the Italian aerodrome at Shijak, near Tiranë. Seymour looked tired and very ill; his moustache flared as bravely as ever but his face was white and sunken, his eyes deeply shadowed. He suggested that I stay with him because there was plenty of work for me in Arbonë. Enver Hoxha and the Central Council were living in a farm-house a few miles back in the hills, but they visited Arbonë daily.

Arbonë was a small village on the southern edge of an open plain bounded on the north by a low wooded ridge, which separated it from Tirana, and on the south by the Peza hills; the plain was bisected by the river Arzen which flowed from east to west between steep banks. From the river's edge to the Peza hills the plain was dotted with Partisans bivouacking with no attempt at shelter or camouflage. Their numbers grew every day with the arrival of fresh Italian deserters from units of the Ninth Army. Colonel Barbi Cinti was working conscientiously to weld the Italians into a composite fighting force, which was to be commanded by General Azzi from the 'Firenze' Division. Azzi proved an unfortunate choice. He explained to Seymour and me that he had never been the same since he had experienced the British bombardment at Alamein; this was understandable but scarcely excused his subsequent conduct: a few months after his appointment to command the Italian Partisans in Albania he absconded to the mountains, accompanied by his Staff, with a considerable sum of money given him by the Allies to feed and equip his men.

For about a fortnight after the surrender of Italy there was one belief held in common by almost everybody in Albania, whether German or Italian, British or Albanian, L.N.C. or Balli Kombëtar: that an Allied invasion of the Balkans was imminent. That this was not so naïve a hope at the time as it seems in retrospect is clear from the pages of Chester Wilmot's *Struggle for Europe*. I have no doubt that had there been an invasion at that time it would have been followed by a general rising in Albania, with the co-operation of most of the Italian army of occupation. We were therefore surprised that our headquarters in Cairo, usually so prodigal of advice and admonishment, failed to give us any directive at this critical moment. Seeing nothing of the larger picture we abused our office savagely for their neglect.

As soon as he heard the news of the surrender, on 9th September, Seymour hurried to Arbonë, where he sent a message to General Dalmazzo in Tiranë requesting his co-operation and asking for a meeting; unfortunately the message was not delivered until the next day, when the Germans were already in occupation of the capital. However, Dalmazzo sent a staff car to Arbonë, which took Seymour, wearing an Italian army greatcoat over his uniform, through the German control posts to Army Headquarters, where he had a long discussion with Dalmazzo's Chief of Intelligence. At the same time, in an adjoining room, Dalmazzo himself was in conference with senior German officers, arranging his own evacuation under German protection to Belgrade; not until Dalmazzo had left Albania did Seymour learn the truth.

This deplorable example was followed by other senior officers of the Ninth Army, including at least two Divisional Commanders; abandoning their men they thought only of saving themselves and their families. The junior officers and rank-and-file, deprived of the leadership they had a right to expect, became hopelessly demoralized. Overcome with terror large numbers allowed themselves to be disarmed and led into captivity by a handful of Germans; others dispersed to farms and houses in the hills, where they worked for the owners in return for their keep; the more virile among them joined the Partisans, who, it must be said, treated them well; a few attached themselves to British missions as cooks, batmen, or grooms, rendering valuable service and often showing great loyalty and courage in the face of severe hardship and danger.

The speed of the German reaction to the surrender surprised every-one in Albania. Within forty-eight hours German troops had occupied every key point in the country; although few they were enough to dominate the people, disarm the Italians and contain the Partisans. In the face of German resolution and Allied inactivity most Albanians outside the L.N.C. followed the old precept, 'When rape is inevitable relax and enjoy it', and adjusted themselves to a German instead of an Italian occupation. Their attitude was reasonable in the circumstances.

Without Allied help they could not hope to expel the Germans, who would in any case be obliged to leave the country if the war continued its present course against them. Better, surely, to bear with patience a temporary inconvenience rather than try to end it prematurely at the risk of property, security and life. Moreover, to many patriotic Albanians it was by no means clear that an Allied victory was in the best interests of their country; they feared—perhaps I should say fore-saw—that it would result not only in the loss of Kossovo but also in their own subjection to Communist rule.

The Germans played cleverly upon these feelings. Firstly they made very few demands on the civilian population, to whom they behaved with courtesy and consideration, and secondly they made much political capital out of the Kossovo question. It is a measure of their success that when they set up a puppet government in Tirana they were able to induce Albanians of high principles and distinction to serve in it. As time went on it became more and more obvious that we could offer the Albanians little inducement to take up arms compared with the advantages they could enjoy by remaining passive. I must confess that we British Liaison Officers were slow to understand their point of view; as a nation we have always tended to assume that those who do not whole-heartedly support us in our wars have some sinister motive for not wishing to see the world a better place. This attitude made us particularly unsympathetic towards the Balli Kombëtar, although the latter was a thoroughly patriotic organization. The Balli refrained from collaboration with the Germans against us; indeed, they gave us much covert help; but they did sit on the fence, hoping to establish themselves so firmly in the administration of the country that the victorious Allies would naturally call upon them to form a government. Indeed, they were naïvely convinced that the British and Americans would be glad to entrust the government to them, in preference to the Communist alternative of the L.N.C. The leaders of the L.N.C. had good reasons for continuing the struggle; but their interests, of course, were not Albania's.

During those days at Arbonë large numbers of German aircraft flew directly over us, taking off from or landing at Tiranë airfield. The plain in front of our house was alive with troops—several thousands of them—who must have been clearly visible from the air and whose camp fires at night could be seen for miles around. Although they were within easy range of German artillery and presented a perfect target for air attack they made no attempt to dig so much as a slit trench for their protection, despite repeated warnings to Myslim Peza and their other commanders from Seymour and myself; nor could we persuade the *Shtabit* to disperse them amid the cover of the neighbouring hills.

I was astonished that we were never awakened in the morning by anything more unpleasant than the singing of the Partisans. After a few days, however, Myslim Peza became alarmed for our personal safety and insisted on moving us to a farmhouse which overlooked the plain from the shelter of the Peza hills—one of the few that had survived the Italian holocaust of the previous year.

Myslim himself had a highly developed sense of personal security, acquired during fourteen years as an outlaw. He never slept twice in the same place; nor, if he could avoid it, would he spend a night in a house, but would move into the hills each evening with an escort. He had recently been appointed Commander-in-Chief of all L.N.C. forces in the field—excluding, of course, those of Abas Kupi. Of all the leaders of the L.N.C. that I met in Albania, with the possible exception of Mustafa Gjinishi, Myslim was the most charming, the most helpful and the most honest. A man of no intellectual ability or pretensions, he understood little of politics—a weakness which his more cunning colleagues exploited to their advantage; but he was a brilliant guerrilla fighter with outstanding qualities of leadership, loyalty and courage.

In his own country his people revered him with a devotion almost amounting to worship; he was known among them as Baba, or Father, and whenever they mentioned his name they would touch their foreheads in the Moslem sign of respect. Peza, where his word was absolute law, was the only region in Albania in which I ventured on journeys without an escort. His frame was slight and emaciated, his dark marmoset's face drawn and sunken; but his small body held enormous strength and inhuman endurance, his black eyes flashed with excitement, enthusiasm, or anger and his thin, delicate hands were never still.

On both of us he bestowed a warm and generous affection, giving us his utmost help in our military and political problems—a refreshing change from the attitude of his colleagues. Himself an enthusiastic and convivial drinker he was delighted to find in Seymour and myself companions who would share his pleasures. We learned to start our work at seven in the morning in order to be finished by eleven o'clock, when we were invariably interrupted. There would be a knock on the door of the room where we lived and worked, and a small procession would enter: first would come Myslim's wife, carrying a roast chicken, followed by Myslim himself, his A.D.C., and his escort, all carrying bottles of raki and plates of mezë. The session would often last two or three hours, while we sat cross-legged on the floor at a low, round wooden table, discussing whatever problems had cropped up since our last meeting. Myslim's wife, who in defiance of Albanian custom sat through these parties with us, was a small slim woman of about forty, dark and wiry like her husband; she always dressed like a man, carrying an automatic at her hip, and had shared her husband's outlawry since its beginning. A less sympathetic participant in these gatherings was Myslim's Political Commissar, a bitter, cantankerous Communist who considered it his duty to the Party to thwart us whenever he had the chance.

We were particularly grateful to Myslim for his 'elevenses' because for a time they provided us with our only meals. The owners of the farm were supposed to feed us in return for our rent; but since it was the month of

Ramadan, which the family strictly observed, they were much too debilitated to cook us any food. In theory our rent included the exclusive use of a large room where we could work undisturbed, but in Albania it is considered most discourteous to leave guests by themselves; however much we desired privacy the good manners of our hosts forbade it. The Albanian code of hospitality does not allow a host to accept payment from his guests; but the demands we were forced to make upon our hosts and the risks to which our presence exposed them put us under an obligation to pay generously. In practice we overcame the difficulty by asking them to accept the money for the benefit of the children.

The first of my tasks when I had re-established contact with Enver Hoxha was to answer a series of questions from Cairo about the political situation in Tiranë. Cairo seemed to attach particular importance to the subject, and so, when I was unable to get a clear picture from the Central Council, I decided without much enthusiasm that I should have to visit Tiranë myself. Since it was impossible for me to go in uniform I signalled Cairo for permission to put on civilian clothes; the only reply I received was a repeat of the original questionnaire. I was now committed.

After a good deal of argument Enver Hoxha reluctantly agreed, on the intervention of Myslim, to provide me with a guide and prepare a safe house where I could stay in the city. He made one stipulation: because he would be responsible for my safety I must only see people approved by himself or by my hosts in Tiranë. He did nothing to raise my spirits by pointing out how conspicuous I should appear in the town, for not only did I look like a foreigner but I even walked like one; to the vast entertainment of Seymour, Myslim, and Stiljan he insisted on giving me lessons in the 'Albanian Walk'. He was not impressed with my progress. On the eve of my departure he turned up at our farm-house with a certain Mehmet Hoxha, ex-Prefect of Dibra, who was lending me a suit of clothes. This gentleman, of whom I was later to see a great deal, was short, broad, and stout—in fact, of quite a different build from mine.

Shortly before midday on 22nd September I set out with my guide, a young Albanian of nineteen or twenty who spoke a little Italian. Mehmet Hoxha's old grey lounge suit hung loosely round my waist, leaving my wrists and ankles to protrude like the stumps of a scarecrow; on my feet were a pair of patent-leather shoes at least two sizes too small for me; my head—and my ears too—were covered by a soft green felt hat. I had grown a sparse blond moustache which drooped discontentedly at the corners of my lip. Seymour tried to console me as he said good-bye.

'I can promise you one thing, old boy: you may not look much like an Albanian, but at least you won't be mistaken for a British Officer.'

It was a day of blazing sunshine; the plain of Arbonë lay shimmering under the noonday heat. We plodded slowly and in silence across the fields, over the narrow bridge spanning the river, and up into the hills. I was surprised to meet no one on the way, until I remembered that this was the time of day when sensible people rested; perhaps that was why my guide had chosen it. After the first half-hour my patent-leather shoes pinched and galled at every step, so that I had to call frequent halts to take them off. At first I was glad when we reached the hills and began to climb in the shade of the woods; but each time I stumbled on the steep and broken track, crying out with the pain that gripped my feet, I longed for the sun-baked but easy paths of the plain.

Every moment I cursed more savagely the foolhardiness that had sent me on this journey; I reflected that I was involving myself and my friends in a great deal of trouble and some hazard in pursuit of information of uncertain value. I preferred not to dwell on the consequences of capture. As a parachutist and saboteur I knew that my chances of survival would be slender enough if I were taken in uniform; in civilian clothes I faced the prospect of a squalid and painful end accompanied by every circumstance of ignominy and ridicule.

Before leaving the cover of the hills we halted in a small copse on the outskirts of Tiranë to cool down, recover our breath, and brush the dust of the journey from our clothes. I carried no papers, and so we had agreed that if we ran into a German picket or were stopped by a patrol I was to look stupid and say only, '*Shqypëtar. Skadokument.*'[1] We trusted that this simple phrase would allay suspicion, because I could not hope to run away in those shoes of Mehmet Hoxha's.

I could feel my heart pounding as I accompanied my guide into the first streets. I tried to look indifferent to my surroundings and pay no attention to the groups of townspeople who passed; they, I noticed, were paying a great deal of attention to me, scanning me closely and gazing after me with expressions of hilarious astonishment. The only people who paid no attention whatever were the few parties of German soldiers who passed us, marching in step, their heads held high, looking neither to right nor left. My guide, who kept shooting me sombre glances out of the corner of his eye, was getting more and more nervous, obviously sharing my own feelings. Suddenly he brightened; following his gaze I saw a lone carozza standing on a corner, with a tired looking horse and sleepy driver. Painfully but thankfully I climbed in and sank back on the cushions as my guide gave an address to the driver. We rattled through dusty side streets, turned into a broad avenue and after a few hundred yards turned off again into a quiet road flanked by prosperous modern villas with bright tidy gardens. At one of these we halted, and after paying the carozza, rang the bell. In a second the door was opened

---

[1] 'I am Albanian. I have no papers.'

and my guide hustled me into the cool twilight of a large, comfortably furnished room.

A tubby, middle-aged man dressed in a Palm Beach suit rose from an armchair and greeted me warmly in English, introducing himself as the owner of the house; for security reasons I was not allowed to know his name, but I gathered that he was a prosperous businessman who owned some copper mines east of Tiranë, and that he was a member of the Greek Orthodox Church. He told me later that he had joined the L.N.C. for patriotic reasons although he detested Communism; he seemed to be a staunch Anglophile and treated me during my visit with exuberant hospitality. After nearly two months in the hills I wallowed in the luxuries of a comfortable bed and a hot bath, of good food and wine, of thick carpets and soft chairs.

My fellow-guests were two members of the Central Council, Ymer Dyshnica and Njako Spiro, both of whom I had met in Shtyllë; they were close friends, who had worked together in France during the first year of the Italian occupation of their country, editing a newspaper for Albanian exiles. Dyshnica was a young doctor of great ability, intelligence and charm;[1] Spiro, by contrast, was a sour-faced, black billed fanatic who would heap abuse and hysterical invective upon all his countrymen who were not members of the L.N.C. I had disliked him in Shtyllë but was forced to a reluctant sympathy when I learned that he suffered from a chronic and incurable disease of the liver.

During the three days I stayed in this house I was occupied with a succession of visitors. Although Enver Hoxha had stipulated that I should meet only people approved by himself or my host, they did their best between them to show me a representative selection of Tiranë opinion. Most of my visitors were professional or business men; none, apart from Dyshnica and Spiro, was a Communist or fellow-traveller; all spoke English, French, or Italian and so I was able to converse without an interpreter.

Hitherto, it seemed, the new occupation had weighed very lightly on the people of Tiranë, who were therefore disinclined to take any active steps against it. The imposition of a curfew, the establishment of check points on the roads, and the compulsory registration of private cars were the only restrictions; civilians were supposed to carry identity cards, but were seldom required to produce them. In the last few days, however, as a result of a number of attacks on Germans in the countryside, the control had tightened considerably; some houses had been searched and the streets were watched by security police in plain clothes. At the same time the German authorities circulated through their Albanian agents grim stories of the ruthlessness of their reprisals and the grim fate that would overtake any Albanian found 'consorting with the enemy'.

---

[1] It is reported that he has been executed by Enver Hoxha.

No Colours or Crest

One of my objects was to find out what aircraft were using Tiranë airfield. Among my visitors was a young man of an illustrious Albanian family, Liqa Bey Toptani; belonging to no political party he maintained good relations with the L.N.C., even with Njako Spiro. Now he volunteered to take me for a drive in his car along the road past the airfield, where I should be able to see all I wanted. On the afternoon following my arrival he turned up with a companion in a small black Fiat saloon; he asked me to get into the back, adding apologetically that I should attract less attention there.

We drove through side streets and into a broad avenue, past the Dajti Hotel, Tiranë's last word in modern luxury, and the chrome stucco palace of King Zog sprawling in its neglected gardens; after half an hour's drive round the town Toptani brought us out on to the road leading towards the airfield.

'You'll easily be able to see the aeroplanes through the fence,' he explained. 'We can drive past very slowly and then perhaps on our way back—' he broke off with a gasp, putting his foot on the brake.

Leaning over his shoulder I saw through the windscreen a car drawn up at the side of the road about fifty yards ahead, with German soldiers standing around it.

'I am afraid it is a control post,' he muttered and began to put the car into reverse. At this moment the car in front began to move on; one of the soldiers noticed us and signalled us to approach. We had no alternative, for behind was a long stretch of straight, open road. As he put the car into gear Toptani whispered to me:

'Sit back and look as stupid as you can. I will do the talking—do not say anything.'

Ramming my green hat well over my cars I huddled in a corner, looking cautiously from under my eyelids for cover in case we had to run. There was not so much as a ditch or a tree; there was nowhere we could flee in safety. I had come to Tiranë unarmed, believing that a gun was more likely to get me into trouble than out of it. I watched Toptani's companion slide his right hand inside his coat and, leaning forward for a moment, saw his fingers close over the butt of an automatic. I felt quite helpless, numb and sick with fear.

A corporal with a slung Schmeizer put his head through the driver's window and spoke quite civilly in German to the two in front; then he came to my window, looked at me searchingly and asked for my papers. I stared back oafishly at him from under the brim of my hat and hissed my piece:

'*Shqypëtar. Ska dokument.*' He gave me a long, puzzled stare and turned back to Toptani. He was clearly dissatisfied about something, and I felt a surge of panic when he turned away as though to shout to his men. At that moment Toptani had an inspiration; from his wallet he pulled out a crumpled piece of paper and waved it in the corporal's face. The German scanned it for a moment and evidently found what he wanted; for he handed it back with a friendly smile and waved us on. When at last we were out of sight and I was mopping my sweaty face Toptani began to laugh.

'Really, that German was very unobservant!'

'Why?' I asked.

'Well, he was asking for the registration paper of this car, which has to have the *Feldkommandatur* stamp on it. Unfortunately there are no papers for this car, but I suddenly remembered that I was carrying a document belonging to another car—a Lancia with a Durazzo number plate. Luckily he only looked at the official stamp and did not notice that this is a Fiat with a Tiranë number plate.'

He stopped the car, and while my two companions pretended to be fiddling with the engines I managed to have a good look at the aircraft scattered on the field. They did not seem very interesting—a few Messerschmitt 109s, half a dozen Stukas, about twenty Junkers 52 troop-carriers, and some old 3-engine Savoias. When we passed the control post on our way back to the town the corporal recognized us and gave us a spectacular salute.

The following evening Dyshnica and Spiro were not present at dinner. My host explained that they had gone back to the hills, adding:

'This evening we received information that the Germans are going to impose a much stricter control in this city; they have already begun to search the houses, section by section. I do not think it is safe for you to stay here any longer. You cannot leave tonight because of the curfew, but you will forgive me if I order your guide to be here after breakfast tomorrow morning to take you back to Arbonë.'

Although I had thoroughly enjoyed my visit I was not inclined to linger after my host's warning. I had the answers to almost all of Cairo's questions and I had been promised some useful introductions in Kossovo should I be allowed to go there. At nine o'clock the next morning, having taken an affectionate leave of my host, I climbed into the carozza which was waiting outside the gate with my guide; after our experience of two days before we had decided that this was a safer method of travel in the city than a car. We returned by the same route as we had entered, making our way out of the city unchallenged. By midday I was back with Seymour in the farm-house, where I thankfully discarded the patent-leather shoes and bathed my blistered and swollen feet. Myslim embraced me warmly and laid on a special celebration in honour of my safe return.

I was alarmed to hear that during my absence Roberts had been taken gravely ill with malaria and bronchial pneumonia. The three N.C.O.s at Grecë had been seriously overworked; not only did they have to deal with a heavy two-way traffic of signals between Cairo and ourselves, but they also had to receive supply drops at all hours of the night. Moreover the dropping ground, although the only possible one in the area, was much too small, with the result that stores were often scattered among the woods on the neighbouring hillsides the N.C.O.s had to spend hours searching for them.

The whole region had a bad name for malaria, against which the only medicine we possessed was quinine. Roberts was a man of frail physique, and for a few days there were fears for his life. However, Seymour had sent an Italian doctor to him as soon as he heard of his illness; when, the day after my return from Tirana, I visited the camp the doctor told me that Roberts was out of danger.

For the next fortnight my time was fully occupied by my liaison work with the L.N.C. Central Council. These duties were exacting, dull and uncongenial. When I had met the Council at Shtyllë I had been able to leave the brunt of the discussion to McLean, speaking only if my advice was asked; now that I was their official link with Cairo they regarded me almost as their servant. They would often fail to turn up for meetings they had arranged; they would fritter away hours of discussion with petty complaints—usually directed against the B.B.C. for some favourable reference to a leading member of the Balli Kombëtar or for failing to denounce one of their political opponents; their claims of military success against the Germans—always unsupported by evidence—grew daily more inflated, their demands on my credulity more absurd. Despite all our protests they refused to allow Seymour or myself to attend any of their operations, leading us to the conclusion that they did not welcome any check on the accuracy of their reports; the few simple requests I passed to them from Cairo were ignored.

Perhaps their most irritating habit was the opening of our letters. Seymour and I kept up a correspondence with Neel in the north and McLean in the east, as well as with our N.C.O.s at Greece. Our letters had to pass through L.N.C. territory, and on every occasion they were delivered with the seals broken and the unvarying excuse that they had been 'opened in error'.

It was sometimes difficult to treat seriously their childish reflections on our own good faith. On one occasion, after I had left the country, a certain British Liaison Officer prepared, at the request of Enver Hoxha, a list of the names and regiments of British officers in northern Albania. The list read something like this:

Lieutenant-Colonel N. L. D. McLean, The Royal Scots Greys.
Major David Smiley, The Royal Horse Guards.
Major Richard Riddell, The Royal Horse Artillery.
Captain Anthony Simcox, The Royal Horse Artillery.
Captain The Honourable Rowland Winn, 8th King's Own Royal Irish Hussars.

When he came to read it to the Central Council the British officer noticed that at each mention of the word 'Royal' Enver Hoxha shot a significant glance round the table at his colleagues, who all nodded in understanding: officers from such regiments must obviously be reactionaries and Fascists. With a disarming smile the B.L.O. ended his recital:

'But *my* regiment is the *Manchester* Regiment—the *People's* regiment!'

The two most serious problems were arms and money. It was quite true that we were very short of arms, for our Italian deserters had brought none with them; but I pointed out to the Council that there was a shortage of arms in every theatre of war at this time, and one or two successful operations with the equipment we had already given them would be more convincing to Cairo than all their eloquence or mine.

Their appetite for money was insatiable. Since my arrival at Arbonë we had already given them three thousand sovereigns to buy food, equipment, and—where possible—arms for their new Italian allies; now they demanded a further fifteen thousand sovereigns. This sum, they blandly assured me, was the bare minimum necessary for the upkeep of their troops—they had just declared 'general mobilization' throughout the territory under their control; for the maintenance of their soldiers' families; for the relief of Albanian refugees from Kossovo and Macedonia, and for the purchase of grain to avert famine in the coming winter. I passed on their request to Cairo, unaware that the E.A.M. in Greece had used identical arguments to obtain funds which they had then misapplied to the use of the Communist Party. Cairo agreed to drop the money, but in small amounts, and to disperse it among the various British missions in the country, hoping thus to control its expenditure. The result was the same: most of the money was diverted to finance the Albanian Communist Party, who took exclusive credit for such relief work as was done.

It was not until much later that we learned how much care the Albanian Communist leaders took to see that the people were kept in ignorance of the source of their relief. When the Partisans entered Tiranë after the German withdrawal at the end of 1944 a certain British Liaison officer with the Partisans arranged a large-scale drop of food and clothing over the airfield to succour the starving population. Enver Hoxha and Mehmet Shehu insisted that the aircraft should not carry British markings. This stipulation was not understood by the R.A.F. The aircraft flew low over the city, their red, white and blue markings clearly visible to the crowds watching from below; as the containers floated down it was seen that each one was brightly painted with an enormous Union Jack. White and almost speechless with rage Mehmet Shehu turned to the Englishman and spat in his face.

'If only I had anti-aircraft guns I would order them to shoot down your planes!'

Enver Hoxha presided at our meetings, acting also as interpreter for me. Mehmet Shehu was still in the south with the First Brigade, so that on purely military matters I dealt with the Chief of Staff, Spiro Moisi, a silent, unassuming little man who understood his own subject and kept silent on others.

The most colourful member of the Council, whom I now met for the first time, was Mustafa Gjinishi, one of the heroes of the 1941 rising and one of the architects of the Mukaj agreement with the Balli Kombëtar. Cheerful and witty, highly intelligent, and incorruptibly honest Gjinishi commanded the affection and respect of all his country-men, of whatever political complexion. Now in his early thirties he had spent much of his adult life abroad and could converse fluently in English, French, Italian, and German. At the invitation of Myslim Peza, who was devoted to him, he came often to our farm-house, where we found him a delightful and stimulating companion. An avowed Communist but a sincere patriot he urged conciliation on the L.N.C., believing the liberation of his country to be more urgent than the struggle for political power. This attitude branded him as a Right deviationist in the eyes of his fellow Communists; his personal courage, his friendship with the British, and his popularity with the Partisan rank and file, to whom his wit and audacity made an irresistible appeal—all aroused the jealousy and suspicion of Enver Hoxha, who saw in Gjinishi his most serious competitor for the leadership of the movement. Enver Hoxha never deviated from Stalinist orthodoxy, particularly in his treatment of political rivals. At the end of August 1944 Gjinishi was murdered in an ambush near Dibra, on the Jugoslav frontier. The incident took place some distance from the battle area; no one saw the murderers or heard of them again.

A very different character was Tito's representative with the L.N.C., Ali Gostivari, alias Ali Dušanović, alias Dušan Mugoša. A tall, heavily-built Kossovar, with a thick, black 'Uncle Joe' moustache, he had seemed to us a ridiculous figure at Shtyllë, earning from McLean the nickname of 'The Shop Assistant' on account of his fussy manner. Now he appeared in a different light, speaking at meetings with an authority that commanded even Enver Hoxha's respect and adopting an angry, hectoring manner whenever his opinions were questioned. To Seymour and myself he was formally polite, affecting an ignorance of any language other than Albanian and Serbo-Croat. However, an incident at the end of September revealed his true attitude with alarming clarity.

One morning Seymour and I were working in our room when we were surprised by the arrival of Sergeant Smith from Grecë; he looked extremely worried. Two days ago Ali Gostivari and another member of the Central Council, whom the N.C.O.s knew by sight and who spoke English, had arrived at the camp, saying that they had come on our behalf to see if the N.C.O.s needed anything; naturally no one had thought to question their statement. They had stayed two nights, during which time they had read through all our papers, interfered with the wireless operators at their work by questioning them about wave-lengths, skeds, and other technical details, asked them numerous leading questions about our work and the reports we sent back—and—here Smith could not control his indignation—had tried to indoctrinate the three of them with Communism.

Myslim, furious, sent for Gostivari as soon as he heard our story. Unabashed, Gostivari assured us that he and his companion had stayed in our camp at the pressing invitation of our N.C.O.s; they had not looked at any of our papers or engaged in any political discussion, apart from a few words of praise for Mr. Churchill.

At the beginning of October Tony Neel joined us on a visit from the Zogist country north of Tiranë; he brought with him an escort of Abas Kupi's men. At the time of the Italian surrender Neel was in the Mati country, maintaining an uneasy contact between Abas Kupi's followers and a force of Partisans under Haxhi Lleshi, nephew of a famous Dibran chieftain. After the surrender they were joined by the Firenze Division. With their combined forces Neel planned to occupy the old fortress town of Krujë, the birthplace of Skanderbeg, preparatory to an attack on Tiranë in conjunction with the troops of Myslim Peza.

They occupied the town, only to be driven out by a German attack powerfully supported with artillery. Neel himself narrowly escaped death when a shell hit the house he occupied, killing a woman in the next room. He told us that Abas Kupi, who had at first been reluctant to co-operate with the Italians, fought like a lion, killing a number of Germans with his tommy-gun and inspiring his tribesmen to a stubborn resistance that provided the only serious fighting of the battle; the Partisans, Neel added, fought indifferently and the Italians never fought at all. Soon after the Partisans and the Firenze Division entered the city four German soldiers drove up in a lorry; they got out and began to move among the Italians, disarming them with magnificent self-confidence and an insolent contempt for the Partisans. Nobody tried to stop them until Abas Kupi himself appeared on the scene and dispatched them with a few bursts of his tommy-gun. Neel was certain that if the others had fought as well as Abas Kupi's men they would have held Krujë. After the battle they had all suffered terribly from hunger, and were eventually reduced to killing their mules for food.

Neel went on to tell us that Abas Kupi was indignant with the L.N.C. Central Council, who had given him neither the arms nor the money they had promised him when he had joined them in 1942; Kupi was convinced that all the power in the movement was in the hands of the Communists, who were using the organization for their own political ends, regardless' of their country's interests. I was not entirely surprised when Enver Hoxha came to see me the following day to tell me, with a confidence surprising in one who had not been present, that the Partisans had borne the brunt of the battle and that Abas Kupi had done no fighting at all.

Having met Neel in Egypt I was shocked at the change in him now. His face was sallow and drawn, the skin stretched tight over the cheek-bones; his eyes were yellow, and he ran a temperature; there remained no trace of his old high spirits. Even to us it was evident that he had jaundice. Luckily we were able to find a competent doctor among the Italian troops in Arbonë, who treated Neel with such medicines as we could get by courier from Tiranë. The heavy, steamy heat that had lasted now for several weeks was affecting Seymour and myself; our room was close and airless, the plain and the encircling hills broiling under the harsh sun. Seymour's exhaustion increased with a sharp attack of dysentery, while I with a temperature and a sore throat squirmed also under the fiery irritation of prickly heat.

Upon this scene of distress Bill McLean entered unexpectedly a few days after Neel's arrival. He brought us the news that a brigadier would soon be arriving to co-ordinate the activities of all British Liaison Officers in Albania; McLean had just finished preparing a dropping ground and headquarters for him and his staff on the plateau of Biza in the wild mountains of Cermenikë, east of Tiranë.

The following day the weather broke in a deluge of rain which continued all day. Myslim now insisted that we move from our farm-house, where he said that we were no longer safe. We set up a temporary headquarters under canvas in a valley near the house occupied by the Central Council. While we were on our way there three German tanks swung off the main road about five miles west of Tiranë, debouched into the plain and for twenty minutes shelled a hamlet close by the farm-house we had just left. We had barely completed our move when Seymour went down with malaria. Luckily there was an Italian army doctor to look after him.

Weak and ill as he was, and badly though he needed rest, Neel refused to let us detain him more than five days; he insisted that his work in Mati could not wait, forgetting Chesterton's observation that cemeteries are full of indispensables. However, he asked me to accompany him as far as the village of Zall i Herrit in the hills five miles north of Tiranë, in order to meet two members of the Central Council of the Balli Kombëtar who were anxious to talk with me. Neel believed that my views had been influenced overmuch by the extremists of the L.N.C., and that now I ought to see the other side of the picture.

At dusk on the evening of 8th October Neel and I set out on foot accompanied by the eight men of his escort. We had the best part of fifteen miles to cover that night, working our way round to the west of Tiranë; we must cross two main roads and pass close by some well guarded petrol dumps and a German barracks; and so we had no time to waste if we wanted to reach the cover of the Mati hills by daylight. Neel was so weak from illness and lack of food that I wondered how he would manage the journey; nor was I very strong myself. But our guides refused to let us take horses, saying that only on foot could we hope to get through the German outposts.

It was a journey I still remember with distaste. We were hardly surprised that our guides were not ready to start at the appointed time, but we were indignant when they delayed us for two hours in Arbonë while two of them had a drink with Myslim Peza. Crossing the roads at night was not usually a difficult business, nor could we believe that we were in much danger from the German guards at the petrol dumps; but our companions regarded each of those obstacles as a major hazard and wasted a great deal of time in frequent pauses to work up their courage; they made much more noise hushing each other up than we should have made talking in our normal voices.

They seemed afraid of the dark, for they cheered up wonderfully soon as the moon rose, chattering happily to each other while Neel and I plodded on in grim, exhausted silence.

About one o'clock in the morning storm clouds hid the moon, enveloping us in thick darkness; heavy rain soaked our clothes and chilled our bodies as a violent thunder-storm broke overhead. For two hours we struggled on, unable to see anything except when a flash of lightning momentarily lit the sky. The storm passed but the rain continued in a steady downpour, turning the paths and fields into thick, slippery mud. Soon after half-past three we stumbled on a deserted shepherd's hut of clay and wattle. Our guides now told us that they had lost the way and suggested we should shelter in the hut until daylight.

As the first light paled the sky we staggered outside, damp and shivering, to continue our journey. From the south, beyond Tiranë, came the sound of gun-fire, a distant rumble of battle which continued all the morning. Luckily we had not gone far out of our way in the storm; we were now over the main roads and past the petrol dumps. Refusing to make a detour, we passed the barracks unchallenged in the early morning light. At ten o'clock we came in sight of the cluster of houses on a hillside that was the village of Zall i Herrit. We were taken to the house of a friend of Neel's, an ex-captain of gendarmerie who spoke English. He had prepared us a magnificent breakfast, which Neel was too ill to eat but which put new life into me.

In the evening a Rumanian doctor arrived from Tiranë to look after Neel; he ordered him to stay in bed for as long as possible, which Neel feared would not be very long. He ascribed my temperature to a local fever and kindly gave me a bottle of grappa, which he said might be taken at night with advantage.

I spent all the following day in conference with the Balli representatives, Halil Maçi and Vasil Andoni; the latter was the secretary of the Central Council of the Balli Kombëtar. I believed their assurances that they had never countenanced active collaboration with the Germans, notwithstanding Enver Hoxha's efforts to persuade me that they had; but I was unable to shake off the feeling that they intended to keep one foot in the German camp in order to conserve their strength for the real struggle for power with the Partisans. In the light of events it is impossible to blame them; but I could not feel much sympathy for them at the time. I did, however, exact from them a promise to send representatives to our brigadier at the end of October in order to discuss plans for operations against the Germans.

I had intended to return to Arbonë the day after the conference; but in the morning I awoke with a splitting headache and a high temperature. The Rumanian doctor thought it might be malaria but he had nothing to give me except aspirin. I spent the day in bed. Next day, 12th October, my temperature was down and so I decided to return that night. My host insisted on lending me a horse, overruling all the objections of my escort; for this solicitude I was soon profoundly grateful.

We left Zall i Herrit at half-past four in the afternoon. The malaria returned two hours later, striking with alarming suddenness so that my temperature seemed to soar in a matter of minutes. Soon I was unable to sit my horse without support; for the rest of the journey one of the escort walked on either side to hold me in the saddle. Fortunately there was no danger of losing our way, for the night was clear. I took no interest in the journey, concentrating only on trying to stay on my horse. Around midnight we stopped to rest at a farm-house, where I drank a cup of milky coffee. I remember that as I shivered and sweated in a feverish doze whole passages of Boswell's *Life of Samuel Johnson* flashed through my mind with extraordinary clarity, and I would jerk awake to find myself declaiming one of the magisterial pronouncements of the Great Cham.

About two in the morning we reached a village in the hills above the plain of Arbonë; here I told my escort that I must stop, for I felt too exhausted to continue our journey. But the villagers were too frightened to let me stay. It seemed that three days previously—the morning when we had heard the gun-fire—the Germans had attacked Arbonë; although they had been repulsed they were still patrolling these hills and would certainly find me if I stayed there.

I told my escort to return to Zall i Herrit immediately, for they would be taking a needless risk by accompanying me further; in any case we were too large a party to move in safety through an area infested with German patrols. Two of them, however, insisted on staying with me until I could find shelter. For another two hours we wandered through the woods, until we reached a lonely house whose owner was willing to take me in. He affirmed stoutly that he would never turn a British officer from his door, but admitted that he was very frightened, for he was certain that the Germans would be there in the morning. He carried me to a room at the top of the house, imploring me to be on my way by daylight. My two companions, seeing me safely lodged, turned back with my horse towards their own country.

I left the house at first light, thanking my host warmly for his courage and kindness; he walked with me for ten minutes to put me on the track that would bring me down to the plain. Revived by the fresh, chill morning air and spurred by the danger of my position I reached the edge of the plain in an hour. There was no sign of activity, German or Albanian. I crossed the plain without meeting anybody and reached Arbonë at about eight o'clock, only to find that Seymour had moved his headquarters back into the hills. However, a Partisan agreed to take me to the headquarters of Ulysses Spahiu's Third Brigade at the village of Haxhijas on the way to Grecë. After a three mile walk I staggered into Spahiu's tent, where I collapsed.

I rested for two or three hours while Spahiu found me a guide and a horse to take me on to Seymour's camp at Grecë. I have no memory of the ride there and only a faint recollection of my arrival and of Seymour's warm greeting as he hustled me into a comfortable camp-bed in his tent, while a small bearded Italian doctor fussed around with tablets of quinine and atabrin.

Seymour's camp at this time resembled a convalescent home rather than a military headquarters. He himself was recovering from the malaria he had started at Arbonë, but was still very weak; Roberts was just beginning to pull through his illness, and Hill was in bed with influenza. The Italian doctor worked tirelessly to look after us, making his rounds at all hours of the day to ensure that we took our medicines at the right time; through his conscientious care we all recovered remarkably quickly. Although the wireless traffic was no longer so heavy we still had to receive supply drops; however, we had collected a large body of Italian servants and camp-followers, who not only took much of the work off our hands but, unlike the Partisans, refrained from looting the stores.

From Seymour's account it was evident that the Partisans had put up a much better fight at Arbonë than they had done at Shtyllë. During the early hours of 9th October the Germans infiltrated strong patrols through the hills between Tiranë and the plain; Neel and I were very lucky not to run into them, and I felt ashamed of my contempt for our guides' caution. At dawn they crossed the river Arzen and were in Arbonë almost before the Partisans had woken up. After the initial shock, however, the Partisans rallied and held the Germans until Ulysses Spahiu's Third Brigade arrived, about eleven o'clock; Spahiu was a brave and competent officer who like Shehu had fought in the Spanish Civil War. By midday the Germans had been driven from Arbonë and were withdrawing northward, pursued by the Partisans. During the afternoon the Germans launched a second attack and retook Arbonë; again the Partisans counter-attacked and, after some close fighting, drove them from the village. By nine in the evening the Germans had fallen back into the hills, leaving thirty-five killed and twelve wounded. The Italians fought very well, showing discipline, courage, and an intense hatred of the Germans, but they suffered heavy casualties.

Seymour calculated that the enemy forces engaged were rather less than one battalion of infantry, supported by artillery, heavy mortars and a few tanks; the Partisans of course heavily outnumbered them, but had only a few mortars and two anti-tank rifles in support. They captured from the enemy seven machine-guns and six mortars. The Germans must seriously have miscalculated the numbers as well as the fighting spirit of the Partisans; we wondered how long they would be content to leave their defeat unavenged.

The heroes of the day, according to Seymour, were Spahiu and Gjinishi; the latter was in the thick of the battle the whole time and was twice wounded, fortunately not seriously. Gjinishi's example obliged the other members of the Central Council to come down from their retreat and join in the fighting, although not all of them showed his enthusiasm. At one moment Seymour found himself firing from a ditch with Enver Hoxha on one side of him and Ali Gostivari on the other; since he had recently quarrelled seriously with both of them, his predicament caused him some anxiety.

'They were damn funny to watch' he told me, 'when you remember the way they used to swagger around festooned with pistols, tommy-guns, and bandoliers. There was no swank in them that morning. Enver's fat cheeks were flapping like sheets in a wind and he could hardly hold his gun, while the Shop Assistant had a sort of crestfallen look as though his richest customer had just cancelled her account.

VIII

ON THE RUN

One morning a week later I was lying under the trees outside the tent I shared with Seymour, watching the dappled sunlight on the pine needles and happy to be feeling well again, when Roberts brought me a signal from Cairo which he had just deciphered. I read it with some satisfaction.

'George!' I called into the tent. 'The Brigadier wants to see me right away. From the wording of this signal it looks as though I may be going to Kossovo.'

'Good show, old boy! When will you leave?'

'The signal says as soon as I'm fit enough to travel—that's any time now. The Central Council have already left for Biza, so there's nothing more for me to do here. I'll have to leave Roberts and the wireless set with you because I've only got one mule; but I'll come back for them as soon as the Brigadier lets me have some more.'

That evening Seymour and I buried two canisters of gold in a secret hide-out, which we marked carefully. We had been visited every day by a German reconnaissance plane, and although we had done our best to camouflage the camp we could not be sure that it was invisible from the air. Lying in a rough triangle between three main roads, the area was peculiarly vulnerable to any German drive; if it came we should have neither time nor transport to remove the gold. Our efforts, however, were in vain, as Seymour told me much later; the gold was found, not by the Germans but by the people of Grecë.

After lunch on 21st October I began my journey to the Brigadier's headquarters at Biza with Stiljan and my Italian groom, a quiet young Florentine called Tomaso: he was an intelligent and reliable servant and a cheerful companion. I took my horse and mule with a minimum of personal kit for the three of us. On the way we stopped to have a drink with Myslim Peza and ask him for a guide to see me as far as the Tiranë-Elbasan road, the limit of Myslim's territory. He gave me a guide with a message to some friends who lived in a village near the road.

I spent the first night at Haxhijas in the house of a poor peasant; the guest-room was used as a store for maize—also, it seemed, as a breeding-ground for a million fleas, whose attentions made sleep impossible. Stiljan and Tomaso, who had the sense to sleep outside, were undisturbed.

The following afternoon we reached the tiny hillside village which was the home of Myslim's friends. These were three old men who shared a house but whose precise relationship to each other I could not determine. They gave us an enthusiastic welcome, plying us with raki and turning out a large room for our use. They gladly promised to see us across the road as they had been doing for Myslim's friends for many years; but they insisted we stay the night in their house while they reconnoitred the road to discover the latest positions of the German pickets; if all was well they would take us across the next evening. They added that the Central Council had passed their way two nights before with General Azzi and forty mules. They also warned me that the Germans were now operating in these hills in patrols of fifty men; but I could sleep easy because they were used to that sort of thing and would post reliable guards.

In the morning my new friends told me that they had made all their arrangements to take us across the road at dusk. Meanwhile, as I had so kindly expressed appreciation of their raki the previous night, perhaps I would care to see how it was made? We went down to a stream below the village, where a very small, wizened old man crouched over a crude pot-still, blowing with a bellows on a fire of wood shavings; on the ground beside him stood a number of small flasks filled with the clear spirit. Delighted at our interest the old man handed me a measure, explaining that the raki in it had just been distilled; he cackled with pleasure when he saw me choke over my first swallow. When I had recovered he handed me a measure from another flask; this, it seemed, was what they usually drank themselves—'not a drop is sold till it's two weeks old.' Finally, with enormous pride, he made me sample his oldest raki, thrice distilled and matured a full year; when, quite sincerely, I praised it he gave me a flask for the journey.

We crossed the road in the last faint twilight with a speed, efficiency and silence that I never saw before or since in that country. On the other side ran the river Arzen, spanned by a narrow wooden bridge; beyond, a steep track climbed into thickly wooded hills. Here our guides left us, embracing us with many assurances of friendship and begging us to return soon to try some more of their raki. We followed the track for two hours until we came to the village of Gurrë, a cluster of houses and a mosque, where we spent the night.

All the next morning we climbed steeply, until at midday we came out of the woods onto a bare, open ridge. We were now on the borders of Cermenikë, the most savage and inhospitable region of central Albania. Picking our way down a precipitous, winding track into a valley hemmed in by wild jagged peaks we followed the path that ran eastward beside the foaming Arzen; at half-past four in the afternoon we halted at the village of Shengjergj, sprawled in a hollow amphitheatre topped by frowning grey cliffs.

Shengjergj was disputed territory between the Partisans and the Balli Kombëtar; the lower half of the village had declared for the Partisans, the upper half for the Balli. Each side had built a line of rough fortifications facing towards the other. The Partisan commander, who lent me a guide to take me on to Biza, told me confidentially that he expected to clear the Balli Kombëtar from the village within the next few weeks.

Passing through the Ballist lines we climbed steeply for an hour to the top of the pass that led to Biza. On the bleak, windswept summit we crossed a disused motor road built by the Italians. At the cross-roads stood a small stone obelisk with an inscription in memory of the travellers who were frozen to death there a few years before. Darkness was falling and a fierce east wind numbed our faces as we came down the gentle incline on the other side onto a wide grassy plateau, at the far end of which lay the Brigadier's headquarters.

A fortnight previously the only habitation on the plateau had been a derelict shepherd's hut; but Smiley had set Italian soldiers to work on the preparation of a camp. In the course of two days they had built three large wooden huts, covered with camouflage parachutes, on the eastern edge of the plain at the foot of a thickly wooded mountain. Tents had also been improvised from parachutes to serve as sleeping and kitchen quarters, leaving the huts for the offices and mess. In the largest hut the Brigadier and his staff were sitting down to dine when I arrived on this evening of 24th October.

Brigadier Davies, usually known to us as 'Trotsky',[1] was a regular soldier of considerable seniority. His experience of guerrilla warfare had been, as it were, on the receiving end; for he had served before the war on the North-West Frontier and in Palestine. Stout and stocky, with a ruddy complexion and a bluff and friendly manner, he relied on his training and common-sense rather than on intuition or intellect to guide him through the complexities of Albanian military and political affairs. Though kind and considerate to his subordinates he tolerated neither inefficiency nor affectation. He detested sloppiness in dress or personal appearance, and discountenanced the wearing of beards—'None of that Wingate stuff here,' he would say. He listened carefully to the opinions of his officers, and once he had given them his confidence he was prepared to back them to the limit.

Resolved that his headquarters should function with strict military efficiency, even in such unpromising conditions, Trotsky had brought with him a formidable complement of staff officers, including a G.I, D.A.Q.M.G., Signals Officer, and Chief Clerk; their equipment comprised, among other things, several wireless sets, camp furniture for offices and mess, a typewriter, and two containers full of stationery. In the transport lines were more than a hundred mules.

The G.I, Lieutenant-Colonel Arthur Nicholls, Coldstream Guards, was an old friend of mine from pre-war days. Having been a staff officer at S.O.E.

---

[1] He had acquired this nickname as an officer cadet at Sandhurst from a reference in an instructor's report to 'a kind of disciplined bolshevism' in his character.

headquarters in Baker Street for the past two years, he had asked to be sent on operations, in the belief that every S.O.E. staff officer should spend at least six months in the field in order to understand the problems of those whose destinies he had to control. Tall, thin and very delicate he had not the constitution to withstand even normal conditions of service in a Balkan country in winter. From his first days in Albania he suffered continuously from dysentry, but his spirit and determination drove him to endurance far beyond his strength.

The D.A.Q.M.G. was Captain Alan Hare, Household Cavalry Regiment, a versatile young officer of outstanding ability and acumen. In charge of demolitions was Major Chesshire, R.E., of signals Lieutenant Trayhorn, an engineer who had lived in Istanbul and spoke Turkish. Other officers present at the time of my arrival were Major Alan Palmer, Captain Victor Smith, and Captain Smythe; Palmer and Smith left the morning afterwards to join the First Partisan Brigade in the south; Palmer later became senior British Liaison Officer with the Partisans. Among the N.C.O.s I found my paramilitary specialist, Gregson Allcott.

There was a fresh and friendly atmosphere among the officers and N.C.O.s despite the austere regime imposed on them by Trotsky and Nicholls, whose ideas of routine were suitable enough for a Brigade Headquarters but a little incongruous in a guerilla camp among the mountains. With touching consideration for my health the Brigadier excused me the most irksome of our duties—that of standing-to each morning an hour before sunrise, presumably in expectation of an enemy attack; at the time I ridiculed this piece of regimentation but within a few weeks I was to regret that I had not adopted it myself. Trotsky confided to me that his past experience of guerrillas had left him with few illusions about their fighting qualities; but even he was shocked when, two days after his arrival at Biza, all his Partisan guards vanished on receiving a false alarm of the approach of German troops. McLean and Smiley, who were still there at the time, assured him that this was their usual habit.

I was sorry to learn that I had missed McLean and Smiley by thirty-six hours; Trotsky was sending them out to Italy, where S.O.E. had established an advance base, to give a personal report on the situation and to enjoy some well-earned leave at home. I was sorry, also, that they had left behind Frederick Nosi to act as official interpreter. His natural arrogance, swollen by the importance of his new position, soon caused trouble in the camp. Encouraged by Nosi the Partisan guards, who had previously been willing and helpful even if not very efficient, suddenly refused to do manual work of any kind for the Mission; when asked for an explanation Nosi came out with the astonishing reply: 'Partisans do not work; their job is to fight.'

When the Albanian cook complained to Hare that the Partisans were openly stealing the rations he was warned by Nosi that as soon as the English had left he would be liquidated for his temerity; the poor fellow was so frightened that he asked to be released from our service. A few days later our N.C.O.s complained that Nosi had ordered them to salute him as 'an officer of the Albanian Army'; when they indignantly refused he called on the Brigadier to discipline them. It required all Nicholls's patience and tact to restore an appearance of harmony.

I spent my first morning at Biza writing a report for the Brigadier on the political situation in the country. When he had read it he sent for me.

'I have two pieces of good news for you,' he began. He indicated a large map on the wall. 'As you know, my parish includes not only the old frontiers of Albania, but the new regions incorporated into the country by the Axis; that is, the whole of Kossovo, the western fringe of Macedonia from the Vardar valley to Lake Ohrid, and a small corner of Montenegro. I'm going to send you to make a reconnaissance of those areas. I want you to be my eyes and ears. I want to know all about the political situation, with particular reference to the chances of starting resistance among the Albanian irredentists. I leave it entirely to you how you go about it. You will send your reports by wireless to Cairo in the usual manner for onward transmission to me; but I hope that later on we'll be able to arrange a courier service between us for letters.

'The second piece of news which I think will cheer you is that your majority has come through with effect from the first of the month. My best congratulations! Now I want you to be thoroughly fit before you start this job, so you'd better rest here while your interpreter goes back to Seymour's place for your wireless and kit.'

This was better than I had dared hope. I was still young enough to find a romantic glamour in the idea of exploring a disputed frontier, while the opportunity of studying at first-hand one of the most complex political problems in the Balkans made an irresistible appeal to one who was still attracted by the glitter of coffee-house politics; moreover, I was delighted to know that I should be working on my own. The next day Stiljan left for Grecë with Partisan guides and enough mules to transport Roberts and our kit. I never saw any of them again.

All the time I was at Biza Trotsky and Nicholls were fully engaged in conferences with the Central Council of the L.N.C., Abas Kupi, and the Balli Kombëtar representatives; I was not required to attend. The Brigadier was working for agreement between the three factions for a combined plan of operations. Kupi, whom the Brigadier liked and respected, was only too ready to agree; the Balli Kombëtar were with difficulty persuaded to sign a written declaration that they would immediately begin open hostilities against the Germans. But when, in order to commit them irrevocably, Trotsky wished to have their declaration broadcast by the B.B.C. Enver Hoxha flew into a rage and arrogantly commanded him to suppress it. At the same time he denounced the Mukaj agreement and issued orders to all Partisan units to attack and destroy the forces of the Balli Kombëtar wherever they could be found. The Civil War had begun.

Enver had repeatedly told us that he would gladly co-operate with the Ballists if they would give an undertaking to join in the War of Liberation. This flagrant duplicity therefore stupefied and shocked the Brigadier after all his patient work for reconciliation. Enver, however, seeing that the Germans were not trying to extend their control beyond the main towns and the roads, had decided to take advantage of his freedom from attack to liquidate his main political rivals.[1] With their superior armament, discipline and training the Partisans soon drove the Balli Kombëtar to take refuge in the towns under the guns of the Germans, so that Enver was able to represent the L.N.C. as the only effective guerrilla organization. For the moment he left Abas Kupi alone; his turn would come next.

The town of Dibra, or Debar, as it is called in Serbo-Croat, stands on the frontiers of Albania and Jugoslavia some thirty miles north of Lake Ohrid; part of Jugoslavia before the war, it had been incorporated into Albania by the Axis Powers. Flight-Lieutenant Hands had been the British Liaison Officer there until mid-October, when he had moved north, his place being taken by a new Mission under Major Riddell and Captain Simcox. At the end of October the Brigadier received disquieting reports of the situation in the area, which he ordered me to investigate.

After the fall of Mussolini, Haxhi Lleshi's Partisans had occupied the town, of which they were still in possession. At the same time some of the local Bajraktars[2] had formed a 'Committee of National Defence' with the avowed object of making war on the Italians, but with the real aim of preventing encroachment by the L.N.C. on the Bajraktars' territory. The headquarters of the Committee was the town of Peshkopijë, some thirteen miles north-west of Dibra; its leader was Colonel Fiqri Dine, formerly a Zone Commander in King Zog's Gendarmerie and one of the original quadrumvirate of chiefs that had helped Zog in his early days of power. There were also several volunteer bands, each numbering between fifty and three hundred men, under minor chieftains who belonged to neither faction and who had offered their services to the British.

The two rival factions had long been on the verge of hostilities; but Hands had achieved a precarious compromise whereby the authority of the Partisans was recognized in and around the town of Dibra and that of the Committee

---

[1] See also Amery, op. cit., p. 65.
[2] The word means 'Standard-bearer', an ancient hereditary title. Later it came to have virtually the same meaning as Chieftain.

in the country to the north. But from across the old frontier another danger threatened, in the shape of a certain Xhemal Gostivari,[1] an Albanian who had made himself powerful in Macedonia with Italian and German help. Riddell now reported that Gostivari was preparing an attack on Dibra with German support and—according to the Partisans—with the connivance of the Bajraktars' Committee.

When he heard the news Trotsky sent for me. 'I want a personal report on this situation as soon as possible. Riddell and Simcox are new to the country, so they may be glad of a bit of help. You'd better take Alan Hare with you—you'll find him very useful. I suggest you leave tomorrow.'

On 1st November Hare and I left the camp on horseback, accompanied by a local guide. Our route lay north-east over a high range of mountains to the village of Martanesh; thence it dropped into a valley where a disused motor road ran from west to east towards Peshkopijë. I had hoped that with good luck we might reach the valley by nightfall. Our guide had other ideas: determined that we should spend the night at the house of his uncle among the mountains he lost the way half a dozen times until, when darkness was falling and our tempers were becoming dangerous, he conveniently hit upon a track that led us straight to uncle's door.

We rode next morning through miles of silent beech forest over a carpet of gold and russet leaves beneath an ice-blue autumn sky. The air on these lonely uplands was clear and sharp; the pale sunlight filtering between the smooth boles, the soft gloom of the shadows and the stillness of the great woods induced a mood of quiet contentment and hushed our talk.

In the late afternoon we came down into the valley, forded a shallow river and climbed an embankment onto the old motor road. From now on the going was easy. Darkness found us at the village of Homesh, two or three miles from the west bank of the Black Drin. Here we heard that there had been fighting around Dibra for the past two days between the Partisans and Xhem Gostivari. We decided to spend the night at Homesh, and immediately sent a message to Fiqri Dine asking him to meet us next morning at the crossroads of Maqellarë, five miles north of Dibra.

Next morning we forded the Drin without difficulty, and reached Maqellarë, a small village with a mosque, at ten o'clock. At first sight Fiqri Dine reminded me of an evil, black, overgrown toad; his manner was reserved and barely friendly, his speech patronizing. He denied any collaboration with Xhem Gostivari, adding that he had restrained his own forces from joining in the battle against Haxhi Lleshi; but he complained bitterly of the Partisans, saying that they terrorized the people of Dibra and were threatening to attack the Bajraktars.

---

[1] Xhemal, or Xhem, Gostivari, was the *nom-de-guerre* of one Xhemal Hasa; he must not be confused with the L.N.C. delegate, Ali Gostivari.

'Their aggressive behaviour will certainly bring the Germans upon us,' he concluded obscurely.

He told us that Simcox was in Peshkopijë and Riddell with Haxhi Lleshi in Dibra. He would give us an escort for a few miles down the road, but his men would have to leave ns at the approaches of Dibra, or they would certainly be fired on; we ourselves must carry sticks with handkerchiefs tied to them, which we must display prominently on approaching the town unless we wished to be shot. We took our leave after obtaining his promise that he would come to the help of the Partisans if they were attacked by the Germans; but he gave it so reluctantly as to inspire us with little confidence.

After parting from our escort about a mile from the town we rode along a straight, open road across the plain, feeling very foolish and conspicuous as we waved our white flags all the way. However, nobody fired at us and we met nobody until we came to the first houses of Dibra, where a Partisan picket challenged us. They took us through almost deserted streets to a barracks on the western edge of the town. In a third floor room crowded with people and thick with tobacco smoke we found Riddell and Haxhi Lleshi; among the party were Mehmet Hoxha—still wearing the same lounge suit that he had lent me for my Tiranë visit—and the Bektashi abbot, Baba Faja. Mehmet Hoxha was on his way to Kossovo to form a Partisan organization on the Albanian-Jugoslav border.

Our arrival broke up the meeting and Riddell took Hare and me to lunch at the hotel, a rickety wooden building kept by an Italian who gave us a most friendly welcome and a very good lunch. Riddell told us that Xhem Gostivari had attacked three days ago. He had driven the Partisans from the hills that overlooked Dibra on the east and had even occupied part of the town; after some street fighting he had withdrawn to his own territory, leaving the Partisans to celebrate a victory. He had been accompanied by a German officer and three or four other ranks. Riddell, who had been in Peshkopijë at the time, had tried to stop the fighting by persuading Fiqri Dine to send a letter to Xhem Gostivari, with whom he seemed to have some influence, asking him to withdraw; unfortunately the Partisans had intercepted the letter, which they were trying to use as proof that Fiqri Dine and his Committee were collaborating with Gostivari.

The fighting had prevented Riddell himself from entering Dibra until early that morning; but the previous evening he and Fiqri Dine had ridden to within a mile of the town under fire from both sides. For the whole morning he had been in conference with the Partisan leaders in a fruitless attempt to reach some compromise between them and Fiqri Dine's Committee; he had found them aggressive and intractable, much more ready to look on the Committee as enemies than as allies.

At five-thirty in the evening we reassembled for a conference with Haxhi Lleshi and his officers. After Riddell, Hare, and I in turn had stretched our eloquence to the utmost, Haxhi Lleshi agreed, rather in the manner of an indulgent schoolmaster humouring his backward pupils, to keep the peace with Fiqri Dine and co-operate with Riddell in his efforts to form a united front against Gostivari and the Germans. Privately we put little more faith in this promise than we had in Fiqri Dine's.

We did, however, obtain from Haxhi Lleshi one hopeful token of good faith: among the prisoners taken by the Partisans in the previous days' fighting was Helmi Beg Karasani, one of the independent minor chieftains who had put his men at Riddell's disposal. Helmi Beg, a cheerful little man with a fair complexion and a frank expression, swore that he had come to help the Partisans; but having lost touch with his men in the confusion he had fallen into the hands of a Partisan patrol. The Partisans swore that they had seen him firing on them, and they therefore intended to shoot him. Whatever the truth of the matter, it would clearly have the worst possible effect on Riddell's plans if they were to carry out their threat, for Helmi Beg was a popular figure with the chiefs and Bajraktars. After a good deal of persuasion, supported by some brilliant argument from Hare, we secured his release.

Although we had a good dinner and comfortable beds in the hotel I slept uneasily; for the night was disturbed by screams and short bursts of tommy-gun fire as the Partisans executed their opponents. Next day Riddell returned to Peshkopijë and Hare and I started our journey back to Biza. The autumn rains had been late this year, but they made up for it now as we rode slowly back over the mountains shivering and sodden. It was after dark on 6th November when, hungry and dispirited, we staggered into the Brigadier's mess, to be revived by Trotsky's formidable cocktails of raki and vermouth.

I was alarmed that there was no news of Stiljan and Roberts; Cairo reported that Seymour had been off the air since 30th October, and there were rumours of a German drive against Myslim Peza. For a week I waited at Biza while the rains deluged us with the sustained violence of a tropical monsoon and a murderous cold wind swept across the three thousand foot high plateau; thunder-storms burst among the mountains around us, echoing like artillery through the rocky gorges, while forked lightning lit the camp in brilliant violet flashes.

'Don't think I want to get rid of you,' Trotsky said to me one day, 'but if you're going to get to Kossovo this year you'd better start immediately—wireless or no wireless. Winter's coming on, and pretty soon the snow will stop you getting over these mountains.'

'Not only that,' added Nicholls, 'but once the Drin's in flood you'll never get across; I should think the water's high already.'

Both these points had occurred to me, but I wondered what use I could be in Kossovo without a wireless.

'If Roberts arrives in time,' said Trotsky, 'we'll send him after you. Meanwhile you'd better base yourself on Riddell and use his wireless; you can work your area from Dibra, starting with Macedonia.'

Summoning Gregson Allcott and Tomaso I told them to be ready to leave in twenty-four hours. I planned to spend the first night at Martanesh, the home of Baba Faja, whom the Brigadier wished me to see; it was a four-hour journey, and so I should have plenty of time if I left Biza immediately after lunch.

The next day, 13th November, I was standing outside the mess saying good-bye to Trotsky and his officers when somebody called our attention to a pair of figures limping wearily across the plateau towards us.

'Looks like Bulman and Corsair,' said Nicholls. 'Now we'll get some news of Seymour. They both look dead beat.'

Bulman and Corsair were two officers who had left Biza for Grecë about the same time as I had started my journey in the opposite direction; we had missed each other on the road. They had a grim story to tell. The Germans had cleaned up the Peza area, beginning their drive a few days after Bulman, Corsair, and Stiljan had reached Grecë. Seymour had immediately moved his headquarters to Myslim Peza's base in the hills, where he felt reasonably safe from surprise; Partisan guards were posted on all the heights commanding Myslim's camp. Early one morning, when the camp was barely stirring, they were alarmed by a single pistol shot close at hand; thirty seconds later the Germans opened fire with machine-guns and tommy-guns from the very hills where the guards were supposed to be stationed. Seymour's wireless operator, Bombardier Hill, was killed instantly; the rest of the Mission was forced to scatter, abandoning the wireless sets and all equipment. For six days, they were on the run; several times they were ambushed; but eventually all of them, including Stiljan, rejoined Myslim Peza, whom no trap was strong enough to hold. Now Roberts had pneumonia and was too ill to move; Stiljan had gone to Tiranë 'to tranquillize himself' and was unlikely to return.

The news of Roberts's death reached me two months later. He had been taken prisoner by the Germans but had escaped, shooting one of his guards with a pistol he had hidden in his stocking and pushing another over a cliff. But the ensuing days of hunger and exposure had proved too much for a frame that was never robust; if his physical strength had matched his gallant spirit he might still be alive.

I delayed my departure no longer, but set out for the mountains accompanied by Gregson Allcott and Tomaso. The Brigadier had given me a fresh supply of money and equipment and three mules to transport it, so that I need depend on Riddell and Simcox only for wireless contact. At Martanesh, where we arrived as darkness was falling, we were taken to the house of Baba Faja's Political Commissar, who sent a Partisan to warn the

Baba of our coming; the Baba did not like receiving visitors unannounced and his Political Commissar was equally averse to his doing so. By the time we had found lodging for the night the Abbot was ready to see me.

Baba Faja, or Baba Mustafa, as he was sometimes called, was one of the very few Albanian guerrilla leaders whose fame had reached the outside world before the arrival of McLean and Smiley; he had fought a vigorous and unrelenting war against the Italians from the first days of their occupation. A native of Martanesh, where his monastery had been burnt down by the Italians, he was revered by the people of Cermenikë more for his prowess than his piety. I found him sitting in a low, ill-lit, smoky room with a half-empty bottle of raki by his side and rows of empty bottles round the walls; his great black beard streamed over his battle-dress blouse. Rumour—not only the whispers of his enemies—credited him with two Partisan mistresses, but now he was alone. He was, as I had been warned to expect, very drunk.

Intoxication had not improved his temper. Returning my greeting with perfunctory courtesy he launched into a series of contentious questions and complaints: why had the English general given him no war material? How long had Abas Kupi spent at Shengjergj, and how much had the General given him? Why did we continue to help the Balli and Fiqri Dine when there was 'documentary proof' that they were working for the Germans?

I was amused to find that the 'documentary proof' was no more than the letter Fiqri Dine had written to Xhem Gostivari at Riddell's request. However, I made a careful note of each complaint, promising to retail it to the Brigadier; then I said good-night with my smartest salute, which he returned with a scowl.

It was half-past eleven next morning before the escort and guide promised by Baba Faja were ready to leave. We aimed to spend the night at Zerqan, a large village on the northern slopes of these mountains, a little way above the old motor road; the guide, who was a Partisan courier, told me that the journey would take at least eight hours and so we could not hope to arrive before dark; yet there was no shelter for the night nearer than Zerqan. The day was cold and cloudy with a threat of snow and I did not look forward to spending the night in the open at an altitude of six or seven thousand feet.

All day we scrambled up and down steep mountains covered in beech forests, climbing higher with each successive ridge. Dusk came upon us as we were crossing a wide, snow-covered plateau strewn with rocks and intersected by countless small streams; thick clouds were swirling around us, bringing a chilly rain. Our guide chose this moment to tell me that he was no longer certain of the way. We struggled on, past a smooth, black tarn onto a wooded ridge where darkness wholly enveloped us. Here the guide gave up; he was sure the track was not very far away, but he could never find it at night and so we must make up our minds to stay where we were until morning. It was hardly a suitable camping place that he had chosen—a steep slope exposed to a bitter wind that pierced right through our clothing. We unloaded and tethered the animals, lit several large fires and cooked a hot meal. Then, piling the fires with wood, we lay down and tried to sleep.

I had barely settled myself when the night was shattered by a violent explosion. I leaped to my feet, drawing my pistol, only to find that one of the Partisans, thinking he had heard a bear prowling around the camp, had thrown a grenade to scare it away. Sleep was impossible for any of us; whichever side we turned to the fire, the other, exposed to the icy wind, felt more miserably cold by comparison. Snow fell during the night.

At dawn I sent the guide to find the track; at seven he returned to tell us that after walking in circles for the last hour he had found it only fifty yards away. After a steep descent through the woods we came out onto open grassy slopes leading into Zerqan.

This was a pretty little village of modern white, red-roofed houses, in one of which the local L.N.C. Committee were waiting to receive us; all of them were followers of Abas Kupi. Their leader, a captain of artillery, showed us into a clean, well-furnished guest-room with a dais at one end and chairs as well as cushions to sit on. By the time we had washed and shaved an excellent breakfast was ready—tea, boiled eggs, a chicken, bread, butter, and jam; we felt ashamed to be eating what were probably their last supplies, but the laws of hospitality forbade us to refuse what they offered. When we had finished the captain brought in three minor chieftains, each of whom commanded a body of a hundred men; they were anxious to help the British and asked me how they could best employ their men in our cause. After what I had seen on my previous visit to Dibra I could only advise them to join the Partisans, for I doubted that Fiqri Dine would use them against the Germans.

We left for Dibra at half-past two, warmed by the kindness and hospitality of our hosts; they lent us a guide to see us across the Drin and a horse for Gregson Allcott—a relief to me because I should no longer have to share mine. On the motor road we met groups of civilians coming from Dibra, the bundles on their backs and the grim, resigned expressions on their faces identifying them as refugees. Among them, riding by himself, I recognized a young man whom I had met on my last visit; he seemed a little drunk. He was on his way, he told me, to Biza, to put a safe distance between himself and the Germans.

'What Germans?' I asked.

'The Germans who are coming with Xhem Gostivari to take Dibra.'

'I don't hear any fighting.'

'You will tomorrow—they haven't arrived yet. Look up there!' He pointed to the sky above the Drin.

Looking through my glasses I saw two Me 109s flying up and down the valley between Dibra and Peshkopijë; they did not seem to be attacking any target and so I supposed they were simply showing the flag. Hurrying on we reached the river at dusk, to find it greatly swollen; we waited, therefore, on the near bank while the guide waded across to see if it was fordable. When he was satisfied he came back for us. We put the horses and mules to the stream, a man holding the head of each; in mid-stream the current tugged fiercely at us, the water foaming around the horses' flanks, so that for a few moments we feared we might be swept away. As we stood on the farther bank, while the horses shook the water from their coats, our guide said with a smile:

'Two or three days more and nobody will cross the river unless by boat.'

At half-past seven we dismounted outside the hotel in Dibra and paid off our guides. Riddell was dining at the hospital with some Italian officers, but I found Haxhi Lleshi seated at a table drinking raki with his Political Commissar, Ersat Ndreou, the brother of a powerful Dibran chieftain. They invited me to join them.

'You have come at a very interesting time,' said Ersat in English. 'We are expecting to be attacked any day now. We have information that Xhem Gostivari has arrived at a village on the other side of the mountains, only four hours' march from here, with a large force of Albanians and Germans.'

'But you need not worry,' interposed Haxhi Lleshi airily. 'We have concentrated our troops around here to meet the threat and we have taken all precautions against surprise.'

As we were finishing supper Riddell returned with his interpreter, Bungurri—a mournful-looking Dibran—and Captain Michael Lis, a lively, thick-set Pole who had been dropped into Albania recently to try and open an escape line from Poland through the Balkans; having found this task impossible he had attached himself to Riddell as an extra Liaison Officer.

Riddell did not share Haxhi Lleshi's confidence in the ability of the Partisans to hold Dibra in the face of a determined attack supported by German troops. He suggested that I send Gregson Allcott, Tomaso, and the mules with all our kit to Peshkopijë next morning, where they could set up a temporary base with Simcox; then Riddell and I could go to see Cen Elezi, the brother of Haxhi Lleshi's Political Commissar, whose house was in the hills north of Peshkopijë and who had valuable contacts across the frontier in Tetovo and Gostivar. I could then reconnoitre that area before going north to Kossovo.

I shared a room with Gregson Allcott and Tomaso, and slept solidly for ten hours. While we sat over the remains of our breakfast, Riddell recommended me to take a sulphur bath—a specialty of the town; he intended to inspect the aerodrome. As I sat there contentedly smoking a pipe, savouring the prospect of a few days' comfort after the hardship of the mountains and planning my forthcoming visit to Macedonia, a Partisan entered the room with a note for Riddell. When he had read it Riddell flicked it over the table to me. It was a message from Simcox at Peshkopijë, relaying an urgent warning from Fiqri Dine: 'It is dangerous to remain in Dibra after 10.00 on Tuesday, 16th November.'

'What's the date today?' I asked.

'Tuesday, 16th November. And the time is ten minutes to ten.'

'This may be a false alarm, but there's no harm in being prepared. I think we'd better find Haxhi Lleshi and tell him.' I turned to Gregson Allcott.

'Where's Tomaso?'

'Gone to feed and water the animals, sir.'

'Good. "When he comes back tell him to bring the lot here. Then you and he get all our stuff loaded and push off along the road to Peshkopijë. There's no point in your staying here, anyway.'

By good luck we ran into Haxhi Lleshi and Ersat Ndreou in the street outside the hotel, and took them inside to show them Simcox's letter. They were amused.

'We've told you there's no need for alarm,' they laughed. 'Every-thing is foreseen. The bridges over the rivers to the south and east are already destroyed, as you know; but in any case we have pickets there and scouts further down the roads to warn them. We have troops on those hills over there to the east. Every possible approach to Dibra is guarded. We shall get at least two hours' warning of an attack.'

I started to shrug my shoulders but was interrupted in mid-shrug. A spatter of bullets struck the walls of a neighbouring house as a machine-gun opened up from the eastern hills. The room emptied in a flash; Haxhi Lleshi and Ersat seized their tommy-guns and ran into the street followed by their guards. Riddell, Lis, and I stood in the doorway scanning the hills through our glasses. The sound of small-arms fire grew in intensity, a few bullets whistled over our heads or smacked against the walls and roofs of neighbouring houses, but the enemy was still invisible to us. From the direction of the barracks a pack gun began firing—one of two that the Partisans had captured from the Italians.

"While we were watching the hills Tomaso arrived with Riddell's Albanian servant, Myftar, and the horses and mules. I ordered Gregson Allcott to start for Peshkopijë as soon as the mules were loaded, leaving Myftar at the hotel to guard our horses. Then with Riddell and Lis I walked to the barracks to see Haxhi Lleshi.

Forcing our way through the crowd of armed Partisans and Italians who were standing round the doorway, we climbed to the third floor room which was Haxhi Lleshi's headquarters. We found him with Ersat and a mob of Partisan and Italian officers, commissars and guards, all of whom had plenty to say and were saying it volubly. I sat down by an open window which faced towards the sound of the fighting while Riddell, having with difficulty attracted Haxhi Lleshi's attention, explained to him the plan on which the three of us had agreed.

Riddell wanted me to go at once to Fiqri Dine and his Committee and urge them to fulfil their undertaking to help the Partisans with every available man; meanwhile he himself would rally his friends among the independent chieftains like Cen Elezi, Helmi Beg Karasani and Ramadan Kolloshi. With our combined forces we would attack and occupy the hills to the east of Dibra, cutting off Xhem Gostivari's retreat and, we hoped, inflicting on him a decisive defeat. We reckoned to be back with our troops about noon the next day if the Partisans could hold out so long; Lis gallantly volunteered to stay with them. Haxhi Lleshi replied that he could certainly hold out; but at first he refused to accept help from Fiqri Dine, whom he called a 'fascist collaborator'. However, recognizing the absurdity of his position, he at length agreed to Riddell's plan.

Back at the hotel we mounted our horses and, accompanied by Myftar and Shaban, a young French-speaking Partisan, rode northward out of the town. A few bullets came our way, none of them very near; the fighting was still confined to the hills to the east and there seemed no reason to suppose that this attack would be heavier than the last. After an hour we overtook Gregson Allcott and his party approaching the cross-roads of Maqellarë. At the entrance to the village we were accosted by two peasants who had come that morning from Peshkopijë; they warned us that German troops were already there. Soon afterwards we met Fiqri Dine's brother, who told us that Fiqri was in Peshkopijë with Simcox and Faik Shehu, another Dibran chieftain on whose help Riddell was counting. He had heard nothing about the presence of Germans in the town.

On our journey we heard more conflicting reports of German troops ahead of us. If indeed they were there and if they advanced on Dibra from that direction we should look very silly, caught on the road with a string of pack animals. We asked Bungurri and Shaban if they knew of a village off the main road where we could safely hide the mules and our heavy kit; they suggested the house of a friend of Haxhi Lleshi's near the village of Dovollan, which lay between the main road and the Drin, about two miles farther on.

We turned off to the left down a muddy lane and came after half a mile to a handsome house with a huge courtyard, where four Italians were working. The owner of the house willingly agreed to look after our mules, promising to hide them and our kit. We decided to leave Gregson Allcott and Myftar in charge of the animals while the rest of us went on towards Peshkopijë.

It was mid-afternoon when we rejoined the road. The noise of battle had been steadily increasing from the direction of Dibra, with a crescendo of automatic fire from which Riddell claimed he could distinguish the continuous chatter of the new German heavy machine-gun; the sound of artillery was louder and more insistent than could be accounted for by the two light pieces which were all that the Partisans possessed. From the top of a rise we looked back across the plain; I saw a series of flashes on the hills overlooking the town, followed a few seconds later by heavy explosions and puffs of smoke around the barracks; coloured ground flares, marking the positions of forward troops, showed where the German attack, creeping towards the banks of the river, was gradually enveloping the defenders. With the Germans so heavily committed I thought it very doubtful that Haxhi Lleshi would be able to hold Dibra overnight; he must either withdraw across the Drin under cover of darkness or be surrounded and annihilated. Clearly our help would arrive too late to turn the scales now. As we rode on our way there came to my uneasy mind some lines of Housman:

> *Behind, the vats of judgment brewing*
> *Thundered, and thick the brimstone snowed;*
> *He to the hill of his undoing*
> *Pursued his road.*

Poor Bungurri was in tears, wringing his hands and lamenting the destruction of his city and the fate of the women and children exposed to the shells and bullets. We did our best to console him but he would not be comforted. On the road we met groups of peasants who repeated warnings that the Germans were in Peshkopijë, one of them adding that they were on their way to Dibra. We decided to leave our horses at the next village and continue our journey on foot to give ourselves a greater chance of concealment or escape if we ran into trouble.

Before we had time to implement our decision matters were taken out of our hands. In the dusk we came to a bend where the road ran between high banks. As our party turned the corner a band of about a hundred armed men sprang from behind the banks on either side and with swift and silent movements surrounded us. They wore the peasant dress of Dibra—black coats, tight woollen trousers, broad, multi-coloured cummerbunds and fezzes of white felt; each man carried a rifle and bandolier. Their manner was determined but not menacing and they made no move to disarm us; yet, as I wondered whether we were in the hands of friends or enemies I saw Bungurri's ashen face, and my heart sank as I heard him mutter the name Halil Alija.

This chieftain had been mentioned to me by Riddell as one of a pair of 'robber barons' who—some said with Italian help—had risen from poverty to a position of local prominence and wide unpopularity; his partner was a certain Selim Kalloshi, cousin of Riddell's friend, Ramadan Kalloshi, with whom, however, he was at feud. The reasons for their unpopularity were not precisely known to Riddell—there were whispered stories of robbery and abduction—but he had made no response to their previous offers of help, fearing that nobody else in the neighbourhood would work with him if he took them for his allies. It was possible that Riddell's information, coming from prejudiced sources, had maligned them; in any case we could only pray now that they had not taken their rebuff to heart. With no chance either of resistance or of flight we must reconcile ourselves to the will of Providence and the mercy of the robber barons.

Such philosophical detachment came easier to us than to Bungurri. As our captors hustled us up the bank and off the road he gave way to unashamed tears of fright, convinced that they were going to shoot him; in reply to our reassurances, given with more confidence than we could feel, he gasped between his sobs:

'I know, and you don't know! I tell you, they are going to kill me. I am Faik Shehu's nephew and these men have *Hakmarjë* with my uncle!'

Our confidence was not increased by the hysterical behaviour of an ugly-looking fellow who stumped up to Riddell, waving his arms and screaming:

'Why did you never come to see our leaders—the chiefs of the People?'

Suddenly there was a murmur of 'Halil Alija!' and the hubbub died down. A small, sturdy man with a hooked nose and merry, dark eyes set in a fleshy face broke through the throng and, squinting up at us with a cheerful, roguish expression, shook us each warmly by the hand. Through Bungurri he told us that he was glad we had met at last; that we had fallen into the hands of friends, and that this was lucky for us because the Germans were even at this moment coming down the road from Peshkopijë. Now he would have us taken to a safe place while he and his men went on to Dibra to 'fight any Partisans or Germans we can find.' After this masterpiece of ambiguity he bade us an affectionate farewell and detailed a large escort to take us to the house of Selim Kalloshi.

Meekly we went with the escort, partly because we had no choice, partly because in the same village lived Selim's cousin Ramadan, on whose promise we were counting to raise men for the relief or recapture of Dibra. After telling Tomaso and young Shaban not to worry—quite unnecessarily, for they showed no signs of it—Riddell and I planned with them to shoot our way out at a given signal if it should seem likely that we were to be killed or handed over to the Germans.

Leading our horses we struggled for an hour across difficult country intersected with streams and gullies, until we saw the lights of Peshkopijë on a hillside ahead of us. For a moment I feared we were to be taken there; but our guides turned away to the left and led us over open country to a hamlet where we stopped for a drink of water. When we moved on we found that all but four of our escort had vanished; the prospect of murder or betrayal receded.

When we halted again Bungurri announced that we had reached the village of Helmi Beg Karasani, the chieftain whom Riddell and I had saved from a Partisan firing squad; but when we asked to be taken to his house our guards angrily refused, threatening to prevent us by force from going there. Irritated beyond distraction by worry and fatigue Riddell and I drew our pistols, swearing to shoot our way through them if necessary; their anger gave way to uncertainty but they begged us not to delay, pleading that they did not know the way to Helmi's house.

'That,' I shouted, 'is something we can easily find out. We will knock at the next door and ask.'

We knocked for nearly five minutes without answer. Then a shutter was slammed back; there was an orange flash, a deafening report and a bullet hummed past us into the darkness. After a moment's frightened silence Bungurri, Shaban and our guards broke out in angry complaint, apparently to some effect for the door was opened and an old man stood glowering at us, an ancient Turkish rifle in his hands. He lowered his gun, explaining none too graciously that he had thought we were bandits; he told us that Helmi Beg had left the village and added that it would be as well if we did the same.

Some time after midnight we reached the village where the Kalloshi cousins lived in mutual hostility. Standing in the little square in front of the mosque we began a bitter argument with our guards: we demanded to be taken to Ramadan but they answered that they could not go to his house, being at feud with him; nor would they accept our suggestion that we go by ourselves. They had the strictest orders to take us to Selim and to nobody else. When the quarrel was at its height their leader suddenly cocked his rifle and covered us. Provoked to a childish display of temper I dropped my horse's reins and ran at him, flourishing my riding crop. If I had struck him he would have shot me. Fortunately both Bungurri and Shaban intervened to tell us that we should be gravely offending against the custom of the district if we went to Ramadan; Halil Alija's men had brought us here safely, and we should be disgracing them if we left them now to go to his enemy.

This matter was settled by the appearance of Selim himself, pulled from his bed by the news of our arrival. He looked old and sick and limped heavily from a recent bullet wound received in battle against the Partisans; but his charm and friendliness calmed our seething tempers as he promised that we should see his cousin tomorrow. Even Bungurri had lost his former fear. We were taken to Selim's stronghold, a tall stone keep, well loop-holed for defence but too bare and grim for comfort; it was two o'clock when we lay down on the floor of the guest-room to sleep.

After four hours' sleep we were awakened with a breakfast of warm sweetened milk, bread, and goat's cheese; our host apologized that the milk was from a cow and not, as was usual, from a sheep. Having given us directions to find Ramadan's house, because his own men could not accompany us there, Selim bade us an affectionate farewell, gave us his besa—his pledge of friendship—and assured us that we should always find a safe refuge in his house.

Ramadan's home was quite different in appearance and atmosphere from his cousin's. It consisted of two long, low, white buildings, clean-looking and well designed, set in a spacious courtyard surrounded by a white wall; over the door of one building, the guest-house, hung a shield bearing the emblem of Albania—the black double eagle of Skanderbeg on a red background. Ramadan himself, a grave, dark, delicately-featured young man, led us inside to a cheerful and comfortable room with clean, white walls, furnished with brightly coloured rugs and cushions.

He was overjoyed to see us and laughed at our abduction by his cousin, for whom he seemed to feel contempt rather than enmity; but he warned us to put no trust in him. The Germans, he went on to tell us, were in Peshkopijë and Dibra; Haxhi Lleshi had withdrawn his men safely across the Drin in darkness, and Lis was with him. Simcox and Faik Shehu had gone to Cen Elezi's house in the hills at Sllovë, north of Peshkopijë. Ramadan suggested that we follow them and establish a new headquarters there; the house was comparatively secluded, and there was a suitable dropping ground near by. We agreed readily; Cen's house seemed an ideal base both for Riddell's operations against the Germans and for my expedition to Macedonia. Having dispatched messengers to bring Gregson Allcott and the mules to Sllovë, Ramadan made preparations to conduct us there himself.

In the early afternoon we set off across the plain with an escort of nearly a hundred men—Ramadan, Riddell, and I on horseback, the rest on foot; our numbers were swollen on the way as more of Ramadan's followers flocked to us from the countryside. He had wisely sent scouts ahead and detailed strong flanking parties to guard against surprise from prowling German patrols. However, the only sign of the enemy was a solitary Me 109 which flew over us very low and circled several times, apparently reconnoitring Kastriotë aerodrome. It was a bright autumn day with a fresh wind from the south-east and small, fleecy clouds in a pale blue sky; the disappointment and irritations of yesterday faded as I gazed across the brown fields to the majestic range of blue mountains that marked the old Jugoslav frontier.

After two hours we left the plain and climbed high into the hills. At dusk we came to a crest where a great valley lay spread before us, falling steeply to a river bed beyond which rose a formidable wall of mountains. Two hundred yards below the crest we halted at a large square stone house where we were greeted by Cen Elezi's brother, Xhetan; there we left Ramadan to spend the night. Xhetan apologized for not accompanying us to Cen's house but he showed us where it lay, only three hundred yards further down; although brothers and neighbours, Xhetan and Cen were not on speaking terms.

After crossing two fields and an orchard we entered a long, narrow yard covered by a trellis, where we were welcomed by a tall and sturdy man of about thirty who introduced himself as Cen's son, Xhelal; with him was Tony Simcox. I was touched by the obvious relief with which Simcox hailed Riddell's arrival; he had believed us dead or prisoners of the Germans in Dibra. Simcox himself had barely escaped from Peshkopijë, climbing the hills a few hundred yards away as the first Germans entered the streets. Warned by Fiqri Dine of their approach he had lingered to organize the defence of the town in the mistaken belief that the people would fight; on the contrary, it seemed that they had lined the streets to welcome the invaders. He had come straight here with Corporal Davis, the wireless operator; they had brought their wireless set but were obliged to leave everything else behind. In Dibra, we subsequently heard, the Germans had received a similar ovation; disgusted with the behaviour of the Partisans and grateful to the power that had united them with their kin in Albania, the Dibrans had turned their backs on the Allied cause.

Xhelal led us inside and up a narrow staircase to the guest-room, where his father was awaiting us. Cen Elezi was a thin, fierce-looking old man with white hair, bright blue eyes and a querulous, arrogant manner; his vigorous personality was reinforced by qualities of initiative and courage for which I was soon to be thankful. With him in the room were three more of his sons: Islam, tall, dark and cheerful; Gani, silent and morose, and a boy whose name I never learned. All were dominated by their father, whom they treated with a deep respect noticeably tinged with fear. 'You must understand' Xhelal confided to me, 'that in the mountains we follow a patriarchial rule of life.' The remaining guests were Faik Shehu and Corporal Davis, a cheerful youth whose fragile appearance concealed remarkable strength and resilience.

Removing our boots we settled ourselves cross-legged on the floor around the hearth while Xhelal, deputizing for his father, rolled cigarettes of fine Skopjë tobacco and tossed one to each of us in turn; Cen produced from inside his cummerbund a long cigarette-holder of chased silver with a large nicotine-stained bulb of amber for a mouth-piece. Our eyes smarted in the smoke that filled the room from the open fireplace, for the few slit-like windows gave little ventilation.

We were saved the usual difficulties of language because the three eldest sons spoke good English, having studied at the American College in Tiranë under the famous Harry T. Fulz. Unfortunately the conversation deteriorated into a prolonged dispute between Cen and Riddell over the deployment of the Elezi forces against the Germans, culminating in a preposterous demand by Cen that the British should recognize him officially as 'the only anti-German military commander in Dibra,' and should undertake to deal with nobody in the area except through him. I took no part in the discussion and was glad when the arrival of raki relieved the tension. Although Cen did not drink, the conviviality seemed to mellow him and he agreed to call up his men, evacuate his family and turn his house into a military headquarters.

No Colours or Crest

After the raki a splendid meal was served, for our hosts had killed a sheep in our honour. The food was placed on an enormous circular wooden table, about six inches off the floor, around which we disposed ourselves with what comfort we could manage; according to custom Cen and his sons would not sit down to eat until we had finished. We all ate out of the same dish, using our fingers for the meat and rice, and spoons for the gravy and vegetables. Riddell, as the senior, was obliged to take the sheep's head to dissect as best he could. It was the custom for the host to give one of the eyes to an especially favoured guest; only by feigning a religious scruple could this delicacy be refused without discourtesy. A bowl of milk washed down the meal, after which we were brought a basin of hot water and a towel.

Xhelal showed great interest in my Macedonian plans. He had already sent for his kinsman and neighbour, Zenel Lita, who had many friends around Tetovo and Gostivar and who would himself accompany me on my journey there; he should arrive at Sllovë tomorrow. Xhelal stressed the many and grave dangers of the enterprise. 'And so', he concluded with a charming smile, 'you must be sure to give him a good present of money.'

Riddell and Simcox left the next morning with Faik Shehu and Ramadan Kalloshi to begin operations against the Dibra-Peshkopijë road, leaving me to await the arrival of Zenel Lita. While Davis made several unsuccessful attempts to get through to Cairo on the wireless I strolled outside the house, returning before lunch to share a flask of excellent Prizren slivovic with him and Xhelal.

Although larger than most houses in the Albanian highlands the home of Cen Elezi was built on a plan common to nearly all of them. Set in a walled courtyard, whose main entrance was barred by a stout timber gate, it commanded a wide field of fire in three directions; only on the southern side was it overlooked by the hills we had crossed the day before. The building consisted of two storeys, of which the ground floor was taken up by animals, fodder and women. We seldom saw and never spoke to the women. The top floor contained the men's sleeping quarters and the guest-room, which in every house was the largest and most important room—the only room a guest would normally see. There were no bathrooms in the mountains; the lavatory was usually a narrow hole in the planks of a tiny penthouse that projected over a yard in which fed poultry and, in the Catholic country, pigs.

These houses contained no furniture; the only concessions to comfort by day or night were cushions, rugs, mattresses, and quilts. Even the family valuables were usually stored in one wooden chest. Such simplicity was in part a legacy from the nomad instincts of the Turks; Sir Charles Eliot, describing a Turkish gentleman's house in the last century, wrote that it contained no more furniture than could be carried off at a moment's notice on a wagon into Asia. But it derived also from the perpetual insecurity of life in the mountains, especially on the frontiers; there were very few families whose houses had not been burnt at least once this century by Turks, Serbs, Greeks, Austrians, Germans, Italians, or fellow Albanians.

In the afternoon Gregson Allcott appeared, so exhausted that he could barely stand. His opening words to me were a severe shock:

'I'm sorry to report, sir, the loss of the rest of "Stepmother".'

At eight o'clock that morning, while he was crossing the plain with Ramadan Kalloshi's guide and our mules, a German patrol had spotted them and given chase; he naturally had to abandon the mules and flee. That was only the start of his troubles; no sooner had he and the guide shaken off their pursuers than they ran into another patrol. For four hours they were on the run, almost without rest and continually under fire from parties of roaming Germans. They had reached the safety of the hills at last, but Gregson had escaped with only the clothes on his back.

We were now in a serious plight for stores and money; I could not borrow from Riddell because he had lost nearly everything in Peshkopijë, and it would probably be a week or more before we could hope to receive a supply drop. I had a hundred gold sovereigns in my money belt, but after my talk with Xhelal I could not be sure how long this would last me in Macedonia. My Welgun was lost with the mules, leaving me with my pistol and only one magazine. I prayed that we should be allowed a little peace to replenish our stores.

I was therefore disturbed to hear later in the evening that a force of Germans from Peshkopijë had arrived at a village only two hours' march from Sllovë. About the same time Faik Shehu and Simcox returned, the latter in a black rage because Faik had refused at the last moment to send his men into action; however, he cheered up when he heard this latest piece of news and left again almost immediately with fifty of Faik's men on a reconnaissance towards the village where the Germans were supposed to be. He expected to be back in the morning.

At eight o'clock Zenel Lita arrived, a stocky little man whose appearance and manner reminded me of a friendly badger. He seemed pleased with the idea of accompanying me to Macedonia and suggested that he and I leave the next morning for his house across the valley, where we could plan the journey in detail. I packed a small haversack with a change of shirt and underclothes, socks, washing things, a few candles, and a pocket edition of *War and Peace* bought in London and still unopened.

While we were talking a sudden fusillade of shots brought us to our feet reaching for our guns; it proved to be a wedding in the village, which the guests were celebrating in traditional style with a *feu-de-joie*. When the excitement had died down Zenel, who was said to have the gift of second sight, tried to tell us the future from a sheep's bone—a method I never saw before or since; after a while he looked around with a grin and announced:

'I see a battle.'

I was dreaming that I was at an Investiture at Buckingham Palace, about to be made a Dame of the British Empire in recognition of outstanding services to Albanian agriculture; as I knelt to receive the Accolade I felt a touch on my shoulder and awoke to find the youngest Elezi bending over me:

'Your binoculars please, Mr. Major,' he whispered. 'There are some men coming over the hill.'

He took them off the floor beside me and hurried out of the room;

I turned over, still half asleep. Before I had time to drop off again Xhelal and Gani appeared in the doorway.

'Mr. Major, get up quickly! The Germans are here!'

For a moment I thought they were joking; but a volley of shots and the sound of bullets striking the wall outside soon jerked me to my feet. Rousing Allcott and Davis I pulled on my field boots without pausing to buckle them, struggled into my battle-dress blouse, fastened my belt and pistol and threw my haversack over my shoulder, blessing the impulse that had made me pack it the night before. Down below we saw Cen, holding a rifle in one hand and pointing with the other towards the back of the house; bullets were smacking into the courtyard all round us from the hills above, but no one was attempting to return the fire or improvise a defence. The surprise was so complete, I concluded, that our only chance lay in headlong flight. I was confirmed in my belief a moment later by Xhelal's shout:

'Follow me, Mr. Major! Quickly, this way!'

'Where's Tomaso?' I demanded.

'He is coming with my father. Please, Mr. Major, hurry!'

At that moment I caught sight of Tomaso; shouting to him to follow, I dived after Xhelal and Zenel, who were disappearing with the two N.C.O.s through a small postern in the wall. Ahead of us lay open ground sloping to a narrow, bushy ravine which seemed to offer the best hope of cover. As we came out of the gate we were challenged from both sides and I saw figures in grey uniform running towards us with pointed tommy-guns; Zenel fired his rifle from the hip and I took two running shots with my pistol at the nearest German; but I did not stop to watch the effect. From both directions bullets whistled past our ears or spattered on the rocks all round us; at such short range it seemed inevitable that one of us should be hit. Davis, I suddenly noticed with astonished admiration, was struggling to carry the heavy wireless set; I shouted to him to ditch it and save himself, but at that moment he tripped and fell headlong, smashing the set against a rock. He scrambled to his feet unhurt and threw the useless equipment into a bush.

The distance to the ravine could not have been more than two hundred yards; but it seemed like a mile as I laboured over the broken ground with pounding heart, dry throat and bursting lungs. At last I reached the edge of the gully and, throwing myself down among the bushes by a small stream, looked around for my companions. Allcott and Davis were beside me, panting but unharmed; Zenel was crouched a few yards away, smiling to himself like a badger that has just dodged the dachshunds; but of Xhelal there was no sign. Then I heard him shouting up on the right and, peering over the edge of the ravine, saw him waving to us to join him.

As we broke cover and ran after him our pursuers caught sight of us and opened fire, this time with a machine guns as well as Schmeizers. Plunging down the hill amid the flying bullets I was pulled up by a stout wooden fence beyond which was a tangle of brambles; with an athletic prowess that I have never achieved before or since I vaulted clean over the fence but stumbled on the other side and landed on my face in the brambles; sobbing with rage and fear I scrambled to my knees and forced my way through, in the manner of a swimmer doing the breast stroke. Davis cleared both obstacles in his stride, but Allcott fell over the fence and, caught by his belt, hung upside down for a few seconds before toppling on his head in the bushes. A minute later we were all bunched with Xhelal in the safety of a piece of dead ground. Together we hurried down towards the river valley.

We were joined by the youngest Elezi and two retainers, but there was no sign of Cen, his other sons or Tomaso; they must have been trapped in the courtyard, unable to break out before the German cordon closed. The house was no longer in sight, but from above us came the rapid, intermittent firing of machine-guns interjected with sharp explosions that sounded like mortar bombs. Xhelal would not hear of our turning back. He was bound by his father's orders and the traditional law of hospitality to escort us to safety; if any thing were to happen to us now he and all his clan would be disgraced. Zenel supported him and I yielded; in any case it was too late to help in the defence. But I felt bitterly ashamed each time Xhelal stopped to look backward, the tears running freely down his face.

Crossing a wide river bed at the bottom of the valley, we began a difficult climb by a narrow track hewn almost perpendicular in the rocky face of the cliff. Heavy rain began to fall, soaking us within a few minutes and almost blinding us as we struggled upwards in the teeth of a fierce storm; the rolling thunder and vivid lightning flashes added their infernal accompaniment to this drama of battle and disaster.

After half an hour we halted at a small hamlet on the cliff top which commanded a view across the valley; shivering and dispirited we sat in one of the doorways and surveyed the ruin of our recent sanctuary. Cen's house and his brother Xhetan's above it were in flames; otherwise the fighting seemed to have died down except for isolated bursts of machine-gun fire and a few mortar bombs exploding in the ravine we had recently traversed. The rain had ceased; but the storm clouds still hung low over the valley. The harsh, cold colours of that rain-washed landscape glowed luminous and steely in the lambent light. A pillar of smoke, dirty white and grey-brown, hung above the burning houses, blending into the sombre blackness of the sky. Lightning flickered on the mountain tops and thunder echoed menacingly along the dark ravines and watercourses. I seemed to be staring at some nightmare canvas of El Greco—a far ghastlier storm than the one he painted over Toledo.

I could not imagine how we had been so easily taken by surprise. But Xhelal explained that, counting on protection or at least warning from Simcox's patrol, he had not troubled to post any guards; so that the Germans were able to approach within a hundred yards of the house before the alarm was given. Much later I learned that the Germans had come by a different path from the one Simcox had taken, and Simcox knew nothing of our danger until he heard the sound of fighting; by the time he arrived the battle was over.

Remembering Shtyllë I reflected bitterly how much more dangerous and demoralizing were the German methods of pursuit than the Italian. The Germans were not afraid to penetrate into the hills with only a company of infantry and a few mortars; against such police tactics, directed with skill and vigour, we could take few effective precautions.

Gani Elezi, who joined us soon after midday, relieved some of our anxiety with the news that his father and Islam had shot their way through the enemy to safety; Cen had two bullet wounds—in the shoulder and wrist—but was not in serious danger. But Gani brought me bitter news as well: Tomaso was dead, shot through the heart at point-blank range as he ran out after us.

Both Gani and Xhelal swore that Halil Alija, despite the *besa* he had pledged us, had accompanied the Germans to Sllovë with a large force of his own men and some two hundred Dibrans. After looting and burning the Elezi houses the Germans had rounded up a group of villagers and their wives and children, lined them against the wall of the school and massacred them with machine-guns. This piece of *furchtbarkeit* seemed to me as stupid as it was sickening; it must have shocked the Germans' own allies, for even in their blood-feuds the Albanians would respect the lives of women and children.

We were now within the borders of Luma, the territory of the powerful Muharrem Bajraktar, one of the most important of all the Gheg chieftains. Zenel told me that Allcott, Davis and I must lie low for a few days because the Germans were sure to search the countryside for us; at this moment their patrols were probably on our track. His guides would take us to a hide-out in the mountains to the north, where we must remain until he sent for us. Before we parted he took pains to impress on me that we must on no account let it be known that we carried gold.

Accompanied by two grim and silent tribesmen we walked for three and a half hours along an easy track following the line of beech-covered heights above the Black Drin. We met nobody; the distant calls of herdsmen were the only signs of human life in these wild, dark, precipitous mountains. In the evening we came to a small stone hut about fifty yards below the path, beside a ravine that ran steeply down to the deep river gorge. An old, emaciated shepherd met us in the doorway and bowed us into a bare and windowless room dimly lit by an oil lamp, where three blankets were spread on the floor for our beds. Without a word our guides departed.

We hid in the hut four days, getting up each morning an hour before dawn to take cover in the ravine until an hour after sunrise. Those were the hours of danger, when a German patrol might surprise us; at other times—or so we understood the shepherd to say—there were watchers who would warn us of the enemy's approach. It was said that the Germans never moved through the mountains by night; but I slept uneasily, jerking into wakefulness whenever a dog barked in the distance. Years afterwards that sound would still wake me from the deepest slumber.

We ate once a day, grateful for the coarse maize bread and skimmed milk that was all our host could offer us. Undismayed either by the danger or the discomfort of our situation Allcott and Davis joked or slept away the daytime hours. I read *War and Peace* by the light of a candle; absorbed in the problems of Pierre and Natasha I was able for a while to forget my own.

IX

THE MARCHES OF KOSSOVO

On the morning of 24th November our two guides returned to conduct us to Zenel. We retraced our steps along the track we had used five days before, past the hamlet from which we had watched the burning of the Elezi house to a village two hours' journey further east, beneath the black and snow-crowned mass of Mount Korab.

We found Zenel with Cen Elezi and his sons. Ceil greeted me with surprising cordiality seeing that I was largely responsible for his misfortunes; he looked very frail, sitting in a corner swathed in bandages, but his wounds were healing well under the usual local treatment, which was to plug the bullet-holes with goat's cheese. I asked Xhelal if they had any plans for the immediate future.

'As soon as my father is well,' he replied, 'we shall go to another part of Drin and raise men against the Germans.' Zenel's enquiries had convinced him that it would be folly for us to attempt a reconnaissance of Macedonia at the present; the Germans were on the alert and a great deal of time would be needed to prepare for such a journey. In the meantime he suggested that I accompany him to his brother-in-law, Muharrem Bajraktar, after which I might be able to visit Gjakovë, Prizren and other parts of Kossovo.

This plan suited me very well; the Brigadier had asked me for a report on Muharrem Bajraktar. Unquestionably the most powerful chieftain in eastern Albania he could, I had heard, raise at least a thousand fighting men from his own territory of Luma, and could probably call on as many more from his allies in Mirdita and the mountains further north; moreover, he was reported to have influential friends in Kossovo and Macedonia and to be in touch with Mihailović in Jugoslavia.

I was relieved to hear that Riddell and Simcox were safe with Ramadan Kalloshi somewhere near Peshkopijë; the Elezis promised to send Davis to join them as soon as possible. I decided to leave Gregson Allcott in their care with instructions to carry my report on the recent fighting to the Brigadier at Biza as soon as he could cross the Drin; although I was reluctant to lose him it seemed unlikely that I should need a paramilitary specialist in the immediate future.

Zenel and I started on our journey in the freezing blackness before dawn on 26th November; with us came his two cousins, Malik and Ismail Lita. Over my battle-dress I wore an old green Italian army greatcoat, with a tattered pair of puttees wound round my field boots; Zenel intended to pass

No Colours or Crest

me off to strangers as an Italian deserter seeking work with Muharrem Bajraktar. At the shepherd's hut where I had lain in hiding we halted for refreshment, and I was at last allowed to reward the old man for his kindness; even so, I could barely persuade him to accept the ten sovereigns which I pressed upon him. Afterwards we climbed steeply among woods of stunted mountain oak; through gaps in the forest we caught occasional glimpses of the Drin, brown and swollen, racing between the smooth granite walls of its narrow gorge far below on our left. The sky was overcast and heavy with the threat of rain, deadening the colours of earth and rocks and dulling the yellow of the maize stubble in the miserable scattered fields roughly terraced out of the stony mountain-side.

In the middle of the afternoon we stopped again, at a long, low, white house whose handsome, well-kept appearance contrasted strangely with the savagery of the surrounding hills; it belonged to Myftar Ahmedi, a vassal and close friend of Muharrem Bajraktar. Myftar, a lean, wiry man in early middle age with a mop of black hair and flashing, humourous eyes, received us joyfully and led us into a spacious guest-room with tall arched windows and clean, white-washed walls on which hung a horse's bridle, an old rapier, and an eighteenth century bayonet. We drank glasses of warm sweetened milk and smoked Bulgarian cigarettes with long, gilt cardboard mouthpieces while Myftar sent a messenger to tell Muharrem Bajraktar of our approach.

From this house we climbed through more oak woods until we came at evening to a crest that overlooked a broad valley sloping down towards the Black Drin; below us lay the village of Ymishtë, beyond it the fortress home of Muharrem. Hurrying through the village we came to a group of buildings surrounded by a high stone wall; on the battlements of the tower above the main gateway stood two armed sentries, who shouted the news of our arrival to someone in the court-yard below. As we entered I saw that all but two of the buildings had been gutted by fire. Before I had time to observe more a quiet voice greeted me in English, and I turned to see a small man with an olive complexion, a thin moustache and a wisp of beard; extending a frail and yellow hand with an ugly scar on the wrist he introduced himself as Muharrem's brother, Bairam. Leading the way across the courtyard he pointed to the gutted buildings and explained that they were the work of an Italian punitive expedition, as also was the bullet wound in his wrist.

Climbing a flight of stone steps we found ourselves in a dark, smoky room dimly lit by a small fire at one end; from the floor beside it a stocky figure rose and welcomed us with a stiff bow. I replied with the customary greeting of '*tungjatjeta*!' and he motioned me to a seat on the floor opposite him. He addressed me in French with short, jerky sentences uttered in a quiet, squeaky voice. When I mentioned my visit to Kossovo he pursed his lips and rose:

'Let us go upstairs where we can talk alone,' he ordered.

No Colours or Crest

I followed him up a broad stone staircase into a spacious, well-lit room with a large open fireplace flanked by scarlet silk cushions, on which we sat facing one another. For the first time I was able to see him clearly, a short, middle-aged man with a ruddy, fleshy face, iron-grey hair and moustache, and small, very bright eyes. His manner was friendly if a trifle condescending, as befitted a powerful chieftain and experienced politician when talking with an ignorant and ingenuous young stranger.

I listened with respect, for I knew that he had played an important part in recent Albanian history and that he could be of great value to us in the future. Originally one of Zog's allies in the revolution of 1924 he had subsequently plotted to overthrow him and had been forced to flee the country. After a period of exile in Belgrade, Vienna and Paris he had returned to his house in Luma when the Italians occupied Albania in 1939; but he had stoutly refused to tolerate Italian rule in his own territory. After the surrender of Italy he had raised his tribesmen to occupy the important town of Kukës on the Scutari-Prizren road, at the confluence of the Black and the White Drin; within a few days, however, a strong German counter-attack had driven him into the hills.

He told me that the Germans had sent troops against him a week ago, shooting up some of his villages in what seemed a curiously inept attempt to persuade him to accept office in the puppet Tiranë government; he had spurned collaboration but had been sufficiently frightened to come to an agreement whereby he would not engage in hostilities against the Germans or allow his territory to be used as a base for operations against them, provided they did not again invade Luma. He was frankly terrified of their power and emphasized that we must not think of undertaking any action against them during the winter, but must build up our strength until the spring, when, he blandly supposed, an Allied invasion would drive them out.

His plans for the future, in contrast to his present fears, were coloured by a strange *folie de grandeur* which convinced him that he could unite the Balkan peoples in a federation under his leadership, to counter what he described as the twin dangers of Russian domination and Pan-Slav Imperialism; these two phrases recurred constantly in his talk during the evening. He admitted that he had received emissaries from Mihailović, who had proposed that they should join forces against the Partisans; negotiations, however, had foundered on the Kossovo question.

On the subject of my journey to Kossovo he was practical if not encouraging. At first he begged me to abandon the project, arguing that the area was overrun with German spies, that the Drin would be impassable and that, in any case, I could just as well study the Kossovo situation from his house. But when I persisted he promised to take me in person to his brother-in-law, Mehmet Ali, Bajraktar of Hass, the territory north of Kukës; there they would put me in touch with Hasan Beg Kryeziu, the influential Gjakovë landowner who had been one of the leaders of the abortive rising in 1941.

No Colours or Crest

This was splendid news; Hasan Beg's had been the first of the names mentioned to me as valuable contacts in Kossovo during my Tirana visit, and I knew that he stood well with both nationalists and L.N.C. For the first time since the disaster at Sllovë I felt cheerful and confident; nor was I dismayed by Muharrem's frequent pauses in the conversation to look at me, shake his head sorrowfully and exclaim: '*J'ai beaucoup de peur pour vous!*'

Before dinner we were joined by Zenel and his cousins and by Muharrem's son Ibrahim, a solemn but friendly youth of twenty-two who brought us a bottle of slivovic; while we drank Muharrem sipped a cup of coffee and treated me to a dissertation on the perils of alcohol. At nine o'clock, after a very good meal, a mattress and quilts were spread for me on the floor and I was left alone to sleep.

Zenel and his cousins returned to their homes the next day; I was very sorry to see them go, remembering the risks they had taken to help me at a time when my fortunes were at their nadir. I spent the day resting and listening to Muharrem's account of Albanian history since the time of Philip of Macedon—a subject on which he claimed to have exhausted the authorities. He maintained that the Albanian language was still close to that of Philip and Alexander the Great; which of course I was in no position to dispute.

Muharrem and I left Ymishtë on Sunday morning, 28th November, accompanied by Myftar Ahmedi and an escort of twelve stalwart tribesmen dressed in short jackets and white woollen jodhpurs embroidered in black. Muharrem, wrapped in a long, dark blue cloak with a flat skull-cap of black silk on his head, bestrode a fine chestnut horse captured from the Italians; Myftar rode a grey cob, and I was mounted on a big grey mare which he had lent me for the journey. In addition to their rifles our escort carried a Fiat light machine-gun—picked up in Kukës, Muharrem explained with the complacent air of a collector exhibiting a fine piece of Chippendale.

We rode slowly up a steep, rough track climbing between high, jagged peaks to a broad plateau, which we skirted, following a line of hills along its eastern edge. Below us on our left was a disused flying field pitted with craters; beyond, on a hill across the river, was the ruined castle of the ancient Bajraktars of Tej Drinit. Muharrem evidently put little faith in his pact with the Germans, for he moved at a slow and cautious pace, throwing out scouts to front and flanks to watch for enemy patrols. At each village and hamlet the people turned out to give us a tumultuous welcome, saluting Muharrem with obvious affection and deep respect as 'Bajraktar'; as well as the title of a northern chief, Bajraktar was also the surname of Muharrem's family, deriving from some incident of medieval history.

We halted for two hours at the village of Shtiqën beneath the eight thousand foot peak of Mount Gjalicë. After a lunch of eggs fried in batter, followed by cheese and sour milk we descended towards the gorge of the

Luma, skirting the steep side of the mountain. Muharrem began to show signs of nervousness, shouting angrily at his men when-ever they bunched together, which was frequently; he explained that there was a German post a mile downstream from the ford. The Luma flowed swiftly between wide banks of shingle overhung by wooded cliffs down which we made our way with difficulty on foot, leading our horses. At the bottom we remounted and, led by Muharrem, trotted across the shingle into the river. Our mounts floundered in the deep and swirling water and Muharrem's was almost swept away in mid-stream; I felt that we should have done better to imitate the Tartars, who let themselves be ferried across rivers clinging to the tails of their swimming horses.

In the late afternoon we found ourselves on the top of the heights overlooking the town of Kukës, five miles to the west, where the Black Drin from Lake Ohrid joins the White Drin from Kossovo. Turning north-east we traversed open, rolling hillsides sloping towards the valley of the White Drin, and at dusk we came to a village where Muharrem announced that we should spend the night; the river ran beside the Prizren-Scutari road, and he wished his men to make a thorough reconnaissance of the crossing before we attempted it.

Our host, Rashid, killed a sheep in our honour, serving me to my disgust and embarrassment with the head and eye; before dinner I overheard Muharrem tell his men to find me some raki, but this they were unable to do. I was sufficiently stimulated, however, by listening to his interpretation of Albania's territorial claims—what he called the frontiers of an 'ethnical Albania'; they seemed to include most of the Balkan peninsula between Salonika and the Adriatic, between the Gulf of Corinth and the northern boundary of Montenegro.

In the morning Muharrem's precautions of the previous day proved justified, for we heard that a German patrol had visited Shtiqën soon after we had left; they had asked for information about 'British officers and Communists'.

At noon we sent a small party to watch the ferry over the White Drin; at half-past two we started ourselves. Moving at a leisurely pace, with frequent halts at houses on the way, we reached a grassy knoll above the valley as the sun was sinking behind the western mountains, splashing the snow-topped heights across the river with bars of delicate rose which faded while we watched to a dead and toneless white.

We paused while Muharrem gave instructions to his scouts. When they had gone he said to me:

'If anything happens while we are crossing the road, come back with me. If we are separated, see that you come back by the same route.'

We followed a steep spiral path down the hillside and came out of the trees suddenly onto an open grass bank. A few yards below us ran the road, a broad grass verge on either side; beyond raced the yellow, swollen river. We handed over our horses to Myftar Ahmedi and two tribesmen, and crouched behind the bank while Muharrem gave a series of orders and I scanned the road for possible cover; finding none I prayed that we should have an undisturbed crossing. The men listened to their orders quietly, but broke into a loud, excited babble as each explained and embellished them to his neighbour. Shouting them down, Muharrem launched into an angry lecture, apparently on the need for keeping silence; then he signed to Myftar and his two companions, who mounted and jogged down the path onto the road. As soon as they reached the tarmac they swung left and galloped for about two hundred yards before turning towards the river.

When they had vanished we followed at the double, leaving two men to cover us with the light machine-gun; we found Myftar and the horses in a clump of willows by the water's edge. From the opposite bank a broad punt was approaching, steered by an oarsman in the bow; it was attached by a pulley to an overhead cable slung across the river and so propelled by the force of the current. As we tried to scramble aboard Muharrem slipped on the muddy bank and slid into the water; I caught his arm and started to pull him out while two of the guards ran to help me, slinging their rifles on their shoulders as they bent to grasp him. In the excitement one of the rifles went off, singeing my face; the report rang down the valley echoing among the rocks on either side.

'If that doesn't bring the Germans upon us,' sighed Muharrem when he was safely on board, 'we can be sure that there are none around.'

Apparently there were none; for we ferried ourselves and the horses across in two journeys without hearing so much as a lorry on the road, although the operation lasted well over half an hour. On the other side we climbed a track up a steep, wooded ravine running towards the crest of the dark mountain mass that formed the northern wall of the valley. After an hour's journey we came to a poor village, whose inhabitants, however, received us hospitably and gave us food and shelter for the night.

We left next morning at ten, after a breakfast of maize bread and milk, and climbed slowly up the face of the mountain through woods of small oaks. The ranks of snowy peaks across the Drin glistened in the sunlight against the clear blue of the sky; the sharp, frosty mountain air brought the blood to our cheeks and put vigour into our limbs. On the road below us a column of horse-drawn artillery moved slowly towards Prizren with a platoon of infantry a few hundred yards ahead of the guns—a splendid target for an ambush.

Shortly before midday we came out upon a bleak plateau covered with coarse grass and studded with outcrops of rock and patches of snow. Above us loomed the squat bulk of Mount Bishtrik like a brown cottage loaf crowned with icing sugar; along the top ran the old Jugoslav frontier.

Shivering in the sudden cold I was glad when we stopped at a miserable hamlet for lunch. We entered the largest of the houses through the stable on the ground floor and climbed a ladder to a surprisingly clean and cheerful guest-room, where a bright fire blazed a welcome. We seated ourselves on a raised dais at one end of the room while the owner, an old man who had known Muharrem when the latter was commanding the gendarmerie in that region, brought us cups of camomile tea and showed us photographs of Muharrem looking very handsome in his uniform at the age of thirty.

When we left after lunch grey clouds were racing low over Bishtrik; on an upper slope of the mountain a splash of sunlight lingered on the grass beside a clump of pines in a lovely contrast of pale golden yellow and dark viridian. In the middle of the afternoon we reached the northern edge of the plateau and looked down upon a deep valley enclosed by high precipitous mountains; a steep, snow-covered track brought us down through thick woods to the head of the valley and the village of Vlahën, home of Mehmet Ali Bajraktar. His high stone tower stood on a mound, which we had barely started to climb when we were halted by a shout from above: a very tall, bent old man in a short black coat, white woollen jodhpurs and conical white skull-cap ran down the slope towards us flinging his arms wide in welcome. He embraced us each in turn, reserving a special hug for Muharrem, who introduced him as Mehmet Ali, the Bajraktar of Hass.

Friendliness and hospitality bubbled from him as he led us up the hill to his house where his son, a tall, dark man of about forty-five, was waiting to conduct us to the guest-room; the son, also known as Mehmet Ali Bajraktar, was married to Muharrem's sister. The old man, who combined the dignified appearance of a patriarch with the hearty manner of an English country squire, took pride in the fact that neither he nor his son could read or write; but he admitted that his grandson could do both, adding regretfully that the boy could even speak a little Italian.

In the guest-room, which contained, besides some fine Persian and Turkish rugs, the unusual feature of a table—although this, we were assured, was scarcely ever used—we were served with rich *mezë* and bottles of smooth but potent raki while father and son entertained us with stories of their embattled history. The old warrior had fought Turk, Montenegrin, Serb, and Italian with impartial vigour and enjoyment. On the last occasion, when they were hunted by the Italians, the whole family had taken refuge with thirty others in a cave in the Catholic country, where they had hidden for three weeks, existing on a little maize bread and water brought them each evening by the villagers.

'That Catholic bread nearly killed me,' chuckled the old man. 'I couldn't chew it with my ancient teeth!'

As the principal guest I must give my assent before the evening meal could be served. To have given it the first time I was asked would have been a grave discourtesy, for there was seldom any conversation after dinner; on this occasion I judged it tactful to delay a while longer than usual, because Muharrem and our hosts had much to discuss with each other and with me. During pauses in our talk an old man sang us harsh mountain threnodies to the accompaniment of the primitive two-stringed *çeteli*, and as a climax to our entertainment old Rasim Domë, the most ancient of Mehmet Ali's retainers, fuddled with the mellow raki, pranced and postured round the room, mouthing ludicrous grimaces from beneath his drooping black moustache, while his companions cheered his buffoonery and the *çeteli* screeched a faster, wilder rhythm.

Young Mehmet Ali told me there was a party of Englishmen at the village of Deg, near the bank of the river Drill, two days' journey to the west. This must be Flight-Lieutenant Hands's mission, which had moved north from Dibra in October. I decided to go straight there from Vlahën to refit myself with money and clothing and regain wireless contact with Cairo and Brigadier Davies; I should also need a properly equipped base from which to make my reconnaissance of Kossovo. I therefore sent word to Hands to expect me within the next few days, as soon as I had seen Hasan Kryeziu, whom Mehmet Ali had already summoned to his house to meet me.

On the evening of 2nd December, two days after our arrival at Vlahën, I was sitting over my raki talking with Muharrem and our hosts and trying to distract my mind from the activities of the colony of lice that had infested my clothes for the last month, when the barking of dogs and a clamour of voices outside announced the approach of strangers. A minute later there was a shout of welcome and a short, chunky man in a knickerbocker suit of grey pepper-and-salt tweed and stout leather gaiters stumped into the room, shook himself like a sheep dog and began to call out greetings in a deep, hearty voice. He extended his hand to me with a stiff bow:

'Kryeziu!' he boomed.

'Kemp!' I replied, coming stiffly to attention as I returned the bow and handshake.

With his white hair, square, heavy-jowled face, bulky figure and bluff good nature he looked like a prosperous farmer, which indeed he was. But I had heard also of his shrewdness, honesty and courage, of his friendship for the British, and of the wide affection and esteem he enjoyed on both sides of the frontier.

It was not until next morning that we were able to discuss the business that had brought us together. Ever since August, when I had heard that there was a chance of my going to Kossovo, I had set myself to study the problem of that disputed territory; I had questioned men of every shade of political opinion, but Hasan Kryeziu was the first Kossovar with whom I had been able to talk and the first person who enjoyed the confidence of nationalists and Partisans alike. Muharrem and Mehmet Ali were manifestly his close friends, and Enver Hoxha himself had told me that he was the 'unofficial president' of the L.N.C. in Gjakovë, whatever that meant. Kryeziu's views, then, should represent those of the great majority of Albanians.

The term Kossovo in its strictest application refers to the plain near Priština in Serbia where the great battle was fought in 1389 between the Serbs and the Ottoman Turks which brought Serbia under Turkish rule for more than four hundred years; more commonly—and in the sense in which I use it—it includes also Mitrovica and the region of Metohija—that is the towns of Peć, Gjakovë and Prizren. As the heart of the medieval Serbian kingdom the Serbs claim that it is indissolubly linked with the history of their nation; for which reason, more than any other, it was included in the frontiers of Jugoslavia. Albania s claims are based on two generally admitted facts: that it is her natural granary, and that the majority of the inhabitants are Albanians—the proportion is between seventy and eighty-five per cent. Jugoslav rule between the two World Wars unfortunately tended to suppress rather than encourage or even tolerate Albanian customs, religion, and language.

My principal task was to explore the chances of forming a resistance movement among Albanians in Kossovo. When I sounded him on the subject Hasan Beg warned me, as I had feared he would, that the majority of Kossovars preferred a German occupation to a Serb; the Axis Powers had at least united them with their fellow Albanians, whereas an Allied victory would, they feared, return them to Jugoslav rule. Therefore, although most believed that the Germans would eventually be beaten, few would risk their lives to help in the process without some combined declaration by the Allied governments, guaranteeing the Kossovars the right to decide their own future by plebiscite. I already knew from a previous interchange of a signals with Cairo that such a declaration was out of the question; instead, I had been advised to 'tactfully avoid the subject of the future of Kossovo'—not a very practical suggestion, as it proved. In my talks with irredentists the future of Kossovo was invariably the first point they raised; nor could I hope to arouse their enthusiasm or allay their fears by a vague reference to the terms of the Atlantic Charter, which was as far as I might commit myself.

Nevertheless, Hasan Beg seemed delighted that a British officer had come to Kossovo, and he promised to do everything in his power to make my visit a success. He emphasized the importance of my keeping in touch with him while I was at Deg, and to this end he detailed one of his retainers, Shpen Zeçeri, to act as courier between us. This Shpen Zeçeri was a tall, very silent man with undistinguished features whom I generally recognized by the way he wore his white 'egg cup' cap tilted well forward on his head. His master described him as exceptionally trustworthy; I certainly found him discreet, for I hardly ever heard him speak and only once saw him smile.

Hasan Beg also promised to arrange for me to visit Gjakovë in the near future; he would put me up in his house and invite a number of influential Kossovars to meet me. Afterwards we could plan a journey further afield. He would send Shpen to me at Deg as soon as he was ready.

Finally, he warned me that the Partisans were most unpopular in Kossovo and their influence was negligible; I should achieve little if I entered the area under their aegis, for they were regarded as agents of Tito, who, like Mihailović, was detested as an instrument of 'Pan-Slav Imperialism'. Coming from the 'unofficial president' of the L.N.C. in Kossovo this warning was not to be ignored.

Snow was falling heavily when I awoke the following day, obscuring the mountain tops, covering the roofs and blanketing the ground. Perhaps it was the weather that made Muharrem more than usually fussy. One of Mehmet Ali's servants arrived from Gjakovë with some shopping I had ordered; Muharrem seized the parcels from him and unwrapped them one by one, throwing the loose contents across the room to me and clucking anxiously as he inspected each item:

'Now look after this, and see you don't lose it!'

When the last parcel was open and I was sitting on the floor beside a pile of matchboxes, packets of cigarettes, candles and other odds and ends he sighed:

'Well! Now you have the things you wanted, but I'm afraid you'll lose them.'

I wondered whether he was thinking of my incompetence or the rapacity of his fellow-countrymen.

On 5th December we separated: Hasan Beg left for Gjakovë, Muharrem for his own territory, and I for Hands's headquarters at Deg. Before we parted Hasan promised to send me a reliable interpreter within a few days; Muharrem lent me one of his escort, Zenel Ahmedi, to act as my servant and bodyguard for as long as I needed him. Zenel's father had been a great warrior in his time and one of Muharrem's closest friends; in the end I was more grateful to Muharrem for this cheerful, loyal and courageous young man than for all his other kindnesses.

The morning was crisp and clear after the previous day's snow as I struck westward down the valley from Vlahën, accompanied by Zenel, Shpen Zeçeri and three of Mehmet Ali's men. At the far end the valley widened into open rolling grassland sloping towards the River Drin, beyond which the mountains of the Catholic country of Jballjë glittered frostily in the sunlight. At noon we met Corporal Brandrick, Hands's paramilitary specialist, with the messenger I had sent from Vlahën four days earlier. They brought with them two horses, a complete change of clothing for me, two tins of English pipe tobacco and a warm letter of welcome from Hands.

At five in the evening we reached a small village, where we decided to spend the night because darkness was already falling. Our escort brought us to a small house belonging to three young friends of theirs; in the tiny, stuffy guest-room there was barely enough space for the seven of us and our three hosts to lie on the floor. I had not been long asleep when I was awakened by the sound of three rifle shots in quick succession; grabbing their weapons Zenel and the others ran outside, to return in a few minutes with the comforting assurance that it was only a tribesman settling accounts with his blood-enemy.

After a small cup of acorn coffee—the usual breakfast in the poorer villages of these mountains—we left the open grasslands for the steep and forested marches of Bityç. At the end of a stiff three-hour climb we found ourselves on a high shoulder of rock overlooking the valley of Deg; behind us to the south-east stretched mile upon mile of shining mountain peaks. Zenel pointed to the horizon where a great mass of grey rock, scored with countless dark watercourses and barred with snow at the summit, swept proudly into the sunlit sky.

'There is Gjalicë of Luma,' he cried, 'and below it lies Shtiqën, my village!'

We walked down through thick beech woods along a track so steep and rough that I feared for the safety of our horses, until we came to a stream that flowed from north to south through the valley to empty itself into the deep ravine of the Drin. Deg stood about half-way down the glen, a few poor dwellings grouped around a small mosque.

Brandrick led us to a white farm-house surrounded by a low wall of brushwood and standing a little way apart from the other buildings; at the entrance stood Hands, a broad grin of welcome on his face.

When I had met him in Egypt in July he had seemed a cheery, self-confident fellow with a trace of brashness in his manner; five months of discomfort and insecurity in the mountains had drained much of his vigour and ebullience, etching deep lines of strain under his eyes and round his mouth. Almost his first words were of trouble.

'Old man, it looks as though you've walked out of one spot of bother straight into another. There's a blow-up expected here any day between the Partisans and the local chiefs.'

He led me up a rickety wooden staircase to a small, ill-lit, and dusty room in the centre of which was an improvised table of boards laid across parachute canisters, with more canisters to serve as seats. In a corner by the tiny window was a wireless set, at which the operator, Sergeant Smith,[1] was finishing a 'sked'; on the dirty floor were four old and greasy mattresses, one of which was for me. There was no other furniture. The remaining room in the house was used as a kitchen and sleeping quarters for the four Italians

---

[1] Not the Sergeant Smith who was with Seymour.

who waited on the Mission. The horses and mules were stabled underneath. The owners of the house had left or been ejected long ago.

Most of the other houses, including the mosque, were occupied by detachments of Partisans, who provided Hands with an inefficient and often troublesome guard. But there were a few villagers left; under the leadership of their *hoxha*, or priest, they maintained a precarious but apparently satisfactory livelihood by looting Hands's stores whenever he received a supply drop and stealing from his headquarters in the intervals; when such methods failed they would come to him and beg.

Their depredations, together with others on a larger, better organized scale by the Partisans who were supposed to help him receive his drops, had left Hands with scarcely enough food and clothing for his own needs. No supplies could be bought locally. Bad weather was holding up the sorties he expected and for which he had prepared a wide and level dropping-ground a few hundred yards below his house, where the valley opened into gently sloping meadows before tumbling into the Drin.

When we had finished tea Hands thrust a piece of paper at me with a sardonic laugh:

'You're dead, old man, in case you don't know it. We had this signal in from Cairo last night, but thought you might like to answer it yourself.'

The message simply said that I had been killed in street fighting in Peshkopijë. I drafted a brief reply:

'Still alive please refrain from wishful thinking.'

A year later I heard details of the rumour from Hare.

'A wounded Partisan turned up in our camp at Biza,' he explained, 'Saying that he had witnessed your death with his own eyes. Major Kemp, he told us, was creeping up a street, close to the wall, with his machine-gun (your Welgun, of course) at the ready; suddenly, round a corner he came face to face with a German, also with his gun at the ready. Both fired simultaneously and both fell dead. The others,' Hare concluded, 'were suitably impressed and sad. I alone knew the story couldn't be true: for one thing, you would never have been wide enough awake to fire at the same time as a German, and for another, your Welgun would certainly have jammed.'[1]

There were some three hundred Partisans grouped in *çetas* between Deg and the valley of the Valbonë about six miles further north; most were from Kossovo but a few had come from the Prefecture of Scutari, which they had made too hot to hold them. All were controlled by a newly formed organization, the 'Kosmet [*Kos*sovo and *Met*ohija] General Staff', under the military command of the renowned guerrilla leader, Fadil Hoxha, who had

---

[1] Brigadier Davies records that while he was a prisoner in Tiranë the Germans showed him photographs of dead bodies in British battle-dress which they alleged to be Riddell's, Simcox's, and my own. *Illyrian Venture* (The Bodley Head), pg. 171.

made a name for himself fighting the Bulgars in Macedonia; the political direction—and the effective power—was in the hands of the Chief Commissar, Mehmet Hoxha—the same man whose suit I had worn in Tiranë and whom I had last seen in Dibra. He in turn received directives from Tito.

The ostensible purpose of their presence was to establish a secure base for the winter; their real objects, according to Hands, were to co-ordinate operations with Tito's Montenegrin Partisans and to clear the frontiers of Montenegro and Kossovo of all 'reactionary elements.' Hands's view of their intentions was shared by most of the local Bajraktars and inhabitants, who regarded the Kosmet with undisguised suspicion and hostility—in which, unfortunately, they included Hands. He had been obliged to move his base twice in the last month under pressure from the chiefs.

It was useless for him to protest that he was only there to help anyone who would cooperate with him against the Germans, because nobody was prepared either to fight the Germans or invite their reprisals by allowing Hands to annoy them; even the Kosmet had rejected his proposals for attacking the Prizren-Scutari road. The local Bajraktars had gone further: after a conference presided over by a certain Mal Shabani the day before my arrival, they issued an ultimatum to the Kosmet and to Hands, either to leave their territory at once or be driven out—if necessary with German help.

If we had to leave Deg it was difficult to see where we could go. Beyond the Drill was Catholic country where the people, if not actively hostile, would certainly not receive us as friends; for they followed the lead of Gjon Marko Gjoni, the Captain of Mirdita and the most powerful chieftain in northern Albania, who was the ally of the Germans. Hands therefore asked me to mediate between himself and Mal Shabani and try to arrange a truce that would at least allow us to remain at Deg; he suggested that I should also have a talk with Mehmet Hoxha. I should find them both in the same village; Mehmet was staying with Salimani, *Bajraktar* of Krasniqi, the mountainous region beyond the Valbonë, and Mal Shabani's house was close by. Salimani was the only chieftain who supported the Partisans; I subsequently learned that he and Mal Shabani had long been at feud.

On 8th December I left for Krasniqi. A six hours' ride over difficult stony tracks brought me to the Valbonë, which I crossed by a flimsy wooden bridge, marvelling at the brilliant turquoise colour of the water pouring over the boulder-strewn river bed and the harsh grandeur of the bare limestone cliffs that frowned above the further bank.

I reached Salimani's house just before dark to find him celebrating the festival of Greater Bairam with Mehmet Hoxha and other officers of the Kosmet—an ironical situation, I thought. The eighty-year-old Bajraktar was the finest looking Albanian I had seen; six foot tall, lean and erect, with a fierce white moustache and silvery hair, he towered like some Homeric hero above the paunchy, puffy-faced Commissar.

No Colours or Crest

The news Mehmet Hoxha gave me was disquieting: a force of six hundred Kossovar mercenaries under Xhafer Deva, the puppet Minister of the Interior, was poised on the frontier, ready to invade Krasniqi and Bityç and drive us into the Drin; of course they might not come this way if Mal Shabani and his friends did not invite them. It was too late for me to do anything that night, but I had better see Mal Shabani in the morning.

While Salimani was out of the room I told Mehmet of my plan to visit Hasan Beg in Gjakovë; he seemed to approve, warned me to be careful of 'fascist agents' and wished me a pleasant visit. I did not mention the matter in front of Salimani because he had a feud with the Kryezius, dating from the 1920s when the eldest Kryeziu, Cena Beg, had invaded Krasniqi with a force of gendarmerie to hunt down his outlawed rival, Bairam Curi. I heard more of this tale later.

After a good sleep in a large four-poster bed, damp with long disuse, I set out with Mehmet to tackle Mal Shabani. Apprised of my coming he was awaiting me with two of his confederates; the three of them eyed me with deep suspicion as Mehmet introduced me. I felt at a disadvantage in being dependent on Mehmet as interpreter and thought it probable that he was using me as a stalking-horse in his game of power politics; but I only realized the extent to which Hands and I were compromised when Mal Shabani, who spoke some Italian, told me bluntly that I was not a British officer but a Russian, because he knew that all British officers had been withdrawn from Albania, and in any case what would they be doing with Communists? It took me the whole morning to convince the three dour chieftains of my *bona fides* but I departed with assurance that they would leave us in peace.

Mehmet Hoxha's report about the six hundred mercenaries proved to be a false alarm, one of many that kept us in a constant state of alert during the next two months. Despite Mal Shabani's promise we were several times asked to remove ourselves from Deg, and on one occasion Mehmet himself advised us to leave the district. Nevertheless, the Partisans remained and so did we; chiefly because, as I have said, we had nowhere else to go.

The next morning, while I was having an uncomfortable bath in one of the canisters that did alternative duty as chairs, Hands came into the room:

'Your interpreter's arrived from Hasan Kryeziu. Scruffy-looking bastard if you ask me.'

The description, though inelegant, was apt. Eles Yusufi was a dark, emaciated, untidy youth with a sallow complexion, shifty eyes and the furtive, apologetic look of an ill-used dog. He spoke little and in a quiet, frightened voice. He had only the sketchiest knowledge of English, but tried to conceal his ignorance by mistranslating what he could not understand. He would have been pathetic if he had been less incompetent and untruthful. Hasan Beg had sent him, I discovered later, because he was sorry for the boy and because there was no one else.

No Colours or Crest

Later in the day I was approached by a young man in a blue uniform tunic, who gave his name as Sadri Dorçë and claimed to have served as an officer in the French Army in 1940; his father, who knew the Kryezius well, had told him to offer his services to me in any confidential capacity. Impressed by his command of French I asked him to stay as an extra interpreter; I felt the need of another to supplement the deficiencies of Eles. He agreed to take up his duties as soon as he had spoken to his father; for, he assured me, he did nothing without his father's approval.

On the evening of 13th December Shpen Zeçeri arrived from Gjakovë with two equally silent companions to escort me to Hasan Beg's house. Next morning I put on a civilian overcoat to hide my battle-dress and changed my green beret for a flat Bulgar fez of black lamb's wool. Our party consisted of Zenel, Eles, Sadri Dorçë, and his father, and a mule which Hasan Beg had considerately sent in case I wanted to ride; Dorçë *pere*, I thought ungraciously, might have been content to give his approval without adding himself to our already swollen numbers.

We had only gone a few paces when we were stopped by a body of Partisans under Rexheb, the Political Commissar of the Scutari *çetas*, an arrogant fellow whose manner and conversation, as well as his position, proclaimed him a sound Party man. He now demanded that I postpone my visit until I had seen Tito's delegate to the Kosmet, a certain Rada, who was expected shortly; he added insolently that the Kosmet had no interest in 'private individuals' like Hasan Kryeziu, and that if I went to Gjakovë I must go with Partisans and see only those people of whom the Partisans approved. I replied, as politely as my anger allowed, that I took orders from the Allied General Staff, not the Kosmet. After a long argument, watched by Shpen and his friends with silent disdain, I agreed, on the advice of Eles and Sadri, to take three Partisans for some of the way, though not into Gjakovë. Detailing three of his men—one of whom spoke French—to accompany us, the Commissar turned his back on me and stalked away.

I regretted bitterly my mistake in telling Mehmet of my plans; I had only done so because both he and Hasan Beg had led me to believe that they were allies, and because I did not want the Kosmet to accuse me of working behind their backs. In my innocence I had supposed them to be as interested as I in building up resistance against the Germans in Kossovo; whereas they were only concerned to consolidate their power at the expense of all other parties. Never again, I resolved, would I confide in them; but my wisdom had come too late.

It was mid-afternoon before we had climbed to the top of the water-shed between Deg and the grassy vale of Bityç. Skirting Vlad, a large village where there was a gendarmerie post, we arrived in the gloom of a wintry dusk at the foot of a steep slope, where we halted to eat the food we had brought from

Deg. It had been much too cold to ride but the mule had slowed our pace considerably; when I asked Shpen how far we were from Gjakovë he answered with glum satisfaction:

'Four hours by day; eight hours at night.'

Before I could make any comment a fruity voice hailed us out of the darkness; an intoxicated gendarme lurched down the track leading towards Vlad. He had only come to exchange gossip and so I kept out of sight, screened by Zenel and Sadri, until Shpen had satisfied his curiosity; he was unlikely to be hostile, but he would probably have spread the news of my presence if he had noticed me.

We climbed a steep and rocky path to the head of the pass, where a small stone pinnacle marked the old frontier between Albania and Jugoslavia. While we rested to get our breath Shpen and his two friends told me that they used to make a good living before the war smuggling tobacco across the frontier from Jugoslavia; now that Kossovo was part of Albania they had lost their livelihood.

The descent was precipitous and dangerous in the dark; several times we lost the track, but our smuggler guides seemed to feel their way back to it by instinct before we could stray far. Gradually the slope levelled and the track became a wide and muddy path running through woodland, easy to follow in the light of a rising moon.

At our next halt a heated argument broke out between Shpen and the three Partisans, at the end of which Shpen announced that he was going to take us back to Deg; it seemed that Rexheb had ordered the Partisans to accompany us into Gjakovë, and had told the one who spoke French that he must stay with me all the time I was there and be present at all my meetings. I was sorry for the three Partisans, who were only obeying orders, but I had not come all this way to have my plans upset by the duplicity of Rexheb; I ordered them to return to Deg at once, adding that the Kosmet could do what they liked about it. What they did, I soon discovered, was to send word to the Germans that I was in Gjakovë.

We left the foothills and, after fording a shallow river, came onto a dirt road running between hedges with what seemed to be hopfields on either side. We passed several isolated houses but met no one. The countryside was soft and peaceful in the moonlight; only the faint thud of the mule's hoofs and the distant barking of farm dogs disturbed the stillness.

We had been going for two hours across the plain when Shpen suddenly stopped and began whispering with his friends; I noticed some scattered buildings ahead, on our right. Eles sidled up to me and murmured:

'We must go very quietly now because we are entering the city and there are Germans in that white house on the right.'

Keeping well into the side of the road we advanced stealthily in single file; Shpen was in the lead, with Zenel and the mule bringing up the rear. We crossed a bridge over a river, lit by a lamp at each end; straight ahead ran a wide, well-lit street, which we avoided by turning right along a path by the river. After two or three hundred yards we turned sharp left again up a hill until we came to some large white barracks guarded by a pair of sentry-boxes. At this point our behaviour degenerated into burlesque. Shpen and his friends crept forward crouched over their rifles, which they carried at the hip with their fingers on the triggers—each one looking, to paraphrase a famous epigram, far more like a guerrilla than a guerrilla has a right to look. I wondered fearfully whether we were in greater danger of arrest as bandits or as lunatics. Fortunately the sentry-boxes were empty; the barracks housed only workers from the chrome mines.

Soon we were prowling through the twisting, cobbled streets of the town like small boys playing Red Indians. Shpen would stop at each corner, peer round it carefully, and hurriedly beckon us on; at every street lamp Eles, whose laboured breathing was heavy on my neck and whose Sten gun, I noticed unhappily, was pointed at the small of my back, would trot forward and steer me forcefully across the street in the full glare of the beam, until I told him irritably to leave me alone; and whenever one of the mule's iron-shod hoofs clattered against a cobblestone everyone stopped in his tracks and hissed 'sh-sh-sh!' so loudly and with such agonized urgency that the poor beast stood still and hung its head in shame.

But for the noise we made ourselves no sound disturbed the quiet of the sleeping city; nor did we see any movement other than our own shadows on the pale, moon-bathed walls of the houses. At midnight we came to a halt in front of a large wooden door in a high, whitewashed wall. Shpen knocked and called up to a lighted window in the house behind; a minute later the bolts were drawn back and a very old man with a long, drooping white moustache let us into a wide courtyard. At a doorway on the far side Hasan Beg was waiting.

He took me upstairs to a living-room furnished with armchairs, a large divan and a table; a double bedroom and a bathroom completed my luxurious quarters. I was too tired to eat but was persuaded to drink some unusually powerful home-distilled raki.

Hasan Beg had shed the breezy bonhomie of our first meeting; he was unmistakably nervous. His face darkened and his manner became more agitated as Shpen told him of our trouble with Rexheb; turning to me he reproached me sharply for having told Mehmet of our meeting at Vlahën. The Partisans had been trying for a long time to make him leave his house and join them in the mountains, seeking thus to deprive him of his contacts among the various Nationalist and Irredentist groups in Gjakovë; now they would spread the news of my presence, hoping that I should be discovered and he would be obliged to flee. Looking back I realize how simple-minded I must have been to suppose that because Hasan Beg was the unofficial president of the L.N.C. he would want to share his plans with official members; events were to prove him tragically justified.

I was horrified at Hasan's reproaches; he was already taking a grave risk in sheltering me, and the knowledge that I had thoughtlessly aggravated his danger was a heavy burden on my conscience. The old servant, on the other hand, who had been listening to our conversation, made light of our fears:

'If you want to play at politics, Hasan Beg,' he teased, 'you must be brave!'

I was roused next morning by Hasan himself carrying a flask of raki—to keep the cold out, he explained, while I dressed. He had recovered his good humour but warned me that I should have to curtail my stay in Gjakovë and postpone a journey to Prizren, Priština, and Peć which he had planned for me. There was another reason for his alarm, which he now confessed: the six hundred mercenaries who had threatened us in Krasniqi had imposed a reign of terror throughout Kossovo, and the memory of their executions was still fresh.

Despite his fears he kept me in his house for three days, treating me with a rare hospitality that I had not experienced in years; more important, he brought to see me some of the most influential of the Kossovar leaders. It was typical of Hasan's integrity that he included among them men who differed from him politically, and one or two who were his rivals; he had promised to help me in the formation of a common front of Kossovars against the Germans, and this object alone guided him in his choice.

Our talks convinced me that we should achieve no more than isolated military action in Kossovo without some Allied declaration on the future status of the Province; it was obvious that the Kossovars did not trust us. Nor might I use the one argument that would have appealed to them—that by fighting now they could obtain arms from us, which they could use later to defend themselves against Communists or Serbs. The most I obtained was a promise from the commander of the Albanian Army garrison at Peć to put his men at my disposal in the event of an Allied invasion or a German withdrawal, and an undertaking from the others to furnish me with military and political information in the meantime. One of my visitors was the Chief of Police at Peć, and so I should at least receive warning of any German operations against us. Two leaders of the Irredentist Party, Ejub Binaku and Professor Sulejman Riza, promised me a second visit to Kossovo with a wide itinerary; as soon as the situation improved they would send for me at Deg.

I left Gjakovë in the early hours of 17th December with the same escort and in much the same manner as I had entered, though without the embarrassing company of the mule. When I reached Deg I was told of the Kosmet's treachery. I smothered my resentment, not wishing to provoke an open breach; but I derived some consolation from the hypocritical enthusiasm with which Mehmet and Tito's delegate, Rada, congratulated me on my safe return.

With Hands I found Tony Neel, who had arrived the previous evening after a dangerous reconnaissance of the country near Scutari, followed by an equally hazardous journey across the Catholic territory west of the Drill. He would never have reached us safely but for the influence and diplomacy of his escort, Ymar Bardoshi, the Bajraktar of Pukë who, although a Moslem, had allies among the Catholic tribes.

'It was pretty rotten, you know,' Neel told us, 'to see how unpopular one was. The only time I was well received in a village was when old Ymar told them I was a Hun officer; then they were all over me.'

I had not been back at Deg twenty-four hours when Smith handed us a signal warning us to stand by that night for a sortie of three aircraft; as well as stores they would drop three parties, each consisting of an officer and a wireless operator.

As soon as we heard the engines in the distance we ran to the drop-ping ground, where Partisan guards were already stationed, and lit the signal fires. At the same time the villagers thronged from their houses in search of loot, while the tracks leading to Deg from all the surrounding countryside filled with shadowy, hurrying figures; some came on horseback, others on foot, the richer ones leading mules to carry their plunder. In some places men laid out their own patterns of fires in the hope that the aircraft would be deceived into dropping their loads.

It was a successful drop, executed with superb skill by the Royal Air Force pilots. The parachutists landed safely on the dropping ground, the containers not far away, but the 'free drops', of which there was a large number, gave us some bad moments; it was an uncomfortable experience to stand in the open in the chilly, moonless night and hear the bundles whistling through the air towards us. The greatest excitement came when a Partisan guard fired on a looting tribesman; the man fired back, frightening the Partisan out of his life, and vanished with his spoil into the darkness.

Instead of bringing the stores to our house the Partisans took them to the Mosque, where they rifled the personal kit of the men who had just landed and stole most of the food; our protests were useless, for they were acting on the orders of Commissar Rexheb, with whom my disobedience still rankled. On the intervention of Mehmet Hoxha next morning we recovered most of the military stores and some of the food; but the parachutists' introduction to Albania was the loss of all their belongings.

The new officers were Captain Hibberdine, Lieutenant Merritt and Lieutenant Hibbert; Hibbert was to join Riddell near Dibra, Merritt would work with Neel, and Hibberdine was attached to me. For the moment we were faced with an acute shortage of space, with twelve officers and N.C.O.s and four Italian servants in one very small house; although our Albanian staff had found themselves billets in the village there was no other house that we could requisition.

However, resolved that if our Christmas must be uncomfortable at least it should be merry, we sent couriers to Gjakovë and Prizren to buy food, drink, and cigarettes and to the Catholic country to bring us a pig. On Christmas Day we entertained successively representatives of the Kosmet, led by Mehmet and Rada, and of the villagers, led by their *hoxha*. The majority of the villagers stood outside in a body while I made them a speech of thanks, translated by Sadri Dorçë; but several came inside and wandered round the room, fiddling with the wireless and picking up anything they fancied to take away. One old man sat down with us and drank a whole bottle of cough mixture which Neel had put in front of him; he giggled weakly after each swig and reeled out at the end, apparently quite drunk.

X

BETRAYAL

On 27th December Eles Yusufi, who had been away on a visit to his family, returned with the news that Ejub Binaku was awaiting us in the house of the Sub-Prefect of Tropojë; this town was the district capital, lying some nine miles north of Deg and a mile or two from the frontier of Kossovo. Leaving Corporal Clifton, our wireless operator, at headquarters Hibberdine and I set off the same afternoon, accompanied by Zenel and Eles.

John Hibberdine was an officer in the Cameronians of slight but sturdy build and quiet, thoughtful manner. Several years younger than myself he combined great physical endurance with unusual intellectual maturity; his shrewd judgment, unruffled temper and dry sense of humour made him an invaluable partner in adventure and a strong stimulus to morale. That some such stimulus was needed became apparent to me from the frequency with which I found myself losing my temper over trifles.

Even Hibberdine's patience was strained on this journey; Eles, who was supposed to know the way, repeatedly lost it, bringing us at length to Tropojë angry, hungry, and exhausted, nine hours after we had started. The Sub-Prefect, a cheerful little man who had lived in the United States, soon revived us with food and raki. Although himself a member of the Balli Kombëtar he had protected the Kosmet so far as he could, even to the extent of sending an official report to the German authorities stating that there were no Partisans in his area and therefore no need for police action.

We stayed indoors next day until darkness had fallen on the town; then, taking leave of our host, we followed Ejub at a hurried pace through the streets and began the steep ascent of the Pass of Morina towards the frontier. The snow, which had been falling lightly when we left, increased as we climbed the pass to a full blizzard blown in our teeth by a howling east wind that froze our hands and faces and seared our lungs at every gasping breath; icicles formed in our noses, encrusted our moustaches, and hung from our eyebrows. As we neared the summit the snow lay deeper, until we were plunging above our knees in the drifts; every step was an effort. The shimmering flakes threw back the light of our torches in our eyes so that we frequently wandered off the path. As a little boy I had been thrilled by tales of trappers and Mounties in the Rockies or the forests of northern Canada, and in my day-dreams had sometimes pictured myself a member of an intrepid party of explorers crossing some wild and unmapped range of mountains. Now I found the reality hideously different, staggering blindly up the slope, my head bowed against the storm, my limbs numb with fatigue, my lungs bursting and my mind clouded with the fear that we should lose our way and perish horribly in this desolate, wind-swept waste of snow and darkness.

It was nearly midnight when we knocked on the door of a farmhouse at the mountain hamlet of Morina, on the Kossovo side of the frontier. We waited in the snow while Ejub and the owner whispered anxiously together for nearly ten minutes. There were visitors in the guest-room who must not see us, and so we were taken to sleep in a disused granary under the roof; but not even the attention of the vermin in which the room abounded could keep us awake for long.

By the time we were dressed next morning the other guests had gone, and so we moved into the comfortable guest-room. Ejub left for Gjakovë to discuss with Hasan Beg the final arrangements for our journey and reception there; he bade us await his return in patience and not on any account stir from the house without an escort—even then we must not wander far.

The fear of informers was so great that throughout our stay in Kossovo, even in the country districts, we were isolated from all contact with—and as much as possible from the sight of—people other than the family with which we happened to be staying and visitors specially summoned to meet us. When we wanted a walk to clear our heads—the guest-rooms were seldom ventilated, for the Albanians could not endure fresh air in their houses—someone would first make a reconnaissance to see that there was nobody about; we had always to take an escort, not so much for protection as for camouflage and in order to answer any awkward questions if we should happen to meet strangers. Lastly, Ejub insisted that we should always wear some kind of peasant head-dress and put on civilian overcoats to hide our uniforms; I wore my black Bulgar fez, but Hibberdine preferred the white Albanian 'half-egg'. To complete my disguise I usually wound puttees over my field boots.

Irksome though these restrictions were we could not reasonably refuse to obey them; for the consequences to our hosts and companions if we were taken would be far more serious than to ourselves. We were astonished at the unselfish courage of these people—whether powerful landowners like Hasan Kryeziu, intellectuals like Professor Sulejman Riza, government officials, small shopkeepers, or poor artisans—who risked their lives to accompany and shelter us in an area where even Albanian Partisans could not move in safety. Certainly people faced far graver dangers in other occupied countries, but in Kossovo there was no reason why men should expose themselves to any danger to help us. It may seem strange that we troubled to wear uniform at all when we must expect to be treated as spies if caught. The reasons were, first that we had a directive from Cairo not to remove our uniforms; secondly that Hasan and Ejub both thought the sight of them would have a useful effect on our visitors' morale.

Like most of the members of the Irredentist Party Ejub belonged also to the Balli Kombëtar. He told us very little about himself beyond the fact that he had been an outlaw since the Italian occupation of Kossovo in 1941 and that he had a wife somewhere. What his occupation was in peacetime we never discovered; but now he was military commander of the Irredentist *çetas*. They were still 'underground', but Ejub offered to call up a nucleus of two hundred men to act as our bodyguard in the mountains whenever we needed them. Despite his melancholy and secretive manner he was a simple man with a warm and generous nature who spared himself neither trouble nor risk in our service.

As chief bodyguard, guide, and constant companion on our journey Ejub appointed his closest friend, Ramadan, a dark, red-faced, thick-set highlander who spoke little and drank a great deal; he was friendly enough, although in his cups he was subject to fits of moroseness, when he would sit by himself with his head in his hands ignoring the rest of the company. But his story, which Ejub told us, proved him a loyal ally and a stout fighter. He had been an outlaw in these hills for twenty years, ever since the gendarmerie had killed his friend, Rustem Bairami; bound by his *besa* to protect Rustem he had fought a stiff battle with the gendarmes, killing six of them and only escaping himself after his friend had fallen. Since then he had been a hunted man without a home to shelter or a wife to comfort him. When there was nothing to do he would let his misfortunes prey on his mind; he would start drinking at seven in the morning and continue until lunch time, when he would pass out quietly until it was time to start the evening carouse.

New Year's Day 1944 found us still at Morina, impatient with the delay and worried by the continued absence of Ejub. He arrived without warning in the afternoon and told us to be ready to start for Gjakovë at dusk; he insisted that Eles and Zenel should stay behind, saying that they would make us too many to travel in safety. We should not need Eles because Ejub spoke French; but it required all my authority to persuade Zenel to return to Deg.

We left the house in the late afternoon and walked a few hundred yards down the hill to a narrow road, where an open fiacre was waiting. At our backs the gigantic bulk of Shkelzen, the eastern bastion of the North Albanian Alps, soared eight thousand feet above us, its southern face shimmering in the fading sunset with a pearly light. The name means 'shining'; and the people who dwell beneath it hold the mountain in deep veneration, investing it with a mythology of ghostly legends. A saint is buried on the upper slopes. In the calm yet menacing grandeur of that mighty massif looming through the twilight I saw embodied all the splendour and savagery of the Balkans; all the harsh nobility and fierce endurance of the land shone in the opalescent beauty of those ice-bound, snow-wrapped cliffs.

Well muffled against the cold Hibberdine and I climbed into the carriage; Ejub and Ramadan sat half on the seat, half on top of us. The driver, a cheery, deep-voiced fellow with a huge pair of moustaches, flicked his whip and the horse started down the slushy road at a spirited trot, in half an hour we had left the hills and were running across level, open country; we swept through the villages at a fast canter in a musical jingle of bells, the driver cracking his whip and shouting to clear the way. The carriage must have excited some comment, overloaded with the five of us and festooned with weapons; Ejub had brought a sub-machinegun for each of us in case we should have to fight, and the driver had a rifle slung across his shoulder.

We entered Gjakovë about seven o'clock, driving up the main street with a flourish that caused me acute alarm, which nearly turned to panic when we were halted at a control post manned by Albanian gendarmes; however, Ejub gave a signal to the N.C.O. in charge, who waved us on without a question though with several curious glances. We turned down a quiet side street, dismounted and began to creep through the streets like conspirators without, however, attracting attention from the few people we met. After a quarter of an hour we knocked on a wooden door in a wall, and were admitted to a courtyard leading to a discreet but comfortably furnished house. This proved to be the back premises of a small cafe and hotel of which our host was the owner.

Our first visitor, an hour later, was Gjakovë's Chief of Police, which accounted for our easy passage through the gendarmerie post. He told us over a glass of our host's smooth slivovitz that the Germans had reinforced their garrison by a thousand *Sicherheitsdienst* during the last few days and had considerably tightened their controls, both on the roads and in the towns. They knew of the parachute drop which had brought Hibberdine and the others, but their reports greatly exaggerated the numbers and they believed that a party of fifty British parachutists had arrived. Our friends thought they were planning an expedition against Deg, but they feared there would also be a house-to-house search through the town in the near future. The Chief of Police hoped to give us at least one hour's warning of any search, and Ejub had a small force of his men in readiness to fight our way out if the worst came to the worst; but we must always be ready to move at a moment's notice and must be prepared to change our lodgings every night.

Accordingly, we left the following evening for Hasan Beg's house, walking through the streets in pairs in a more sensible manner than usual; in the dusk no one seemed to pay us any attention, least of all the two or three German patrols that we met. This was just as well, for Ejub told us that the Kosmet already knew of my visit; only that morning he had met a schoolmaster belonging to the L.N.C. who stopped him in the street.

'How is Major Kemp?'

'I haven't seen him,' replied Ejub as innocently as he could.

'Oh yes, you have! We know he's in Gjakovë with you.'

Late that evening we listened on Hasan's wireless to the B.B.C.'s account of the sinking of the *Scharnhorst*; it was thrilling to watch the respect with which his guests heard the news. Hasan and Ejub we knew to be our friends and devoted to our cause, but the sympathies of the others were still in the balance; such an incident as this would impress them far more than any words of ours.

We moved house every evening for the next three days, covering the whole of the city in the course of our journeys. Ejub and Ramadan would point out the places of interest we passed—the Town Hall, the Prefecture of Police, and the German officers' mess among others. They had gained confidence since our first furtive entry into Gjakovë, but I was never entirely happy in the streets; Hasan Beg had impressed upon me that the German garrison had a most efficient counterespionage service among the civilians. The German soldiers we met seldom looked at us, but we attracted—I particularly—many curious stares and backward glances from Albanians. Only once did our guides show alarm—when Hibberdine unthinkingly pulled out a handkerchief to blow his nose. Ramadan whipped it from his hand, crushing it out of sight in his fist; while Hibberdine, realizing at once that no Albanian peasant would use a handkerchief, blew vigorously through his fingers, wiped them on the seat of his trousers and, to complete the picture, spat noisily on the cobbles.

During this time our hosts and most of our visitors were minor civil servants and small tradesmen, from which classes the Irredentist Party seemed to draw its greatest strength. The tradesmen made up to us in professional services what they lacked in political influence; for a barber arrived each morning to shave us, and at one house a tailor called to measure Hibberdine for a pair of breeches. Some of our visitors had come to see us from the farthest limits of Kossovo, so that we began to wonder how long it would be before the Germans came to hear of our presence. However, there was no doubt of the enthusiasm which our arrival had excited, for promises of help flowed in from every quarter.

From our conversations, especially from those with Army officers and government officials, our hopes grew of organizing a nucleus of resistance among Albanians throughout Kossovo. Our friends under-took, when they returned to their districts, to recruit their sympathizers into cadres which would receive clandestine training from officers of the Albanian Army, to choose sites for secret dumps of arms and food, and to reconnoitre suitable dropping grounds. In imagination we already saw ourselves controlling an underground army with cells in every town and large village from Gjakovë to Priština, from Mitrovica to the borders of Macedonia.

On the evening of 6th January we tramped for half an hour through snowy streets to the house of a leading member of the Irredentist Party, where we were to hold an important conference on the following day. I had a momentary pang of anxiety when I saw our reception committee, which consisted of our host and four uniformed gendarmes; however Ejub explained that one policeman would remain in the house with us for the whole of our visit while the other three kept watch outside. The one appointed as our personal bodyguard was a bibulous, red-faced fellow with an enormous 'Kaiser Bill' moustache; he spoke little but sat all day cross-legged on the floor, his rifle across his knees, regarding us with a benevolent and boozy leer which he interrupted at intervals to swallow raki from a flask by his side. Whatever use he might have been in an emergency there was no doubt that he took his duties seriously; for whenever either of us went to the lavatory he would follow across the courtyard and stand swaying and hiccupping in the cold until his charge was ready to return. It seemed that he was an equally conscientious husband, for he confided to us that he had begotten twenty children on his wife, although only seven of them had survived.

The conference which assembled the following evening was, in the hateful jargon of those wartime years, on a high level; there were present the Mayor of Gjakovë, the Colonel-Commandant of the Albanian Army in Kossovo, and Professor Sulejman Riza, the *Eminence Grise* of the Irredentist Party. Our purpose was to discuss the final arrangements for our journey through the rest of Kossovo—a matter which we had been pressing since our arrival in Gjakovë.

We were therefore bitterly disappointed to hear that we must postpone our journey for the present. Our friends at first pleaded the excuse that the recent heavy falls of snow had blocked the roads; but it was not long before they admitted the truth—German controls on the roads had been so severely tightened that they could not accept the responsibility of escorting us. Sulejman Riza, who did most of the talking, told us that the enemy knew of our presence and was on the look-out for us. Although we argued and pleaded, offering to absolve them in writing from any responsibility for our safety, the Irredentists were adamant; and we, knowing that these men were no cowards, were obliged in the end to give way. Reluctantly we agreed to remain a few more days in Gjakovë, and then return to Deg to await a better moment. We had to content ourselves with a promise from Sulejman Riza to prepare his party for immediate action against the Germans, and a further promise from the army commander to supply the Irredentists with weapons and instructors. It was midnight when the conference broke up; Hibberdine and I looked sorrowfully at each other.

'It's time to go home,' I sighed.

The next evening, sped on our way by the good wishes of our police guards, we returned to Hasan Beg's house; it was a short distance but Ejub, who seemed to have become much more nervous since our conference, took us on a long detour—in order, he said, to shake off any German agents who might be following us. Hasan welcomed us with unusual cheerfulness; we detected more than a little bit of 'I told you so' in his manner as he listened to the account of our disappointment.

We found a courier from Hands awaiting us with a parcel of books and tobacco from a recent sortie and a signal from Cairo blandly instructing us to keep Lake Scutari under observation. Forbearing all comment on the bizarre sense of geography displayed by Headquarters and hoping fervently that their message did not represent the true sum of their knowledge of the country or our whereabouts, we detained the courier until we had drafted a signal describing our present situation and future plans.

We stayed six days in the Kryeziu house, confined indoors during the hours of daylight but allowed to walk in a walled garden at dusk; we needed the exercise, for Hasan's rich pilaffs, strong red wine, and raki were taking the edge off our fitness. In the evenings we played poker with Hasan or listened to his wireless; and once, after he and his friends had heard the B.B.C. News in Serbo-Croat, we tuned in to Tommy Handleyand shook with laughter under the solemn, uncomprehending gaze of our companions.

For all his kindness we noticed in Hasan's manner a rising tension as the days went by; his expression grew more harassed and from time to time he would mutter 'Gestapo! Gestapo!' under his breath. He was worried also by the indiscretion of our interpreter, Eles, who had followed us to Gjakovë and had been seen flaunting our gold in the cafes of the town. But although his fears for our safety increased with every day he would not let us leave until he was sure that we could circumvent the controls on the roads. We were all relieved when, on 13th January, Ejub arrived with the news that he had arranged for us to travel south on the morrow to Rogovo, a village half-way on the road to Prizren. Ejub admitted that he was not happy about the journey, but told us frankly that he dared not let us stay longer in Gjakovë.

I slept badly that night, waking often to fret about our escape from the town and the journey that lay ahead. These days I seemed to jump at shadows, but I was worried not only for our own safety but because we were risking the lives of so many good friends who had much more to lose than ourselves. Bright morning, however, scattered my fears and I relaxed happily watching the grey-and-white fan tail pigeons flash their wings among the bare trees in the garden under the pale blue sky. A pretty, dark-haired little girl carrying a basket on her arm trotted gaily along the path below our window, her tiny wooden shoes clattering like a pony's hoofs on the stones.

Hibberdine and I were left to ourselves all the morning. Hasan arrived to join us for lunch—an anxious but genial host. When the meal was over we prepared to depart: I wound puttees round my field-boots, donned an Italian army greatcoat and put on my black Bulgarian fez—an incongruous and ridiculous figure that could hardly escape attention; Hibberdine, in an old civilian overcoat and white skull-cap, should pass fairly well for an Albanian. Hasan, who was not accompanying me, found my appearance much more diverting than Hibberdine, who was.

At four o'clock Shpen Zeçeri came to fetch us, accompanied by Ismail, the old white-haired servant who had teased Hasan on my first night in the house; now the old man surprised me by taking my hand between his two withered claws and kissing it. Hasan said a hurried good-bye in the courtyard, promising to keep in touch with us. Shpen opened the gate, shooed away a crowd of small children who were playing in the porch and beckoned Hibberdine to follow; taking my arm Ismail hustled me after them, the two of us keeping about thirty yards behind.

After the semi-darkness in which we had lived for so long the glare of the afternoon sunlight on the white walls of the closely huddled houses struck painfully on our eyeballs; so that for a few minutes I was glad to let Ismail guide me by the arm. School-children with satchels over their shoulders were playing on an open space below Hasan's house; they let us pass without a glance. When we entered the narrow, twisting streets I bent my gaze on the cobbles, but even so I could not help noticing the curious stares that I attracted. Ismael, however, was quite unperturbed, even prodding me into calling a *'tungjatjeta!'* to a pair of gendarmes whom we passed on the outskirts of the town.

Half an hour's walking brought us to a broad dirt road where a fiacre was waiting, similar to that in which we had left Morina; standing beside it were Ejub and Ramadan. Taking an affectionate farewell of our two guides we squeezed into the back. While we rattled over the flat, snow-bound countryside, from which the colour was slowly draining as the sun sank in a fiery glow behind the western mountains, Ejub explained the reason for our hurried daylight departure: the previous evening the German garrison commander had ordered our friend, the Chief of Police, to put a cordon round the town and search every house. The Chief of Police gave Ejub twenty-four hours to get us out of the town, warning him that the search must begin at six o'clock tonight and that the *Sicherheitsdienst* would take part.

Ejub had scarcely finished his story when we came to a control post: turning a corner we saw, about two hundred yards ahead of us, a rough barrier across the road, guarded by a party of Albanian gendarmerie and two grim-looking figures in field grey. Ejub had evidently planned our journey carefully, for our driver, without checking his pace, turned down a rough track to the right which, after a few hundred yards, crossed a river and ran parallel to the road. Although they must have seen us, the Germans made no attempt to interfere. A mile further on we were met by a fine-looking man mounted on a spirited grey stallion with a high-pommelled saddle and scarlet and silver trappings. When he came up to us he wheeled his horse and shouted a greeting; Ejub told us that he was the owner of the house where we were to stay in Rogovo and that his name was Dobrushi.

About eight o'clock we saw the white walls and lighted windows of a large farm-house gleaming through the darkness on our left. Following Dobrushi we dismounted in front of a handsome, two-storeyed house with broad bow windows protruding beneath thatched eaves. After food and raki in the guest-room we were shown into a bedroom with three wide and comfortable beds; despite our hosts apologies for what he called such inadequate accommodation I slept better and longer than I had done for many weeks.

The Dobrushis were a rich Albanian family with property in Gjakovë and Prizren as well as the large estate on which we were now staying. Their wealth, however, had brought them little happiness. Next morning we were shown the tomb of our host's elder brother, Rexheb, which lay in the garden beneath the windows of the guestroom. One day during the German invasion of Jugoslavia a party of Serbian soldiers came to the house; they were well received and entertained with food and drink. After their meal they ordered the whole family outside and shot Rexheb in front of them.

The suspicion and hostility in which Serbs and Albanians had for centuries held each other flared into open violence when the former saw their country and their power disintegrating under foreign attack; the Pan-Serb intransigence of successive Jugoslav governments between the wars, which had frustrated all hopes of unity within the kingdom, now expressed itself in the persecution of all minorities whose loyalties to the central power were suspect. The Mussulman populations in Bosnia, Montenegro and Kossovo provided the principal victims of this flood of fear and hatred. In their turn they reacted savagely against their former oppressors, under the benevolent protection of their new German and Italian masters.

The tragedy of the Dobrushi family deepened soon after Rexheb's murder, when the son of the house, conscripted into the Jugoslav Army, was taken prisoner and transported to Germany, since when there had been no word of him. Our host, shattered by this double blow, abandoned himself to a silent despair alleviated only by the temporary consolations of the bottle. With our guard, Ramadan, he would start drinking at daybreak and continue until both were unconscious; as soon as they awoke they would start again.

'He is always like this now,' whispered his mother to Ejub. 'Although he has a beautiful house in Gjakovë and another in Prizren he will not go near them; he just comes here with a few servants to drink.'

To escape from this stricken atmosphere Hibberdine and I each borrowed a gun and some cartridges and, accompanied by two servants, went duck shooting by the river. We killed no birds but the walk in the flat open country, the sunlight sparkling on the snow and the tingle of the sharp frosty air on our faces more than compensated for the lack of sport. Ejub, who complained of influenza, went to Prizren to see a chemist. He returned in the evening disgusted. The chemist had given him a draught whose nauseous smell and bright orange colour had aroused his suspicions, which were confirmed, he told us, when he saw that the chemist was a Serb. Leaving the draught untasted he stalked from the shop.

Much more serious was the confirmation he brought that the German authorities knew of our presence in the area; they were combing Prizren and Gjakovë for us, and had taken over all controls on the roads. If we stayed in Kossovo it would only be a matter of time before we were found. We decided to return to Deg until the hunt had died down.

We left Rogovo at dusk next day, 17th January, striking due west across country on foot until we reached the shelter of the foothills and a small village on the Jugoslav side of the old frontier. While resting there the following afternoon we received a courier from Hasan Beg with a long letter from Hands and a sheaf of telegrams from Cairo. From these we learnt the melancholy story of the death of Corporal Roberts, my wireless operator whom I had left behind with Seymour, and of the dispersal of Brigadier Davies's Mission by the Germans.

During the winter of 1943 the Germans launched a series of determined drives against areas known or believed to harbour British Missions or their allies. Those operations, combined with the fierce cold of one of the severest winters of the war, virtually paralysed the guerrilla movement for four months and forced British and Partisans high into the mountains, where they had a painful struggle even to survive. Trotsky was obliged to leave his camp at Biza and jettison his equipment, including essential supplies of food and clothing. Pursued by the Germans, abandoned by the swifter-moving Partisan General Staff—deserted even by the Partisan guards who were supposed to protect them—exhausted, starved, and frost-bitten, Trotsky and his companions were ambushed on the morning of 8th January by hostile Albanians while they were taking refuge in a high and lonely sheep-fold. Trotsky and two of his officers were wounded, captured, and handed over to the Germans; they remained prisoners until 1945. Nicholls and Hare, both suffering severely from frost-bite, escaped from the trap; but the former survived only three weeks before exhaustion and gangrene extinguished his incomparable spirit. He was awarded a posthumous George Cross. Hare, whose courage and steadiness throughout that terrible journey earned him the immediate award of the Military Cross, escaped to the south.[1]

A courier from Hasan Beg brought us another piece of grim news: our former host, the sub-Prefect of Tropojë, had been shot dead by Partisans

---

[1] A fuller account of Davies's disaster is given in his own book, *Illyrian Venture*, pp. 147-153, and by Julian Amery, *Sons of the Eagle*, pp. 68-70.

outside his own house a few days after our departure. His murder was the measure of the Kosmet's gratitude for the protection he had given them, nor did they ever try to justify it; it was a clear warning to other Albanians of the consequences of befriending us: to ourselves it was a scarcely concealed threat.

We recovered from total despair when we heard later in the evening that Hasan's brothers, Gani and Säid, had just arrived at his house in Gjakovë after escaping from their internment in Italy. This was thrilling news indeed. Devoted friend as Hasan had proved himself he did not pretend to the military qualities of Gani or the political ability of Säid. With these two new allies our chances of organizing an effective resistance movement in Kossovo were immeasurably increased. The recent messages from Cairo were enthusiastic over our progress in this direction and our plans for the future. I wrote at once to Gani asking for an early meeting.

Next day, 19th January, we moved further west towards the mountains of the frontier, walking across pleasant, gently rolling country under a bright sky. Ahead of us loomed the sugar-loaf bulk of Bishtrik; thirty miles to the south we could see the snowy bastion of the Sar Planina, a formidable line of white peaks, corrugated with deep black clefts, running away to the east—the barrier separating the plain of Kossovo from Macedonia; to the north the sunlight glanced on the top of Shkelzen, 'The Shining'.

We halted for the night in a large and isolated house where the guest-room had a curiously carved and painted wooden ceiling and a floor alive with fleas. We left early in the morning because there was a wedding nearby and we could not risk being seen by the guests—'Besides,' Ejub whispered to us, 'the food in this house is extremely bad.'

Inspired by Cairo's enthusiasm we spent the next two days reconnoitring the neighbourhood for a suitable base near the frontier. On the afternoon of the 21st we scrambled up the side of a steep, forested ridge, crossed the old frontier and came down into the valley where stood the house of the District Magistrate of Has, who was to be our host that night. As we sat over our raki before the evening meal Ejub pointed out a small man with long drooping moustaches who was standing by the window.

'That fellow,' he told us, 'has been in hiding from the gendarmerie for many years—ever since he killed a man who raped his sister.'

'Admirable. But how is it that we find him here in the District Magistrate's house?'

'But you see, he was a great friend of the District Magistrate; and of course the District Magistrate would have done the same thing himself.'

While we were preparing for bed a messenger arrived with a letter for me from Gani Beg Kryeziu, assuring us of his devotion to the Allied cause and his resolve to collaborate with us personally; he and Säid were leaving

Gjakovë that same evening for Vlad, where they would await us in the house of their friend, Halil Hoxha.

An eight-hour walk through splendid mountain scenery brought us late the following afternoon to Vlad. The courtyard of Halil Hoxha's house was crowded with Kryeziu retainers and friends who had come from town and countryside for miles around to bid them welcome; already, we heard, more than three thousand people had come to offer their congratulations to Gani and Säid on their escape. Inside the stifling guest-room the oil-lamps flickered mistily through a thick haze of tobacco smoke; above the continuous murmur of conversation rose the crackle of a brushwood fire and the coughing, hawking and spitting of the close-packed throng of neighbours and servants. We waited in the doorway while Ejub fought his way through the press to the group seated on the floor around the fire; a moment later Hasan Beg himself hurried forward to embrace us and led us to join his brothers by the hearth.

Gani Beg Kryeziu was short and sturdily built, with a high, prominent forehead, strong features and a candid, determined expression; he spoke clearly, without evasion or embellishment, in short, pungent sentences. Although he would make up his mind quickly and carry out his decisions with speed and vigour, he was at the same time a shrewd and careful planner. Säid was of lighter build, tall and dark, quiet and sparing of speech, by inclination a diplomat and scholar rather than a soldier. Detesting the methods and mistrusting the leadership of the Communists he had yet some sympathy for the political Left, with whose literature his French education had made him familiar. As an intellectual he had a passion for political philosophy and had many friends among the Partisans; as a politician he proposed the formation after the war of an Albanian Agrarian Party.

With them was sitting a quiet man with a gentle manner, a sallow face, delicate features and a melancholy expression who was introduced to us as Lazar Fundo, the Kryezius' companion in prison and in their recent escape. He had once been an important member of the Communist Party, with influential friends in Moscow, including the veteran Bulgarian Communist, Dmitrov; but a visit to Moscow during the great purge trials wholly disillusioned him and in 1938 he renounced all connection with the Party. Returning to Albania he was arrested by the Italians in 1939 and imprisoned on the island of Ventotene, where he was later joined by the Kryezius. His brilliant and objective mind, his integrity and his courage earned him their trust and admiration and led them to appoint him their chief political adviser in the field; his knowledge of seven languages, including English, made him particularly useful in this service.

All three carried on their worn faces and emaciated bodies the marks of extreme privation and suffering; Gani held a handkerchief to his lips, into which he coughed convulsively while he talked, and Säid's overbright eyes and waxy pallor were more suited to the sickroom than the mountains.

Their escape had indeed been remarkable. Transferred from Ventotene to the mainland when the Allied invasion of Italy seemed imminent, they had escaped to Rome in the confusion following the Italian surrender. There Mehmet Bey Konitsa, the Albanian Minister, had provided them with false papers and arranged their repatriation; they had travelled in a sealed carriage with other Albanian exiles in a German military train through Italy, Austria, and Jugoslavia. When, after a journey of three weeks, they arrived at Hasan Beg's house in Gjakovë the Germans were still ignorant of their real identities.

However, after a rest of three days they judged it prudent to leave the town; Hasan sent his family to a place of safety, shut his house and, with his brothers and Fundo, took to the hills, where he told me they intended to remain until the enemy should withdraw from their country. The immediate German reaction was to loot and burn his house.

While we listened to this story Hasan sat opposite us on the floor with a smile of pure happiness on his chunky face, occasionally leaping up to salute some new arrival who had come to offer congratulations. Despite the sufferings of more than two years' rigorous imprisonment and their present ill-health and anxieties Gani and Säid were in high heart and impatient to go into action with us against the Germans. At present they had with them about a hundred men under arms but they had already sent couriers to rally their friends and kinsmen and hoped soon to have a thousand men at their command. Gani listened sympathetically to my account of our journey in Kossovo and our disappointment when it was curtailed; after a moment's thought he said with decision:

'Do not worry, you will make your journey. I promise it. We will go together to Prizren, to Priština—even to Mitrovica. Only give me five or six days to make preparations while you are at Deg; then I will send you word. There is nothing I will not do for you; I have been waiting two years for this moment.'

Over the raki and goat cheese we talked late into the night—of suitable targets for attack, of the stores we should need, of a joint battle headquarters for the Kryezius and ourselves, of dropping grounds and arms caches, and of plans for a speedy and reliable intelligence service; we discussed the political situation in Kossovo and the measure of support we could expect from the people in each district; and, of more immediate importance, we debated the chances of active cooperation with the Kosmet Partisans. Gani and Säid were willing, even anxious, to sink all political differences and work with them, but from our own experiences Hibberdine and I were not optimistic about the Kosmet's response; however, we kept our doubts to ourselves.

When at last we had eaten we all settled down to sleep on the floor; but excitement and the incessant coughing of poor Gani gave me, at least, a disturbed night. I was thrilled at the prospect of continuing our journey through the whole of Kossovo, and I never doubted Gani's ability to perform what he had promised. Moreover, although the messages from Cairo had been warm in their praise I knew that military action was what our staff officers expected; now it seemed they were going to have it, for Gani convinced me—as he later demonstrated—that he meant to put all his energy and talent into the struggle.

Jubilant, Hibberdine and I set out next day for Berishtë, where Hands had established a new headquarters in a hamlet above the bank of the Drill, about three miles south-west of Deg. With us came the Kryezius, Fundo, and a large escort. We arrived in the afternoon to find Neel and Hands with the wireless operators, our two interpreters, and my servant, Zenel Ahmedi; Hibbert and Merritt had left, the former to join Riddell near Dibra, the latter to work with a Catholic chieftain near the Montenegrin border. I wasted no time in sending a signal to Cairo with the good news that we now had a formidable ally in the field, and asking that at least one of our supply drops be allocated to equip Gani Beg.

There was interesting news awaiting us: first, Hands told us that the Kosmet, enraged by what they called our 'defiance' of them in visiting Kossovo without their escort or permission, had threatened to 'report us to Tito'—a threat whose implications became clear to us soon enough; secondly, two days ago Neel had narrowly escaped capture by a party of fifty Germans.

On the other side of the Drin stood the Catholic village of Dardhë; about a mile further south Neel had his headquarters in the hamlet of Trun. Neel had thought himself safe from surprise, for although the Prizren-Scutari road lay no more than five miles south of Trun, the only paths across the wild and mountainous country that separated him from the road were guarded by the followers of his friend, the Bajraktar of Pukë. On this occasion, however, the guards were either too careless or too frightened to give the alarm. Swiftly and silently the Germans moved up the steep and twisting track towards the house where Neel was comfortably taking his lunch. He would certainly have been caught had not the commander of a gendarmerie post on the road received early notice of the German plan; a friend of the Bajraktar, he immediately dispatched one of his men to warn Neel. This man reached Trun half an hour ahead of the Germans, giving Neel and his staff just enough time to hide the wireless set and all traces of their presence and reach the cover of the hills before the first Germans surrounded the hamlet. Neel ferried his party across the Drin to Berishtë; the Germans, after spending the night in Dardhë and plastering the walls with anti-British slogans returned to their base.

The enemy was certainly taking an unhealthy interest in our movements. Next morning Hands received a letter from the Kosmet, warning him that German troops with strong forces of Albanian auxiliaries were massing around Plav and Gusinje on the Montenegrin border; their ostensible purpose was to attack the Montegrin Partisans in Andrijevica to the north, but the Kosmet feared that their real intention was to come down the Valbonë valley and attack us at the same time as the Germans in Kossovo launched a drive from the east.

From all we had heard such a plan seemed more than likely; if it were synchronized with a German advance from the Scutari-Prizren road along the path followed by Neel's fifty Germans we should have no way of escape. The Partisans claimed to be watching all the approaches from the east, but after Neel's recent experience and my own at Sllovë I felt we could hardly hope for much warning. I was a little reassured by Gani, who undertook to put his own guards on the tracks and send us word as soon as danger seemed imminent. He and his party returned to Vlad late the same evening.

I shall not easily forget that 24th January. The Parish priest of Dardhë came across the river to lunch, a quiet, taciturn figure who seemed to have little liking for our company. Hands and Neel had invited him in the hope that he might be persuaded to influence his villagers in our favour. Although Neel was protected at Trun by his friendship with the Bajraktar, Ymar Bardoshi, he was far from welcome in Dardhë, where the people would not even sell him food; indeed we had all been warned by the priest himself not to enter his village, even to go to church. But our lunch was not a success; although coldly polite to his hosts he would not listen to any of our arguments, quoting texts from the Pope's Christmas broadcast and twisting them to justify his own hostility to the Allies. To his mind we were clearly the agents of Communism. We escorted him back to the ferry in silence.

The signal that shattered all my hopes came over the evening wireless sked' from Cairo. Its opening words are fixed for ever in my memory 'Kemp to break tactfully all contact with Kryezius and Irredentists.' The message went on to explain that my activities in Kossovo were causing an 'unfavourable impression' among Tito's Partisans and ended with the sentence, 'Our relations with Jugoslav Partisans are of overriding importance.' Mehmet Hoxha's threat had produced quicker and more effective results than the worst we had feared.

With horror and incredulity Hibberdine and I read and re-read the decoded words on that dirty bit of paper. Only staff officers, we commented sardonically, would suppose that we could 'tactfully' abandon men who had risked their lives to help us; moreover, to desert the Kryezius at the very moment when, exhorted by Cairo and ourselves, they had taken up arms for the Allies, was not only base but foolish.

'And so,' I stormed to Hibberdine, 'we are to ditch Gani Beg, the one man in this part of Albania who really means to fight the Germans and has got the guts and ability to do it; the one man who can rouse the Kossovars to fight; a man who has just suffered two years' imprisonment for his loyalty to the British—just to please Mehmet Hoxha and his bunch of scheming thugs who hate the British anyway!'

'If Cairo's relations with the Jug Partisans are really so important,' added Hibberdine, 'why the hell didn't they warn us off before, instead of encouraging and praising us in everything we've done? After all, there isn't a step we've taken that hasn't had their approval.'

For all our anger we could not believe that these instructions had the approval of Philip Leake; and we proved to be right. We later discovered that Mehmet Hoxha's report was passed by Tito, with a strong protest, to the headquarters of the British Liaison Mission in Jugoslavia; in consequence, the order for our withdrawal came from a much higher quarter than the Albanian Country Section.

In desperation I drafted a 'Most Urgent' signal, begging at least to be allowed to keep in touch with Gani Beg now that he was in arms against the Germans; the answer was a categorical No. It was clear to me that my usefulness in the country was now over, my position no longer tenable. I was already discredited with the Kosmet Partisans, whose knowledge of their triumph would only increase their intransigence; besides, I did not believe that they contemplated any operations against the Germans, but were resolved to keep their forces intact for the subjugation of their own people, including those who had been my friends and protectors. On the other hand, if I could get out of Albania quickly it was just possible that I might be able to help both my country and my friends by personal interviews with our staff officers; thus naively I reasoned. Sadly I sent my last signal, asking permission to return to Cairo and report. Hibberdine, who was much less compromised than myself, was willing to remain.

He and I spent the next two days with Neel among the pine woods at Trun high above the swift flowing Drin, shaking off some of our depression in his cheerful company, and relaxing in the crisp mountain air and the splendid scenery that rolled away south of us towards the mountains of Luma.

At lunch-time on the 27th Hands arrived with a signal for me from Cairo approving my request to return and report. Hibberdine was ordered to remain and carry out general intelligence duties in the area—a vague assignment which I did not envy him.

Hands was very excited about a visit he had received the previous day from Mehmet Hoxha, who had arrived seething with rage against me for what

I had done in Kossovo; after a tirade against me and my dealing with 'traitors, collaborators, reactionaries, and enemies of the Albanian people' Mehmet had concluded with the revealing statement that if it had not been for his relations with Hands he would have 'taken measures against me'.

Hands suggested that I should join him at a meeting with the Kosmet General Staff the following afternoon at Deg, to which I agreed. We went on to discuss the question of how I was to get out of the country. I could not go south, for the Shkumbi was in flood; the only possible route was across the North Albanian Alps to Berane in Montenegro, where Tito's Partisans held an airfield from which I could be flown to Italy. But there was a difficulty here: in the words of Cairo's message, 'Berane Partisans have been receiving unfavourable accounts of your activities probably from Kosmet.' However, Hands believed that if I could avoid an open breach with the Kosmet at tomorrow's meeting, they would be so glad to have me out of the country that they would themselves arrange my journey.

After breakfast next morning Hands and I left Trun; we reached Deg in the early afternoon. At the entrance to the village we came upon a group of Partisans practising with an old Hotchkiss machine-gun under the supervision of a burly blond whose thick hair, beneath a brown fur Montegrin hat, reached to the shoulders; as we approached the blond turned round, revealing a fine pair of handle-bar moustaches that would have been the envy of any pilot in Bomber Command. He told us that the members of the Kosmet were assembling in the house of the village *hoxha*. Hands went on ahead of me to have a quiet word with Fadil Hoxha and Mehmet and soften the impact of my arrival.

So effective was his diplomacy that Mehmet and his colleagues greeted me more like an old friend and comrade than the Fascist beast of their denunciations. We maintained our facade of friendliness throughout the meeting; for the Kosmet were too happy at the thought of getting rid of me to be deliberately offensive, while I was determined not to be provoked into argument. There were, nevertheless, moments when I could hardly restrain my laughter; as when Mehmet propounded quite seriously the amazing theory that the civil war had been brought about solely by British encouragement of 'collaborationists and reactionaries,' and ended with a jewel of double-think: 'there was no civil war in Albania until the arrival of the British Military Missions.'

With genuine enthusiasm the Kosmet agreed to escort me to Berane, but warned me that the German and Albanian forces concentrated around Plav and Gusinje had started an offensive against the Montenegrin Partisans; a Kosmet patrol had been sent to report on the situation and should return within the next few days. If I would return to Hands's headquarters at Berishtë they would send for me as soon as it was safe to move.

While at Deg I received information that sickened me as much as anything I had heard in Albania: the miserable Eles, my interpreter, had been a frequent visitor to the German *Kommandatur* in Peć while Hibberdine and I were travelling in Kossovo. Instead of returning home when we left him at Molina at the beginning of January, he decided to earn some money by reporting our movements to the Germans; only Ejub's precautions had saved us from capture. I was at first unwilling to believe the story of his treachery, for I distrusted all evidence from Kosmet sources; but when, after examining the witnesses, I tackled Eles on my return to Berishtë, he burst into tears and admitted the charges. I was angry enough to have shot him on the spot; but I had no wish to start a blood-feud between his village and Berishtë. I sent him home feeling sure that either the Partisans or the Kryezius, whom he had also betrayed, would exact their own revenge.

From Berishtë I wrote a letter to the Kryezius, which I sent by the hand of my other interpreter, Sadri Dorçë: I tried to explain 'tactfully' that I had been recalled suddenly to Cairo for consultations, that I would never forget their kindness, and that I would do all in my power to secure them British arms and supplies in support of their operations. I felt too deeply ashamed to write more.

Our meeting with the Kosmet had taken place on 28th January; on the 31st, while I was still awaiting news of my journey, a signal came from Cairo informing me that there was a good chance of an aircraft landing at Berane airfield soon to pick up a party of British officers who had arrived there from Mihailović's territory. I decided to start immediately for Salimani's house in Krasniqi. There I should be much nearer the frontier, and I hoped that the old Bajraktar might have his own means of getting me across to Montenegro. After sending a fast messenger ahead to warn the Kosmet of my need for haste I left Berishtë at eleven the same morning; my servant, Zenel, mindful of Muharrem Bajraktar's charge, insisted on going with me.

We walked at a brisk pace in the cheerful morning sunlight across rolling hillsides above the gorge of the Drin. Although I was sorry to part from my friends it was a relief to turn my back on the disappointments and frustration of Berishtë. I was turning my back, also, on my six months' work in the country; but now that the decision had been made for me and I knew that I could do no more, I began to shed some of the gloom and apprehension which lately had almost overwhelmed me. I even looked forward to the adventure of crossing the frontier; and the prospect of leave and rest beyond was delightful.

We reached Salimani's house soon after dark, to find the Bajraktar seated in his guest-room among a group of Partisans, including Mehmet and Fadil Hoxha. They had received my message, and introduced me to their courier, Idris, who had just returned from Plav with his report on the offensive against the Montenegrin Partisans. An unassuming young man of slim and wiry build who spoke good French, he told me that the attacking 'reactionaries and Chetniks' had been routed, suffering extremely heavy casualties, chiefly from frost-bite and avalanches.

'In consequence,' he added, 'the repression up there is very severe.'

Mehmet, however, more affable than I had ever seen him, agreed to send me on my journey the following evening with Idris and two Montenegrin Partisans as escort. I must take only what kit I could carry easily on my back. Zenel, when told that he must stay behind, refused with such eloquence and determination that he persuaded Mehmet to let him accompany me as far as the frontier. We were warned to follow the courier's instructions without question; we should have to travel mostly by night, avoiding contact with people on the way. The frontier was closely patrolled by volunteer bands of Albanian 'reactionaries,' but we might be able to bribe one or two of their leaders to let us pass.

February 1st was a day of cloudless sky and brilliant sunshine in which the great peaks to the north beneath which I should have to travel that night shone in frosty but friendly grandeur. During the morning I reduced my kit to a small haversack, an overcoat and a couple of blankets; for defence I should have to rely on my .45 automatic and the rifles of my escort. Before lunch Fadil and Mehmet took their leave in the same sunny mood which at another time I might have thought suspicious.

In the late afternoon the five of us began our northward journey. It was safe to travel in daylight the few miles to the small town of Kolgecaj; but at a house on the outskirts we halted to eat and to await the fall of darkness. We left at eight and walked for an hour across open country until the track entered the deep gorge of the Valbonë, which runs north-westward along a narrow cleft through the mountains to within a few miles of the old frontier. Idris called a halt.

'Let us rest a few minutes,' he said. 'Ahead of us lies a march of six hours.'

Under a bright moon we resumed our journey, following a narrow path which wound along the cliff-face above the right bank of the river. Below us the torrent foamed and bubbled among the boulders and over the rapids, the roar and hissing of its passage echoed and amplified by the steep, confining walls; above, the moonlight glistened white on the mountain tops outlined starkly against the indigo sky and glinted evilly on the bare rock faces which plunged hundreds of feet into the shadows of the gorge.

On our side the overhanging wall of rock blotted out the light, so that we stumbled helplessly among the loose stones and boulders which littered the path. Soon the going became harder as the track dropped down to the river, then rose and fell again steeply in a series of vicious switchbacks. Hour after hour we struggled on, with only an occasional halt for a drink of water, until my eyes ached with the strain of following the track and I could no longer control the movements of my aching legs; as though drunk I began to stagger and lurch from side to side. I was painfully reminded of the local name for these mountains—*Prokletijë*, or Accursed.

The moon was already down when we came to a widening of the valley where a ravine ran in from the north. We forded the river and, after climbing several hundred feet up the opposite hillside in order to avoid a village, crossed the ravine and continued up the valley. If there was a track we failed to find it in the darkness; but after an agonizing scramble over broken, rocky ground, which drained my endurance, we suddenly found ourselves beneath the white walls of a farm-house. The owners were evidently expecting us, for the dogs were quickly silenced and we were hustled inside; Zenel and I were pushed into a small room by ourselves because there were strangers in the guest-room. The time, I noted, was a quarter past four.

Zenel awakened me to another bright morning with the news that the strangers had left. Soon afterwards Idris entered, followed by a giant of a man with huge black moustaches; tin's was our host's brother, a Capo Band or leader of one of the bands that had taken part in the attack against the Montenegrin Partisans. He greeted me warmly and told me that he would come with us to see me over the frontier.

'We have nothing against you English,' he added. 'Only we don't want the Communists here; and so we collaborate with the Germans, who help us to drive them out.'

Idris, I reflected, was an honest interpreter as well as a skilful diplomat.

After a brief lunch of sour milk and maize bread we left the house at half past three in the afternoon, retracing our steps as far as the ravine we had crossed the night before. Here we turned north and climbed steeply towards the head of the ravine, following a track which ran along the mountain-side through a forest of beeches above a narrow, stony stream. Throughout the afternoon we penetrated deeper into the heart of the North Albanian Alps. On every side rose great walls of shining rock pitted with crevices in which grew clusters of stunted pines. Darkness fell and a bright moon swung into the clear sky, glinting with a steely radiance on the naked rock and bathing the peaks in the still, white beauty that moonlight brings to deserts and mountains and all lonely places.

After four hours' march we crossed a wide, level valley carpeted in snow and began to climb a steep, beech-covered mountain—an exhausting business, for our feet slithered continually on the frozen track. Half an hour's climb brought us out of the trees onto an open, windswept crest where a small stone pyramid marked the old Montenegrin frontier. Here, while we rested, I looked back over the moonlit mountains and dark, deep valleys of Albania, so beautiful in that clear February night that all the fears and disappointments I had suffered there vanished from my mind; in that moment of rapture I felt a futile longing to return.

Led by our guide, the *Capo Band*, we set off downhill at what seemed to me a mad pace, for the narrow, twisting track of beaten snow was as slippery as an ice-rink; quite unable to control my speed or direction I continually slithered off to bury myself in the deep drifts at the side or land up hard against a tree. We progressed in a series of these terrifying descents, interrupted by arduous climbs up narrow paths on the side of mountains above sheer precipices, until at half past one in the morning we reached our destination, a wooden cabin at the bottom of a steep hill. Unable to keep my feet on the slippery gradient, I made the descent from the crest to the cabin on my bottom.

Our host, a fine-looking, dark Montenegrin, showed us furtively into a small room at the front of the house, apologizing in whispers for not being able to offer us the guest-room, which was occupied by strangers whom he dared not let us meet. Throwing myself on the floor without undressing or removing my boots I slept soundly until late in the morning.

We were now on the most dangerous part of our journey, Idris told me, in the heart of enemy territory. Through the little window of our room he pointed out to me a broad lake a mile or two below us, and beside it a cluster of houses among the trees; this was the lake and town of Plav. There was a German military headquarters in the town, he explained, and the country all around was thick with fascists. Our friend the *Capo Band* had already left for the new frontier to find out whether I could cross that night; meanwhile I must stay in the room, being careful not to show my face at the window.

At six in the evening the *Capo Band* returned to say that his friends would not be on duty until the following night, but that I could certainly cross then. I had resigned myself to another twenty-four hours of waiting and was preparing to go to bed after an excellent dinner when there was a loud knocking on the front door, and I heard a voice shouting for Idris. He hurried out, to return a minute later with a serious face, accompanied by the *Capo Band*, who looked a little frightened.

'Listen! We must hurry away from here! The German authorities in Plav know of our presence and are searching for us at this moment. We'll move to a village an hour's journey from here—back on the way we've come—please hurry!'

Wondering if one of our own party had betrayed us or if Mehmet's affability at our last meeting had been a mask for treachery, I hurried out of the house with Zenel at my heels. We scrambled breathlessly up the steep slope I had descended so fast the night before, until we came to a track running along the crest. From here we made good progress, only pausing at each bend in the path to send two scouts ahead. Keeping my eyes fixed on the track I lost all sense of direction and time; but at last we halted near a small cabin while one of our party went in to talk with the owner. Ten minutes later we were inside a dim, stuffy little room with grimy plaster walls and a dirty wooden floor on which a young man and three small girls were lying in a jumble of dirty bedding. We threw ourselves beside them on the ground and slept.

Daylight revealed that our new hiding place had been well chosen, tucked away in a fold of the mountains at the head of a narrow valley with no other house in sight. Thick fir forests clothed the mountainsides, their foliage a soft green in the morning sunlight. In the afternoon the *Capo Band* appeared, accompanied by a tall, swarthy Albanian whose head and jaw were wrapped in cloths as though he had toothache; he was, it seemed, the *Capo Band* in charge of the sector of the frontier where I should have to cross.

Through Idris they told me that I could not leave until the following night, when the hue and cry should have died down. Then, for the sum of fifty gold napoleons, they would arrange my journey. This was more money than I had; but after some bargaining they agreed to accept thirty napoleons and my promise that I would commend them favourably to the Allied High Command. I handed over the money on the spot and took a note of their names, which I subsequently passed to a staff officer in Bari.

Next day it was snowing. Fearful that the weather would provide another excuse for delay I paced morosely all morning up and down the little room, my every movement followed by the grave, saucer eyes of the three little girls. Zenel and Idris joined me for lunch and Idris relieved my anxiety.

'Major,' he said, 'you leave for the frontier this afternoon. Zenel and I can accompany you no farther, but the two Montenegrin boys we have brought with us will escort you to Andrijevica, where Tito's Partisans will take care of you. The *Capo Band* and his friends will go with you as far as the new frontier. Between this frontier and Tito's territory is a wide no-man's-land infested by patrols of Albanians, Partisans and Mihailović's Chetniks—all hostile to each other. There will lie your greatest danger.'

In the early afternoon my escort arrived, shaking the snow from their clothes. There were six of them in all, including the two Montenegrin Partisans. Idris was leaving immediately for the south; Zenel, in tears, begged me to take him with me, even to Andrijevica, swearing that he could make his own way back through the mountains to Muharrem Bajraktar.

I knew as well as he did that he could not hope to survive such a journey alone. I sat down and wrote a letter to Muharrem thanking him for giving me so faithful a servant; sternly I ordered Zenel to take the letter to his master, telling him that it was a message of great importance. Only thus could I persuade him to leave me. Then, unable and unwilling to conceal my own tears, I took leave of that greathearted young man who combined in himself the finest qualities of the Albanian tribesman: patience, loyalty and courage. Every night he had lain down to sleep across the doorway of my room; on the march he had always placed himself where the first bullet from an ambush would be most likely to strike. Now, obedient to his *besa* and his chieftain's command, he wished to accompany me on a journey from which he knew he could not return.

We climbed steeply through the forest until we reached the top of the mountain behind the house. The thickly falling snow blotted out our view but the *Capo Band* set a fast and sure pace over the hills, along a very narrow track between high walls of frozen snow. At dusk we halted for an hour at a small house overlooking the lake of Plav and swallowed in silence a meal of eggs and milk provided by the Albanian owners.

It was still snowing when we resumed our journey in the darkness; but the moonlight, filtering through the clouds, was reflected from the snow to diffuse a weird, pale light over the landscape. Soon we descended from the hills into the broad valley of the Lina, following the course of the river northwards over open meadows bounded by hedges. Crossing the flat, snow-covered ground in single file we must, I felt, be easily visible to any hostile patrols or sentries. The two Montenegrin Partisans acted as scouts, moving about fifty yards ahead of us. Luckily they had sharp eyes. As we were crossing a field they halted suddenly, then signalled us frantically towards the cover of a hedge. Crouching in the ditch beside it I watched a file of men approaching on our left; I had counted a dozen of them when I felt a tug on my sleeve and found the *Capo Band* at my elbow:

'*Tedeschi!*' he hissed. 'Over there, too!'—he pointed to a field on our right, where I could make out another and larger party moving parallel with the first—'But they haven't seen us—not yet.'

Slowly, agonizingly slowly, the two German patrols stalked across the fields on either side of us. Silent and motionless we lay in the shallow ditch, holding our breath and sweating with anxiety. Once we were spotted we could not hope to escape across the open snow; nor could we fight our way out against such odds and without one automatic weapon between us. Fervently I prayed that they would not notice our footmarks.

They plodded steadily past us, seeming to look neither to right nor left. We lay hidden for a full five minutes after the last files had disappeared into the night; then we moved forward in a series of bounds from hedge to hedge, floundering across the open fields as fast as we could pull our feet through the deep snow. Nearly two hours later we came upon the main road from Plav to Andrijevica, a broad band of beaten snow between low banks.

After a brief rest we set off along the road at a good pace; our guides seemed confident that we should not run into trouble on this stretch of the journey—a feeling which, after our last experience, I could not share. But as it turned out they were right, for in two hours of walking we met no one.

Half a mile short of the frontier we turned up a steep track into the hills. We climbed slowly through thick pine woods, picking our way with difficulty in the darkness and striving to make no sound that might attract the attention of the frontier guards. Emerging suddenly from the woods we found ourselves on the top of a precipitous slope among some deserted earthworks. We stood now upon the frontier. At our feet lay a deep valley; a steep, bare hillside rose beyond—a no-man's-land of uncertain breadth and unknown danger.

For a moment we halted, crouched among the earthworks, while our Albanian guides held a whispered consultation with the two Montenegrins. Then, with a word of farewell to the Albanians, I sprang to my feet and launched myself downhill in the wake of the two Partisans. So steep was the slope and so slippery the snow that I was soon careering downhill quite out of control; unwilling to finish up with my head in a snowdrift I tobogganed on my bottom for most of the way, pulling up only when I came to a belt of trees beside a stream at the foot of the mountain.

I found the climb on the other side a nightmare, stumbling painfully upwards through the snow and tormented by the knowledge that our figures were clear targets against the bare hillside. However, although the ground was honeycombed with footprints we reached the top of the mountain without being seen. While I sat down to regain my breath the two Montenegrins added considerably to my alarm by lighting a fire in order to signal the *Capo Band* that we had crossed the valley safely. I made them put it out.

We walked for half an hour through the hills, seeing many more footprints but meeting nobody, until my guides, who knew the country well, brought me back onto the main road. We were now in Partisan territory, where our only danger lay in being shot by a trigger-happy sentry. We therefore kept to the middle of the road, walking in line abreast, singing and talking loudly with a confidence which I, at least, did not feel. Beside us ran the River Lim, swift and dark and noisy in the night. Suddenly, as we rounded a corner, a voice called peremptorily out of the darkness ahead.

'*Stoj!*'

We stopped in our tracks. My companions answered the challenge, exchanging a stream of words with the unseen sentry. At last we advanced slowly towards an improvised pill-box beneath an overhanging rock; two very young Partisans seized my hands and shook them over and over again amid a torrent of friendly greetings.

After a few minutes' rest and talk we continued down the road for two or three miles, challenged repeatedly by sentries, until we came to a collection of small wooden huts which formed Battalion Headquarters. In a narrow, smoky room, almost entirely filled by an incongruous four-poster bed, I found a crowd of soldiers, among them the Battalion Commander and his Political Commissar. The former, a lean, weather-beaten Serb, immediately subjected me to a sharp interrogation in Italian, strangely relaxing from suspicion into friendliness when he learned from my escort that I held the rank of major; the Commissar was a small, squat man with very bright eyes and a *Struwwelpeter* shock of black hair who sat on the bed swinging his legs and smiling into the light. I was handed a large piece of stale bread and an army water-bottle full of raki, from which I was repeatedly urged to drink, by the crowd of Partisans who pressed close around me. Overcome with relief at our safe arrival, exhausted by the journey, and stupefied by the heat, smoke, and fumes of alcohol I soon began to nod. Friendly hands removed my boots and carried me to the four-poster bed, where I lay beside the Political Commissar, scarcely aware of his presence.

At dawn I was shaken into consciousness by a very pretty girl wearing battle-dress and a Partisan forage cap; she gave me some soap and poured water over my hands, fluttering her eyelashes and giggling 'Aristocrat!' as I washed. At eight o'clock I took the road to Andrijevica, following the valley of the Lim, past burnt-out villages where the blackened shells of once prosperous farm-houses bore gloomy witness to the hatred bred by political cleavage and religious intolerance.

Soon after midday I reached Andrijevica, a cluster of brown and white houses with broad gables standing upon a hill above the river. In a house in the main street I lunched with a major and two captains of the old Royal Jugoslav Army, now serving on the Staff of General Peko Dapčević, Tito's commander in Montenegro; the walls of the room where we ate were plastered with such slogans as: 'Death to the Chetniks of the bandit Draža Mihailović—the general under whom my hosts had been proud to serve less than three years before. They told me that there was a party of British officers at Berane, eight miles up the road, awaiting evacuation by air to Italy, 'after escaping from Draža's territory.' I had, it seemed, arrived in time.

During the afternoon I received calls from various Albanians whom I had met with the Kosmet, among them a serious young schoolmaster who treated me to a long lecture in French on the 'ethnic identity of the Albanian and Montenegrin peoples'; Montenegro, he explained, his sad eyes enormously dilated behind the thick lenses of his glasses, was ethnically a part of Albania and would certainly be administered as such under the new Partisan regime. After dinner that evening I was treated to a similar lecture from a keen young Montenegrin Commissar, who explained to me that all Albania north of the Drin belonged economically and ethnically to Jugoslavia and would be so administered under the new Partisan regime. These fraternal sentiments did not seem to be shared by the people of Andrijevica; they pointed out to me the surrounding fields which had recently been the scene of fighting between the Partisans and. the attacking Albanians, and rejoiced that the former, even if they were Communists, had managed to repel the invading 'Turks'.

After lunch the following afternoon, 7th February, I started on the last lap of my journey to Berane. A walk of four hours through a thick snow-storm brought me in darkness to a sad and silent town straggling on either side of a broad main street in the middle of a valley dominated by high forested mountains. My guides left me at a dismal two-storeyed building with a courtyard opening off the street. Climbing a wooden staircase to the first floor I entered a dingy, ill-lit room furnished with a table, a few chairs and three narrow beds; through a thick haze of tobacco smoke I saw four or five men sitting round the table. A tall, lean figure in British Army battle-dress, wearing the badges of a lieutenant-colonel, rose and introduced himself with a charming smile.

'Good evening! You must be Kemp. I'm Hudson. We've been expecting you for some days now. Let me introduce Colonel Seitz of the United States Army, Captain Wade, Northamptonshire Yeomanry, and Sergeants Roberts and Ross, who operate our wireless. Have some raki. Do you play bridge?'

I never returned to Albania. Within the year the Communist forces of the L.N.C. and Kosmet had overrun the country. Implacable in their hatred of the British who had nursed them they were determined to destroy all those whom they considered to be our friends. In the eyes of the new rulers of Albania collaboration with the British was a far greater crime than collaboration with the Germans. The fury of the new regime was directed especially against those Albanians who, as our allies, had submerged their political differences with the Communists in a united effort to win their country's freedom. Such men were marked for destruction because their fighting record gave the lie to the Communist claim that the Communist Party alone represented the Albanian people in their fight for independence.[1]

From this murderous holocaust only a few of my friends escaped. The Kryezius, as I have told, declared open warfare against the Germans during my last days in Albania; and later conducted a brilliant campaign against them which nearly drove them from the town of Gjakovë. The Germans in reprisal burnt the Kryezius' house in Gjakovë, plundered their property and destroyed their fortune. But it took the Partisans to kill Hasan and Gani, torture to death their friend Lazar Fundo, and drive Saïd into exile.

Ejub Binaku, my companion and guide in Kossovo, escaped into Greece with his friend, Professor Sulejman Riza, when Tito's forces overran Kossovo and massacred or imprisoned all the Albanian Irredentists who fell into their hands. My servant, Zenel, returned to Muharrem Bajraktar in Luma; I have had no news of him since, nor do I know if he escaped to Greece with his master.

Of the Partisan leaders with whom I worked some have survived to enjoy power and privilege: others have been devoured by the monster they helped to rear. Mehmet Shehu, Prime Minister of the country, and Enver Hoxha, First Secretary of the Party, ride an uneasy see-saw for the supreme position; the ruthlessness and cruelty of the one matched by the treacherous subtlety

---

[1] For a detailed account of this sad saga see Julian Amery, *Sons of the Eagle*, p. 307 et seq.

of the other. Dušan Mugoša, alias Ali Gostivari, was murdered in Kossovo by an Albanian, who was afterwards hanged by Tito; Frederick Nosi, undismayed by his uncle's death at the hands of the Party executioners, was rewarded for his loyalty with the post of Chief Justice of Albania;[1] Baba Faja, the 'Whisky Priest', was shot dead by one of his own Bektashi Dervishes when he tried to impose obedience to the Communists upon his Order; Myslim Peza has found refuge if not peace under the Hammer and Sickle.

Albania, now the most abject of the Russian Satellites, was a totally unnecessary sacrifice to Soviet imperialism. It was British initiative, British arms and money that nurtured Albanian resistance in 1943; just as it was British policy in 1944 that surrendered to a hostile power our influence, our honour, and our friends.

---

[1] There is a rumour that he is now in disgrace.

XI

MONTENEGRO

I need not have hurried to reach Berane. It was nearly two months before an aircraft arrived to take us to Italy—two months of dispiriting inactivity during which we were confined within the limits of the town by the conditions of winter, rumours of an impending German attack and the hostility of our Partisan hosts. I was at least fortunate in my new companions.

The senior British officer of the party was Lieutenant-Colonel Bill Hudson. He was a man in his early thirties, of splendid physique and unusual powers of endurance, who had led an adventurous and exhausting life in peace-time and in war. I was to see a great deal more of him before another year was over. A South African by birth and a mining engineer by profession he had completed his technical studies in England before taking up a series of posts in some of the most unattractive and unhealthy parts of the world. The outbreak of war found him engaged in mining operations in Jugoslavia. When that country was invaded he was sent to Cairo, where his knowledge of the Balkans and command of Serbo-Croat immediately obtained him a commission in the British Army. According to the stories I have read about the fate of such people in the First World War, he should then have been posted to Iceland or Abyssinia; in fact, he was recruited by S.O.E. for service in Jugoslavia.

In the autumn of 1941 he was landed by submarine on the coast of Dalmatia—the first British officer to be sent into the country after the occupation. His orders were to get in touch with General Mihailović, at that time the only Jugoslav resistance leader known to the British Government. Slipping past the Italian coastal garrisons he arrived, after a long, hard and hazardous journey over the mountains, at the General's headquarters; his presence there as a British officer in uniform wonderfully stimulated the morale of that gallant but erratic soldier. Soon afterwards he met Tito, then an obscure guerrilla leader with a small but growing band of followers. Hudson was the first to report Tito's existence and potentialities to London, an achievement for which he was never given due credit by either party. Now, after two and a half years of unrelieved hardship and danger, he was looking forward to some leave in England.

Captain Bob Wade might have stepped straight from the pages of Surtees. About my own age, of medium height and broadly built, with a bright red face, a wide, humorous mouth and a rich throaty laugh he had a vitality and zest for life that no hardship or adversity seemed able to subdue. At the beginning of the war he left his fanning and his horses to join the Northamptonshire Yeomanry and went with them to North Africa; there, after a period of regimental soldiering, he volunteered for service with S.O.E. In April 1943 he was dropped into southern Serbia to one of Mihailović's less reliable commanders. In that area the occupying forces were Bulgars—ferocious enemies whose treatment of the few B.L.O.s they captured was notorious and horrible. Wade had some narrow escapes from them, being surprised on one occasion literally with his trousers down. He was adored by the people of Berane. I can still see his stocky figure striding along the street, his face a glowing beacon against the snow, accompanied by two grinning, bearded Montenegrins, each with an arm round his shoulder.

Sergeant Roberts, who was Wade's wireless operator and worked the set which was our only link with S.O.E. headquarters in Cairo, and so with the outside world, was a quiet, competent young man who treated us all with an easy familiarity that was never offensive. Sergeant Ross, a perky little Australian with an irrepressible sense of fun, had been taken prisoner by the Germans in Greece in 1941 but had managed somehow to escape and join a band of Chetniks. He helped Roberts with the wireless.

Colonel Al Seitz of the U.S. Army was a regular soldier, a serious but amiable officer of considerable seniority. He had dropped to Brigadier Armstrong, the senior British Liaison Officer with Mihailović, in the previous autumn; for General 'Wild Bill' Donovan, the American O.S.S.[1] Commander, was anxious to attach American officers to S.O.E. missions in the Balkans. Seitz confessed himself no politician, but would listen with a fatherly interest to what we had to say before giving us the West Point angle. As time passed he fretted even more than the rest of us; for he was convinced that the 'boys in Washington' were gnawing their nails in their anxiety to have his report in time for what he continually referred to as the 'Spring Offensive'. I must admit that in those days we all shared a simple faith in the value of our reports to the architects of Allied policy.

There was another British officer in the area who sometimes paid us a visit; this was Major Anthony Hunter, Royal Scots Fusiliers, now acting as liaison officer to General Dapčević. He had long been away from his regiment, having commanded a troop of David Stirling's S.A.S. in the desert before he came to S.O.E.; but he retained the regular soldier's healthy horror of politics and, being a guileless young man, took at face value everything told him by the Partisans. Later on his innocent enthusiasm for his job nearly cost us our lives.

Berane was full of troops, Partisan and Italian; these were the 5th Partisan Brigade and the remnant of the Italian Army Corps that had occupied Montenegro in 1941 and surrendered in 1943 to the Partisans. The Italians

---

[1] Office of Strategic Services, the American equivalent of S.O.E.

No Colours or Crest

carried arms and were supposed to fight beside their new allies, but they wore little of the look of fighting men. In tattered uniforms they shuffled about the streets, their sorrowful, starved faces gazing apathetically at the ground; the feathers stuck saucily in their dirty, shapeless Alpini hats seemed only a mockery of their wretched-ness. Whenever we spoke to one of them he would ask us the same sad question:

'When will the Allies come, so that we can go back to our lovely Italy?'

Their new masters treated them like helots; every morning a dismal procession of Italians would amble past our windows in the direction of the Partisan Brigade Headquarters, carrying logs the size of tree-trunks to feed the Comrades' fires. I sighed, remembering the gay *Vincitori di Málaga* whom I had seen swaggering about Spain during the Civil War. The humiliation of the proud ones may be a useful moral lesson, but it is not a pretty sight.

The Partisans, on the other hand, stalked haughtily about the town like men who owned the world—as indeed they did own this little part of it. The townspeople were terrified of them. The new regime had conscripted all the young men and women; the girls who declined military service were put to the hardest and most unpleasant work that the Brigade Commissar could find; for which, of course, they received no kind of payment.

Our own troubles were principally with the Partisan high command, represented by the Brigade Commander and his Political Commissar; the latter was a loud-voiced, dictatorial fellow with a shaven head, long drooping moustaches and a most aggressive manner. The two of them were never at a loss for some complaint against us.

We knew that the Partisans disliked and suspected us: myself for my activities in Kossovo, the others for their contacts with Mihailović, and all of us because of our nationalities; but we had not supposed that they would make their feelings so plain. They abused us to our faces as 'collaborators', 'Fascists' and 'reactionaries'; invited us to concerts where anti-British and anti-American songs were sung and insulting speeches made about our countries; watched our movements and put a guard on our house—officially to protect us but really to keep a check on our visitors. Alone of the Partisan leaders General Dapčević, on the one occasion when he came to Berane, showed us some courtesy. Small and dark, with a firm, handsome face, great personal charm and an alert, lively manner which gave the impression that he moved on springs, the General had won himself a name throughout the country for his leadership, skill, and courage.[1] Before the war he had commanded a battalion of the International Brigade in Spain; if he knew that I had fought on the other side he gave no sign of it.

Most of the time the weather was bitterly cold, with a dead grey sky and frequent falls of snow. The hideous modern town seemed to congeal into a

---

[1] He is now Marshal Tito's Chief of Staff.

gloom that matched our own; the harsh white mountains and the bare black skeletons of the forests hemmed us in, savage and hostile as the faces of our gaoler-hosts. We spent long hours in our cramped quarters playing endless games of bridge for stakes that were illusory, since we knew the winnings would never be collected; we had soon exhausted the few books there were among us. Except for Hudson, who had been in the country much too long, we really had little reason to complain; but it was not the disappointment or the boredom that irritated us—not even the needling of the Partisans—so much as the knowledge that we were sitting idle in a backwater while great things were happening in the war outside. I thank heaven that I was never so unfortunate as to become a prisoner of war.

As though to tantalize us, frequent signals arrived from Cairo assuring us of an aircraft to fly us to Italy as soon as the weather cleared. From time to time it did clear, giving us a day or two of brilliant sunshine; then we would listen all morning and afternoon for the sound of engines in the sky. On the first morning we heard them we ran into the street, to see a flight of old Savoia *trimotori* circling overhead, their Italian markings clearly visible through our glasses. We watched them descend slowly towards the airfield a quarter of a mile out of the town. We were about to run indoors and pack when from the belly of the leading aircraft fell a cluster of gaily-coloured parachutes; the red, yellow, and green canopies made a brilliant splash of colour against the sky and mountains. Each plane made several runs; then they climbed, circled once more over the town and flew off in the direction of the Adriatic.

The Savoias returned on several occasions to drop supplies; we always hoped until the last moment that they would land. In fact, the drops were badly needed, for they contained food, clothing, and medical stores, all of which were cruelly short in Berane. These supplies came from the Americans, but the Political Commissar used all his ingenuity to persuade his men and the peasants that they came from Russia. He went to the trouble of explaining that the initials, U.S. which were clearly stamped on the packages stood for 'Unione Sovietica'; had not the planes been Italian? Then of course the labelling would be in Italian.

The Partisans tried to discourage the local population from making friends with us, but in this they were unsuccessful. Peasants and townspeople would stop us in the street and invite us into a cafe for a glass of *rakija*; the bolder ones asked us to their houses. All told us that they were King Peter's men and hated the Communists. They told us, too, grim tales of night raids in the town by Partisan patrols and of men and women dragged screaming from their beds to the firing squad.

Generally, however, for the sake of our hosts, we avoided all talk of politics, especially when we were in a cafe; for the Partisans, knowing how little they were loved in Berane, employed a flock of *agents provocateurs*. These creatures were a persistent pest. One of them, a Croat, would follow us around from cafe to cafe, however hard we tried to shake him off; pretending to be drunk he would join our table and nothing would shift him because the proprietors were too frightened to make him leave. One day he overstepped himself by making a sickening pass at one of their daughters—a little girl of eleven—whom he had taken into a dark corner. Wade threw him into the street.

Sometimes, tiring of the ugly rectangular buildings of the new town, we crossed the river to the old Turkish quarter, a charming district of small white houses with glimpses of brown gables peeping through the snow. There we drank slivovic or rakija with two old Mussulmen who seemed to feel no more religious scruples about alcohol than their co-religionists in Albania. On other evenings we would join some of our older friends, who had fought in the Serbian Army in the first war, and listen to their stories of the great retreat through Albania to Corfu and their songs of the Salonika front. There was one song I still remember, about the lemon trees of Corfu; it had a sad and haunting lilt:

> *Tamo daleko, daleko kraj mora*
> *Tamo je selo moi, tamo je lubov moia.*[1]

We often wondered why the Germans never bombed Berane, for they must have known of the presence of so many troops. Presumably they had more important targets for their dwindling air force. But they sometimes sent over a reconnaissance plane, which strengthened the rumours of an impending attack from the north; it seemed unlike the Germans to leave a serviceable airfield for long in Partisan hands. We could not see how the Partisans could hold Berane, for they had neither the equipment nor the discipline to stand against the Germans, who could bring armour and artillery down the road from Bijelo Polje. We should have to take to the hills, which would mean leaving many of the sick and wounded to be massacred.

The Partisans and Italians maintained their own hospitals, over-flowing with casualties from the last few months' fighting. It was hoped to fly the most serious cases to Italy. Meanwhile, in the middle of February a new danger arose, more immediate and graver than the German threat: typhus broke out in the Italian hospital. Among the starved and debilitated patients it spread fast. Then it struck the town. There was nothing the civilian doctors could do to check it because, as one of them told us, the Partisans had requisitioned their entire stock of drugs. We ourselves trusted to luck and plentiful applications of delousing powder to keep off the disease; and we were lucky.

---

[1] 'There far away, far away by the sea, There is my village, there my love.'

No Colours or Crest

On 20th February our relations with the Partisans exploded in an incident that nearly ended in murder. Although we resented having guards posted on our house we had never protested, because they had not interfered with us or our visitors. The sentry on duty stood on a landing at the top of an outside staircase leading up from the entrance courtyard of the building; his comrades usually lounged in the court-yard. On the morning of the 20th, hearing the sound of an argument from the landing, we went outside, to find the guard—a new man—refusing admission to the boy and girl who did our marketing. He explained to us, none too politely, that no one was allowed to see us without a written pass signed by the Staff at Brigade.

Hudson immediately sent Sergeant Ross to Brigade Headquarters. Ross returned with an apology from the Commissar, who said that the sentry must have misunderstood his orders. Hudson, Seitz, and I then went back to see the sentry, and Hudson passed him the Commissar's message. The sentry was unimpressed; leaning against the balcony with his hands in his pockets and puffing cigarette smoke in our faces, he replied contemptuously that he knew his orders perfectly well and nobody was going to get by him without a written pass.

Provoked beyond endurance by the deliberate insolence in his manner Hudson seized him by the scruff of his neck and booted him half-way down the stairs. Recovering swiftly from his surprise he turned on us, released the safety-catch of his rifle and pulled back the bolt—thereby ejecting a live round which he had forgotten was in the chamber; then he slammed another round into the breech and took up an 'on guard' position half-way up the stairs. He had the good sense not to level the muzzle at us; for Colonel Seitz had his .45 out and was squinting at him along the barrel.

There followed a few tense seconds. Seitz's face had turned a dangerous dark red and for a moment I feared for the sentry; then the other guards clattered up the stairs to see what was the matter. Hudson explained and asked for the guard to be changed.

'If we find this man on duty again,' he warned them, 'I promise you that we shall disarm him.'

Ten minutes later I passed the landing and saw the same man on guard. We had no difficulty in disarming him, for by now he was thoroughly scared. His rifle was laid on my bed, where it remained until the afternoon; then it was claimed in person by the Brigade Commander and the Commissar. I do not ever remember seeing two more angry men.

'That's all very well,' said Hudson when they had left. 'But it's obvious that the sentry's orders came from the Commissar and that he made no move to alter them. He just put Ross off with an excuse to get rid of him. I should never have gone for the sentry if he hadn't been so insolent. It's a terrible thing for a Montenegrin to have his gun taken from him. They have such exaggerated pride that even the peasants here refer to themselves as *junaci*—heroes.'

The question of passes for our visitors was never raised again. But Hudson was sure that we had not seen the end of Partisan hostility.

'You wait,' he warned us. 'The next thing they'll do is try to collar our wireless set. They knew that as long as we have a wireless link with Cairo there are limits to what they can get away with. So they'll find some excuse to get it from us. Then they can treat us like dirt.'

'Well, it's my bloody set,' said Wade, 'and they're damn well not getting it.'

A week later General Dapčević arrived in Berane. With great tact he asked us not to allow our recent misunderstandings with the 5th Brigade to spoil our relations with the Partisan movement; for a while we thought that the incident was closed.

On the afternoon of 15th March we heard the sound of aircraft overhead; someone ran into our room to tell us they were landing. In a few minutes we had packed and were on our way to the airfield, myself dragging behind the rest because I had another attack of gout. But when we arrived our hopes vanished, for there were only two Savoias on the ground; there would not be nearly enough room for all the wounded, let alone ourselves. The Italian officer in charge told us that his orders were to take only the worst cases, together with the Italian General and his secretary, but that we could have two seats. Hudson declined on our behalf; but after some discussion Colonel Seitz, who was in a state bordering on anxiety neurosis about his report and the 'Spring Offensive,' decided to go. He was not happy about going, but he believed it to be his duty.

By now the scene around the aircraft resembled a popular fair-ground; Partisans, Italians, peasants—men, women, and children—swarmed in a tightly packed circle to get a closer glimpse of the machines, ignoring the angry protests of the crew, who were trying to service them. More sightseers streamed towards them from the town until the field looked like an enormous wheel, with the aircraft as the hub and the converging lines of troops and villagers as the spokes. Everyone was screaming at once in excitement, anger or pure enjoyment.

Suddenly above the din I heard, close overhead, the unmistakable whine of fighters. I looked up in fear, for I knew that the Germans had fighters at Mostar, only a hundred miles to the north; I knew also that a German fighter had once before destroyed an aircraft on this field. Now I could see them—there were two of them—banking in a steep turn to bring them into a dive. People began to scatter in all directions to get away from the Savoias.

'This will be a bloody massacre!' shouted Wade to me as we made for the edge of the field.

No Colours or Crest

Hitherto I had been hobbling slowly and painfully, for my foot was very sore and swollen; now, according to Hudson, I covered the ground like a racehorse. When I thought I was out of the danger area I looked round, just in time to see one of the fighters dive low over the Savoias, pull out and climb away. There was no shooting. My glasses, picking out the red, white and green markings, confirmed that we had made fools of ourselves.

The dive was a warning to the Savoias that the fuel reserves of the escort were running low. At this moment a dispute arose between the Commissar and the senior Italian pilot concerning the proportion of Italian to Partisan wounded in the aircraft. Disregarding the pilot's plea that he must leave at once or fly home without an escort, the Commissar kept the Savoias on the ground for another half-hour before he was satisfied. They took off at last, long after the fighters had gone, and their crew swore never to return.

I was forced to spend the next week in bed, for I could not get my foot into a shoe. My companions cheered me with the latest rumours of the expected German offensive. We should certainly have to take to the mountains, they smugly prophesied, and in a hurry too. How could I possibly come with them in my present state? There was no help for it, they would just have to leave me behind to be taken prisoner. It would provide Lord Haw-Haw with broadcasts for a week:

'Units of the Wehrmacht occupied Berane yesterday and captured a British major in bed with the gout.'

They found this hugely funny.

It was the afternoon of 25th March, and snowing hard outside, when Sergeant Roberts brought us the decoded message from Cairo:

'In view of misunderstanding between Partisans and yourselves reported by Hunter which may endanger British relations with Partisans in Montenegro you are instructed to hand your wireless set to Major Hunter within twenty-four hours of receiving this.'

The signal ended with the information that wireless contact with us would be broken off the following evening. For half a minute after Hudson had finished reading it to us there was complete, shocked silence. We could not have been more astounded if we had been ordered to hand ourselves over to the Germans.

It was not a pretty prospect. We needed little imagination to guess how the Partisans would treat us once the restraint of our wireless link was removed. Hudson was fairly certain that they would arrange an accident for us—or at least for himself, Wade, and me. Nothing could be easier for them, especially if the threatened offensive were to materialize: nothing, in their present mood, would suit them better. We cursed the innocence of Major

Hunter and the cynicism of the Staff in Cairo that had placed us in so dangerous a situation;[1] we could not feel that 'British relations with Partisans in Montenegro' were as important as our lives.

'We have a little over twenty-four hours,' Hudson pointed out, 'in which to get this order reversed. If we send a strong enough protest on our next sked, and send it highest priority, we should get Cairo's reply before the close-down.'

The signal he drafted was long and bitter. After listing the promises he had received from Cairo over the last two and a half years he concluded:

'At least refrain from treachery to your officers in the field. Such conduct is unworthy of prostitutes let alone S.O.E. Staff Officers.' He very rightly rejected my amendment, which would have read:

'Such conduct is unworthy of prostitutes or even S.O.E. Staff Officers.'

His anger must have roused some torpid conscience; for at noon next day we received the most abject apology I have ever seen from any headquarters. We were to retain our wireless, communications would be reopened and—a sting in the tail, but a welcome one—the next aircraft to land at Berane would take us all to Italy.

Two days later, on 28th March, three Savoias landed. While two of them embarked wounded we clambered aboard the third. We said good-bye to the Brigade Commander and the Commissar—one of the happiest partings of my life; a few minutes later the aircraft was climbing steeply towards the mountains. After half an hour's flying the dead black and white of snow and forest gave place to the deep blue of Lake Scutari; far away on our left the houses of the city gleamed in the sunlight. A few minutes later we were over the Adriatic.

To our uncritical minds the first few days in Bari seemed a paradise of gaiety and comfort. We were surrounded with friendliness and flattery; senior staff officers congratulated us, junior officers bought us drinks, and gorgeous secretaries and F.A.N.Y.s asked us to their dinner parties.

We were billeted in the S.O.E. holding camp at Castellana, a group of villas in open country a few miles south of Bari. There we met other B.L.O.s back from the Field, among them Anthony Quayle who had been on the Staff at Gibraltar when I was there in 1941. Quayle had just come out of Albania from the Valona area, where his life had been an uninterrupted nightmare in which the Germans had played only the smallest part. Persecuted alternately by Partisans and Balli Kombëtar, pursued, threatened, robbed, and on several occasions nearly murdered, he had been reduced to living like an animal in a

---

[1] In Justice to Major Hunter I must record that experience soon altered his view of the Partisans. When I met him in London a few months later he was even more virulent about them than I.

cave. He had been rescued by sea on the day that we had flown out of Berane; when I saw him he was suffering from malaria, jaundice, and nervous exhaustion.

There was also a tough little Canadian major, a veteran of the first war, who had been with the Partisans in Bosnia. He had taken to his work with such single-minded enthusiasm that the authorities in Cairo had decided to pull him out for a rest. It seemed that he used to preface his signals with the distribution order: 'Personal to Mr. Churchill following for President Roosevelt.'

Our party soon dispersed. Hudson and Wade flew to Cairo on their way to London, where Hudson's presence was required by the Foreign Office, Roberts and Ross went on leave, and I moved into Bari, where with the help of two patient secretaries I started work on my report.

When I entered the office of the Albanian Country Section the day after my arrival I found nobody there that I knew. Philip Leake was still in Cairo, although he was expected shortly in Bari; Mrs. Hasluck was in Cyprus. The officer in charge was Captain Watrous, an amiable young American with a commission in the British Army who took endless pains to ensure my comfort and peace of mind. He told me that Bill McLean and David Smiley were on their way to Bari to drop into Albania again, this time on a mission to Abas Kupi and the Zogist tribes; as their political officer they were bringing Julian Amery, whom I had met when he was a war correspondent in Spain. I was delighted at the news, for I reasoned that the British Government would not send so powerful a mission to Kupi unless it was intended to give them full support.

Another newcomer to the office was Lieutenant John Eyre, a serious young Communist whose courteous manner could not altogether conceal his disapproval of my Albanian record. Like his co-religionist, James Klugman, he was his Section's Intelligence Officer, and like Klugman and so many other Communists he had great sincerity combined with charm. I saw little of him in Bari but I heard a great deal of him later, when I was in Java. There, while attached to the 5th Indian Division in Soerabaja, he landed himself in trouble by editing a seditious newspaper for the troops; in consequence he was sent home by the G.O.C., General Mansergh.

In the intervals of writing my report I was conducted by Watrous on a round of official visits. The first of these was to the Major-General commanding S.O.M., or Special Operations, Mediterranean. S.O.M. directed, among other activities, all S.O.E. operations based on Italy. Its headquarters was in a village on the coast road south of Bari, where the Major-General had a suite of offices managed by four or five very tall, very beautiful F.A.N.Y.s known as the Potsdam Grenadiers. I have always been nervous of officers above the rank of lieutenant-colonel, and the Major-General did little to put me at my case. For a minute he stared at me across his desk in silence; then he asked:

'Whereabouts were you in Albania?'

I told him. There was another pause.

'Were you with Hands?'

I said that I was.

'Humph! Well, I'm glad you got back all right.'

With that we were dismissed.

Watrous was most apologetic. 'I'm afraid the General is a little vague about Albania. I've shown it to him on the map, but . . .'

Much more friendly and useful were my interviews with the officers of P.W.B., the Psychological Warfare Bureau, an Anglo-American organization which gave valuable help to S.O.E. in the work of undermining enemy morale in occupied countries. One of its stars was the great Harry T. Fulz, who had been Principal of the American College in Tiranë and who was now reviled as a Fascist and a spy by the Albanian Partisans whose leaders included some of his own pupils, notably the ineffable Frederick Nosi. Another whose talents certainly lay in the right direction was my friend Archie Lyall. His work involved him closely with recent events in Albania, and I was disturbed to find him pessimistic about the future of Western influence in that country. He seemed to enjoy living in Bari although, like most British officers I met there, he could not stomach the inhabitants.

'I have an anthropologist friend in this office,' he told me, 'whose researches have convinced him that the *Baresi* are the authentic missing link between the Egyptians and Man.'

Personally I shall always associate Bari with the sharp lesson I learned there on the folly of indulging in outbursts of moral indignation. A short distance away was a rest camp for officers and men of the Eighth Army, where soldiers of Britain and the Dominions were sent to relax for a few days after the horrors of Cassino and the Sangro. For some of their relaxation they came into town, where the rough red wine and poisonous brandy supplied by the shopkeepers sent them literally spinning. It is scarcely an exaggeration to say that at this time the streets, pavements and gutters of the town were strewn day and night with inert khaki bodies.

I suppose that eight months in the Balkans can be lethal to anyone's sense of proportion. That must be my excuse, for it was certainly no business of mine. However, I took it upon myself to write a pompous letter to the Area Commander, in which I said that, having just returned from an enemy-occupied country to one under Allied occupation, I was horrified at the difference in behaviour of the occupying forces. Even today I blush at the memory. I sent the letter through the usual Army channels, and three days later it reached the General.

Meanwhile, for two days I sweated over my report, working well into the dog watches each night. On the third evening I put work aside and went to a party. It was late when I walked out of the Miramare Hotel and paused at the top of the steps to breathe in the cold night air. I took a pace forward, stumbled, and fell headlong onto the pavement, at the precise moment when a patrol of military police was passing.

In the D.A.P.M.'s office a young subaltern of the Brigade of Guards received me with a mixture of respectful courtesy and anxiety. After closely questioning the sergeant in charge of the patrol, who seemed particularly shocked that I had been found without my cap, he noted the details on a large sheet of official paper.

'I'm very sorry, sir.' he told me, 'but we shall have to send in a report on this incident to the Area Commander.'

'The Area Commander!' I exclaimed. 'But surely I didn't resist arrest or create any disturbance?'

'No, sir. On the contrary you were very quiet. But—' he squirmed with embarrassment—'you see, sir, a day or two ago we might have been able to overlook the matter. But since the General received a complaint about the behaviour of troops in Bari he has issued orders that all cases of drunkenness on the part of officers be reported direct to him.'

Luckily for me the General had a sense of humour. But I brooded bitterly on my humiliation—the story was soon known all over Bari—until the arrival of Philip Leake and, shortly afterwards, of Bill McLean and his party put an end to my gloom. I was disturbed to learn that Leake, in whom we all had such confidence, intended to drop into Albania in a last effort to persuade Enver Hoxha to sink his differences with his political opponents and call off the civil war.

'Why do you have to go yourself?' I asked him. 'After all, you're the only experienced Staff Officer we have in the Section.'

'Peter,' he sighed, 'for a year now I've been sitting on my bottom, sending other people into the field. Now I feel I must go in myself—and apologize.'

Six weeks after he dropped he was killed in a German air raid: an irreplaceable loss.

Bill McLean's mission was leaving on 16th April. Thankful as I had been to escape from the Balkans less than three weeks before, I now felt there was nothing I wanted more than to return to Albania with these old friends. McLean agreed to take me, but Leake would not hear of it.

'Certainly not until you've had some leave in England,' was his answer. But he said I might fly over with them in the aircraft.

We took off from Brindisi at nine in the evening in a U.S. Army Air Force Dakota with an American crew. As we were boarding the plane I asked the pilot:

'Who is doing the dispatching?'

'Why, you are, I guess,' was his reply.

'No, he damned well isn't!' chorused McLean, Smiley, and Amery. Not until one of the crew told us that he had dispatching experience could they be persuaded to climb aboard.

We flew over Tiranë and, less than an hour after take-off, saw the fires on the dropping zone where the mission's stores were to be jettisoned—near to the plateau where Brigadier Davies had set up his headquarters the previous October. It took us eight runs over the target to drop all the stores. This dropping zone was too small for parachutists, and so the party was to land on another one, a few miles away. When we arrived there we could see no fires. It turned out later that the officer in charge had lost his nerve and put them out.

For two hours we cruised around, sometimes approaching much too close to Tiranë for comfort or safety. It was not long before searchlights picked us up and the aircraft began to lurch and shake in the flak. We believed that the Germans had no night fighters in Albania, but the anti-aircraft fire was unpleasantly close, and so we raised no objection when at length the pilot told us that he was turning for home. We reached Brindisi at two in the morning and went straight to bed.

It was not until 19th April that the mission was able to drop, by which time I had been recalled to Bari.

XII

POLAND

> Where war is holier than peace,
> Where hate is holier than love,
> Shone terrible as the Holy Ghost
> An eagle whiter than a dove.
> - G. K. Chesterton

Mr. Evelyn Waugh in one of his stories has referred to S.O.E.—though not by name—as an organization engaged in setting up hostile and oppressive governments in the countries of eastern and south-eastern Europe. There was, however, one Section of the organization to which his criticism never applied—the Section controlled by Lieutenant-Colonel Harold Perkins, who directed operations in Poland, Hungary, and Czechoslovakia. To him I reported in London in the middle of June, a month or so after my return from Italy.

Perkins and I had been friends at Weedon. When our course ended he was given the task of coordination with the Polish High Command the recruitment and training of Poles for S.O.E. work, their dispatch to Poland, and the planning of operations inside the country. Later on his responsibilities were extended to cover Czechoslovakia and Hungary. Having arrived back in England too late to take part in any operations connected with D-Day I hoped that Perkins would find me something to do in his territory.

I was not disappointed. He proposed to send me to Hungary to work with a non-Communist resistance group near Gyöngyös, north-east of Budapest. I should have to drop in the Tatra mountains in Slovakia, where the Slovak army was in revolt against the Germans, and cross the frontier to Hungary. It sounded an interesting assignment in a part of Europe that I had always wanted to visit.

Before releasing me to Perkins the Albanian Section suggested that I should meet King Zog, who was living near Marlow. Mrs. Frank Stirling, whose husband, in the course of his distinguished and adventurous career, had commanded the Albanian gendarmerie, took me there to tea. The ex-King lived in a large house above the river surrounded by woods patrolled by grim-faced bodyguards and Alsatian dogs famous for their ferocity and strength. He and the beautiful Queen Geraldine received me with extreme friendliness and almost excessive hospitality; for instead of a cup of tea I was given a tumbler of neat Scotch.

The courage, ruthlessness, and cunning that had raised King Zog from a small chieftain to be ruler of Albania were concealed in a mild manner, a soft voice, and considerable charm. Our conversation centred round the danger of Communist domination of his country—a danger of which I was only too well aware. He was disgusted with the Foreign Office, who had not allowed him to give McLean a letter to take back to Albania calling upon all Zogists to rise against the Germans.

Perkins sent me in July on a fortnight's refresher course in 'cloak and dagger' technique at the training school in the New Forest where I had been in 1941. There I found Hudson and Wade, the latter destined for the south of France, the former for Poland. The following month I spent in London trying to improve my German and learn a little Hungarian, and studying the brief prepared for me by Perkins's two assistants, Major Pickles and Captain Auster. My Hungarian studies were not a great success; the only words I learned were *Nem bezélek Magyarul* (I don't speak Hungarian).

Early in August, twenty-four hours before I was due to leave London, the operation was cancelled. I went on leave to Cornwall to get over my disappointment, but I had only been there a few days when a message from Perkins brought me hurrying back to London. On 1st August the Polish Underground Army,[1] commanded by General Bór-Komorowski, had risen in Warsaw. Perkins was sending them a British liaison mission under Bill Hudson, which he wanted me to join. This operation would be mounted from Brindisi and we must be ready to fly out there in a fortnight.

There were to be six of us, including Hudson and myself: the second-in-command, Lieutenant-Colonel Alim Morgan, was to meet us in Italy, where he had been engaged in liaison work with Polish agents. Next in seniority was Major Peter Solly-Flood, a quick-witted and quick-tempered young Irishman who had served with Hudson in Jugoslavia; a career diplomat, he had with difficulty persuaded the Foreign Office to release turn for the duration of the war. Captain Tony Currie, a British officer of Polish extraction, was to be our interpreter and signals officer; he was an amiable, studious young man who wore glasses and spoke in careful, precise accents; we immediately nicknamed him the Professor. Among his many valuable qualifications was that of a trained wireless operator, although the two wireless sets on which we should depend for our communications with London and Italy were in the care of Sergeant-Major Galbraith, a young and very competent N.C.O. of the Royal Corps of Signals.

We were ready to leave in a fortnight, but political difficulties arose with the Kremlin. In the years since the disruption of that curious manage a trois,

---

[1] In Polish 'Armja Krajowa' (Home Army), abbreviated to A.K.

the Anglo-American honeymoon with Russia, the various instances of Soviet treachery have faded from our memory, dulled either by the passage of time or by the frequency of repetition. The story of the Warsaw rising, however, provides a particularly odious example. In July the Red Army summer offensive across Poland was halted on the Vistula by the German Army Group Centre under Field-Marshal Model; on 1st August Russian forces under Marshal Rokossovsky—himself a Pole—were only five miles east of the capital. At this critical moment the Polish Home Army rose in revolt, joined by the entire civilian population of Warsaw.[1]

It may be that the rising was premature and that supply difficulties and heavy German reinforcements held up the Russians; perhaps the Poles were unduly sanguine if they forgot for the moment that it was the stab in the back from the Red Army in 1939 that brought about the final collapse of their resistance to the Germans, or if they expected Stalin to forget the great Polish victory on the Vistula in 1920 which drove the Red Army from their country. Nothing, however, can excuse the Russian failure to lift a finger in support of Bór-Komorowski; most infamous of all, the allied aircraft flying from Britain and Italy to drop supplies to the beleaguered Poles were refused permission to use the Russian airfields near the city. Knowing that the Armja Krajowa was opposed to Communism in Poland, Stalin was delighted to watch its destruction at the hands of the Germans; in the words of Dr. Isaac Deutscher, usually a sympathetic biographer, 'he was moved by that unscrupulous rancour and insensible spite of which he had given so much proof during the great purges.'[2] After a few weeks of lonely and heroic resistance, during which the Germans systematically reduced Warsaw to rubble, the remnant of the Polish garrison surrendered.

Having paralysed allied help to the Home Army by the denial of their airfields the Russians were equally adamant in their refusal to countenance our own small operation. Describing the Poles as 'Fascists' and 'bandits'—they could scarcely call them 'collaborationists'—they fiercely opposed the idea of sending a British mission to report on the fighting; for they rightly feared that the report would reflect little credit on themselves.

It was not until October that Major-General Colin Gubbins, now in command of S.O.E., was able to prevail upon the Cabinet to let us go without Russian approval. By that time General Bór was a prisoner and Warsaw—what remained of it—was again in German hands.

---

[1] Unlike the Hungarians who revolted in even more desperate circumstances twelve years later, the Poles had accumulated a stock of arms, partly from old Polish Army sources and partly from supplies dropped over the previous four years by S.O.E.

[2] *Stalin* (Oxford), p. 524.

The disaster proved, as the Russians hoped it would, the end of the Underground Army as an offensive fighting force. At the height of the insurrection the A.K. was able to mobilize, apart from its troops in Warsaw, some fifty thousand men throughout the country; but for the shortage of arms it could have mobilized more. In the middle of August these territorial units marched to the relief of the capital; none got through and few returned. The survivors remained mobilized until November, when the fighting formations were reduced to skeleton strength. Their main object during the winter was to maintain their existence.

There was one of these formations in the thickly forested country between Czestochowa and Kielce; Perkins decided that this was the most suitable area for our reception. Obviously much of the value of our mission was lost with the fall of Warsaw; but both the Foreign Office and S.O.E. still required independent information, to supplement reports from purely Polish sources, about the political and military situation in the country, in particular about the strength and morale of the Armja Krajowa. Our reports, it was hoped, would indicate how the British Government could best help the Poles in the face of increasing Russian pressure to abandon them. Perkins impressed upon us that our new role was simply to observe and report; we must not become involved in battle unless we should be trapped and have to fight our way out. He also passed on these instructions to the leaders of the A.K. The Russian Foreign Office and High Command were kept informed of our movements, because we should probably meet the Red Army on its next drive westward from the Vistula.

From the moment we received permission to go we had little time in which to complete our preparations for departure; most of it we spent in learning a new system of coding messages. The greater part of our operational kit awaited us in Italy, but we drew our personal arms from Baker Street; we chose American .30 calibre semi-automatic carbines, because they were light, easy to handle, and accurate up to three hundred yards—ideal weapons for forest warfare. We were also handed, in an atmosphere of grim and silent sympathy, a small supply of 'L tablets', each containing enough cyanide to kill a man in half an hour if swallowed, in a few seconds if chewed; the idea was that we might find ourselves in circumstances where suicide would be preferable to capture. Fortunately or unfortunately we somehow mixed them up with our aspirin tablets and so decided to destroy our store of both.

We flew to Italy in the middle of October; there we were quartered in the village of Selva, on the edge of the hills above the coastal plain between Bari and Brindisi. Had we arrived a few hours earlier we could have left for Poland immediately, for on that day the weather reports were good on both sides of the Carpathians—a very rare coincidence—and an aircraft was leaving to drop a party of agents near our area.

As it turned out, perhaps we were lucky, for the sortie was marked by an ugly accident caused by the inexperience of the dispatcher. While hooking up one of the agents to the wire strong point in the aircraft he somehow passed the static line through one of the straps that held the man's parachute to his back; when the agent jumped, the static line, instead of pulling open his parachute, held him swinging in the slip stream. Although the aircrew tried desperately to pull him back the slip stream was too powerful; he remained hanging in space until he froze to death.

Nevertheless, having missed that opportunity it was more than a month before we had another. At first it was the weather that defeated us. The flight from Brindisi to our target area took five and a half hours—eleven hours' flying there and back, excluding the time spent over the target; therefore the weather had to be good at Brindisi for take-off, clear over the target and good enough for landing at Brindisi on return. In winter this very seldom happened.

Soon, however, fresh political troubles intervened. When we left England the Polish Prime Minister in London was Mr. Mikolajczyk, in whom the British Government had the greatest confidence as a man who had done his utmost to co-operate with the Russians. His moderation, unfortunately, had met with no response from Stalin and had undermined his influence with his own countrymen. Russo-Polish relations were further embittered by Stalin's 'Curzon Line' declaration, when he annexed to the Soviet Union the territories in White Russia and the Ukraine from which Marshal Pilsudski had ejected the Red Army in 1920. Mikolajczyk therefore resigned in favour of Mr. Arciszewski, a Socialist as well known for his hatred of Russia as for his patriotism and integrity. As allies of the Russians the British Government naturally hesitated to accredit a military mission to an organization now under the direction of an acknowledged Russophobe. Stalin's reaction to Arciszewski's appointment was to denounce the Polish Government in London and give diplomatic recognition to a puppet government of his own, composed of Polish Communists and known at first as the 'Lublin Committee'.

It is a considerable nervous strain to have to sit for long in idleness when you are keyed up for an operation of great importance and some hazard; but it is an experience to which most officers of S.O.E. became accustomed. Throughout November we controlled our impatience while our future was fought out in London. We lived in a *trullo*, one of the beehive-shaped dwellings that are typical of the Apulian hill country. These quaint and cosy buildings, warm in winter and cool in summer, are said to date from pre-medieval times when taxation was levied on every house with a roof; their ingenious construction requires no mortar, the bricks supporting one another from foundations to ceiling, so that the roof could be quickly removed on the approach of the tax collector and as quickly replaced after his departure.

From the terrace of our *trullo* on the hillside we looked eastward over silver-green olive groves to the lead-coloured waters of the Adriatic.

We had, of course, too much leisure. Some of it we spent learning Polish with the help of Tony Currie; sometimes we went to Bari to dine with Archie Lyall or drink at the Hotel Imperiale, the transit hotel, where we met our friends on leave from the Eighth Army. Nearly every day we drove to Monopoli on the coast-road halfway between Bari and Brindisi, where Perkins's advanced headquarters under Lieutenant-Colonel Henry Threlfall occupied two floors of a building in a muddy lane. An undistinguished village, Monopoli has one claim to recognition: it is the birthplace of Al Capone—'from mud hut to glasshouse,' as Lyall expressed it.

Occasionally Alun Morgan and I would take a jeep and drive into the mountains to buy wine for our mess. Morgan was an established civil servant who, like Solly Flood, had persuaded his Service to release him to the Army. At Oxford he had been an enthusiastic Socialist and, coming down from the University just before the outbreak of the Spanish Civil War, had all but enlisted in the International Brigades; electing instead to enter the Civil Service he had received a white feather from his girlfriend, a poetess who rowed stroke in the Oxford University Women's Eight.

We fretted, of course, at the erratic arrival, or failure to arrive, of our mail; I also missed the London newspapers. But one unfailing con-solation was the news-sheet Union Jack, published daily for the fighting services in the Central Mediterranean. Its editor was a well-known Fleet Street journalist, who with his anonymous staff of sub-editors managed to extract the spiciest headlines from the dullest items of news. Thus, soon after the liberation of Greece we were treated to GREEK PRIME MINISTER ADDRESSES TRIUMPHANT GATHERING OF LESBIANS IN ATHENS, while another small paragraph, tastefully headed 'DROIT DE SEIGNEUR', informed us that 'Field-Marshal Montgomery today accepted the freedom of Maidenhead'. The pearl of all headlines was found by my brother-in-law—and no doubt by many others—towards the end of the European war, on the front page of one of London's leading dailies: SOVIET PUSH BOTTLES UP ONE HUNDRED THOUSAND NAZIS IN LOWER BALKANS.

In Bari I found Bill McLean, David Smiley and Julian Amery back from their unlucky mission to Abas Kupi. Denied the support they had been promised in London they felt they had also been betrayed by their Country Section in Bari. They had reason to be bitter, because the staff officers of the Albanian Section had received them with undisguised contempt and had referred to them openly as 'Fascists'; worse still, messages which they had sent—and which under their terms of reference they were entitled to send—to the Foreign Secretary and to the Minister of State for Middle East Affairs had been suppressed by the office in Bari. Philip Leake's death in battle had proved a most fortunate accident for the Communists.

At last, early in December, we received permission to go. A few days afterwards, in the late afternoon, we boarded a Liberator of a Polish squadron at Brindisi. Wearing thick clothing under our flying suits—for the aircraft was unheated—and with our parachutes already strapped to our backs we climbed with difficulty through the narrow hatch under the fuselage and settled ourselves half lying, half reclining on the metal floor. I experienced again the claustrophobia I had first known when climbing into the Halifax at Derna; this time there was less room and I felt that we were being packed for immolation in a tin coffin.

The dropping zone, which we had settled in detail on the map, was a stretch of open country surrounded by forest near the town of Zarki, about twenty miles south-east of Czestochowa. We asked to be dropped from six hundred feet, which should give us plenty of time to look around on the way down. The two hazards of the journey, we were given to understand, were a German night fighter belt over Hungary and the possibility of icing up while crossing the great mountain barrier of the Carpathians. We must be careful, also, not to stray over territory held by the Red Army; for the Russians had given warning that they would fire on all aircraft flying to Poland.

When we were over Jugoslavia the two waist gun ports were thrown open and the gunners took up their positions behind the Brownings. One of the gunners started talking to Currie in Polish; he was a squat young man with long dark hair and a perpetual smile on his face, although when I heard his story from Currie I wondered what he had to smile about. His brother had been killed by the Germans in 1939 and his sister sent to a brothel; his mother and father had been arrested by the N.K.V.D. and deported to Siberia. He was the sole survivor of the family.

'Now I have only myself to worry about,' he told us with a little laugh; and he caressed the barrel of the Browning.

We met with no night fighters and we cleared the Carpathians without incident; but on the far side we ran into thick mist. The navigator, Wing-Commander Krol, who was also Captain of the aircraft, came aft and told us:

'It's just like flying through milk. I can't even see our wing tips.'

For an hour we cruised low over the target area, hoping to catch a glimpse through some break in the mist of the fires that would show us the dropping zone. Our fuel reserve allowed us to stay no longer; in deep gloom we resigned ourselves to another five and a half hours of cramp and cold. We landed at Brindisi at four in the morning, just twelve hours after take-off.

I have described this flight in some detail because it was typical of two more unsuccessful attempts we made that month, the last of them on Christmas Day. We had hurriedly swallowed a little cold turkey and plum pudding on the edge of the airfield and were on our way to the aircraft when two signals arrived from England. One was for Tony Currie, announcing the birth of his son; the other was an order to Alun Morgan to stand down and await transport to England, where he was urgently required for duty with his former Civil Service department. Morgan was so indignant that for a moment he seriously considered defying the signal and coming with us. It was as well that he didn't, because we were back in our *trullo* at dawn the next morning.

I had scarcely fallen asleep, or so it seemed, when I was shaken awake to see bright sunlight flooding the room and Hudson standing over my bed. It was half-past ten.

'Get dressed quick! The op's on again this afternoon. Weather reports are good everywhere, so we've an excellent chance of making it this time.'

Alun Morgan and Archie Lyall drove with us to the aerodrome. As we stood talking near the aircraft Morgan remarked cheerfully: 'The last person I saw off from here was Philip Leake. Six weeks later he was dead.'

Lyall shook my hand solemnly and said with impressive gravity: 'Well, good-bye, Peter. I trust you've made arrangements that if you croak I get your Spanish cloak.'

It was nine o'clock when the dispatcher came aft to open the exit hatch in the floor; he told us that the fires were clearly visible on the dropping ground.

'It is a beautiful night,' he smiled. 'Just like daylight, so bright is the moon.'

When it came to my turn to jump and the red light flashed for 'action stations' I sat on the edge of the drop praying that I might make a better landing than I usually managed, calming my fears with the thought that I should have at least twelve seconds in which to get ready for it, and repeating to myself the password Michal by which I must make myself known to the reception committee. According to our information the Germans had a garrison of eighty S.S. at a village six kilometres away and another of fifty gendarmerie ten kilometres away; if they had been alerted by our aircraft the night before we ran the risk of an unfriendly reception.

The red light turned to green, the dispatcher tapped my shoulder and two seconds later the slip-stream hit me as I cleared the exit. When I felt the pull of the opening parachute I looked down for the ground. To my horror I saw that it was very close and coming closer fast. I had just enough time to pull on my lift webs to break my fall before I crashed onto what felt like concrete. For a few moments I lay still, winded and shaken, on the ice-bound ploughland; my left knee hurt abominably and when I tried to get up I found that it would scarcely bear my weight.

At first I thought my parachute must have been late in opening; but it turned out that the pilot, either through an error of judgment or in the excitement of finding himself so close to his native land, had dropped us all from a little over two hundred feet. If any of our parachutes had failed to open immediately there would have been a fatal accident.

While I was pulling off my harness and flying suit two figures came running towards me across the dropping ground. When we had exchanged passwords they asked in French if I were badly hurt; after a moment's doubt I replied that I wasn't. Shaking my hand vigorously and slapping me on the back the two young men each put an arm round me and, laughing and chattering, helped me to hobble towards the trees that fringed the field. In fact, I had suffered no more than a severe bruising and a fright; for a while I forgot my pain in the exultation that swept over me as I realized that at last I was in Poland.

It was a fine, clear night, the air dry, bracing and intensely cold. The wide, level expanse of snow-patched fields where we had landed gleamed with a pale radiance under the glittering stars, in sharp contrast to the black outline of the surrounding forest. Gazing upward for a moment at the bright pattern of the sky I thanked God from my heart that despite all difficulties we had arrived and should now have the opportunity of helping these gallant people who had done so much to help themselves.

In a few minutes we came upon the rest of the party with a group of fifteen or twenty Poles. Hudson, who had knocked himself out on landing, was dazed and groggy from concussion; he wandered about, muttering in a bewildered, plaintive voice, 'I've wet my pants.' Solly-Flood had hurt his back, and Currie and Galbraith had minor injuries. Currie, who was the first to drop, had been dispatched too soon; arriving on the ground at the edge of the field he had found nobody there. Making his way through the woods he almost blundered into a village; luckily he met a party of youths on the outskirts who, although not members of the A.K., guided him back to the reception committee.

The leader of the committee told us that his men would collect all our kit and bury it in a hide-out in the woods in case the Germans, their curiosity aroused by the drop, should send troops to investigate; it would be delivered to us safely next day. Accustomed to the Balkans we were pleasantly surprised when it was. We lingered only long enough to recover our personal arms before setting off along a track through the woods for about half a mile, until we came to a long, low-built farm-house. We were shown into a large and well-lit room crowded with men and women of different ages, all of whom gave us such an enthusiastic welcome that I was unable to decide which were our host and hostess. The majority, we heard, were refugees from Warsaw.

Everyone sat down at a long table in the middle of the room loaded with plates of food and bottles of vodka and wine; I found myself next to a handsome middle-aged woman who encouraged me to drink more than was good for me and to eat more than I wanted; excitement or exhaustion had taken away my appetite. Fortunately she spoke French, for my Polish was unequal to conversation. A bright, intelligent woman, she was surprisingly well informed about events outside Poland. Although the Home Army maintained a news service its bulletins contained very little information and seldom reached the country districts; wireless receivers were almost unknown in the villages, so that most of the war news came from the German-controlled Press.

My neighbour, however, must have had some other source, for she challenged me on a matter which I was to hear raised frequently during the next few weeks and with some bitterness. Earlier in the month there had been a debate in the House of Commons on Poland and in particular on the Curzon Line. In his speech the Prime Minister, anxious to say nothing that might damage relations with Russia, had remarked that Stalin's action was largely a result of the intransigence of the Poles. Most people in Poland recognized that Britain could do little to restrain Stalin, since Russian troops were already on the Vistula; they were resigned to making the best of a bad job, for partition was not a new thing in their history, but they were indignant at being blamed for the treachery and rapacity of which they were the victims.

The meal ended with speeches of welcome, to which Hudson, somewhat recovered from his concussion, replied on our behalf. Soon after midnight we continued our journey northward, escorted by some twenty armed men and three girl partisans.[1] Nearly all wore some kind of uniform, usually an old army tunic—either Polish or converted German—with a leather belt and ammunition pouches, breeches, puttees, and boots; a few had British battle-dress. Most of the men wore Cossack hats of grey fur, sometimes with the Polish eagle and crown embroidered on the front.

My knee was too painful and swollen for me to walk, and so I was laid on a pile of hay in a farm cart pulled by an old horse. After three miles we stopped at a peasant's house in the village of Kacze Bloto, where an old man and his wife were awaiting us. Within a minute of lying down I was asleep.

Early next morning the leader of our escort woke us with the surprising news that two Russian officers were waiting to see us. We found a captain and a lieutenant, both of them quite young, who told us that they had been dropped three months before and were now living in this village. They spoke Polish and German, which Currie and Solly-Flood interpreted for the rest of us; although shy at first, they were friendly and freely answered all our questions. They were wearing civilian clothes, and almost their first words were to recommend us to do the same; advice which, as it turned out, we were wise not to take. It seemed that they lived on excellent terms with the villagers and with the Armja Krajowa, on whom they relied for their intelligence and for warning of German movements. They appeared to have no very active duties.

---

[1] The word 'partisans' in this chapter refers to any armed guerillas under military discipline, and has no political connotations.

No Colours or Crest

It may be useful here to give a brief description of the paramilitary forces operating in Poland at this time. The Russians began to drop small parties of officers and N.C.O.s in the country west of the Vistula during the spring of 1944; although well equipped with arms and wire-less they were not supplied with food or money; they were obliged, therefore, to live off the country, requisitioning what they needed from the peasants. To the unpopularity thus imposed upon them they added the grave mistake of avoiding all contact with local resistance groups; in consequence they received no warning of German attacks and were soon destroyed or forced to abandon their equipment and go into hiding. Later the Russians dropped a few large parties, of a hundred men and upwards, who concentrated on railway demolition. These took care to cultivate good relations with Polish resistance, particularly with the A.K., establishing mutual warning systems against German attack; but like their predecessors they had to depend on requisitioning for their food. There had been two of the larger parties in this area, but they had moved east before our arrival.

Our Polish friends told us that all the Russian officers used to recite the same few words of propaganda, which they seemed to have learnt as a set piece; they make ironic reading against the background of subsequent events: 'We Russians have not come to occupy your country. We do not care what kind of regime you choose for yourselves, so long as it is not Fascist. We have only come to beat the Germans and then go home.'

It is well known, although it can bear repetition, that Poland alone among the countries occupied by Germany produced no Quisling. But Polish resistance was never united under a single command; there were several movements inside the country, each pursuing its own policy. Of these by far the most popular and powerful was the Armja Krajowa, which commanded the passive support if not the active participation of more than ninety per cent of the country. Originating at the end of 1942 with the fusion of four large resistance groups, each of which represented some political party of pre-war days, it was at first a purely underground movement, whose members remained in their homes but carried out secret military training. It was organized on a territorial basis in platoons of from thirty to a hundred men. Its principal objects were to prepare for a general rising at a suitable moment to expel the Germans; to weaken them in the meantime by sabotage and guerrilla actions on a small scale; and to protect the population against oppression. Later the A.K. developed its own political machinery, in collaboration with the exiled London Government, to administer the country after liberation. One of its leading politicians M. Retinger, parachuted in from Italy shortly before us, making the first drop of his life at the age of fifty-two.

Partisan units were mobilized as the need and opportunity arose for direct action; their ranks were swelled by young men who had fled from the towns and villages to escape conscription or forced labour. These units lived in the woods and, whenever possible, wore some trace of uniform. Their weapons were of all kinds: some came from old Polish Army stocks; others were dropped from Britain and Italy; a few were traded from Russian partisans for food, information or money, and many were captured or stolen from the Wehrmacht. The A.K. also maintained specialist sabotage groups, an elaborate intelligence system and its own nursing and courier services; the couriers were nearly always women and children. The higher ranks of the movement were drawn from officers of the Polish Army who had remained in Poland; some junior officers and many saboteurs and agents were sent by S.O.E., all of them Poles. As far as I know we were the first and only British officers to be dropped into the country.

Next in importance to the A.K., though greatly inferior to it in numbers, efficiency, and influence, was the A.L. or 'Armja Ludowa' (People's Army). As its name implies, this was a Communist organization, supplied and directed by the Russians. Its principal aim was to form a cadre capable of taking over the country's administration, with Russian help, after the arrival of the Red Army. In the meantime it attempted road and railway sabotage on a small scale and issued a great deal of propaganda designed to discredit all other resistance movements. Its partisan units wore red-and-white armbands and the Polish eagle without the crown. They were poorly trained and led, and their intelligence and warning systems were inadequate, with the result that their casualties were heavy. Moreover, having no funds they had to loot in order to live, and their levies pressed heavily on landowners and peasants alike. Relations with the A.K. were cold but correct; there was no fighting between them and they gave each other warning of enemy attacks. In Warsaw there were detachments of A.L. who fought very well, at least in the early stages of the rising.

Lastly, there was the N.S.Z. (National Armed Forces), a small political and paramilitary organization derisively nicknamed 'The Colonel's Party'; politically it was so far to the right that even the A.K. called it reactionary. Its members were sometimes accused, especially by the A.L., of collaboration with the Germans, but they fought gallantly enough in Warsaw. Relations between the N.S.Z. and Armja Ludowa were as bad as they could be; they fought each other whenever they met, taking no prisoners.

The Germans treated members of all three organizations as rebels, so that any Pole taken in arms was likely to be executed. But our friends in the A.K. told us that they stood some chance of survival if captured by the Wehrmacht, none at all if taken by the S.S.

Most savage of all were the German auxiliary troops belonging to the army of the renegade Russian General Vlasov. Vlasov was a Cossack who was captured at the beginning of the German offensive against Russia in 1941 when, according to some figures, eight hundred thousand Russian soldiers were taken prisoner. From these Vlasov recruited an army of Cossack,

Ukrainian, Turkoman, Mongol, and other Asiatic troops, which the Germans employed chiefly on garrison and security duties in occupied countries. Knowing that they would receive no quarter if taken, these men fought to the last; such was their barbarity towards the civilian population that they were feared and detested throughout occupied Europe. In this part of Poland there were Ukrainian and Turkoman divisions on the river Pilica and Cossack patrols everywhere. The A.K. shot any of Vlasov's men whom they captured, as they also shot all S.S. men; prisoners from the Wehrmacht were usually deprived of their arms and uniforms and then released.

The country here was not well suited to guerrilla warfare. It was quite flat and, at this time of year, covered in snow. The Germans could bring tanks, armoured cars and lorried infantry to almost any part of the area with very little warning; the partisans, on the other hand, were seldom more than five miles from a German garrison. The great fir forests, carefully cultivated for their timber, were intersected at regular intervals by long, straight, broad rides which could be swept by machine-guns; there was scarcely any scrub or undergrowth and the trees were bare of branches from the ground to a height of more than twelve feet. They gave concealment from a distant enemy but little protection from close range. The only dense cover was to be found in plantations of young firs that had not yet been thinned.

German operations against the Poles took two forms; the *pacyfikacja*, a punitive expedition against partisans, and the *lapanka*, a round-up of young men and women in the towns and villages for work in Germany; Cossack and Ukrainian troops were usually employed in both. The tactics of the *pacyfikacja* were as simple as they were frightening. The area of forest in which the partisans were hiding was tightly cordoned; tanks, armoured cars and heavy machine-guns were stationed where they could command all the rides; then infantry in close formation beat through the woods, driving the partisans, like game, onto the guns. The A.K. claimed that their warning system usually gave them time to leave the threatened area, or that their knowledge of the terrain enabled them to slip through the cordons by night. The *lapanka* was harder to counter, in winter especially, because the partisan units were then reduced to skeleton strength and could provide neither food nor protection for the fugitives.

We left Kacze Bloto at dusk on the 27th with an escort of twenty men under a Lieutenant Twardy;[1] I was still unable to walk far and rode again on the farm cart, which also carried our heavy kit. It was a fine but freezing night and despite my American army windbreaker jacket, heavy whipcord trousers, and thick gloves and socks I was soon numb with the cold. The creaking of

---

[1] Nearly all the names of A.K. officers mentioned in these pages are *noms-de-guerre*.

the wagon, the crunch of footsteps in the snow and the gusty whinnying of the old horse sounded as if they must carry for miles in the stillness. Propped upright against a pile of rucksacks, my pipe in my mouth and my carbine resting on my knees, I fancied myself an early settler travelling into the heart of some unknown continent; I certainly felt jumpy enough, for whenever the men at either end of the column called out directions or orders in their loud, harsh voices I found myself gripping the carbine with my thumb on the safety catch and peering anxiously from side to side into the dark and silent forest.

At length we came to a cottage on the fringe of forest and open fields. Here we were welcomed by a middle-aged Pole who wore the armband of the German-controlled Forestry Service, a taciturn but hospitable fellow. In his small but comfortable parlour his wife gave us a warm greeting, which she immediately reinforced by making us sit down and drink two bottles of cherry vodka. An enormous meal followed; and we slept in clean sheets.

We were surprised at the quantity and excellence of our food, for we had understood that the severity of the German agricultural levies had left the peasants on the verge of starvation. However, we learned that the peasants, with the help of the A.K., contrived to evade the levies, or at least to mitigate their effect; and an ingenious system of barter and black market in the surplus produce ensured that, in the country districts at least, the people did not go short.

We stayed the next two days in the forester's cottage, but we were not idle. Most of the first day we spent encoding telegrams to Italy, which Galbraith immediately dispatched, announcing our arrival and recording such of our first impressions as we thought might be useful. We had visits from A.K. officers, including the local battalion commander and an officer who had recently returned from a campaign of sabotage in northern Silesia—a dangerous area owing to the hostility of the population. A young lieutenant was attached to us to act as our liaison officer with the A.K.

In the early afternoon we heard the sound of machine-gun fire about two miles away across the fields. Lieutenant Roman, the liaison officer, immediately sent out a patrol and posted double guards on the approaches to the house. In the evening he told us that a troop of Cossacks had been carrying out a *lapanka* in a village nearby.

'One or two villagers were shot, and I hear that a girl was raped.' He smiled and shrugged his shoulders.

However, he was sufficiently worried to suggest that we should move away from this area; he told us that the Germans had heard our aircraft two nights ago and were already making inquiries, and that the partisans here were not strong enough to protect us. He proposed to take us the following evening to the neighbourhood of Radomsko, where they were more numerous.

Next morning, 29th December, Currie and Galbraith, accompanied by Roman and his men, carried all our heavy kit except the two wireless sets and their necessary equipment into the woods and buried it in a concealed dug-out. We could send for it later when we were more securely established. In fact we never saw it again; Roman was killed by the Germans a fortnight later while he was trying to recover it for us.

We began our journey at dusk, accompanied by Roman, Twardy and the escort. Nearly all our journeys in Poland were made at night, because the enemy had too healthy a respect for the partisans to venture into the country after dark; the dangerous hours for us were from dawn until late afternoon. Even so, we moved carefully as a small tactical unit, with scouts ahead, an advanced section and a rearguard. On this occasion two hay carts accompanied us and carried not only our kit but our entire party and all of the escort who were not required for scout or guard duty; for the paths were deep in snow and if the Germans were searching for us we should be wise not to leave too many tracks. As a further precaution we had to remove our badges of rank and parachute wings; in order to keep our identity from the peasants our guards were going to pass us off as escaped prisoners of war. There was little, I reflected, that the Poles did not know about their favourite word, *kotispiracja*.

We travelled all through the night, sometimes along forest tracks scarcely wide enough for the carts to pass, sometimes across open country over fields shining in the snow, with the faint lights of distant villages blinking at us through the dark. Three times on the way we stopped at peasant houses— twice for a glass of vodka and something to eat, and once when a cart broke an axle in a deep rut. Dawn was near when we came to a group of farm buildings, part of a large estate. Here we had hoped to sleep, but the manager would not have us; Cossacks came there every morning, he told us, to collect hay and so we should be well advised to move on quickly.

It was bright daylight when, tired and frozen, we stopped at a peasant's house in a village five miles further on. The two small rooms were already filled with people sleeping on the floor, all of them refugees from Warsaw. Indeed, all the country districts in this part of Poland were overcrowded with fugitives from Warsaw and from the eastern provinces occupied by the Red Army; it was a serious problem, which had already caused one epidemic of typhus and a general deterioration in health, aggravated by an acute shortage of medical supplies.

Late in the morning, after we had slept, we made our first wireless contact with London, who had the kindness to pass on to us a few messages from our families and friends. We left again in the evening and marched all night. There was no need now to hide our tracks, and so we walked beside the carts, glad enough to be able to keep warm rather than sit and freeze as we had done on the last journey; luckily we had all recovered from our parachuting injuries. Marching along with these cheerful Poles I began to feel a sense of security such as I had never known before in enemy country; their infectious self-confidence, their efficiency and their inspiring record convinced me that they would neither lead us into unnecessary danger nor fail us if we ran into trouble. In the latter belief I was soon enough proved right.

In cold grey twilight we skirted the small village of Wlynica and approached a large country house standing on a rise in open parkland surrounded by woods. We were evidently expected, for lights were burning in the windows downstairs. Roman went ahead to announce us. In a few minutes he returned and led us up a flight of stone steps into a large high-ceilinged hall dimly lit by oil lamps and filled with the scent of pine logs; there our hostess was waiting. In many countries over many years I have never seen a more beautiful woman than the slim, dark-haired girl who stepped from the shadows to meet us. Her great, dark eyes set in the face of a mourning Madonna smiled a welcome that brightened the gloom of the dying lamps and coloured the ugly neutral light of invading morning.

She greeted us in a soft, clear voice and led us to a small room where a meal was waiting. While we ate she asked us about the progress of the war. Her husband, an officer in the Polish Army, had been a prisoner of the Germans since 1939 in an Oflag in Posen; she counted the days till she could see him again.

We awoke late, relaxed and content. The war seemed very far away in this large and gracious house. Solly-Flood and I shared a room; we had bathed and were finishing dressing, savouring the luxury of comfort and leisure, when Hudson came in.

'There are some men coming up to the house,' he told us cheerfully. 'They're in uniform, and they look to me like Huns. But no one seems to be worrying and so I suppose it's all right.'

'Lots of the A.K. wear Hun uniforms or bits of them,' I pointed out. 'Are we in time for some breakfast, or do we go straight on to the vodka?'

Before he could answer, Roman and Currie hurried into the room, their faces tense.

'The Cossacks are here! We've got to hide. Hurry!'

Behind them I saw our hostess looking anxious but calm; she beckoned to Roman and murmured a few words to him before walking towards the hall.

'Follow me,' Roman ordered and led us at a run up a flight of stairs, along a corridor and up more stairs to a small, bare room with a single high window.

We sat on the floor not daring even to whisper, our ears strained for the sounds of a search; all I could hear was a murmur of voices and the muffled tread of boots in the hall below, but even those sounds seemed faint in comparison with the hammering of my own heart. I did not dare imagine what would happen to Madame Rubachowa if we were discovered in her house; I could not bear to think of her rotting in the horrors of Ravensbruck or Oswiecim—supposing Vlasov's ruffians let her get so far. As for ourselves, we should be lucky to meet no worse a death than a firing squad; Hitler had ordered the execution of all captured parachutists, and we could not hope to pass for long as escaped prisoners of war.

The tension grew in the tiny, dim room as the long drawn-out minutes passed and we listened to the shouts and clatter of boots on the two lower floors. Suddenly, with a wild rush of panic, I heard heavy steps on the stairs leading to our hide-out; I unbuttoned my holster and gripped my automatic as with agonizing deliberation they approached. The door was flung open and two grinning figures stood in the entrance beckoning us out. With almost sickening relief I recognized two of the servants who had waited on us the previous night.

Madame Rubachowa was an excellent hostess and went to a great deal of trouble to ensure our comfort and entertainment. Knowing that we wished to meet as many of her countrymen as might be useful to us in our mission she arranged a large luncheon party, to which she asked a few senior officers of the A.K. and some younger friends of hers who lived or were staying in the neighbourhood. I suppose the latter could be described as a mixture of local landowners and refugee intellectuals from Warsaw. We commented on the lack of interest that all of them, old and young, showed in the personalities of the exiled Polish Government in London—an indifference which we found everywhere in Poland. Mikolajczyk alone seemed to have a considerable following. It has often been remarked that governments in exile tend to lose touch with the people they claim to represent; they tend also to lose their respect.

Among the A.K. officers present was a certain Major Stefan, commanding the 25th Infantry Regiment. This unit, which was disbanded after Warsaw, retained one detachment of about forty men under arms, commanded by a very young and enthusiastic subaltern, Lieutenant Warta; he and his men were to be our escort in future, replacing Roman and Twardy.

That evening, the last day of the year, we left the house of Madame Rubachowa while it was still light; we were to see her again before long, in sadder circumstances. As we plodded across the fields towards the forest I was filled with a curious despondency, I might almost say a premonition of disaster; at the time I put it down to the melancholy of parting from Madame Rubachowa, intensified by the chill of the dead and snow-bound countryside and the grim, cold blackness of the fir trees rising out of the thickening gloom. I tried to shake it off during the three-mile journey through the woods which brought us to the village of Katarzyna; but my apprehension deepened as we approached the outskirts and came upon a wide, straight road whose hard, snow-covered surface was clearly designed to carry motor traffic.

No Colours or Crest

In the village we were led to the house of a Madame Dembowska, a middle-aged widow with a shock of white hair above a mahogany face who fussed unceasingly about our food and comfort. The house, which resembled a small chalet, stood apart from the village, among open fields separating two areas of forest, and was surrounded by stables and outbuildings; the rooms were furnished in the heavy, gloomy style usually associated with aspidistras and antimacassars.

Our escort, whose quarters were in a group of huts on the edge of the nearest woods, invited us to join them after dinner to see in the New Year. When we arrived the small mess room was packed with cheerful, noisy partisans and heavy with the reek of sweat, tobacco and unwashed clothing; the lamplight flickered on the strong faces and sparkled in their fierce, eager eyes. At midnight we all stood to attention and sang the Polish National Anthem, a noble tune with brave words worthy of that heroic and indestructible people.

'Jeszcze Polska nie zginela póki my zyjemy,' (Poland is not yet lost while we are alive) we roared in chorus with more feeling than tune.

Next we sang the *Warszawianka*, the stirring call to battle written for the Warsaw rising of 1830—the rising whose defeat a year later inspired Chopin's 'Revolutionary' study. Bottles of vodka and plates of *zakaska* were passed round; we drank toasts to Poland and Britain, to Anglo-Polish friendship, to His Majesty the King of England, to Mikolajczyk, Churchill, and Roosevelt, and to the damnation of our common enemies; our hosts shook us by the hand, slapped us on the back and warmly if unsteadily embraced us all in turn. The smoky, overcrowded room rang with shouts: 'Down with the Curzon Line!' 'We want Wilna and Lvóv!' 'To Hell with the Lublin Committee!'

The party culminated in a series of *feux-de-joie* from the rifles of our escort. It was this final gesture, I am sure, that brought us trouble in the morning.

Before we went to bed Hudson made it clear to Lieutenant Warta that we should have to depend on him for all instructions concerning our security. He replied that his men made a habit of rising at five every morning and standing to until at least an hour after daybreak; he did not think it likely that the Germans would be very active on the morning of New Year's Day, but he would see that we were alerted just the same. And so ended the year 1944.

I awoke soon after seven with a bursting bladder, a natural consequence of the previous evening. I went outside to relieve it and was on my way back to the house when I heard a dull rumbling from the direction of the road we had crossed the previous evening; distant at first, it became noticeably louder as I listened. It was a sound I had first heard in the days of the Spanish Civil War: the sound of approaching tanks. Hurrying into the room where the rest of the party were sleeping I shook Hudson awake.

'Bill, I don't want to alarm you, but I'm jolly sure I hear tanks. And they're coming closer.'

I had hardly finished speaking when one of our escort burst into the room to confirm my fears. We threw on our clothes, grabbed our carbines and slung over our shoulders the small haversacks containing our signal codes and essential personal kit. Currie and Galbraith seized the smaller of our two wireless sets and the portable hand generator; it would be calamitous if we were to lose our own wireless links with London and Italy. If the Germans were indeed coming after us there was no hope of saving our heavy, more powerful set or any of our equipment that we could not carry ourselves.

We were not left long in doubt. While we made our preparations for flight the sound of the tanks grew louder; we could also hear the roar of heavy lorries grinding along in low gear. From close at hand came Warta's voice rapping curt orders to our escort. Solly-Flood and I ran out to see what was happening. Turning right outside the door I ran for the shelter of a barn and peered round the corner in the direction of the noise.

I saw four medium tanks, their guns pointing straight at us, moving at a tangent across a field three or four hundred yards to my front; behind them, in a clump of trees, several large lorries were disgorging green-uniformed soldiers. Fascinated by these preparations for our destruction I was brought sharply to my senses by the crack of an exploding shell in a ditch a few yards away; at the same time a burst of machine-gun fire spattered the walls of my barn. As I jumped back into cover I heard, from my left, the clatter of a Bren; with astonished admiration I saw that a detachment of our escort had emplaced itself behind a low bank and was firing on the tanks and the advancing infantry: some twenty-five Poles with rifles and one light machine-gun were taking on four tanks and at least a hundred well-armed Germans.

I heard my name shouted and, turning, saw Warta and the rest of our party beckoning to me from the door of the chalet. Warta was talking to Currie in short, urgent sentences; he ran to join his men and Currie translated his instructions.

'We're to make for those woods,' he told us, 'while Warta holds off the Germans. Once we've got clear he will break off the action and try to join us. We have to cross some open ground first, so we must run.'

The patch of open ground between the house and the woods was some three hundred yards wide; we should be crossing it in full view of the enemy and clearly outlined against the snow. Half-way across was a thin plantation of young firs; we sprinted for this, darting from the cover of the chalet like flushed rabbits and sweating with fear as we forced our heavy feet through the clogging snow. If there is any more disagreeable experience in warfare than that of running away under fire I hope I never meet it. There is none of the hot excitement of attack, but much more of the danger; the blood trickled icily in my veins and with each step my muscles contracted, anticipating the impact of a bullet; my throat felt dry and constricted and I had a violent urge to vomit. Bullets in plenty sang over our heads and smacked into the ground all round us as we ran. But fortunately the tanks were concentrating their attention on the heroic Bren-gunner and his companions; one machine-gun would have finished the lot of us. As it was, we were beyond the effective range of Schmeizers, and the riflemen seemed to be poor shots.

We reached the fir plantation without a casualty and paused a moment for breath, sitting in the snow because the saplings were not tall enough to hide us when we stood. Here we dumped the hand generator in a ditch; it was much too heavy for a running man and Currie had done well to bring it so far. It was cunningly hidden and Currie retrieved it himself later the same day.

From behind us broke loud on our ears the sound of battle: long bursts of machine-gun fire, the vicious crack of tank shells and the faint popping of rifles.

'Jesus!' sighed Solly-Flood, 'aren't we the brave boys? Running off to the woods while the Poles stand and take the rap. This is a shit's job.'

'You know our orders,' snapped Hudson. 'What's more, so do the Poles. Come on, let's go.'

All together we broke cover, spreading out as we ran across the last hundred and fifty yards that separated us from the shelter of the great forest. But the fighting now was in Katarzyna village, around the house of poor Madame Dembowska, and no one paid attention to our flight.

Ten minutes later, when we had hidden the wireless at the rendezvous Warta had indicated, we returned to the edge of the wood to peer through the trees at Katarzyna. The firing had died away; thick smoke was rising from Madame Dembowska's farm buildings, and above the roar and crackle of the flames we heard the Germans calling orders in that half-bellow, half-scream which in their army was the voice of command.

Dismally we wandered back to the large plantation of saplings where we had left the wireless. We were sure we had seen the last of Warta and his men, and it was bitter to feel that but for our presence they could have faded into the forest without a fight. Madame Dembowska, too, would be in trouble when the Germans found all our equipment in her house. The fact that she had not invited us was unlikely to be accepted as an excuse.

These painful thoughts occupied us in silence for half an hour. We were the more astounded, therefore, as well as delighted when Warta himself appeared with the greater part of his detachment—the rest, he explained, were on guard or patrol duties. In the whole action he had lost only one man—the Bren-gunner, who had certainly courted death and who had been killed instantaneously by a machine-gun burst from one of the tanks; his body had been recovered and would be buried in the morning. Warta had broken off the action after ten minutes, rightly considering that he had given us plenty of time to get away. He claimed to have inflicted casualties on the Germans, and he must have given them a mauling, because they had not cared to pursue him. By any standards his performance was an epic of skill, self-sacrifice, and valour—those qualities that had forged the grand and tragic drama of Warsaw.

We stayed in the woods for most of the day, with guards posted to warn us if the Germans should return. Now that they knew there was a party of British parachutists in the neighbourhood they might well conduct an intensive pacyfikacja and beat us out of our hiding place; we must therefore be clear of the district before morning.

In the late afternoon we went back to Katarzyna. Madame Dembowska's house was deserted but undamaged; the Germans had confined their destruction to the out-buildings. As we feared, our unhappy hostess had been taken to Czestochowa; we learned later that she was released next day frightened but unharmed. After the battle the Germans had brought their casualties into her house, and Warta pointed with grim satisfaction to the blood-spattered dining-room table on which they had been laid for operation.

All our equipment, of course, had gone; Solly-Flood, who had been a Brigade Intelligence Officer, treated us to a graphic description of German Security Officers examining with painstaking thoroughness each article of our kit and evaluating its military and political significance. From our point of view the most serious losses—we did not then appreciate how serious—were our heavy wireless set and petrol generator; the smaller set had not the necessary power, and the hand generator that Currie had saved gave continual trouble. We were soon reduced to handing our encoded signals to the Home Army for transmission; only when we returned to London did we learn that neither Perkins nor Threlfall had received any of them.

We never discovered what had brought the Germans to Katarzyna. Warta suspected that members of the Armja Ludowa, of whom there were several in the village, had informed on us in the hope that we should be captured and their rivals consequently discredited. There was no evidence to support his theory, and it seems more likely that the *feux-de-joie* on New Year's Eve attracted the enemy's attention.

We did not linger in Katarzyna, but in the last daylight began our journey through the woods. We marched fast and with few halts or rests; although it was unlikely that we should meet Germans abroad at so late an hour we took no chances and moved in our usual formation. Warta's senior sergeant had found himself a fine horse and rode up and down the column all night, checking the distances between the main body and the advance guard and rearguard, keeping an eye on the scouts and encouraging us all in his strong, cheerful voice. He was a man of fine physique and commanding presence with a long experience of partisan warfare; in his fur hat, with his cavalry bandolier and his rifle slung across his back, he looked to me like some famous Cossack hetman—a Mazeppa or a Stenka Razin—as he rode along the line in the thickening dusk.

In the small hours of the morning we reached our destination, the village of Dudki. We had brought with us the body of the gallant Bren-gunner, and at daybreak we assembled to give him burial. There was no priest, but the service was read by the Battalion Commander, whom we found awaiting us at Dudki. As we stood around the open grave on a bare, windswept mound outside the village, blinking our red-rimmed eyes against the harsh and hostile light of that snowbound dawn, I wondered, as I think we all did, how we could hope to justify this man's sacrifice for our safety. When the body, wrapped in a Polish flag, was lowered into the ground, when the volley was fired and the earth sprinkled, then we felt the full shame and bitterness of our flight. On the wooden cross that marked his grave I wished I could have written Simonides's epitaph on the Spartan dead at Thermopylae, who also died defying hopeless odds.

Afterwards Warta told us sadly: 'We can not even tell his family, because they live in eastern Poland—beyond your Curzon Line.'

We left Dudki immediately after the funeral and tramped for two hours through the forest until we came to a collection of scattered farm-houses known as Maly Jacków. In one of these we prepared to spend the day, but at noon Warta hustled us outside and led us at a run into the woods: detachments of *Feldgendarmerei* had arrived at the next village and were asking if any British officers had been seen. Although they did not visit Maly Jacków we remained in the forest until twilight, nursing our ragged nerves among the fir trees.

Our guest at dinner that night was a very senior officer of the Armja Krajowa, the colonel in command of the Czestochowa Inspectorate. A friendly person and anxious to put us at our ease, he frequently assured us that nobody in Poland felt bitterly towards our country because Britain was too far away to give much help to Poland; but, he added fiercely, the Poles would fight to the last man to preserve their independence from Russia. We forbore to ask him how they could hope to fight so powerful a neighbour without a single aeroplane or piece of ordnance at their disposal. At that time, of course, the whole problem seemed academic and unreal; none of us could foretell the hideous future, none of us remembered Stalin's pledge to Hitler in 1939 that Poland should never rise again; least of all could we suppose that those apostles of freedom, Britain and the United States, would underwrite by treaty such an odious conspiracy.

In the middle of our conversation the Colonel quietly informed us that the following afternoon we were to meet the Commander-in-Chief of the Polish Home Army—the successor to General Bór-Komorowski. This romantic and mysterious figure, whose very name was concealed from us until our return to London, was travelling swiftly and secretly throughout the country, reviving and reorganizing those shattered remnants of the A.K. that had survived the catastrophe of Warsaw. Tomorrow he would be staying nearby; twenty-four hours later he might be in Kraków, Lódz, Póznan, or even Warsaw.

In the early afternoon of 3rd January we set off from the farm-house with a strong escort under the command of Warta's senior sergeant; a horse-drawn sledge came with us to bring us home in the evening. It was still light when we arrived at a large and comfortable mansion surrounded by tall trees. Inside we found a blaze of lights and a crowd of people, nearly all of them in civilian clothes; among them I recognized an old acquaintance, Colonel Rudkowski, a close friend of Perkins, whom I had met several times in London and once, briefly, in Italy.

Rudkowski was already a senior officer of the Polish Air Force when war broke out in 1939. He was a short, square man of about fifty-five who combined the fierce patriotism and mature cunning of his race with the irresponsible ana disarming sense of fun of a preparatory schoolboy. His courage was attested by his two ribbons of the Virtuti Militari, the Polish Victoria Cross: his skill by the post he had held until recently of Air Officer Commanding of the Polish Fighter Group in Britain, and by his present assignment, which was to build the foundations of a new Polish Air Force. He had parachuted into Poland on the night of our arrival in Italy.

Looking in his civilian clothes more like a character out of Murder Incorporated than the gallant and distinguished officer he was, Rudkowski pounced on us in the hall and led us directly to a small, trim library where we were presented without formality to the Commander-in-Chief.

Of General Okulicki's appearance I can recall little, and that would probably be inaccurate because I only met him this once; of his history I knew only that he had commanded a Polish division in the field under General Anders. What I do remember well is his soft voice, his courteous, almost deferential manner, his quiet, convincing self-confidence, and his passionate sincerity and belief in his own people and his mission among them. He had no illusions about the difficulties ahead of him and meagre hope for their solution; but as I listened to him I knew that this man would make any sacrifice to nourish the starving spirit of his shattered army, caring nothing for his own safety in the cause of his country's freedom. With his life he was to prove me right.

The details of our talk are no longer important: the German Army order of battle in Poland, the morale of the Armja Krajowa after Warsaw, the military and political intentions of the Russians—all these have long reposed in the waste paper basket of history. But one sentence of General Okulicki's still stays in my mind: despite their treachery at Warsaw, he told us, he would continue to treat the Russians as allies and would do all in his power to co-operate with them; but he could not trust their word. Later, in his anxiety to save his country, he trusted them too much.

After the Russian occupation of Poland and the end of the war Stalin invited the leaders of the Armja Krajowa, who had gone into hiding, to come to Moscow for discussions on the future government of Poland; the invitation was issued through the Chief of the Russian General Staff, who publicly gave his word of honour as a General Officer of the Red Army that the delegates would come to no harm in Russia and would be allowed to return to Poland without interference. In spite of their natural misgivings General Okulicki and the other leaders of the Home Army felt it their duty, in the interests of Poland, to accept this invitation. On arrival in Moscow they were all immediately arrested and imprisoned in the Lubianka. They were brought to trial on charges of sabotaging the communications of the Red Army in Poland and operating clandestine wireless stations; on evidence which in Britain would not even have secured their committal for trial they were convicted and sentenced to penal servitude for life. General Okulicki has died in prison; there is no news yet of his companions.

After the conference was over I found Rudkowski again. He escorted me to a large buffet laid out in a room leading from the hall, and pointed to a pair of decanters, each filled with a clear spirit.

'Which do you like?' he asked me, 'Vodka or bimba?' Bimba is an inferior kind of vodka made from potatoes; it has a filthy taste, a violent kick, and a horrible effect on the head and stomach. But it is cheap and plentiful and so, out of politeness, I asked for bimba. Rudkowski gave me a wicked grin as he handed me my glass.

'I never touch bimba, only vodka.' And he poured himself a drink from the other decanter.

We left Maly Jacków long before dawn, and after a five-mile march reached Redziny, a few small houses on the edge of a great forest.

Our hosts, an old peasant and his wife, moved with remarkable good humour into their kitchen, leaving the other two rooms for ourselves and our wireless equipment. While we were there we worked late every night, drafting and encoding signals to London reporting the action at Katarzyna, our meeting with General Okulicki and information we acquired from our numerous visitors—unaware, of course, that we were losing our sleep to no purpose.

At five o'clock each morning Warta routed us out of bed and led us into the forest, where he kept us until two in the afternoon. This was the usual pattern of our lives for the rest of our time with the Home Army; there were many German and Cossack foraging parties around, and the Poles were taking no more chances after Katarzyna. Throughout the daytime we remained in a perpetual state of alert, ready to move at a minute's notice; we slept, of course, in our clothes.

Our first visitors were two junior officers of the Home Army, Lieutenants Jerzy and Alm; they were to be attached to us in future as liaison officers with the Home Army command. Alm was an intelligent young man with a fresh complexion and reddish brown hair who came from Western Poland; a lively, friendly companion he was gifted with unusual courage and resource, as his story showed. In order to secure the release of his father, who had been sent to Dachau, he had volunteered for the German army and had soon won himself a commission. As an officer he had little difficulty in persuading the authorities to free his father, who went into hiding. Alm then obtained a posting to the Russian front, where he skilfully—or luckily—contrived to get wounded just badly enough to be sent to Poland for convalescence; once he was back in his own country he deserted and joined the Armja Krajowa. Jerzy was a very tall, thin young man with a quiet, serious manner; a brother of the beautiful Madame Rubachowa, he had all his sister's gentle charm. Both officers proved themselves invaluable during the next ten days.

M. Siemienski, our next caller, was a prominent landowner from the neighbouring town of Zytno; he was a saddened, soft-spoken man in his middle or late fifties whose principal interest was farming but who looked more like a university don than a squire. His only son had been killed four months earlier with the A.K. in battle against the Germans. With him came two young women who worked in the courier service of the Home Army; one of them was his daughter, a gay, pretty, dark-haired girl of about twenty; the other was married to a Polish officer now in a German prisoner-of-war camp. Siemienski was a member of the *Uprawa*, an organization of landowners whose principal object was to keep the Home Army supplied with food, money, clothing, and shelter.

On the third evening of our stay at Redziny we were in the middle of supper when there was a commotion outside and the sound of urgent whispering; Warta swept into the house, followed by Jerzy. The latter spoke without preliminary greeting.

'Please hurry with your meal. We have just heard there is to be a *pacyfikacja* in this area tomorrow morning. We are leaving at once.'

We marched all night in grim silence, for we were all short of sleep and only too liable to snap at one another when we spoke. At first light we arrived, grey-faced and bleary-eyed, at a small settlement of poor peasant houses. Before the war the place had been a colony of *Volksdeutsche*—German settlers—but after the occupation these had been moved to richer holdings near Radomsko and the dispossessed Poles resettled here. Our house was filthy and almost bare of furniture and we slept on grubby pallets on the earthen floor; but the owners, a small family reduced to a state of apathy by poverty and suffering, did their best to make us comfortable. In return for their hospitality we gave them a few sovereigns, which they accepted courteously but with apparent indifference; adversity had drained them of all feeling.

During the three days of our stay we became infested with the most prolific and ferocious crop of lice that I at least have ever encountered. For the Spanish, Albanian, and Montenegrin louse I had learnt to acquire a certain tolerance, even affection; but these creatures bit with an increasing and fanatical fury that excluded all hope of sleep and comfort.

On 11th January we returned to Redziny. The Germans, having caught no one in their net, had withdrawn; but we did not relax our security measures during the five days we were there. Any temptation towards slackness that we might have felt was soon dispelled by the regular appearance every morning and afternoon of a pair of Storch reconnaissance aircraft; they flew steadily back and forth over the village, and it was soon clear to us that they were trying to locate our wireless by D/F. General Okulicki had warned us of this very danger. We had plenty of traffic for Galbraith's skeds—every day we received fresh reports from different sources on military, political, and economic conditions; but we could not risk operating the set while the aircraft were around, and so we were obliged to hand most of our messages to Jerzy or Alm to be sent on Polish links.

The presence of the two aircraft seemed to confirm our suspicions that the Germans already had a good idea of our whereabouts; we braced ourselves for an unpleasant period of *pacyfikacja* and pursuit. It never came. Instead, on the night of 13th January we were startled to hear the sound of heavy gunfire rolling towards us from the east. As the hours passed the barrage intensified to such a climax that we knew it could mean only one thing: the Russians were attacking on the Vistula; a new offensive had begun.

Neither the Poles nor ourselves—not even, it seemed, the Germans—had expected the Red Army to begin its drive towards the Oder before the spring; nor could we foresee that it would meet with so little resistance. The bombardment continued all night without interruption. During the next two days numbers of enemy fighters and bombers flew overhead, but the Poles told us that the Germans were withdrawing. Warta kept us in the woods from early morning until dusk, for we were so close to the battle now that he had every reason to fear an intensive round-up by Security forces; but so swift was the German retreat that we were left in peace.

On the 15th we heard that Russian tanks were in Maluszyn, on the western bank of the Pilica, which meant that they had breached the last line of defence before the Oder and the German frontier; we could expect them to reach us within twenty-four hours. Our standing orders, when this happened, were to present ourselves at the nearest Red Army headquarters.

The same afternoon Jerzy brought us an invitation from his sister to a party at Wlynica. We should not be returning to Redziny, and so we piled all our kit onto one farm cart and ourselves onto another and set off soon after dark. We travelled slowly and with extra caution, every man on the alert for signs of trouble; we avoided all villages and roads, keeping as much as possible to the forest and pausing for a thorough reconnaissance whenever we had to cross a patch of open country. The district was crawling with enemy patrols, and we had no desire at this stage for a brush with desperate Cossacks or S.S.; nor could we be certain of the temper of any Armja Ludowa forces we might meet at this moment of their masters' triumph.

We did in fact run into an A.L. patrol soon after we had started, in the depths of a very dark wood; they were belligerent at first and called on us to surrender. We leaped off our wagon and took up battle stations at the sound of peremptory shouting and the menacing clatter of rifle bolts; but after a brief parley they decided that we outnumbered them, and so they let us pass.

Madame Rubachowa's party was going briskly when we arrived.

Her guests included almost everyone we had met there before, and many more of her friends from the district. The atmosphere was much less restrained than on our previous visit; there was music and dancing, and tables laden with vodka, champagne, and food of every kind. But the evening sparkled with a forced, determined hilarity that was terrible and tragic; the underlying tension and anxiety crackled from room to room.

We had hoped for a final interview with General Okulicki, and Hudson had accepted tonight's invitation partly in the hope of meeting some representative of the G.O.C. But he was disappointed, for the only two senior officers present were our old friend Major Stefan, Warta's commanding officer, and the deputy commander of the Czestochowa Inspectorate, neither of whom could—or would—give us any idea of the General's whereabouts. They had received no fresh instructions and therefore proposed to carry out those they had been given several months ago—to disband all partisan units on the arrival of the Russians and go into hiding. Home Army formations were making no attempt to harass the Germans. After Warsaw they could hardly be expected to, even if they had been given warning of the offensive; besides, the hostile tone of recent Russian broadcasts can have left them in no doubt of the treatment they might expect from the Red Army.

As the evening progressed, the pace of the party quickened to a macabre and frenzied gaiety whose implications could no longer be concealed. However much these people hated the Germans—and there was not a man or woman in the room who had not lost at least one close relative fighting against them—they literally dreaded the Russians. Tonight they were saying good-bye to the world they had always known. The German occupation had brought unbelievable hardship and tragedy to their country and their class: Russian rule, they foresaw, meant extinction for both.

The dancing grew faster and wilder: waltzes and foxtrots were abandoned for the whirling, stamping folk dances of Poland—the Krakowiak, Oberek, and Kujawiak; glasses were filled, emptied at once and immediately filled again as people drank with an intense, desperate urgency, as though they would never be drinking again, as though they must not leave a drop for the invading Russians. Beautiful and solitary among these fantastic bacchanals wandered our hostess, her air of gentle melancholy dissolving in a gay and friendly smile as she talked to each of her guests. She told me that she would leave for the north as soon as the party was over, and make for Poznan, where she hoped to find her husband.

It was after midnight when we left Wlynica and took the road to Katarzyna, as we had done on New Year's Eve; Warta and his men accompanied us, for they had been ordered to remain with us until the arrival of the Russians. We stayed in a small cottage near the village: at such a time it might be wise to sleep away from large houses.

We awoke to a noisy morning. From the north, where the main road ran west towards Czestochowa, came the rumble of tanks and the continuous roar of motor transport, often punctuated by bursts of machine-gun fire and the thunder of artillery; the sky above us was filled with the whine and drone of aircraft, and to east and west the air vibrated with the thud of heavy bombing.

Our hand generator had finally broken down, but Galbraith's batteries had just enough charge left in them for a last contact with London; this contact brought us a brief signal, confirming our orders to hand ourselves over to the Russians and reassuring us that our names and location and the nature of our mission had been communicated to the Russian political and military authorities and to the British Military Mission in Moscow.

At noon we learned that Russian armoured spearheads were already well to the west of us; there seemed no reason to keep our escort with us any longer—indeed there was every reason to let them disband and hide themselves while they could. They had refused to leave us the day before when we had made the same suggestion, but now it was easy to convince them; they left us the same afternoon, each one shaking us firmly by the hand and giving us a cracking salute before he marched away proudly into his future of hazard and doom. Sorrowfully we took our leave of these men who had hazarded their lives for so many years to uphold the imperishable honour of their country.

Our problem now was to find the Russians without running into any of the large groups of defeated Germans, Turkomen, and Cossacks that were wandering about the country; Vlasov's troops, especially, would be in an ugly mood. Hudson decided to send Currie and Solly-Flood to try and make contact with a Russian divisional or corps headquarters; they left soon after the Poles, telling us to expect them back in the morning.

Much to our surprise we received an invitation to dine that night with Madame Dembowska; we had thought that after New Year's Day she would want no more of our company. Hudson, Galbraith, and I set off for her house before it was quite dark, keeping a careful look-out on the way. It was well that we were vigilant, because we saw the Russian patrol before they saw us—in a wood a few hundred yards from Madame Dembowska's house; there were two soldiers moving slowly through the trees, their tommy-guns at the ready. It was unnecessary as well as dangerous to try to avoid them, and so we stood still and called to them, waving in what we hoped would seem a friendly, carefree manner.

They came towards us slowly and suspiciously, their guns pointed straight at our stomachs and their fingers on the triggers. When they were close Hudson, who spoke some Russian, explained who we were and showed them a card, with which each of us had been issued in London, displaying a Union Jack and a message in printed cyrillic letters which began, I remember, '*Ya Anglichanin.*'

They shed some of their hostility and accompanied us the rest of the way, still keeping us covered in a manner suggesting that they would stand no nonsense. I hate to speculate on Madame Dembowska's feelings when she opened the door to us; first we had brought the Germans to her house: now we were bringing the Russians. Perhaps she had expected them anyway, and hoped that our presence would have a restraining influence; because she welcomed us with warmth and even affection. One of our guards now left us to fetch his officers, while his companion made himself comfortable squatting on the floor of the dining-room. There were three or four other guests for dinner, all of them farmers or professional men from the district.

We were starting to eat when a Russian captain and two lieutenants walked into the room and saluted smartly; they were all from one of the armoured formations which had been leading the advance and were for the moment resting in reserve. The captain, who acted as spokesman for the others was a rangy, fair-complexioned young Ukrainian with a frank and humorous face; Madame Dembowska asked them rather nervously to join us for dinner—an unnecessary invitation, for they told her in a firm though friendly manner to fetch a lot more vodka and be quick about it.

At the end of the meal we toasted each other and the British and Russian leaders; the captain himself proposed the health of President Roosevelt—as well he might. He then launched into a long set speech, obviously carefully rehearsed because he paused from time to time to ask his colleagues whether he had omitted anything.

In outline his argument was the same as that of the Russian parachutists of whom our friends in the Armja Krajowa had told us: there was a long defence of Russia's attitude to the Curzon Line, coupled with a statement that the Poles would be well compensated on their western borders; there was much praise of the Lublin Committee, and there were repeated assurances that the Russians would make no attempt to impose Communism but would leave Poland as soon as the Germans were beaten.

His concluding words were directed at us: in the most charming way he told us that the Red Army had been holding three hundred German divisions for the greater part of the war, while the British and Americans were even now containing only sixty-seven. When Hudson gently reminded him of the enormous material help Russia had received under Lend-Lease he smiled and admitted that of course Lend-Lease had been very useful, graciously adding that the tanks supplied by Britain had been especially valuable and that one of the Brigades in this offensive was equipped entirely with British tanks.

In fact it was a very successful party for all except poor Madame Dembowska, whose entire store of vodka was drunk in the course of the evening—without, I must add, producing any noticeable effect on her Russian guests. Before we left, the Captain invited us to drink in his mess the following evening.

There was no sign of Solly-Flood and Currie all next day; although anxious about them we thought they had probably been detained by the Russians and would show up in due course. Our party with the tank officers that night was brief but memorable. Their mess was in a small wooden house on the outskirts of the village; about a dozen officers stood at a long table laden with bottles of what appeared to be cherry vodka and plates of zakaska—small pieces of cheese, smoked ham and sausage. When we were seated our glasses—half-pint tumblers—were filled almost to the top with vodka by the Ukrainian captain, who indicated that he expected no heel-taps. We rose as the first toast was called: '*Pobeda!*—to the victory of the Allies!' Jauntily I raised my tumbler and poured the contents down my throat; a moment later, if I had had any voice left, I would have screamed.

Mr. P. G. Wodehouse once described a certain drink as having an effect—I quote from memory—'as though someone had touched off a bomb in the old bean and then taken a stroll through the stomach with a lighted torch.' That is a fair description of what we had just swallowed; it burned like molten lead and tasted strongly of petrol. It was in fact a mixture of the neat spirit used as the basis of vodka, and the petrol on which they drove their tanks—camouflaged with fruit juice.

In fairness to our hosts I must add that they drank the same liquor and seemed to love it; moreover they swallowed several glassfulls, whereas we surreptitiously emptied our refills on the floor. I cannot say what was the ultimate effect on them because we left after half an hour, but I know that I did not recover my voice that evening.

XIII

CAPTIVITY

Early next morning, 18th January, a Dodge truck arrived outside our house to take us to the Russian Army Corps headquarters at Zytno; in it were Currie, a Russian major and two soldiers. The major was far from friendly, and curtly ordered us to pack up our things and get into the truck.

Currie warned us that our reception at headquarters was not going to be an affair of handshakes, vodka and caviare. He and Solly-Flood had been received with arrogance and suspicion; they had been taken before a major-general and subjected to a long interrogation; the general had called them liars, made them hand over their arms and identity cards and sent them under guard to the house of M. Siemienski, where Solly-Flood was now detained.

As soon as we turned into the main road we came upon a continuous stream of Russian trucks, guns, and tanks rolling westward in the opposite direction to ours; all the way to Zytno we passed the same column of vehicles driving nose to tail with scarcely a break. On this and on subsequent journeys we observed that at least two thirds of the motor transport of the Red Army was of American or British Commonwealth manufacture; the fighting vehicles, on the other hand, and the artillery were almost all Russian. It is fair to say that without this aid from Lend-Lease the Russians would not have had the mobility to follow up their victories even if they had been able to achieve them.

The armour was mixed indiscriminately with administrative and supply vehicles, jeeps, civilian cars, and a surprising amount of horse transport. But traffic control seemed to be well organized; road forks and junctions were already clearly signposted in Cyrillic, and traffic police—usually enormous girls in military uniform—were stationed at the major cross-roads.

Apart from a brief delaying action on the Pilica the Germans had put up little or no resistance; their object had been to withdraw their forces intact behind the line of the Oder. They seemed largely to have succeeded, because we saw very little destroyed or abandoned equipment and only two columns of German prisoners, of about fifty men each.

Corps H.Q. at Zytno occupied two small rooms of a peasant's cottage. Forcing his way through a crowd of lounging guards and orderlies, who stiffened to attention as he passed, the major led us to the inner room, where a lieutenant-general and several staff officers were standing before a large coloured wall map of the front. The general, a lean, dark man of thirty-five or forty with a grave, intelligent face and a very quiet voice, courteously acknowledged our salutes and pointed to some hard chairs round a small table; his interest was con-fined to the course of the battle. An officer with a field telephone in one hand passed a series of reports to the Corps Commander, who commented briefly on each, while another officer marked the map with coloured pencils. The General gave his orders confidently and without hesitation; nothing seemed to be put in writing.

We rose to our feet as the door opened to admit a square, thick-set officer with a pale, flabby face who wore on his greatcoat the gilded epaulettes of a major-general. He made no attempt to acknowledge our salutes, but sat down across the table from us and stared at us for a while without speaking; a faint sneer twisted the corners of his mouth.

He brought with him a Polish-speaking subaltern, who interpreted for him, as Currie did for us. Hudson explained who we were, adding that Moscow had already received all our particulars; he showed his identity card, but the major-general refused to look at it, saying that it was probably a German forgery. We were then subjected to a barrage of questions: What was the name of our organization in London, and who commanded it? What were the times of our skeds, what frequencies and what codes were we using? Most sinister of all, who were our Polish contacts?

Hudson answered politely that we were not allowed to give this in-formation, but that our bona fides could easily be verified from Moscow; the general laughed unpleasantly and said that this was a fine way to treat allies. We felt the same. It was clear to us that he did not seriously doubt our story but was going out of his way to be offensive; it was also fairly certain that he was not an officer of the Red Army, but of the N.K.V.D.[1] He concluded the interview by ordering us to hand over our arms, documents, and wireless equipment; our protests were contemptuously dismissed and we were obliged to comply. Hudson's parting threat to take up the matter with higher authority in Moscow met with a very nasty laugh.

We were sent under escort to Siemienski's house, which seemed to have been taken over as the administrative headquarters of the Army Corps. Troops thronged the building; in the grounds were parked vehicles, guns and 'Katiusha' multiple rocket batteries, which we were never allowed to approach. We found Solly-Flood, still seething from his treatment of the night before, and Siemienski and his daughter, his mother, and his niece, who welcomed us with joy and relief—either because they had feared for our

---

[1] *Narodny Komisariat Vnutrennik Dyel* (People's Commissariat for Home Affairs) formerly known as the OGPU and now the MVD. This organization controls not only the secret police and forced labour camps, but all the forces of public order, such as the municipal police and militia. It is independent of the fighting services and has its own aircraft, infantry, artillery, and armour, in which a large proportion of the rank and file are Asiatic troops.

safety or because they hoped for our protection; perhaps both. Siemienski's niece was an attractive blonde of about the same age as her cousin; Madame Siemienska, a small, white-haired old lady with fine, delicate features, walked erect and proud among the noisy Mongol soldiers as though she was not even aware of their presence. As well as their uninvited guests they were housing some forty Polish refugees, most of them from Warsaw.

We lived, ate, and slept in a large ground-floor room at the front of the house, formerly the drawing-room but now denuded of most of its furniture. We were committed to the charge of a Russian major, who in the three days that we stayed there never let us out of his sight. There was, of course, no privacy for any of us—the Siemienskis or ourselves. They bore their humiliation with a fine dignity and good humour.

Apart from the uncertainty of their future, their sufferings were already considerable. Siemienski owned an estate of between four and five thousand acres—most of it timber, the rest farmland; if he was lucky he might be allowed to retain twelve acres and a few rooms in his own house. A committee had been formed of his own estate workers to manage the property, but they depended entirely upon his technical skill and experience. The Russians had requisitioned all the livestock in the district without compensation, and so there would be no means of cultivating the land in the spring; the Red Army's method of living off the country during an advance was as devastating as their 'scorched earth' policy in retreat.

These troops belonged to Marshal Koniev's Second Ukrainian Army; among them was a high proportion of Mongols. I believe their behaviour was no worse than that of other Soviet armies in occupied territory; there seemed to be little difference between their treatment of the peoples they were supposed to be liberating and those they were conquering.

The soldiers quartered on Siemienski behaved towards him and his family with calculated brutality and contempt. They broke up his furniture for firewood, they pilfered every article of value and marked or spoilt what they did not care to take away; they urinated and defecated in every room, sparing only our living quarters because the major in charge of us stopped them; the hall, the stairs and the passages were heaped and spattered with piles of excrement, the walls and floors were splashed with liquor, spittle, and vomit, the whole building stank like an untended latrine. It is a pity that those Communists in France and in Australia who declared a few years ago that they would welcome the Red Army as liberators never saw that army at its work of liberation.

Towards the girls, whenever they were out of our sight, they showed a deliberately boorish and arrogant manner, insulting, threatening, and sometimes hitting them. The officers behaved better; the girls could always put them to shame by the use of the phrase, *nie kulturny*, for the Red Army officer is very touchy about his 'culture'. But the officers had no authority over their men off duty. On parade and in action I am told that orders are obeyed instantly and to the letter; here, however, the officers seemed to mix with their troops without distinction of rank, and their few attempts to check indiscipline and hooliganism were either ignored or—as we ourselves observed—answered with ridicule and defiance. To us they made no pretence of being friendly; one bumptious little captain told us with spiteful conviction:

'Don't worry. When we've beaten the Germans we're going on to fight the British.'

He at least did not doubt our nationality.

For Madame Siemienska, however, the troops displayed a reluctant respect; she was, I have said, an old lady of formidable personality, and her obvious indifference to whatever fate might overtake her, coupled with her unconcealed scorn for her captors, filled them with surprise and awe. On the evening before we left she came into our room and, sitting down at the piano, began to play some Chopin; soon the Russian officers, and then the little Mongols, gathered round until there was scarcely room to move in the close-packed circle. With superb skill and with a fierce, exultant pride she played the *Révolutionnaire*, the 'Death of Poland', the Polonaise and the first two Ballades. She ended with the *Warszawianka* and the Polish National Anthem. Then, with a stiff little bow she wished us good-night and, looking straight ahead of her, walked quietly away through the ranks of applauding Russians.

On the afternoon of 21st January we left Zytno in a truck, escorted by the major and an armed guard. We spent that night in Radomsko, where we dined with two Russian colonels who noted with apparent sympathy Hudson's complaints against our treatment as prisoners instead of as allies. Prisoners, however, we remained and were even prevented from speaking to the owners of the house in which we slept.

Our status was made clearer the next day. In the town of Jędrzejów, some sixty miles to the south-east, we were handed over to a major of the N.K.V.D. and two subalterns, who kept us confined under guard for five days in a small and dirty room; only once were we allowed outside the house, when we were taken for a brief walk under the supervision of one of the subalterns, a supercilious young man with very close-set eyes who wore a Cossack hat and talked German to us in tones of studied insolence. We were firmly segregated from all contact with the Poles; our protests were disregarded and when we asked to speak to a senior officer the major simply laughed and told us to shut up. He was a swaggering, loud-voiced ruffian, clearly happy in his work.

The final humiliation came on 26th January. We were crammed into the back of a lorry with a dozen Russian soldiers and a glum, tubby little man with a red face who wore the blue uniform of General Vlasov's army; he seemed to be an officer and spoke fluent Russian. He sat on the floor in deep gloom, his head on his chest and his hands plunged in the pockets of his greatcoat. The soldiers addressed him as 'Vlasov' and from time to time prodded good-humouredly at his tummy with their rifles, which did nothing to cheer him up. A few miles from Czestochowa, which was our destination, the lorry stopped beside a long, low stone building, and all but two of our escort climbed down.

'Come on, Vlasov!' they shouted cheerfully. 'This is you.'

I felt sorry for the little man as he climbed very slowly and deliberately over the back of the truck, lost and lonely and afraid; his guards marched him through the gloomy prison gates while we drove on our way.

I was beginning to feel quite sorry for myself.

The lorry stopped outside a grim stone building surrounded by a high wall with a gateway guarded by two sentries. The major and his Cossack subaltern led us through, across a courtyard and into a gloomy, dim-lit stone passage with doors along one side. Here they handed us over to a sergeant, who signed a receipt for us and led us to one of the doors, unlocked it with an enormous key and motioned us inside; the guards urged us forward at the points of their tommy-guns. We stepped into the cell, the heavy door crashed to behind us and from the other side we heard the laughter of our captors.

'Well, boys, this is it,' sighed Solly-Flood. 'There's only one question now: which is it to be—Siberia or the firing squad? Personally, I'm not sure I wouldn't choose the firing squad.'

The cell was about twelve feet long, nine feet in breadth and twelve feet high, with a stone floor and bare, whitewashed walls; stout boards nailed across the window shut out the daylight, but a powerful naked bulb hung from the ceiling, throwing a hard bright glare in our eyes day and night, for we had no means of turning it off. Against the wall on each side of the door was a triple tier of bunks with mattresses of straw covered by pieces of old sacking; they were alive with vermin. Through a slot in the door, cut at eye-level and fitted with a shutter on the outside, the guards peered at us and mocked our helplessness.

'*Soyusniki!*' they jeered, 'how are you feeling—*you allies?*'

Seated on the bunks we discussed our fate with indignation and anxiety, in which I am not ashamed to admit that anxiety predominated. We had the greatest confidence in Perkins and General Gubbins, but what could they do if the Russians chose to deny all knowledge of our existence, or to report us as dead? While we were debating, we heard from a few yards down the corridor, a woman crying out in anger and despair; with horror we recognized the voice of the Home Army courier, married to a Polish officer, who had visited us at Redziny with Siemienski and his daughter. We heard her give her name to the interrogating officer or N.C.O.; then we all broke spontaneously into loud and random chatter, for we wished to hear no more. . . .

At six in the evening we dined; that is to say, a pair of guards stood in the doorway and handed us each a piece of stale rye bread a little larger than the average restaurant roll, and a filth-encrusted tin canteen half-filled with lukewarm water in which floated a few grains of barley. This was the staple prison diet, and we had it twice a day; when I asked the sergeant of the guard for some vodka he slammed the door with a volley of abuse which unfortunately I could not understand.

Worry, lice, and the unrelenting glare from the ceiling kept me from sleep for most of the night; a thunderous banging on the door, accompanied by shouts and more abuse, roused us in the morning. The door was thrown open and a couple of guards with levelled tommy-guns ordered us outside. Led by an N.C.O. and prodded on by the guards we were hurried along the passage to wash in the courtyard. On the way we met a group of Poles, among whom we recognized two who had been our fellow-guests at the Wlynica party; we passed them with-out a sign. In the yard each of us was given a bucket of water, in which, after breaking the ice, we washed superficially and with haste, for the temperature at this early hour was well below freezing. After our wash we were escorted to the latrine, a shallow trench surmounted by a wooden pole and only too evidently never cleaned; we had to use it under the cynical stares of our guards. Then we were locked in our cell for the day.

Such was the routine of our prison life. The N.K.V.D. had taken over the building from the Gestapo only two days earlier—with all fittings. Luckily we still had two packs of cards and so were able to vary the monotony, as once before in Montenegro, with endless rubbers of bridge; I have never played the game since. Poker was impossible because we did not even have matches for chips; somebody suggested using lice, but that proved impracticable because they would never stay put.

From time to time, usually at night, we would be called out for interrogation; this burden fell principally upon Hudson—and upon Currie who accompanied him as interpreter—because he had given all of us the strictest orders to answer no questions of any kind. He himself firmly and fearlessly refused to speak to any Russian officer below his own rank, which was full colonel; in the face of threats from the bullying major and his colleagues he remained stolidly silent, to their appeals to reason dourly indifferent. Finally, with our help he drafted a personal letter of protest to Marshal Koniev, which he persuaded the major to forward to Army headquarters.

We never knew whether this letter reached the Marshal; but Hudson's intransigence impressed the Russians and our treatment began to improve. The food remained the same, but we were lodged in a larger, brighter cell upstairs with bars across the windows but with glass to let in the light. The junior officers who visited us were sometimes polite; we even overheard one of them telling an N.C.O. that he considered our previous treatment scandalous. Finally Hudson was interviewed by a Russian colonel—or by an officer dressed as a colonel—who showered him with sympathy and wholly unconvincing excuses.

The guards also became quite friendly; they were Asiatics who felt no embarrassment at being required to switch suddenly from their former hostility. One of them, a cheerful, wiry little peasant from the Soviet Republic of Azerbaijan beside the Caspian, told us that he had thirteen brothers and as many sisters; such was the efficiency of the Soviet school system, he added, that all of them had received as good an education as he.

'What is the capital of England?' asked Hudson.

He scratched his head. 'I know...it is...it is...' for a moment he looked puzzled, but then his face cleared: 'Of course, *jep twaya match*, it is London!'

'When did Lenin die?' asked Currie gently.

Without a moment's hesitation the boy replied: 'On the 21st of January 1924, at six-fifty a.m. precisely.'

On 12th February we were driven to the aerodrome and embarked in a Dakota of the Soviet Air Force; with us came the major—now a model of courtesy and consideration—and his two subalterns; also, we noted, all the equipment we had been made to hand over at Zytno; our identity cards were returned to us.

We flew at five hundred feet, following the course of roads and rail-ways eastward to Mielec beyond the Vistula, where we spent a night; then on to Lvóv in the newly-incorporated Russian territory and thence to Kiev in the Ukraine. All the way the major fussed over us like an old hen, anxious lest we should slip away long enough to speak to any of the inhabitants. At Kiev, a city still in ruins, we were taken early in the afternoon to the station to await the Moscow express, due to leave at midnight. We changed our Polish zlotys into roubles and bought at an inflated price enough food to last the three days' journey ahead of us. We had a second class compartment to ourselves—and the major; it was fitted with bunks and so we slept for most of the way.

At nine o'clock on the morning of 17th February we reached Moscow. After a long wait in the draughty station in a temperature of about ten degrees Fahrenheit an N.K.V.D. police van appeared and whisked us at high speed through the snow-bound streets. None of us knew Moscow, but we all recognized the grim facade of the Lubianka when the van drew up outside its heavily guarded gates. At that moment I think we all tasted the dregs of despair.

Perhaps this was only the Russian idea of a joke; for our driver disappeared into the guard house to return a few minutes later with an envelope, which he handed to the major. We sped off again and stopped ten minutes later in front of another large building—the *Narkomindyel* or Ministry of Foreign Affairs. We were taken up several flights of stairs and shown into a long, narrow room furnished with a green baize-covered table and high-backed chairs. Here the major stammered an embarrassed good-bye and left us.

Two or three hours later we abandoned our game of bridge and sprang to our feet as the door opened to admit a Russian general; he motioned us to sit down and stood staring at us for five minutes in silence. Then all our worries rolled away as a British Army captain stepped briskly into the room, followed by two Russian officers. Our names were read out and checked, salutes were exchanged and a few minutes later we were being driven in an army station wagon to the headquarters of the British Military Mission.

The Mission headquarters was in the street called Ulitza Kominterna; although Stalin had decreed the dissolution of the Komintern nearly three years ago, the memory obviously lingered on. The building itself reflected a freer, possibly happier and certainly quite irresponsible society. Constructed to the plan of a rich merchant at the turn of the century its stone walls were crowned with crenellated towers and battlements, its halls and stairways paved with the rarest marble. The merchant's mother, when invited to inspect the completed product of her son's wealth and genius, simply remarked:

'My son, before you built this only I knew what a fool you were: now all Moscow knows.'

In the entrance hall we were greeted with a warm and dazzling smile by Natasha, the blonde young Russian receptionist who was married to a sergeant in the Mission. Dirty, lice-bound, and unshaven we were rushed to the M.I. Room, where we shed our filthy battle-dress and were deloused under the sympathetic supervision of a young major of the R.A.M.C.; bathed, shaven and dressed in clean, if ill-fitting, uniforms we presented ourselves in the mess before lunch, to be plied with vodka, red caviare, and an endless series of questions.

At no time did we receive either explanation or apology from the Russians for our detention; but at least a part of the true reason became clear to me when I met General Bob Laycock in the mess, on his way back to England from the Yalta Conference. The future of Poland had been one of the subjects under discussion, and so the Russians had made sure that it should not be complicated by any report we might have to make.

We remained in Moscow exactly a month while the applications for our exit visas went through the tortuous channels of the *Narkomindyel*. For the first few days we stayed in the already overcrowded headquarters in Ulitza Kominterna. The Mission at this time was commanded by Admiral Archer, a short, broad-shouldered sailor with an inexhaustible good nature and a refreshing sense of humour, qualities he badly needed in the discharge of his official duties; his chief of staff was a Grenadier officer, Colonel Napoleon Brinckman. They and their subordinates spared no effort to make up to us for the discomforts of the past month; indeed, they succeeded so well that I really believe we were in more danger of death from alcoholic poisoning during those days than we ever had been from enemy or Russian action.

Very much to our surprise we were allowed to move freely about the city, although we were warned that we were probably being kept under discreet observation and that we should be unwise to talk to strangers in the streets or in cafes—more for their sakes than our own. There were a few girl students from the university who were allowed to mix freely with officers of the Mission and were often seen dining in the mess; they were attractive and friendly and spoke good English, but they were all considered to be unofficial agents of the N.K.V.D., and so conversation with them was somewhat restricted. Four years of war—or twenty years of Stalin—seemed to have reduced most of the civilian population to a state of empty-eyed apathy; they shuffled along with downcast faces drained of all interest or hope. With fascinated horror I watched an old man who had lost both his legs at the groin, crossing a street in the snow and slush on his elbows and his stumps. Nobody paid the slightest attention.

We admired from every angle the smooth straight lines of the Kremlin walls and the multi-domed church of St. Vassili in Red Square, whose architect, according to legend, the Tsar rewarded by having him blinded lest he should design another like it. The tall narrow gateway leading from the Kremlin into Red Square was a formidable hazard to cross; a bell would ring and then, with no further warning, one of the long black government limousines would race into the Square at fifty or sixty miles an hour, carrying some high official of police or Politburo safe behind armour and dark, bullet-proof glass.

We were vividly reminded, however, that there was another aspect to this Russia, when we went to the Bolshoi Theatre to see the bewitching Ulanova dance *Giselle* or watched the exquisite Tartar ballet, *Fountain of Bakhchisarai*, or thrilled to the Tartar dancing in *Prince Igor*, led by a pair of Krim Tartars, brother and sister, who whirled round the stage in a symmetry of flashing colour and fierce, ecstatic movement that brought the whole audience to its feet in hysterical, uncontrollable applause.

The difficult problem of our accommodation was solved by Brigadier Hill, the S.O.E. representative in Moscow; he put up Hudson and Currie in his own flat and arranged for Solly-Flood and me to share the suite he kept at the Hotel Nazional. As a young man the Brigadier had been engaged in intelligence work in Russia during the first world war, both before and after the Revolution, and had been a friend of the fabulous Sydney Reilly; between the wars he had published his memoirs in a book called *Go Spy the Land*—a mistake, he told me, that he had never ceased to regret. Whether to atone for his past activities or because he thought it good policy in his present position, he now adopted towards the Soviet government an attitude of uncritical approval and would allow himself no sympathy for our complaints.

Nevertheless Solly-Flood and I were grateful enough for his hospitality. Our suite, which was really a vast double bed-sitting-room with a bathroom, looked across Metropole Square to the Kremlin. There was a legend that from its windows it was possible, with the aid of a telescope or binoculars, to watch Stalin shaving; we had a pair of binoculars, but we caught no glimpse of Stalin.

Life was never dull in that room. We had been warned that the walls were wired for microphones and that all our conversation would be recorded; if that is so the N.K.V.D. must have heard some plain if hardly novel criticism of themselves. When either of us was at home in the evening the telephone was sure to ring; whoever picked it up would hear a husky female voice vibrant with desire—the approach was always the same, though not the voice:

'Darling! I see you today and you are so attractive! Let me come to your room now, please, darling.

Young and foolish and sex-starved we may have been; but we were old enough not to fall into that trap.

We received our visas in the middle of March; at six o'clock in the morning of the 17th we boarded a Soviet Air Force Dakota bound for Baku. None of us had been to bed; for our farewell party, including a boisterous dinner with the Mission, had lasted all night and we had barely time to pack and get to the airport. I was in particularly bad shape and so I remember with undying gratitude the kindness of one of our Russian fellow-passengers, a diplomatic courier on his way to Johannesburg. For a while he listened to my groans and watched my contortions with a sympathetic smile on his smooth round face. Then he tapped me on the knee.

'Butter!' he whispered with a friendly grin. 'A piece of bread, much butter and red caviare. Then I give you a glass of vodka and you will feel wonderful.'

I cried out in my misery and begged him to let me die in peace. But he opened his black brief case and brought out a long roll of fresh French bread, cut off a large hunk, spread it thickly with butter and piled on most of the contents of a tin of caviare; he handed me the *bonne bouche* with one hand and a bottle of vodka with the other.

'First you drink a little vodka—from the bottle because we have no glass. Then you eat this.'

I remembered how one of Tolstoy's characters in *The Cossacks* used to cure her husband's hangovers with platefuls of red caviare, and so I did as I was told. Within the hour I had recovered.

Another example of the many faces of Russia.

We stayed two nights in Baku's wilderness of abandoned oil derricks; we had, of course, a Soviet officer as escort, but he was more guide to us than gaoler and found us rooms in the comfortable In-tourist hotel overlooking the dull grey waters of the Caspian.

The next lap of our journey, and our last in Soviet aircraft, was over the massive range of the Elburz to Tehran; first-class pilots were employed on this run, for it was dangerous in winter. It was a memorably disagreeable experience. We flew at twenty-two thousand feet through thick cloud, without heating and without oxygen. Ambulances met us on the airfield at Tehran and carried away our fellow-passengers—three Field Officers of the Red Army and their wives; very proud of our inexplicable and undeserved stamina we climbed into our waiting staff car and were driven to our hotel.

In Cairo five days later I found David Smiley, *en route* to the Far East on a mission to Siam. Over lunch in a small Arab restaurant he told me that Bill McLean was already on his way to Kashgar in Chinese Turkestan and Julian Amery was in Chungking as political adviser to General Carton de Wiart. Siam appealed to me, and so we agreed that I should apply to join Smiley as soon as Perkins had released me.

There was nothing for us to do in London. We handed in our report to Perkins and General Gubbins; dined at the Rembrandt Hotel as guests of the Polish Government in London—now no longer recognized by the British Government—who decorated us with the eagle and wreath of the Polish Parachute Corps; and prepared to drop into Czecho-slovakia to make contact with some partisans discovered north or north-west of Prague. VE-Day and Perkins had intervened, instead we watched the celebrations in front of Buckingham Palace.

There still remained the war with Japan.

ABOUT THE AUTHOR

Peter Kemp was an English soldier and writer. Educated at Wellington College and Trinity College in Cambridge, Kemp was preparing for a career as a lawyer before, alarmed by the spread of Communism, he volunteered to assist the Nationalists during the Spanish Civil War. Kemp saw extensive combat in both the Requetés militia and later the Spanish Foreign Legion. After the Civil War ended, Kemp was recruited as an agent for the British Special Operations Executive, taking part in numerous commando raids and other irregular warfare activities in France, Albania, Poland, and several colonial territories throughout the Pacific during and after the Second World War. After that war ended, he worked as an insurance salesman and international journalist, continuing his life of distinction and adventure. He passed away on October 30, 1993.

Made in the USA
Middletown, DE
18 July 2021